Politics, Markets, and Mexico's "London Debt," 1823–1887

In 1823 and 1824, the newly independent government of Mexico entered the international capital market, raising two loans in London totaling £6.4 million. Intended to cover a variety of expenses, the loans fell into default by 1827 and remained in default until 1887. This case study explores how the loan process worked in Mexico in the early nineteenth century, when foreign lending was still a novelty, and the unexpected ways in which international debt could influence politics and policy. The history of the loans, the efforts of successive governments in Mexico to resume repayment, and the efforts of the foreign lenders to recover their investment became one of the most significant, persistent, and contentious, if largely misunderstood, issues in the political and financial history of nineteenth-century Mexico. The loans themselves became entangled in partisan politics in Mexico and abroad, especially in Great Britain and France, and were a fertile source of speculation for a wide range of legitimate – and not-so-legitimate – international financiers, including Baring Brothers and the House of Lizardi.

Richard J. Salvucci is Professor of Economics at Trinity University. He has held major fellowships from the Social Science Research Council, the National Endowment for the Humanities, and the American Philosophical Society. In 2006, he was the Peggy Rockefeller Visiting Fellow at the David Rockefeller Center for Latin American Studies at Harvard University, and in 2008, he delivered the Christopher Lasch Memorial Lecture at the meeting of The Historical Society. He has published in the *Hispanic American Historical Review*, the *Journal of Interdisciplinary History*, and *Historia Mexicana*. His books include *Textiles and Capitalism in Mexico: An Economic History of the Obrajes, 1539–1840*; *Latin America and the World Economy: Dependency and Beyond*; and a chapter in *The Cambridge Economic History of Latin America*. In 2001, his article in the *Journal of Interdisciplinary History*, coauthored with Linda K. Salvucci, won the Conference on Latin American History Prize. Richard Salvucci lived in Mexico City from 1976 to 1977 and has returned repeatedly to Mexico for research and other professional purposes since then. He has also spent extensive periods in England, Spain, and Cuba doing historical research.

CAMBRIDGE LATIN AMERICAN STUDIES

General Editor
Herbert S. Klein
Gouverneur Morris Emeritus Professor of History, Columbia University
Director of the Center of Latin American Studies, Professor of History,
and Hoover Senior Fellow, Stanford University

93
Politics, Markets, and Mexico's "London Debt," 1823–1887

(*Continued after index*)

Politics, Markets, and Mexico's "London Debt," 1823–1887

RICHARD J. SALVUCCI

CAMBRIDGE
UNIVERSITY PRESS

CAMBRIDGE UNIVERSITY PRESS
Cambridge, New York, Melbourne, Madrid, Cape Town, Singapore, São Paulo, Delhi

Cambridge University Press
32 Avenue of the Americas, New York, NY 10013-2473, USA

www.cambridge.org
Information on this title: www.cambridge.org/9780521489997

First published 2009

Printed in the United States of America

A catalog record for this publication is available from the British Library.

Library of Congress Cataloging in Publication data
Salvucci, Richard J., 1951–
Politics, markets, and Mexico's "London debt," 1823–1887 / Richard J. Salvucci.
p.   cm. – (Cambridge Latin American studies)
Includes bibliographical references and index.
ISBN 978-0-521-48999-7 (hardback : alk. paper)   1. Loans, British – Mexico – History – 19th
century.   2. Default (Finance) – Mexico – History – 19th century.   I. Title.   II. Series.
HG5162.S27   2009
336.3′435097209034 – dc22   2009007765

ISBN 978-0-521-48999-7 hardback

For Madeline Salvucci
And in memory of Louis Salvucci

Nel mezzo del cammin di nostra vita

An excuse for the war was found in the confiscation of the sums of money that Claudius had given to the foremost Britons; for these sums, as Decianus Catus, the procurator of the island, maintained, were to be paid back. This was one reason for the uprising; another was found in the fact that Seneca, in the hope of receiving a good rate of interest, had lent to the islanders 40,000,000 sesterces that they did not want, and had afterwards called in this loan all at once and had resorted to severe measures in exacting it.

Cassius Dio, Roman History, Vol. 8, Bk. 62

Contents

List of Tables, Figures, and Maps

Tables

Maps

Acknowledgments

If, as it is said, it takes a village to raise a child, how many villages does it take to write a book? We, of course, acknowledge our many debts and make a ritual assumption of sole responsibility for the result. This is as it should be. I wrote this book and, for better or worse, its merits and defects are my doing.

Yet most of us should know a little better. A good book usually benefits from much scrutiny long before, or even well after, the formal referees' reports are in. This book is no different. Herb Klein, let it be said, takes his responsibilities as the editor of the Cambridge Latin American Studies seriously. Not that he was anything other than encouraging or helpful, because he was both. However, he also told me exactly what I needed to hear about an early draft of the manuscript, and without ceremony. I have taken the editor seriously and am glad that I did. The few suggestions that Herb made that I did not follow are the result of my obtuseness.

I honestly do not know how John Coatsworth gets from here to there every day as a serious administrator of serious programs at equally serious institutions. Somehow he found the time to read and comment on what I had written. He made several major suggestions for improvements, and I have followed them closely. Coatsworth is one of the hedgehogs of Latin American history. The foxes, and I count myself as one, end up suitably instructed. For more than one big idea, and for three decades of collegial support, I thank him.

Doctora Josefina Vázquez y Vera of El Colegio de México also reviewed this with the thoroughness and care characteristic of the truly distinguished professional. The political and financial history of the nineteenth century is just treacherous. The documents leave you longing for the "simplicities" of the seventeenth century, and the adage that a week is a long time in politics somehow seems an understatement. Josefina Vázquez knows this better than any other living historian of Mexico, so if you can persuade her of a larger argument, you tell yourself you did something right.

William Summerhill of UCLA has read this entire book, some parts more than once. He is one of the best economic historians working in any field in the United States today, and he tried to keep me honest about bond markets. He usually succeeded, even if I wasn't always sure of what "telling the truth about history" might mean in the context of financial history.

We all give papers, chapters, and presentations. Over the years, their number gets unwieldy. So, with due respect for a listener or discussant whom I have omitted, I would mention only a couple of crucial encounters. The first took place at the University of Texas at Austin more than fifteen years ago. The discussant for my paper was Josefina Vázquez. "Stylized facts" about this subject, she made it clear, would never do. I took her point, and for me, the rest really was history. Much more recently, I had the great honor of talking at the Instituto de Investigaciones Históricas at the UNAM in Mexico City, thanks to Maestra Alma Parra. Doctora Leonor Ludlow and Doctor Silvestre Villegas Revueltas made, for me, very striking observations that forced me to rethink parts of my basic argument at a very late date. Carlos Marichal, of the Colegio de México, the outstanding financial historian of Latin America, has always encouraged my efforts. Finally, I thank Jeff Williamson for inviting me to Harvard's Economic History Workshop, where seminars are indeed a contact sport. These gatherings wonderfully concentrate the mind, whether or not you want it concentrated.

Among economic historians, there is a broad consensus that markets are embedded in institutions and, therefore, so are their outcomes. A book is a good example of this principle, because trying to write in the absence of relevant institutions is likely to mean writing little or nothing at all. At the very least, institutions provide the resources to get the job done. In my case, Trinity University supplied, over a lengthy period of time, the academic leave and supplementary funding that allowed me to begin the basic research and the outline of a manuscript. My department was very helpful in funding research assistance and travel to Mexico and in acquiring scholarly resources including a microfilm run of the Mexican newspaper *Siglo XIX* long before anyone had digitized it. There were two absolutely critical grants that moved me along at crucial moments. The first was a Sabbatical Fellowship from the American Philosophical Society (APS), which essentially allowed me to compose a very rough (handwritten) draft of most of the manuscript. The second was an appointment as the 2005– 2006 Peggy Rockefeller Visiting Scholar at the David Rockefeller Center for Latin American Studies (DRCLAS) at Harvard University. That was an incredible opportunity and permitted me to complete what became the first working draft of this book. Were it not for the generosity of the APS and DRCLAS, these acknowledgments would most likely be appearing as the footnotes to a few good articles, if at all.

Following are special acknowledgments, mainly to generous colleagues at archives and libraries in three countries and across two continents: In

Mexico, these include Linda Arnold in cooperation with Archivo General de la Nación and the Archivo Histórico Diplomático of the Secretaría de Relaciones Exteriores. In the United Kingdom, Dr. John Orbell at Baring Brothers, which was subsequently acquired by ING Bank NV; Caroline Shaw at The Rothschild Archive; the British Library and Manuscript Collection; the Guildhall Library; the Bodleian Library at Oxford University; and the Public Record Office (now, The National Archives of the United Kingdom). In the United States, among others, Walter Brem at the Bancroft Library of the University of California; Martha Whittaker at the Sutro Collection of the California State Public Library; the Quaker and Special Collections of Haverford College; the Baker Library at Harvard Business School; the Special Collections at the Harvard Law School Library; the Widener Library at Harvard University; the Historical Society of Pennsylvania; the Institute Archives and Special Collections at Rensselaer Polytechnic Institute; the Woodsen Research Center at Rice University; the Benson Latin American Collection at the University of Texas, Austin; and the Rare Books and Fine Press Collection at the University of Texas, San Antonio.

My particular thanks go to the seventh Earl of Clarendon for permission to quote from the Clarendon Papers at the Bodleian Library.

The reproductions from *The Illustrated London News* appear courtesy of the Mary Evans Picture Library.

Jeanie Lee and Frank Smith at Cambridge University Press have made the always-mysterious process of getting a manuscript into print much easier by their kindness, patience, and professionalism. I consider myself very fortunate to have been able to work with them.

Finally, I acknowledge the special assistance provided to me by Roberto Beristaín y Rocha, whom I have known since my first day working in the Archivo General de la Nación in 1976. Roberto is one of those remarkable people whose names should appear in quite a few books, but somehow never do. Referring to him as a research assistant does Roberto no justice, because he has spent his life in the archives and libraries of Mexico, to the point where it is difficult to separate what he knows of Mexican history from what he knows of its sources. Roberto uncovered considerable archival material for this project, much of which time, neglect, and "the nineteenth century" had rendered virtually unusable. This would have been a far different and much less interesting book without his help.

I began writing this manuscript watching Martin and Rosie swim in the Alamo Heights Pool. Thanks for not tossing it in the water, guys! And to Linda, for somehow managing it all.

Introduction

Déjà Vu All Over Again

Martín Reyes Vayssade, author of a recent book about Jean-Baptiste Jecker – the Swiss financier whose bonds proved crucial to the French intervention in Mexico in the 1860s – made a revealing comment when asked about the financial maneuverings in which Jecker was involved. "It seems like recent history," Reyes Vayssade commented in a newspaper interview, "It's like the Fobaproa business."[1] To anyone familiar with the politics of high finance in Mexico, the simile is arresting. The "Fobaproa business" to which Reyes Vayssade alluded is one of the largest and most complex financial scandals in Mexican history. It involved a list of public officials and private businesspeople that were a virtual *Who's Who of Mexico* at the end of the twentieth century. It grew out of the catastrophic results of the devaluation of 1995 and involved the government's assumption of the debts and nonperforming assets of Mexico's largest banking, industrial, and financial groups. At bottom, it involved the commingling and conversion of private into public debt at a cost to Mexican taxpayers estimated by Enrique Cárdenas at more than 552 billion new pesos.[2] The scandal generated a heated political conflict between the major parties that eventually involved the national leadership of the Partido de la Revolución Democrática and Andrés Manuel López Obrador, the narrowest of losers in the presidential campaign of 2006.

A cabdriver in Mexico City in his rueful comment on my research on the origins of Mexico's foreign debt on the London market in the 1820s suggested that the Spanish title of my book might well be *La Deuda Eterna* rather than *La Deuda Externa:* a pun on "eternal" and "external," thus *The Eternal Debt* rather than *The External Debt*. Although seemingly an unending problem to Mexicans profoundly affected by the debt crisis of the

1 *El Financiero*, August 8, 2005.
2 "FOBAPROA III," http://www.cddhcu.gob.mx/cronica57/contenido/cont2/fobapro3.htm (accessed April 29, 2007); [Secretaría de Hacienda y Crédito Público] *Fobaproa. La Verdadera Historia* (3rd ed., México, 1998).

1980s, such crises in Mexico and, indeed, elsewhere in Latin America were not so much continuous as cyclical. This was driven home by economists such as Albert Fishlow and Barbara Stallings, but for historians, it was the pioneering work of Carlos Marichal, aptly entitled *A Century of Debt Crises in Latin America: From Independence to the Great Depression, 1820–1930* (Princeton, 1989), that became indispensable. Marichal demonstrated that there had been episodes of foreign lending and domestic default in the past. Their origins and consequences may well have differed, but there were nevertheless earlier examples from which one could draw instruction.

What made the first Mexican debt crisis unusual was that if not precisely eternal, it was long lasting. Sovereign default occurred in 1827, but was not finally resolved until 1887. For a surprising number of the intervening sixty years, the consequences of this default were an active issue. The cast of characters involved changed substantially over time, and there were few major (or minor) figures of historical import who were not involved. Virtually every president, finance minister, and foreign minister from the First Republic through the presidency of Porfirio Díaz spent significant time on what Mexicans called "the London Debt." In one way or another, the London Debt was associated with the defeat of the Spaniards; with the Texas rebellion and annexation; with the War of 1847 and its settlement; with the amortization of church property in 1857; with the reform wars; with the intervention and Second Empire of Maximilian; and with the rise of Díaz, the fall of Manuel González, and the economic origins of the Porfiriato. The London Debt was a heated domestic political issue from the 1820s through the 1850s. It was every bit as divisive in the 1880s – more so, in fact. Some of Mexico's greatest writers and polemicists – Francisco Bulnes, Joaquín Casasus, José María Luis Mora, Manuel Payno, and Guillermo Prieto – all wrote extensively about it. It is no exaggeration to call the London Debt one of the great issues of nineteenth-century Mexican history. Indeed, as late as *1891*, several years after the London Debt had finally been resolved, the great liberal newspaper, *El Siglo Diez y Nueve*, termed the "contracting of the loans of 1823 and 1824 with the houses of Goldsmith and Barkclay [*sic*]" one of the great economic disasters of the century, the fruit of precisely the sort of economic ignorance that the paper had been launched to eradicate.[3]

Nevertheless, this monograph has several specific purposes and is new in the following ways:

First, it is, above all, a financial history. The London Debt involved not just a random series of moratoria, restructurings, and financial maneuverings. These reflected the state of public finance in Mexico in a systematic way. Thus, an implicit argument, and a source of novelty, is the effort made

---

3 *El Siglo Diez y Nueve*, October 10, 1891, cited in Irma Lombardo García, *El siglo de Cumplido. La emergencia del periodismo mexicano de opinión (1832–1857)* (México, 2002), p. 138.

to "read" the history of the debt in the context *of* and as a window *on* public finance. To this end, the study provides estimates, usually for the first time, of the returns to bondholders, of the costs of the debt to Mexico, and of the fiscal sources of Mexican conduct. To do so, it relies on an ongoing analysis of the market for Mexican bonds on the London Stock Exchange, and is especially concerned with "explaining" changes in the price of these securities. Such changes can yield insight into the collective thinking of the Mexican government, its agents, financiers, and creditors, frequently with shifting focus, but always with the conviction that there is some pattern to things. Some accounts of the London Debt give the impression that its history is "one damn thing after another." One damn thing after another it may have been, but the "things" followed a certain logic and displayed an overall coherence that yields to systematic analysis.

Second, the book is both *international* history and international political economy. Many of the primary sources may be Mexican, but there is an equal emphasis on the nature and content of British diplomacy. Neither side operated in a vacuum, but responded to the incentives and disincentives that the shape of international affairs provided. These incentives changed with events, and as the essence of an historian's explicandum, these must be followed carefully and in detail. While studies of the London Debt are not in themselves new, the patterns of interaction between ministers, financiers, markets, and bondholders considered here are, at least insofar as they involve a rewritten historical narrative.

Third, the book incorporates, insofar as possible, the insights and the findings of a new generation of Mexican historians. This synthesis is tentative, sometimes incomplete, and occasionally contradictory, but then so is the work that is emerging. The quickening pace of publication in Mexico, its decentralized nature, and its frequently limited circulation makes nonsense out of claims of comprehensiveness. It is an exciting time to become immersed in the nineteenth century, but a challenging one as well. The intellectual energy that once transformed our understanding of Mexico's colonial past is now also transforming our understanding of much of the nineteenth century. Some regional politics, some institutional changes, and some emerging economic trends are documented far better than others, but that only makes the need to cast a wide net over what is being done all the more imperative. In order to place the London Debt in its broadest fiscal, commercial, and economic context and to avoid duplication of their efforts, I refer the reader to two outstanding Mexican surveys of the period, by Enrique Cárdenas Sánchez, María Eugenia Romero Sotelo, and Luis Júaregui.[4]

---

4 Enrique Cárdenas Sánchez, *Cuando se originó el atraso económico de México. La economía mexicana en el largo siglo XIX, 1780–1920* (Madrid, 2003), and María Eugenia Romero Sotelo and Luis Júaregui, *Las contingencias de una larga recuperación. La economía mexicana, 1821–1867* (México, 2003).

Fourth, the book frames, both in the introduction and throughout the text, a simple but nevertheless powerful framework for considering the relation between domestic finance, foreign borrowing, international diplomacy, and foreign and domestic politics. This is not a new statistical test, an improved means of time-series analysis, or even an event study, all popular and fruitful means of approaching the history of international bond markets. It is, rather, the application of the most basic of economic concepts, *opportunity cost*. This is only to say that one course of action not only precludes another, but that the choice involves a distinct calculation of costs and benefits, or of winners and losers, if you will. Thus this book essentially views the historiography of Mexico's high-yield government finance (*agiotaje*) in a negative light as less a reality, or even a value judgment, but as a reading of the past that was shaped by those *who bore the costs* of *agiotaje*. These were not solely Mexican taxpayers: the British bondholders in the 1830s and 1840s collaborated in forging the view of the *agiotistas* as the "vampires of the Treasury" because it was the British bondholders, among others, who could not be paid if the agiotistas were. Financial resentment helped create if not a Black Legend of Mexican finance, then at least a dark view of it. True enough, there was roguery, thuggery, dishonesty, swindling, and sharp practice – actions that would (or should) swiftly bring down the wrath of financial authorities or complaints of serious fraud in countries with a tradition of prudential supervision. The dark view may well be justified, even accurate in broad outline, but it is not and cannot be objective truth.

Fifth, the book presents two new interpretations in Mexican economic history. One involves a political economy of what is generically (and too simply) termed "centralism," itself a complex movement whose beginnings were played out in the 1830s and 1840s, but whose ultimate realization did not occur until the 1880s and beyond.[5] I show how budgets, debt service, tariffs, and prohibitions – even such hardly perennials as the Banco de Avío – can be regarded as part of a more or less coherent body of practice that I term "centralist political economy." The coherence may have been in improvisation, but it is now clearer as to how these pieces fit together and why the London Debt was the centerpiece of their arrangement. I do not say that the London Debt motivated the centralist reorganization, but it is indisputable that the fortunes of centralism helped drive the London market for Mexican assets. From this I argue that federalist modes of finance – perhaps federalism itself – could never solve the problem of

---

5 A nuanced understanding of the stages of centralism is presented in Mᵃ del Carmen Salinas Sandoval, "Las autoridades de los Poderes centralistas y del Departamento de México" (1836–1846) (Documentos de Investigación, El Colegio Mexiquense, 1998).

the London Debt and, thus, of Mexico's increasingly urgent necessity of reentering the European capital market after 1867.

The second interpretation concerns the end of Mexico's "first debt crisis." How, why, and when did a solution come about, even as Díaz had previously pronounced himself hostile to its refinance? I consider the standard political explanation, which argues that Díaz wanted none of his rivals to be the beneficiaries of a solution to Mexico's obvious "debt overhang," but I also argue that the nature of the Dublán Convention, which led to the resolution of the issue, represented a belated – but logically consistent – recognition by a new generation of British bondholders that the convoluted quarrels of the past were, by the late 1880s, a matter of sunk cost. That is to say, they had become irrelevant to calculating the costs and benefits of a resolution, and hence, no bar to one. And as Leonor Ludlow has observed, the Dublán Convention worked precisely because it undertook a *simultaneous* settlement of both the internal and external debt, and as such represented a very different approach to reconciling the interests of domestic and foreign lenders, interests that had usually been at odds.

Sixth, I have written this book with the conviction that an issue as important as the London Debt, however complex, convoluted, obscure, or difficult, ought to be explained in plain language – the plainer the better. One very important reason why most of us have lost sight of the centrality of the London Debt to nineteenth-century Mexican history is that its narrative of default, renegotiation, refinance, defalcation, and the rest is hard to follow.[6] The intricacies of bearer bonds, their characteristics, and their technical measures (including coupon rate, yield, duration, and more) are something familiar to those who work in the bond market, but few historians do. Most people tire quickly of the intricacies of financial negotiations. Even fewer are interested in the technical aspects of swaps, conversions, or debentures. I sympathize with their ennui. I have tried to spare the reader all, but the most essential, details of these matters, even, perhaps, at the risk sometimes of concentrating on the forest rather than the trees. Prospective woodsmen will undoubtedly find much choice, not to say crooked, timber to fell, and they are welcome to it. No book can be the last word on a subject as vast as this.

Finally, I have consciously tried to avoid the politics and myth of advocacy. One version of the London Debt story, familiar to most Mexicans, concentrates on the injustice, unfairness, and sheer rapacity of both the

---

6 Not everyone, especially in Mexico, is oblivious. As the late Araceli Ibarra Bellon put it in her incomplete, but nevertheless very important, book, "The history of independent Mexico is, in more than one sense, the history of the external debt." *El comercio y el poder en México, 1821–1864. La lucha por las fuentes financieras entre el Estado central y las regiones* (México, 1998), p. 47.

original agreements and their various reincarnations. This is the "Mexico-deceived and abandoned" tale with which some older works present us. While it is true that few financiers, British, Mexican, Swiss, or otherwise, were out to do Mexico any favors, the story of pillaging and looting needs to be put to rest. While various Mexican regimes did not always act wisely and some acted positively foolishly, it is simply wrong to view the first federal republic as the unwitting victim of the conniving British. *Everyone* was conniving and with reason. There was much at stake in 1824 and 1825, the independence of a nation, for one thing, and as Benjamin Disraeli so memorably remarked, fortunes to be made. *Everyone* in this little drama sought to seize the main chance. There were crooks to be sure, and true patriots as well – sometimes in the same person, although rarely at the same time. But a lot of people lost their fortunes – and some their lives – to the process that the British loans set in motion: the victims were *both* British and Mexican, as were the beneficiaries. By 1827, both British merchant banks that had brought the original loans to market had gone bust, and one of them, Barclay, Herring, Richardson, explicitly blamed Mexican duplicity for the debacle. Many observers of the London market said much the same. Of course, it is equally wrong to view this as a story of predatory Mexicans having their way with Scottish widows, although, to be sure, there were predatory Mexican officials and Scottish widows. The cheaters, scoundrels, and thieves were, refreshingly, a diverse lot, some of painfully and deliberately indefinite nationality, the better to confuse the unwitting on all sides. John Womack remarked many years ago that it was time to get beyond civics in these stories. I trust I have or, at least, I have tried.

Finance in the Time of Cholera: An Overview

In 1836, a sophisticated, cosmopolitan, anonymous, and unusually astute observer of the Mexican economy published an analysis entitled *Algunas Consideraciones Económicas*.[7] While modern historians have considered the problems of the early national Mexican economy from a variety of perspectives, this observer took an unusual tack. Clearly, influenced by political economists such as John Stuart Mill and Nassau Senior, the author of *Algunas Consideraciones Económicas* looked to the Mexican monetary system – and more specifically, to the exchange rate – as the root of the country's problem. Mexico was tied to silver and, in conjunction with the productivity of its mines, was at a distinct disadvantage when Great Britain, the world's most dynamic economy, was linked to gold. Briefly, the price of

---

7 Richard J. Salvucci, "Algunas Consideraciones Económicas (1836). Análisis Mexicano de la Depresión a Principios del Siglo XIX," *Historia Mexicana*, 55: 1 (2005), pp. 67–97, for a preliminary treatment of this analysis and a full range of textual citations. Much of what follows is based on this study.

silver in terms of gold was determined internationally, by world supply and demand. But prices in Mexico – in terms of silver – were determined locally, because the great bulk of Mexican production was, by virtue of high transportation costs, nontradable. This implied that wage goods in Mexico, especially foodstuffs, bore no necessary relation to the exchange rate, certainly not as theories based on purchasing power parity would have it. But if food costs were typically the largest part of the wage bill in a manufacturing industry like textiles, this fact constituted a serious structural problem. When expressed in terms of gold, the costs of Mexican industrial production were high. Or conversely, when expressed in terms of silver, the price of imported goods, typically British cottons, were low.

In theory, or at least in the vision of David Hume, such imbalances would get righted by monetary flows. The high-cost country would suffer a balance of trade deficit and lose specie to its competitors. This, in turn, would drive down prices and restore international equilibrium. But Mexico was a mining country, and the mines were, at least in the view of the author of *Algunas Consideraciones*, no respecter of relative scarcity. Their output was strictly exogenous – in modern terms, mostly a matter of happenstance. So there was no guarantee that domestic prices and costs would necessarily move in accord with the Humean mechanism, either. Since the exchange rate (in terms of gold) was exogenous as well, the peculiarities of a mining economy affected Mexico in a number of ways. The most obvious, of course, was the misalignment of the exchange rate. Since Mexico had no control over it, devaluation or depreciation was ruled out.[8] Indeed, modern discussions of the implications of a fixed exchange rate – such as the silver standard – emphasize the general ineffectiveness of monetary policy under such a system. It is, rather, fiscal policy that is effective.[9] Ironically, the fiscal policy that the later Bourbons had imposed on Mexico had been highly contractionary, consisting largely of sending Mexican purchasing power abroad in a series of increasingly aggressive taxes and forced "loans" chronicled in detail by Marichal, who estimates that Mexico sent 35 million pesos abroad between 1780 and 1810.[10] Thus, Mexico in the early nineteenth century suffered from stagnation, an economic contraction brought on by the consequences of what amounted to an overvalued exchange rate,

---

8 It is true that, strictly speaking, Mexico violated the small-country assumption, for disturbances to mining output in Mexico during the instability of the 1810s had repercussions on the international price of silver. But mining was a decentralized, private activity and there seems to have been no effort made to coordinate or direct the production decisions of individual silver miners.

9 This is known as the Mundell–Fleming model. A nontechnical discussion appears in *Finance and Development*, 43: 3 (2006). For an accessible textbook treatment, see Manfred Gartner, *A Primer in European Macroeconomics* (London, 1997).

10 Carlos Marichal, *La bancarrota del virreinato. Nueva España y las finanzas del Imperio español, 1780–1810* (México, 1999), p. 284.

by the crushingly deflationary policies of the Bourbons, by price rigidities, or, most likely, by all of the above. *Algunas Consideraciones* makes for grim, if not fascinating, reading, for it suggests that whatever else ailed Mexico in the early nineteenth century – the heritage of civil war in the 1810s or the beginning of a long period of political instability in the beginning of the 1830s – there were structural foundations to this crisis that virtually no government of the era could have realistically been prepared to confront.

These were the macroeconomics of scarcity, as far as Mexico was concerned. The consequences were clear enough. For example, the author of *Algunas Consideraciones* thought that the backbone of the Mexican countryside, the hacienda economy, had been severely prejudiced by what occurred. The argument went to the root of things, for, historically, the owners of haciendas had drawn on the equity of their properties for finance by the widespread and intricate mechanism of clerical mortgages or *censos*. Rising land prices had encouraged such borrowing in the eighteenth century, but now property values had gone into reverse, especially in those parts of the country, such as the Bajío, where damage from the civil war of the 1810s had been most severe. Here the implications of stagnation were even starker, for they were self-reinforcing. If Mexico was essentially rural and agrarian, with an exiguous share of the population living in cities, the implication of falling property values for aggregate demand was surely disproportional. Unlike other parts of Latin America, and the importance of silver mining notwithstanding, secular movements in output in the Mexican economy were more the product of home than external demand, for in this sense, Mexico was unlike Brazil, Cuba, the River Plate, or what portions of Central America, Chile, and Peru were to become after 1840. And these secular movements had typically been associated with the fortunes of what Victor Bulmer-Thomas calls "domestic use" rather than export agriculture. Enrique Florescano, for example, has famously argued that agricultural crises were the key to understanding economic cycles in the eighteenth century.[11] Here, in slightly different guise, the thesis reappears, but driven by a wealth effect rather than by price shocks propagated by crop failures.

But countries do not grow by aggregate demand alone, at least in the long run. In the short run, aggregate demand drives variations in production. But in the long run, it is aggregate supply, determined by population, resources, and technology, that determines what an economy will produce. *Algunas Consideraciones Económicas*, with its focus on the exchange rate, does think about costs, but costs in the short run. The fundamental importance of the size of the labor force and its level of productivity were not of much interest to its author. But there were Mexicans who were deeply interested in population and resources, just as the wide variety of publications in

---

11 Enrique Florescano, *Precios del maíz y crisis agrícolas en México (1708–1810)* (México, 1969).

the 1830s and 1840s might suggest.[12] Many of these, it is true, were motivated by fiscal considerations, but they serve to provide us with some notion, however imperfect, of the magnitudes at issue.

The best estimates of the day made allowance for the wars, epidemics, and "other calamities" that had struck Mexico since the time of Humboldt. And these put the population of México at about 7 million souls. With contemporary estimates of product toward 1840 at 300 million pesos, this implied an output per head of around 40 pesos. Combining the famous estimates of José María Quirós and Alexander Humboldt would suggest very nearly the same, about 40 pesos per head, around 1810. By the late 1830s, the inescapable fact was that Mexico was not growing, hence the appearance of studies like *Algunas Consideraciones*, which sought to account for this fact.

But the absence of economic growth is a real problem, not just a matter of numbers. It does not require particularly complicated economic models to demonstrate how rapidly problem will arise – an elementary account will suffice.[13] Aggregate demand (AD) determines – and in return, is determined by – production or current income (Y). In a simple closed economy, the largest component of demand is personal consumption (C), itself a function of income. Savings (S) is nothing but "nonconsumed output" ($S = Y - C$). If income is stagnant (abbreviate this $dY = 0$, where "d" is "the change in" what follows), if C rises ($dC > 0$), S must fall ($dS < 0$). Conversely, if greater savings are required ($dS > 0$), then consumption must fall ($dC < 0$).

Under what circumstances would greater savings be needed? There could be many. In a closed economy, private investment (I) must be financed out of home resources. So the volume of savings ("nonconsumed output") limits the size of investment, famously $S = I$, as another equilibrium condition. It is the iron law of common sense: if you consume everything, you have no resources left over with which to create productive assets. This in itself is a serious enough issue, one that bears heavily on Mexican history, because it explains the sharpness of class struggles over distribution, the ongoing tendency for the expropriation of the peasantry, and much more. Yet this is not even the principal focus of our interest, which is public finance.

Define savings (S) as the sum of private (S_{PR}) and public savings (S_{PU}), which occurs when we introduce the idea of public or government expenditure (G). Government savings can then be defined as the difference between

---

12 Virginia Vargas Rangel, "El Primer Presidente de la Sociedad Mexicana de Geografía e Estadística," *Elementos*, 62 (2006), pp. 35–41; *Catológo de documentos históricos de la estadística en México (Siglos XVI–XIX)* (Aguascalientes, México, 2005).

13 Keynes put the matter simply enough in Book III of his *General Theory*. Say's law did not apply to a modern economy because the marginal propensity to consume out of income was less than 1. See, for example, Benjamin M. Friedman, *The Moral Consequences of Economic Growth* (New York, 2005), pp. 400–411, for a nontechnical discussion.

Table I.1. *Budget Balance of the National Government*

Year	Revenue	Expenditure	Balance
1825–1826	11.0	12.2	−1.2
1826–1827	11.4	12.6	−1.2
1827–1828	10.4	11.0	−0.6
1828–1829	11.0	12.2	−1.2
1829–1830	9.8	12.0	−2.2
1830–1831	13.4	16.5	−3.1
1831–1832	11.8	15.7	−3.9
1832–1833	10.3		
1833–1834	11.5	18.6	−7.1
1835–1836	13.8	24.9	−11.1
1836–1837	18.5	17.6	0.9
1837–1838	22.6	24.1	−1.5
1839	27.5	25.7	1.8
1840	19.9	19.9	0.0
1841	21.3	20.3	1.0
1842	26.7	26.6	0.1
1843	29.3	29.2	0.1
1844	15.8	25.3	−9.5
1845	20.4	19.6	0.8
1848–1849	16.7	17.5	−0.8
1849–1850	13.8	15.8	−2.0
1850–1851	7.3	12.6	−5.3
1851–1852	9.2	8.6	0.6

Note: Values are in millions of pesos.

Source: Adapted from http://biblioteca.itam.mx/recursos/ehm.html#finanzas, 17.3.1 (accessed September 25, 2007).

G and taxation (T), or ($T - G > 0$). This is nothing more than a fiscal surplus. A deficit ($T - G < 0$) has the opposite sign and represents dissavings. If a government runs a deficit, it reduces (total) S because the public component (S_{PU}) has a minus sign. A fall in S must reduce I in a *closed* economy, something known as "crowding out." If the reduction in investment reduces the growth of income, private consumption and savings will also stagnate in the long run. So, assuming that foreign capital or increased exports cannot come to the rescue (i.e., this is not an open economy), budget deficits would have exacerbated the problems that the author of *Algunas Consideraciones* had fixed on. And in particular, the distributive conflicts to which we referred could have only sharpened.

The idea that fiscal deficits accompanied slow growth in Mexico is more than a theory. If we look at the sparse data we have on actual deficits of the national (i.e., either federal or central) government between 1825 and 1850 in Table I.1, about two-thirds of the time, the budget was in deficit.

Most deficits were small, certainly, averaging about 2 million pesos per year, but 1835–1836 and 1844 were sizable. Interestingly, comparing the "realized" and "budgeted" deficits shows that the government was generally too pessimistic, or perhaps "optimistic" is the better word. There was simply no way for Mexico to finance large, persistent fiscal deficits, so the "realized" deficits tended to be lower. And if fiscal matters got truly out of hand, as they did in the signal year of 1835–1836, when the Texas campaign and the suppression of provincial federalism were the military order of the day, the consequences were severe, as we see later. Although modern interpretations of government deficits emphasize their expansionary effects, it went differently in Mexico. Deficits are expansionary to the extent they increase aggregate demand. In Mexico, fiscal deficits absorbed what little savings there were and capital markets were small and thin. Deficits did not drive the economy, not even in the short run. Deficits choked off productive activity. Interest rates reported by British consul-general Charles T. O'Gorman confirm the impression that small deficits were difficult to finance. As early as 1825, O'Gorman reported rates of 1–3 percent *per month*, and as high as 4–6 percent per month for short-term credit, even though the legal ceiling was 6 percent a year.[14] If domestic lenders were getting this much in 1825, it is no wonder that the Federation would turn to London in order to borrow!

The sheer magnitude and persistence of the fiscal problem did, as Silva Herzog observed, affect everything. Certainly, one way of interpreting a fundamental political division of the nineteenth century, the conflict between federalists and centralists, is in fiscal terms between the "haves" (the states) and the "have nots" (the Federation). It is no exaggeration to argue that centralism was an attempt to marshal the resources that were unavailable under federalism and that the effort was successful enough to leave its traces in the financial markets. The administrative reorganization of Mexico under centralism signified many things, but it was also a response to the financial inadequacies of federalism. These inadequacies appeared with signal clarity in matters of debt service, one of fundamental themes of this study. Financing deficits and paying debt service raised excruciatingly difficult choices: between paying current and past expenses, or current and past creditors. At the limit, it meant choosing between paying domestic and foreign creditors as well, *agiotistas* (high-risk government lenders) versus *tenedores de bonos*. This was the peculiar syntax and vocabulary of nineteenth-century finance.

---

14 "Interest," México, March 1, 1825, PRO, FO 203/3. I emphasize that we do not have an adequate study of prices or interest rates before 1870, but into the late 1830s, documentary evidence suggests that government borrowing at 3 percent a month was "normal" falling to as low as 1 percent a month in times of serious financial stress, such as during the Panic of 1837.

What exactly, one asks, is the evidence for such an interpretation? While the following chapters provide a detailed account of the argument, we can outline it in general terms here. Under centralism, the effective revenues of the central government grew because the reorganization of state finances allowed for more direct supervision and control. The increase in revenues provided greater latitude in paying debt service, but especially for meeting the demands of the London bondholders. Hence the stock exchange tended to support centralist administrations, even though centralist governments did not inevitably conform themselves exactly to the interests of the London bondholders. There was a delicate balance to be maintained between the interests of domestic and foreign creditors, so that no policy could, in a strict sense, favor one group completely over another. In one case, for instance, servicing the London bondholders was a means of accumulating diplomatic capital when the support of Great Britain appeared crucial in matters of foreign policy. In another, paying domestic financiers (the notorious *agiotistas*) mattered when their complaisance was required to purchase war matériel or political and military support at home – especially when foreign matters were less pressing or amenable to influence. Or there were times, such as the French intervention, when domestic Mexican interests were more or less subordinate to French diplomatic concerns – hence the complexity of the argument and the sharply changing contours of the narrative. The financial and political logic of each distinct situation trumped the general, and largely noncontroversial, assumption that Mexico should pay its British creditors. Mexican finance ministers knew that. Most believed it. And most were unable to do very much about it.

To understand, however crudely, the effect that centralist reorganization had on the revenues of the government, we look at the *ingreso efectivo* provided by Matías Romero in Figure I.1. Admittedly, revenue figures for the period are imperfect, but these are what we have for 1825 through 1870, and the claims we make are modest. If we examine the trend for *ingreso efectivo* produced by smoothing the annual data with a Hodrick–Prescott filter,[15] there is some upward movement as early as 1830, but the real increase comes after 1835, peaking around 1842, the high-water mark of centralism. The fiscal crises of the return to federalism and the post-war collapse are well represented here too. The trend continues to decay until around 1858, at which point a recovery that continues through the conservative "reaction" and the French intervention occurs. Recent studies

---

15 I resort to smoothing here because I am interested in estimating a (nonlinear) trend, for which smoothing is most appropriate. See Francis X. Diebold, *Elements of Forecasting* (4th ed., Mason, OH, 2007), pp. 75, 313. Romero defines *ingreso efectivo* as the income of the central government adjusted for extraordinary income and carryovers. This presumably adjusts for the effects of domestic loans or *agiotaje*. See *Memoria de Hacienda . . . 1870*, par. 3187.

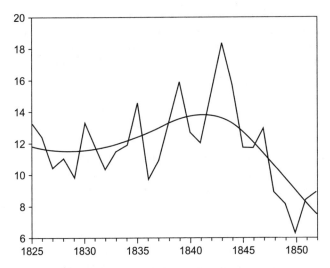

Figure I.1. *Ingreso Efectivo* of the Federation, 1825–1852.

demonstrate that these trends reflect changes in the relation between the states and the central government; the reorganization of state treasuries and their audit and supervision; and attempts to diversify the tax base in favor of direct taxes on real property as an alternative to the maritime customs – a kind of revival of what David Brading once termed the "Bourbon reconquest," but at a purely national level.[16]

Yet even more intriguingly, the financial markets – here the London Stock Exchange – indicated the ability to discriminate between centralist and federalist regimes in Mexico, with the preference given to centralism. This finding runs counter to current trends in the Mexican historiography, which tend to minimize the substantive differences between centralism, federalism, and their adherents.[17] Yet the result was not magical. It is not even counterintuitive. The mechanism was prosaic. The London bondholders were interested, above all, in repayment. Repayment became most likely when Mexico could maximize the revenue it collected. This generally occurred under centralist regimes. So Mexican bond prices rose under

16 See especially the contributions of Jorge Castañeda Zavala and Martín Sánchez Rodríguez in Carlos Marichal and Daniela Marino, eds., *De Colonia a Nación. Impuestos y política en México, 1750–1860* (México, 2001). Matías Romero concurs, pointing out the under centralism or Santa Anna dictatorships, the income of the states was effectively considered the income of the central government – which was not the case under federalist regimes. See *Memoria de hacienda . . . 1870*, par. 3185, II.

17 See, for example, Catherine Andrews, "Discusiones en torno de la reforma de la Constitución Federal de 1824 durante el primer gobierno de Anastasio Bustamante (1830–1832)," *Historia Mexicana*, 56: 1 (2006), pp. 71–116, esp. 105, 109–110.

centralism (or performed less robustly under federalism). A simple but suggestive test of the proposition is to regress the average price of Mexican bonds on *ingreso efectivo*, a crude procedure to be sure, for it uses an annualized bond price from a very volatile market. Nevertheless, even at this level, the *tendency* is apparent.

$$\text{Price of bonds} = 21.0 + 0.65 \text{ } \textit{ingreso liquido}$$
$$(t = 1.8),$$

where the adjusted coefficient of determination is .35, the F-statistic (10.25) is significant at 99 percent, and the coefficient on *ingreso liquido* is significant at 90 percent. This includes the period 1828–1862, or the thirty-five years between default and the French intervention, and is corrected for first-order serial correlation. The point, to repeat, is simple. The London Stock Exchange reacted positively to increases in the collection of Mexican revenues, for these raised the probability of repayment (perhaps even disproportionately in the case of an issue in default, as was Mexico after 1827). The centralist governments generally extracted greater revenues from the states (or "departments") than did the federalist regimes – a government sharply constrained by the representatives of the states in Congress. Therefore, the London market typically "supported" centralism.

Another indication of the impact of centralism on the financial markets was the peso–sterling exchange rate. While we explore the impact of British lending on this rate in 1825 in much greater detail later, it is worth considering a few general features of the exchange market here. The exchange rate of sterling per 100 pesos on London appears here in an annual average form and smoothed to bring out long-term features in Figures I.2 and I.3. Both pictures highlight the steady rise of the peso between 1824 and 1853, as if to underscore the very concerns presented in *Algunas consideraciones*. Yet there are periods when the rise is particularly sharp: on the smoothed graph, one occurs after 1836 and the other roughly after 1850 or so. The coincidence of appreciation with centralism and the Santanista dictatorship (1837–1844) is apparent. The very sharp appreciation at the end of the period comes during Antonio López de Santa Anna's final dictatorship (1853). It would be tempting to assert that this proves that the British had great expectations of Santa Anna, at least while Mexican territory was in play, something taken up later as well. But this is, perhaps, too facile, since the silver standard was a fixed exchange: it could not mirror fluctuations in market sentiment as a floating rate can. However, a fixed exchange will respond to trade and capital flows within the narrow band of import and export points. This, once again, was where the political economy of centralism was in evidence. The regime of high tariffs and prohibitions that began in 1837, continued in 1842 and 1843, and reached its climax in 1853

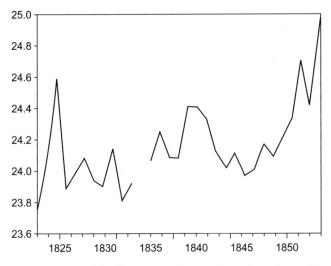

Figure I.2. British Pound Sterling per 100 Mexican Pesos. *Source:* Jurgen Schneider et al., *Wahrungen der Welt* (8 vols., Stuttgart, 1991–1994), vol. 7: pp. 365–367.

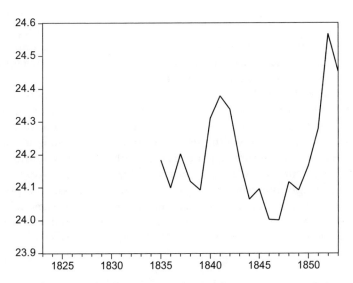

Figure I.3. British Pound Sterling per 100 Mexican Pesos (Smoothed).
Note: Smoothed series begins in 1835 because of gap in data.

had a dramatic effect on trade flows to Mexico.[18] It effectively reduced crucial imports such as cotton cloth, yarn, and thread. The falling demand for imports drove down the demand for foreign exchange – hence the peso appreciated in bursts around the tariffs that defined centralism. The evidence of the effect appears in *both* the asset and foreign exchange markets.

There was, nevertheless, some irony here. As we shall see, not all the elements of the political economy of centralism were equally congenial to the London bondholders. In particular, one of the core constituencies of centralism was Mexico's nascent industrial class. For these, a commercial policy that emphasized protection, not to say complete prohibition, was what they most desired. Yet the *last* thing helpful to improving Mexico's fiscal position was a commercial regime that *reduced* or eliminated imports, because the customs were historically the principal source of government revenue. So while the fiscal, bureaucratic, and organizational reforms that centralism brought might be desirable from a creditor's point of view, the element of protectionism, among others, was not. While it is by no means clear that "liberal," "federalist," and "free trader" were synonymous – or even necessarily overlapping – categories, a credible regime from an international standpoint would inevitably be economically liberal, but politically centralist. One has only to read Francisco Madero's account of politics after independence in *La sucessión presidencial de 1910* to understand why a (historically centralist) government of the stripe of Díaz's would ultimately be required to take Mexico back into the international capital market or what the required political transformation would be.[19] For the economic historian, the genesis of "conservative liberalism" in Mexico was as much a function of international pressure as it was of the exigencies of domestic politics described by Charles Hale.[20] It is also a key to understanding one of the paradoxes of centralist political economy: why the London market supported a protectionist regime (and an ostensible reduction in government capacity to pay), even as the arrears of the debt were growing. As Fishlow has astutely observed, this was a recurring issue in nineteenth-century Latin America.[21]

Mexico's return to the international capital market after a decade of civil war and foreign intervention (1858–1867) was slow in coming precisely because of domestic opposition. Yet when it did come, it came relatively quickly. As we have seen, in a closed economy, fixed capital investment is constrained by available savings ($S = I$). But in an open economy, no such

---

18 Richard J. Salvucci, "The Origins and Progress of U.S.-Mexican Trade, 1825–1884: 'Hoc opus, hic labor est'," *HAHR*, 71: 4 (1991), esp. p. 713.

19 *La Sucesión Presidencial en 1910* ([1908] México, 1985), p. 123.

20 Charles Hale, *The Transformation of Liberalism in Nineteenth-Century Mexico* (Princeton, NJ, 1989), pp. 246–247.

21 Albert Fishlow, e-mail to the author, April 7, 2007.

constraint applies. The crucial identity of international macroeconomics is

$$S - I = X - M,$$

where $X - M$ is the trade balance (net exports of goods and services), or roughly, the balance on current account. This means that investment is no longer limited by domestic resources. In other words, an open economy can draw on the resources of its trading partners. It can consume more than it produces, hence saving less than it invests, by importing the difference; that is,

$$S < I = X < M.$$

Yet this is, in a sense, merely arithmetic. The crucial question is how to finance the external deficit ($X < M$) or how a country persuades the rest of the world to lend to it.[22] In the short run, at least, a country pays by issuing claims against itself – IOUs, in other words. Obviously, a country's bonds, when sold to the rest of the world, accomplish just that. But the Mexicans were well aware that they had little prospect of reentering the international market as long as the "first debt crisis" remained unresolved. What choice did they have?

The pressure on Mexico to resume "normal" financial relations with the rest of the world, especially with Great Britain, was a legacy of how Mexico had operated since independence, or at least, since the 1830s. With negligible economic growth and negative public savings, the domestic resources available to fund capital formation were limited. At the same time, high rates of interest to government lending (*agiotaje*) and elsewhere do suggest some crowding out of productive investment. This was especially true in view of the fact that many of Mexico's major industrialists, such as Cayetano Rubio, Manuel Escandón, or the Martínez del Río, were also major government lenders. Hence crowding out was simply opportunity cost. But Mexico was now entering the railroad age: no other investment was as necessary nor as capital intensive as railroads.

The nature of Mexican endowments made railroads peculiarly valuable. As a country with difficult terrain and high transportation costs, the evidence of an inefficiently low degree of economic specialization was everywhere. As Guillermo Beato has observed in a recent overview of the textile industry in the nineteenth century, factories in Mexico typically marketed their output at the state or regional level. As a result, "a good number of

---

22 In recent years, it has become common to warn developing countries against the dangers of relying overmuch on the dangers of foreign finance because of the possibility of rapid reversals of capital flows and accompanying collapse of demand. In Mexico, practically, the alternative implied an even more rigorous expropriation of the peasantry than actually occurred. Admittedly, this strains credibility, not to say ordinary notions of distributional fairness.

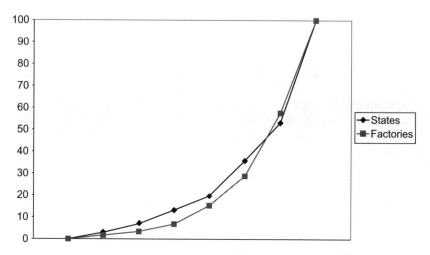

Figure I.4. Lorenz Curves, by Population, Location of Factories, Selected States, around 1840 (see text).

states had factories that did not venture to place their products in distant markets."[23] A graphic illustration of Beato's point appears in Figure I.4. Using population data for 1839 and Beato's data on state factory locations 1843, we have constructed Lorenz curves for seven states (departments). While these are a very crude representation on several counts, it is interesting that the concentration of factories and population more or less follow each other; there is really no evidence of far more specialization (concentration) in factories than in population, which seems to be the larger point. If regional comparative advantage were evident, one would expect significantly more concentration in factories than population, but high transportation costs impeded any such reorganization.

As a consequence, significant productivity gains were to be expected from the reallocation of resources that a sharp reduction in transportation costs would provide – an increase, in other words, in total factor productivity. Thus a potentially large source of domestic savings was contingent on the construction of railroads, and these were, in turn, dependent on the mobilization of significant quantities of capital, and hence, savings.

In theory, there was no reason why such a "vicious circle" or low-level equilibrium could not have been altered by an increase in net exports, because from the standpoint of national income, these would have had (approximately) the same effect as an inflow of foreign capital. But here

---

23 "La industria textil fabril en México. I. 1830–1900," in Mario Trujillo Bolio and José María Contreras Valdez, eds., *Formación empresarial, fomento industrial y compañías agrícolas en el México del siglo xix* (México, 2003), pp. 225–228. For the quotation, see p. 234.

again, the railroads in Mexico proved crucial. The improvement in the barter terms of trade for most of the nineteenth century had been modest, so something was clearly needed to improve the relative prices of the *potential* exportables that Mexico could offer. While a portion of this would come from the decline in international freight rates, something more was needed, or the growth of Mexican exports would have gathered momentum earlier in the nineteenth century than it did. So, again, one hypothesizes that what John Coatsworth termed "indispensable railroads" were important in raising the prices that exporters could expect – hence the importance of negotiating an end to the default on the British bonds. Given what was at stake, one expects that the Mexicans would have been able and willing to offer a substantial premium to reenter the international – especially, London capital – market.

But, one asks, how could anyone in Mexico have realized this *ex ante*? As we will see, the political costs of bringing the London Debt problem were substantial and immediately apparent. How, the historian asks, could the potential benefits (or their present value) have been equally apparent? The answer may be prosaic, but some of the ministers who were instrumental in helping Mexico end its isolation – someone like Romero – in the initial stages were broadly cosmopolitan, well traveled, and above all, intimately familiar with modernity, at least in its material manifestations. Romero, for example, had literally bridged the gulf from Oaxaca to Wall Street in the course of his life. His travels in the United States had taken him to New York and Philadelphia as well as Washington and the things he fixed on were revealing. True, Romero was deeply interested in the staple institutions of nineteenth-century reform, prisons, and asylums, which he visited frequently. But when he went to Philadelphia, he commented on the famous water works on the Schuylkill, spent time in the thriving textile district of Manayunk, and, in particular, admired the bridges, probably truss bridges for railroads.[24] For someone like Romero, who commented with distaste on the slave market of New Orleans – a city where many Mexican politicians had been in exile, but whose institutions seemed less than admirable – this was surely the meaning of "falling behind." The matérial prosperity of the liberal northeastern United States was bound up in its infrastructure and its railroads – artifacts that Mexico could purchase only with capital brought in from abroad. Yet none of this was possible as long as Mexico remained in default. In Romero's mind, the promotion of trade, an open economy, and productive investment were linked to the sorts of humanitarian reforms that interested him deeply in his travels. To dismiss his outlook, in modern

---

24 Emma Cosío Villegas, ed., *Diario personal de Matías Romero (1855–1865)* (México, 1960), esp. pp. 319–322. Also see, in general, Matías Romero, *La promoción de las relaciones comerciales entre México y los Estados Unidos de América* ([1879] México, 1961), pp. 160–164.

parlance, as simply "neoliberal" is to do both the man and the entire notion of economic development a grave injustice.

When the final settlement of the default did come, as we shall see, numerous factors played a role in its timing. For contemporaries, the *political* dimension of the question may have been the immediate catalyst, for as it had done so often previously, political considerations in the short run could outweigh the economic benefits that would accrue in the long. Madero, no friend to Díaz to be sure, but an astute student of the century just ended, argued that Díaz opposed the resolution of the London Debt under Sebastián Lerdo de Tejada precisely because he had no intention of aiding his rivals.[25] Yet in the last analysis, Díaz was ultimately the beneficiary of institutional developments in Mexico that made the historic choice between domestic and foreign finance less of a binding constraint than it had been. In particular, the establishment of banking in Porfirian Mexico, especially the creation of the Banco Nacional de Mexico,[26] effectively furnished the executive in Mexico with a freedom of maneuver that earlier presidents could have only envied. The problem with confronting domestic financiers was not that they would stop lending – ultimately they *had* to lend if they were to recover anything – but that they would not lend to you. Their power over governments was considerable: the roll of finance ministers drawn from the ranks of the *agiotistas* was not unimpressive, especially in the 1830s and 1840s. The creation of a bank of issue that acted as a creditor to the government by no means eliminated the power of domestic bondholders, but certainly reduced it. In 1882, bank notes comprised less than 10 percent of the money supply in Mexico. By 1889, the proportion had reached 45 percent, even as the money supply had not quite doubled.[27] The conclusion is inescapable. Díaz was able to resolve the issue of Mexico's London Debt in no small part because he was the beneficiary of a monetary revolution of the 1880s. Of all of Mexico's nineteenth-century "revolutions," this is perhaps the least recognized, but arguably the most important. It was in precisely this that for the first time since the late 1820s, the countervailing pressures of domestic and foreign lenders – pressures that had so often produced a stalemate or a tendency to lurch from satisfying one group to satisfying another – were overcome.

Plan of the Work

The plan of this book is as follows. There are four chapters that proceed in chronological order. The advantage of a chronological approach is that there is a coherent framework that makes the complex back-and-forth

25 Madero, *Sucesión Presidencial*, p. 115.
26 Created by the merger of the Banco Nacional Mexicano and the Banco Mercantil Mexicano in 1884.
27 *Review of the Economic Situation of Mexico*, 60 (June 1984), pp. 184–187.

of negotiations, reschedulings, and moratoria easier for the reader to follow. There is also another reason for following a chronological approach.
Contemporaries' understanding of the London Debt changed as the world
around them changed. If the independence of Latin America was the touchstone of the initial negotiations, by the 1830s and 1840s, what mattered
was the independence of Texas. In the 1850s, the relation of Mexico and
the United States was openly compared to that of Turkey and Russia, and
so the interests of the British bondholders were accordingly defined. The
British bondholders were certainly the beneficiaries of French ambitions in
the Americas in the 1860s, just as were the Mexicans of rapid postbellum
growth of the United States in the 1870s. There is no point in avoiding
chronology because with the London Debt, context is everything. Hence
this framework rather than, say, a thematic one.

The first chapter opens with the financial world turned upside down,
the great financial crash in London in late 1825. While this is certainly one
of the more interesting episodes of financial history, it bears a more-than-
passing connection to Mexican, and indeed, Latin American, borrowing.
By some accounts, defaulted Latin American issues over the period 1822–
1825 were a critical element in bringing the speculative loan boom to
an end, causing the then astronomical figure of £21 million in losses.[28]
Mexico was no small player in this market, borrowing and defaulting on
£6.4 million, or nearly a third of the total. Hence I carefully analyze the
process whereby the Mexicans determined on foreign borrowing, decided
between alternative offers, negotiated a series of agreements, received the
proceeds of the loans, and began their disbursement and repayment. Yet
each aspect was embedded in bureaucratic and political processes on both
sides of the market. They involved multiple actors with sharply conflicting
ideologies and goals, not to say unequal access to ministers and even official documents. In the context of the day, these conflicts were frequently
disclosed – or understood – as purely personal rivalries, but in reality, they
tell us far more. Similarly, the varying goals of the actors, such as the consolidation of independence and British recognition on the Mexican side,
or pursuit of profit on the British yielded to the limitations of financial
markets, government ministries, and even the mechanics of exchange rate
determination. The result was a classic case of unintended consequences.
Mexico's bid for financial stability in the 1820s was upset by shocks to the
exchange rate. British expectations of profit were similarly frustrated by
lags in the timing of negotiations and signings, or by principal–agent problems: merchant bankers in London and their agents in Mexico City could
and did weigh their own interests differently, especially when disparities

---

28 Frank Griffiths Dawson, *The First Latin American Debt Crisis. The City of London and the 1822–1825
Loan Bubble* (New Haven, CT, 1990).

in access to private information meant large profits for those in a position to know. Finally, I consider two questions that have long defined studies of the London Debt. The first is the question of who profited and by how much. I assess the evidence by a variety of metrics. The Mexicans paid, sometimes dearly, for what they borrowed. Ironically, though, had Mexico paid more regularly, it might well have paid less. The millstone around their collective necks was the compounding of arrears, a sum that each successive interruption and renegotiation of payment enlarged. On the other hand, the original British merchant banks that underwrote the loan went bust and certainly the first generation of what contemporaries called bona fide or buy and hold investors in Britain and elsewhere lost most everything. The conclusion that *everyone* lost money will strike some as not only odd but impossible. Others will be reminded of something that Fishlow said of the debt crisis of the 1980s: "Only the airlines made money."[29] There were no airlines to transport ministers and negotiators around the globe in the nineteenth century, but there were intermediaries then – active traders on the London Stock Exchange – who seemingly got the lion's share of the capital gains. The second question involves both due diligence and accounting controls: was Mexico swindled, historians in Mexico and elsewhere have sometimes insinuated, albeit vaguely?[30] The answer to this question, not surprisingly, turns out to be rather complex. There was undoubtedly hanky panky on both sides, swindlers and swindled wrapped in various flags, but these were more often crimes of opportunity than systematic robbery. Victims there were in abundance, and not just in Mexico. If anything, the Federation revealed itself to be a most astute negotiator when circumstances permitted. The "Mexico as victim" story had its origins in the labyrinthine course of nineteenth-century Mexican politics. It made for good, and quite enduring, rhetoric.

Chapter 2 centers on the first Mexican default in 1827. The Mexican default was not exactly unprecedented: Colombia, the largest of the Latin

---

29 Fishlow made this remark at a seminar in Berkeley in the mid-1980s when then Finance Minister Jesús Silva Herzog was the guest speaker.

30 The most recent study to appear in Mexico in this vein is José Zaragoza, *Historia de la deuda externa de México, 1823–1861* (México, 1996), pp. 40–48. Jan Bazant, *Historia de la deuda exterior de México* (2nd ed., México, 1981), is better balanced, but nevertheless concludes that Mexico was one among many "victims," p. 32. Bazant's view had largely become the received wisdom. See, for instance, Óscar Alatriste, "El capitalismo Británico en los inicios del México independiente," *Estudios de historia moderna y contemporánea de México*, 6 (1977), pp. 9–41. The classic, and in many ways still indispensable, account is Joaquín Casasus, *Historia de la deuda contraída en Londres* (México, 1885), which distinguishes between the loans themselves and the disposition of their proceeds, esp. pp. 79 et ff "Consideraciones acerca de los dos empréstitos." Of those outside of Mexico, J. Fred Rippy concluded that "[Mexico] seems to have been shorn more thoroughly than any of the rest....," "Latin America and the British Investment 'Boom' of the 1820s," *The Journal of Modern History*, 19: 2 (1947), p. 127.

American borrowers, had defaulted earlier in 1826. Nevertheless, a close reading of the Mexican version reveals some interesting and, perhaps, unusual features. We might say that the default was imperfectly antici-pated: a month or so before it occurred, Mexican bonds dropped substan-tially on the London Stock Exchange, but when the formal deadline passed in October 1827, there was little public notice. Nor did Mexican min-isters seem unduly concerned by the default, at least initially. The major impetus to a resolution came only with Lucas Alamán and Rafael Mangino, who served with Anastasio Bustamante's brief government (1830–1832). Alamán was especially willing to accommodate the London bondholders, but his arrangement, the Conversion of 1830, proved fragile. Ironically, the fiscal crisis provoked by the separatist tendencies of the northern states, especially Texas, was to wreck the Conversion of 1830, but prepare the diplomatic environment for its successor, the Conversion of 1837. Indeed, the impetus behind the Conversion of 1837 was Mexico's attempt to enlist British support in its struggle to recover Texas. A series of intricate maneu-vers was played out through 1846 in an effort to balance the support of domestic and British interests, but the attempt would fail. The program "the political economy of centralism" sought stability by binding Mexi-can financial and industrial interests to the state through a combination of administrative restructuring, restrictive commercial policy, development finance, and consistent domestic debt service. Presumably, the enhancement of public revenue would permit uninterrupted service of the London Debt, which had become one of the major irritants in Anglo-Mexican relations. But in the final analysis, the circle proved impossible to square. British industrialists trumped financiers: merchants and manufacturers wielded more influence than the bondholders, even with the great and good of Parliament among them. Perhaps more importantly, capitalizing arrears produced a debt that doubled each decade, even as the Mexican economy stagnated. Something more than juggling was required to hold this set of arrangements together, but in the end, that something, real economic growth, did not materialize.

This chapter also introduces an actor of continuing importance in the Santanista era of the London Debt, the Lizardi merchant bank. Functioning in a variety of roles, Lizardi and Company not only brokered the Conversion of 1837, but may well have been the driving force behind it. The interest of the Lizardi in Mexico stemmed not only from the family's long-standing connection to Veracruz, where it was based, but also from holdings in Texas, from acting as financiers to the First Federal Republic, and from acting as a banker to Santa Anna. With representatives in France, Great Britain, Mexico, and the United States, the Lizardi merchant bank had something of a quasi-public status in Mexico until the ultimate demise of Santa Anna in 1854. Its influence would linger even longer.

Chapter 3 concentrates on the period between 1837 and 1862, an era of failed conversions, partition, national bankruptcy, civil war, and finally, the Tripartite Intervention. In some fashion or another, the London Debt was a defining aspect of all these events. With the continuing conflict over Texas, governments in Mexico continued to seek accommodation with Great Britain over Texas. Even with the War of 1847 lost and the fate of Texas, California, and the other "collateralized" territories of the Conversion of 1837 decided, Mexico continued its pro-British stance. Before the outbreak of the war, Mexico could hope for British mediation, if to prevent nothing more than the annexation of Texas, guaranteeing its continued independence. Yet with war over, Mexico continued to placate British interests. Thus the "indemnity" that the United States paid ultimately passed to Mexico's foreign creditors, of whom the London bondholders were but one of several, and not even the most senior. They received something more than 20 percent of the indemnity. The bulk of the repayments passed to the "convention" creditors, who acted as a further impediment to the solution of the London Debt. Even if Mexico had *wanted* to walk away from its financial debacle and start afresh, it could not. The convention debts were senior obligations concluded at an official diplomatic level – precisely to avoid the fate of the London bondholders. To ignore them would have surely invited British intervention before the corpses of those killed in the War of 1847 had had time to grow cold. So Mexico's debt problems simply multiplied in the 1850s, with very little prospect of solution. But now, through the irony of rising expectations, fueled by the availability of the war indemnity from the United States, both domestic and foreign creditors remained unsatisfied.

Domestic factors in particular reduced the room for maneuver to an absolute minimum. The financial costs of the war for Texas had triggered a crisis within Mexico by 1837, delaying compliance with the Conversion of 1837 until an agreement made in 1842. Yet the agreement of 1842 was financed by the same maneuvering that had occurred previously, in particular the simultaneous suspension of domestic payments. This cleared the way for a resumption of debt service, substantial while it lasted, but temporary nonetheless. The increasing involvement of the Lizardi in government finance, blurring the boundaries between the public and private sector, produced a noisy financial scandal that virtually destroyed Mexican credibility in the international market. So too did the clumsy, inept, and thoroughly corrupt handling of the Conversion of 1846. A dangerous change of perception thus occurred in the 1840s: Mexico, its repeated efforts to service the London Debt notwithstanding, had sacrificed whatever moral capital it had gained through its previous efforts.

A new aggressiveness crept into dealings between Mexico and the London bondholders. Its relations with its erstwhile British allies were now palpably deteriorated. Payments on the debt continued into the early 1850s, largely moved forward after the war by Payno, and then ceased, effectively driving a final wedge between Mexico, Great Britain, and the Continent. Perhaps the only factors that prevented the full reorientation of Mexico's external finance toward the United States was that nation's blundering policy toward Mexico in the 1850s and the continuing fear of its territorial ambitions even by liberal ministers like Luis Cuevas and Mariano Riva Palacio.[31] The outbreak of civil war in Mexico in 1858 and U.S. recognition of Juárez in 1859 signified the opening of a new chapter in the history of the London Debt. The period closed, as it had opened, with another Mexican shock to the Atlantic economy, a halt to shipments of silver from Mexico to Great Britain between January 1857 and July 1858.

Chapter 4 is an analytical narrative of the quarter century between the French intervention and the final resolution of the London Debt in 1887. The rationale and effects of the intervention occupy a significant part of the discussion. While there can be no doubt that relations between Great Britain and Mexico deteriorated over the subsequent suspension of debt service in 1854, we look beyond the strictly bilateral aspects of the conflict. In particular, the French intervention allowed Napoleon III to funnel significant wealth to the British bondholders, most likely to consolidate the Cobden–Chevalier Treaty between Great Britain and France in 1860. Maximilian, in turn, saddled Mexico with enormous debts, a kind of fiscal looting, that surpassed anything the infamous Jecker loan to the conservatives could have envisioned. The British, for their part, did not seek recovery of the arrears of the London Debt, but were concerned to rectify an incident in Mexico that despoiled the bondholders of dividends *already in their possession*. Again, there were broader (electoral) implications for the protection of "British" property at a time at which the implications of reforming the franchise in England had become obvious to the Parliamentary parties. These, rather than a pure "redress of grievances" model, seem a more fruitful explanation for what Mexico experienced through 1867.

The end of the intervention, of course, did not imply the end of the problem. If anything, the "resolution" of Maximilian's ill-fated empire simply added another layer of difficulty. Queen Victoria, a cousin of Maximilian's wife, Charlotte, was famously outraged by his execution at the hands of Juárez.[32] Juárez and his government, for their part, refused to recognize any government that had recognized Maximilian, including Great Britain. This

---

31 Manuel Payno, *México y el Sr. Embajador don Joaquín Francisco Pacheco* (México, 1862), p. 63; Donathon C. Olliff, *Reforma Mexico and the United Status: A Search for Alternatives to Annexation, 1854–1861* (University, AL, 1981).

32 Jasper Ridley, *Maximilian and Juárez* (London, 2001), p. 284.

resulted in the anomaly of having no diplomatic relations with the London bondholders' government, complicating negotiations on both issues. No surprise then that some seventeen years elapsed before a settlement was even possible. Díaz, whose government fashioned the agreement, had been historically (and publicly) opposed to settlement: Díaz assumed an ambiguous position during the civil turmoil that ended negotiations under González, and may have played some role in manipulating it. But after a series of false starts, Mexico was able to reach an advantageous, not to say quite favorable, arrangement with its British creditors. A detailed explanation of this process, and its rationale, which I term a "punters' agreement" suggests that those who gambled on Mexican bonds late in the day profited handsomely. This was a far cry from the dismal fate of the original bondholders, those called bona fide investors, who lost their shirts. Finally, the chapter also considers the fiscal, monetary, and international circumstances that facilitated a resolution in the 1880s. This was in many respects a remarkable decade in Mexican economic history, one in which the forces of commercialization transformed the face of a long-stagnant economy. These changes had everything to do with settling the London Debt, for they made resolution imperative as well as possible.

The conclusion, "Lessons for the Past: The London Debt in a Modern Mirror," draws out the larger implications of the study. By situating the study of the London Debt in the context of contemporary economic historiography, the conclusion illustrates the ways in which Mexican financial history contributes to an understanding of the history of modern bond markets. It demonstrates, in other words, some ways in which Mexican history confirms the larger lessons that international economic historians have learned. It is especially useful in explaining the phenomenon of so-called debt intolerance, or default at relatively modest levels of indebtedness. In Mexico, the illness was self-induced, the product of a fiscal system largely shorn of its ability to mobilize resources in the wake of a massive colonial expropriation of funds. This was no accident. Having been thoroughly mulcted by the Bourbons, the Mexican political elite would not allow the same to happen once again.

But it is also a cautionary story, a warning against inferring too much about the past from our experiences in the present. This is especially true regarding some recent accounts of bond markets that uncritically refer to the ways in which bond markets react negatively to wars and "violence."[33] This was most assuredly not always true in Mexico before 1870, and for

---

33 See especially Paolo Mauro, Nathan Sussman and Yishay Yafeh, *Emerging Markets and Financial Globalization. Sovereign Bond Spreads in 1870–1913 and Today* (New York, 2006), about which more is said in the conclusion.

sound historical reasons. Some conflicts and violence brought people to power in Mexico who were more rather than less interested in repaying the British bondholders. From the perspective of the London market, some instability was, oddly enough, good instability.[34]

34 For which the inspiration, obviously enough, is Stephen Haber and Armando Razo, "Political Instability and Economic Performance: Evidence from Revolutionary Mexico," *World Politics*, 51: 1 (1998), pp. 99–143.

I

A Crazy Contrivance

Ignorance, any slip, could cost thousands of pesos.

Dictamen de la comisión del sistema de hacienda (1823)

The first steps that the Mexican nation took into the financial system were entirely unfortunate. They have led succeeding governments to go from mistake to mistake by a twisted path full of dangers and obstacles.

Dictamen de crédito público (1850)

What Choice Did We Have?

In early December 1825, the worst financial crisis to affect the City of London in more than a century broke, the windup of a bull market in stocks that had gotten under way in the early 1820s. A period of heavy foreign lending had helped fuel speculation, including loans to Colombia, Chile, and Peru, to the imaginary American republic of Poyais and to the very real, if prostrate and war-torn, Republic of Mexico. But while the worst may have passed by Christmas 1825, the lingering consequences of the horrific crash that had occurred were much in evidence. One of these was the death of a certain L. A. Goldschmidt, a principal in the merchant bank of B. A. Goldschmidt, which failed on February 16, 1826. The proximate cause of Goldschmidt's demise, it was said, was cerebral hemorrhage, but one report stated that Goldschmidt died because of "the suffering of his mind."[1]

Poor Goldschmidt! The crash of 1825 may have hastened his death, but his troubles were, in part, Mexico's troubles, and these were no new thing, for they dated to the ill-starred empire of Agustín Iturbide, if not before.

---

1 David Kynaston, "How Rothschild Saved the City from Collapse," *Financial Times*, February 12, 1994; David Kynaston, *The City of London: A World of Its Own, 1815–1890* (London, 1994), pp. 63–73; Frank Griffith Dawson, *The First Latin American Debt Crisis. The City of London and the 1822–1825 Loan Bubble* (New Haven, 1990), pp. 114–124; *Times* (London), February 20, 1826.

28

On December 16, 1822, the Finance Committee of the Junta Nacional Instituyente del Imperio Mexicano met to consider the needs of the public treasury, Iturbide having become Emperor Agustín I a scant six months earlier. Charged to prepare a budget for the imperial government, the Finance Committee declared that "the system of finance [is] always the hardest problem for governments to resolve and if the most civilized nations have often struggled fruitlessly with it . . . what should the Committee fear in current circumstances, without statistics, censuses, or even a knowledge of the wealth of the Empire?"[2] To operate the government, the committee, in round numbers, required revenue of 20 million pesos, of which 2.8 million were required to pay off a forced loan from the previous year "since covering the debt is, in large part, on what the credit of the Empire depends." The immediate problem, it appeared, was that income could be crudely estimated at 14 million pesos, so the remainder – 6 million pesos – was the looming deficit for 1823.[3] Such numbers were in the air in 1822. An anonymous pamphlet of the day observed that those 20 million pesos – the rents, as it happened, of New Spain in 1809 – were the product of "happier times, prosperity and abundance" that "could not now serve as a guide." At most, the pamphlet's author thought, you could raise 8 million pesos and expect a deficit of 2.95 million. "There is a substantial deficit, and as long as there is, the complaining will never stop."[4] In the event, Iturbide's brief empire would experiment with paper money and a proposed direct tax – the first a resounding and disastrous failure; the other discussed, but never imposed. The other expedient to occur to Iturbide's hard-up ministers and Mexico's politicians was other people's, or other nations,' money – a foreign loan, for, as we shall see, the possibility of a domestic loan was, unfortunately, not on offer. Indeed, Iturbide was said to have estimated that Mexico witnessed the loss of 120 million pesos in capital to Europe, the United States, Cuba, and the West Indies in a year's time, starting in 1822. If that figure is even remotely accurate, it alone could explain why the imperial government would have been forced to borrow.[5]

On June 25, 1822, Congress authorized a foreign loan of 30 million pesos to be secured on the general revenues of the empire. A certain James Barry, resident in London, agreed to lend the empire 10 million pesos

2 *Diario de la Junta Nacional Instituyente del Imperio Mexicano* (México, 1822), p. 104, in *Actas constitucionales mexicanas (1821–1824)* [hereafter, *ACM*] (2nd ed., México, 10 vols., 1980), vol. 7: pp. 104, 107.

3 *ACM*, vol. 7: p. 141.

4 *Memoria presentada a S.A.S La Regencia del Imperio Mexicano sobre los principios en que debe fundarse un justo y razonable sistema de Hacienda Pública . . .* (México, 1822), pp. 15–16.

5 William Jacob, *An Historical Inquiry into the Production and Consumption of the Precious Metals* (Philadelphia, 1832), p. 389.

at 10 percent per year. Concurrently, Barry agreed to furnish a million pesos in bills drawn against Thomas Morton Jones, also of London.[6] Barry drew 565,000 pesos in bills for a variety of reasons, including payments to Manuel Gómez Pedraza, "for important attentions to service for which there is no evidence in the file," and to the Conde de Heras Soto "to repay various supplemental loans that he made on behalf of the General Treasury," amounting to 185,000 pesos.[7]

But for reasons that are obscure, Barry turned out to be less than reliable, earning the sobriquet "adventurer" from Lucas Alamán; from the finance minister, in 1823, Francisco Arrillaga; and from José María Luis Mora in his estimable *Crédito Público*.[8] According to Arrillaga, things went wrong very quickly with Barry. Pointing to a "tissue of fraud" that Barry wove, Arrillaga condemned Barry in no uncertain terms. Writing from Tampico in July 1822 and bound for London, Barry had admitted, "I think it would be risky to use the million pesos of bills that I have signed. Hold on to them until I advise you from London, which will be as soon as possible. Otherwise we will put the reputation of the Empire at risk. No money, much less such a meager sum, can compare with a good name."[9]

The guarantors of Barry's letters in Mexico were a Veracruz merchant, Don José Javier de Olazával, and Don Pedro del Paso y Troncoso, who, according to Mora, had an exposure of more than 50,000 pesos.[10] According to Arrillaga, Olazával had guaranteed up to 100,000 pesos, but had gotten nervous about his position in light of Barry's warning. Still, Arrillaga observed, Iturbide's government had tried to put Olazával's mind at ease, abusing Olazával's good faith, saying precisely the opposite of what it knew to be true, thus inducing him to do "what he had offered in service to the Fatherland."

The object of the operation was twofold. On the one hand, a certain Richard (also referred to as Robert) Meade – identified as a banker from Philadelphia, who had offered himself as a candidate for the position of Mexican consul in New York – had been entrusted with purchasing ships for

---

6 *Gaceta del Gobierno Supremo de México*, May 22, 1823; Lucas Alamán, *Historia de México desde los primeros movimentos que prepararon su Independenciaen el año de 1808 hasta la época presente* (1850: 5 vols., México, 1985), vol. 5: p. 667. The *Gaceta* also reported, on May 13, 1823, a loan of 16 million pesos at 6 percent offered by one Dennis Smith, a Baltimore merchant. The agreement was abrogated on April 24, 1823. See, too, *ACM*, vol. 5: p. 283.

7 Razón del préstamo contratado en el año de 1822 por Dn Diego Barry. Letras que se giraron a favor de qué sujetos y su destino [1827], *Hacienda Pública*, 2ª, *Sección de Carpetas Azules*, AGNM. *"de que no hay constancia en el expediente"* is translated as "for important attentions to service for which there is no evidence in the file."

8 Alamán, *Historia de Mexico*, vol. 5: p. 667; Arrillaga, Circular Order, May 15, 1823; José María Luis Mora, *Crédito Público* (1837; México, 1986), p. 456.

9 Arrillaga, Circular Order, May 15, 1823.

10 Mora, *Crédito Público*, p. 456.

the imperial government to blockade the fortress of San Juan de Ulúa, then held by the remaining Spanish garrison in Mexico. According to Arrillaga, Meade had the foresight not to try to negotiate Barry's bills on London because if he had, "this new incident would have brought us to even greater grief... thanks to the poorly planned and worse executed measures of the previous [Iturbide's] government."[11] According to Arrillaga, Iturbide's government had bungled things in the United States as well, where the empire had ordered several *balandras cañoneras* in Philadelphia, not all of which could be purchased because of the same lack of funds – funds that Barry was ostensibly to provide.[12]

The other aspect of the plan, according to Arrillaga, was frank speculation by the Treasury. The standard commission on negotiating a bill was 8 percent, but Olazával had agreed to retain only 2.5 percent on bills he handled. Thus the Treasury stood to earn 5.5 percent on as much as 10 million pesos, or 550,000 pesos, which was about 6 percent of its income in 1822. It was obvious why the empire had found Barry's blandishment difficult to resist: he had provided money and ships, both of which were highly prized in 1822 and 1823. But things turned out very badly. As Alamán put it, "not only were Barry's bills of exchange not paid, but the person on whom they were drawn [Morton Jones] could not even be found."[13] Nor could any other way out of the mess be devised. On April 30, 1823, the Supremo Poder Ejecutivo gave up on Barry, leaving poor fish, like the merchant Olazával, holding the bag. Of the 56,000 pesos in bills that Olazával (and Paso y Troncoso) had guaranteed, they had recovered no more than 12,000 pesos by 1827. They were among the first, but hardly the last, to be burned by Mexico's search for capital in Europe.[14] And while Barry may have been the empire's specific doing, other "adventurers," who would demonstrate that Iturbide's mistakes were far from unique, were soon to follow.

Indeed, the proclamation of the Plan de Casa Mata and the fall of Iturbide in the spring of 1823 did nothing to alleviate Mexico's fiscal distress.

11 Arrillaga, Circular Order, May 15, 1823. On Meade, see *Los primeros consulados de México, 1823–1872* (México, 1974), p. 25. Richard was probably the father of Union General George Gordon Meade. He was the son of Richard W. Meade who served in Cádiz as an agent of the U.S. Navy. George Gordon Meade was born in Cádiz in 1815. See the biography of George Gordon Meade at http://www.nps.gov/gett/historyculture/people.htm (accessed May 23, 2008).

    Samuel Chew, a Philadelphia lawyer, acted as agent for the corvette *Kensington* (*Tepeyac*), built for the Mexican government, and for which Mexico eventually defaulted payment. Some account can be found in the *Samuel Chew Papers, 1826–1850*, Historical Society of Pennsylvania.

12 *Memoria que el secretario de estado y del despacho de marina presenta al soberano Congreso Constituyente Mexicano. Leída en sesión pública de 13 de Noviembre de 1823* (México, 1824), p. 6.

13 Alamán, *Historia de México*, vol. 5: pp. 667–668.

14 See Josef de Presas, *Memoria sobre el estado y situación política en que se hallaba el Reino de Nueva España en agosto de 1823* (Madrid, 1824), p. 36.

During the discussions of the Congreso Constituyente, one delegate, Francisco Manuel Sánchez de Tagle, spoke at length about the problems the interim government faced.[15] The Treasury, he said, was empty, "without resources," but obliged nevertheless to meet its day-to-day obligations. The government had tried to raise funds domestically. The Finance Committee of the Congreso Constituyente had consulted with the biggest merchants (*primeros comerciantes*) of Mexico City in search of funds with which to operate the government.

In fact, we had a long meeting with them and we offered them highly advantageous terms. We didn't ask for the entire loan at once. We were happy with 100 thousand or 200 thousand a month. We offered 10 to 12 percent interest, a general mortgage on government receipts, and their choice of taxes to fund the debt. What's more, we offered to let them administer the *temporalidades*, 2 or 3 million in total. But they resisted, claiming that they didn't have the money to lend they once did, and that the most they could come up with in hard cash was 12 or 13 thousand pesos. We gave them six days to think it over, think about how well they could do, that they themselves could negotiate a foreign loan. Even though we told them that if they didn't answer in the prearranged time, it would mean they could not or would not get involved with the loan, I urged them to respond. They were given copies of some of the proposals made by English houses. But, at the end of the day, they said they couldn't make the loan.

The Finance Committee echoed and modified these sentiments.[16] The Treasury had no resources and scant prospect of getting them "by ordinary means in light of its vast and urgent needs. A general lack of confidence, deeply rooted, can only be cured in the long run and with great difficulty. Business is at a standstill. . . . Capital has disappeared or been destroyed. The disorder of the Treasury is matched only by its impoverishment."

Why negotiate with merchants for loans?

Even before we talked with them, we knew we could not get them to lend. There is not enough hard cash around and the lack of confidence is impossible to overcome. That is why we made no progress even though we offered [the merchants of Mexico City] very advantageous terms. What choice do we have but to go to foreign houses, just as did Spain, France and Colombia on other occasions?

The Finance Committee then concluded in words that its members would surely live to regret: "Fortunately, this government has the expertise necessary to carry out such a sensitive matter. Ignorance, any slip, could cost thousands of pesos . . . And so the nation places its justly merited – even blind – faith in it."

---

15 *Diario de las sesiones del Congreso Constituyente de México*, in *ACM*, vol. 5: p. 389.
16 *ACM*, vol. 5: p. 384 (Session of April 29, 1823).

So here, then, was the justification for a foreign loan. There was no choice. Faced with pressing fiscal needs, such as driving the remaining Spanish forces out of San Juan de Ulúa, the nascent republican government thought that extraordinary measures were justified. Yet Mexico's domestic capitalists showed little interest in funding such a risky venture, even at 10–12 percent. Could 10 or 12 percent compensate them for the possibility that their funds could, quite literally, go up in smoke? In this sense, the merchants of Mexico City were no match for, say, the Rothschilds, who financed the Duke of Wellington and the British army in the campaign against France in 1814, or more importantly, British allies like Russia, Prussia, and Austria. True, the Rothschilds thereby amassed the beginnings of a huge fortune, but as Niall Ferguson puts it, "[war finance] was a strategy fraught with risk."[17] Yet it was a risk the Rothschilds were prepared to take for they were international financiers in the largest sense, engaged in exchange arbitrage and even speculation in the various combatants' bonds. They were no mere hostages to the fate of a single government, shipping bullion to Wellington and hoping for the best. The merchants of Mexico City had fewer options. They may well have concluded in 1823 that lending to the Mexican government was a bad bet, given the scale of its needs and its exiguous resources. Foreign lenders, with broader horizons and more diversified portfolios, were in a better position to lend a hand or, as it turned out, a pound. Or maybe they simply knew no better.

And so it was that the Finance Committee authorized a foreign loan of 8 million pesos *for 1823*, giving preference to whichever foreign house would offer money "with greatest alacrity." The loan was to be authorized immediately, secured on the whole of the Mexican government's income and, in effect, prepayable without penalty. The committee also pledged to find a source of repayment "whose proceeds were dedicated solely to paying interest on the loan and to amortizing its principal."[18] Still, the decision to look abroad for a loan was not taken lightly and was made only over considerable objection – not simply to the proposed size of the loan, but to its very necessity.

One way of viewing the fiscal situation in 1823 might be as follows: in Table 1.1, we use data provided by Alamán to compare the resources available to the state under the last Bourbons as opposed to what was available to Mexico when it first became independent. The evident disparity is tremendous. At the end of the eighteenth century, the viceregal government had access to about 20 million pesos per year. But in 1822, income was scarcely 9.3 million pesos, or less than half of what Mexico under the

17 Niall Ferguson, *The House of Rothschild. Money's Prophets, 1798–1848* (New York, 1998), pp. 92–95, 99.

18 *ACM*, vol. 5: pp. 384–385.

Table 1.1. *Income of the National
Government in Various Eras According to
Alamán, Historia, V, "Estado Comparativo"*

New Spain	
1795–1799 (mean)	20,562,307
Mexico	
1822 (total)	9,328,740
1825–1830 (mean)	13,411,220
1831 (total)	12,909,059[19]
1844 (total)	29,323,423[20]
1851 (total)	13,113,383

Note: Values are in pesos or dollars.

Spaniards had enjoyed. And even if one argues that the capacity of Mexican society to supply resources went well beyond 20 million pesos per year, as it did during the crisis of the Bourbon monarchy, the politicians and ministers of the empire or the first federal republic enjoyed no comparable power to tax. This was a consequence, argued Matías Romero in 1870, of a broad reduction in the level and number of taxes available to regimes after independence and in effect a reaction to the literal expropriation of Mexican wealth at the end of the colonial era.[21]

In late 1821 and early 1822, when a regency was constituted under the Treaty of Córdova (essentially, the formal declaration of a Mexican "Empire"), some of the first steps in dismantling the financial structure of the ancient regime were taken. These included sharp reductions in the internal sales (*alcabala*) and import taxes (*aduana*), as well as the hobbling of the very lucrative royal tobacco monopoly. Alamán commented that the regency's actions "seem to have had no other object than to increase expenditures . . . while reducing resources," only to intimate that the purpose of these policies and others like them was "to popularize the revolution."[22] Leonor Ludlow has come to much the same conclusion: Iturbide's nascent government had no independent fiscal base outside the former colonial elites of Mexico City and the port of Veracruz, and their support, in turn, came at a price. A bit prematurely, perhaps, Ludlow concludes that the die was cast by 1824, when the new federal republic came into existence. From the beginning, federalism in Mexico thus became synonymous with the capture of what had been the fiscal basis of the Bourbon monarchy. Hence,

19 Adjusted for carryovers and advances on customs house.
20 Include state ("department") income.
21 *Memoria de Hacienda . . . 1870*, par. 221. Also see, more generally, Carlos Marichal, *La bancarrota del virreinato. Nueva España y las finanzas del Imperio español, 1780–1810* (México, 1999).
22 Alamán, *Historia de México*, vol. 5: pp. 413–414.

in Ludlow's view, any reasonably solvent, centralized (or centralist) system of public finance was "an impossible undertaking" after Iturbide's failure.[23]

When the foreign loan of 8 million pesos was authorized in 1823, it would have restored the balance between income and outgo to its late colonial levels, that is, $9.3 + 8.0 = 17.3$ million (vs. 20.5 million), or using 1825–1830, $13.4 + 8.0 = 21.4$ million (vs. 20.5 million). Foreign borrowing was, in this sense, an attempt to restore the fiscal status quo ante. Could we thus conclude that New Spain taxed, but Mexico borrowed? It does not appear that Mexico's nominal fiscal capacity ever approached that of the late colonial period until the 1840s, even allowing for the incorporation of state revenues into those of the national government under centralism. And, on closer examination, these nominal revenues were just that – nominal and, indeed, notional. Bookkeeping gimmicks, the anticipation of customs revenues, the panoply of financing mechanisms that were *agiotaje* (high-interest, short-term lending): all conspired to maintain the disposable or liquid income of the central government at levels that at best reached 12 million pesos as late as 1838, but at no more than 9.8 million pesos in 1840![24] If, as historians are inclined to think, gross domestic product (in nominal terms) did little more than stagnate in this period, one is forced to conclude that the decline in revenue approximates a substantial decline in the share of revenues in gross domestic product. Here was the beginning of Mexico's "revenue problem."

There was little agreement about the merits of the proposed loan. One member of the Congreso Constituyente from the state of Mexico, José Agustín Paz,[25] thought that the proposed loan was far too large. "Sir," he announced, "I would like the loan to be reduced to what is necessary to cover the current deficit. I believe that 8 million pesos are not necessary." The 8 million pesos, Paz continued, included the expenses associated with the now-defunct imperial household. Moreover, he expected the return of political peace to generate an increase in customs revenues, and this, in turn, would render predictions of the deficit incorrect.

But the most trenchant criticisms were offered by José María Covarrubias,[26] from Jalisco. "The moment that the country becomes a debtor to the Europeans is the moment that it becomes their slave." Or, "there are three kinds of tyranny: iron, under which we were a colony;

23 Leonor Ludlow, "Elites y Finanzas Públicas Durante La Gestación del Estado Independiente (1821–1824)," in José Serrano Ortega and Luis Jáuregui, eds., *Hacienda y Política. Las finanzas públicas y los grupos de poder en la primera república federal mexicana* (México, 1998), pp. 79–110, and esp. pp. 109–110.

24 [J. Espinosa], *Bases del plan de Hacienda pública que en clase de especiales de los diversos ramos de ella deben fijara marcha de desarrollo* (México, 1841), "Estado que demuestra el juego de todos los valores que han compuesto las cuentas del ministerio en los seis y medio años que expresan. . . ."

25 *ACM*, vol. 5: p. 392.

26 *ACM*, vol. 5: pp. 393–394.

golden, when a fool governs; and fraudulent or monetary, when one country gets mixed up with another by borrowing . . . [and] it is into this one
that we have fallen because of the stupidity and blockheadedness of the previous government [i.e., Iturbide's]." Covarrubias stated that Mexico would
end up paying interest of 960,000 pesos per year (i.e., 12 percent of the
principal of 8 million) and that even the 8-million-peso loan would prove
illusory because once the Mexican government had its credit established,
it would then borrow from the domestic merchants who had previously
refused it. These merchants would lend the government four or five times
as much, but at much higher rates of interest, thus charging the government as much as it would have borrowed from Britain to begin with. "I
don't know why it is that we fall victim to Europe's schemes – we're like the
stupid fish that takes the bait. What more do we need to end up ensnared
by the Carthage of modern times with the papers of its damned bank circulating among us." Covarrubias concluded with a warning that amounted
to a prediction of disaster. Let the British gain a foothold in Mexico, he
suggested, and their merchants and manufacturers will overwhelm us, leaving us "like the blacks in Cuba" or the moribund manufacturers of Buenos
Aires. It was not an inviting prospect.

The discussion continued pro and con. Most of it focused on the putative
effects of a large foreign loan. Covarrubias seemed to think that a foreign
loan would drive up Mexican demand, that excess demand would be satisfied
by imports, and that a flood of imports would somehow produce generalized
bankruptcy. "Never buy abroad what you can make at home," Covarrubias
warned. In response, Finance Minister Arrillaga denied that a British loan
would bankrupt Mexico's infant industries. Instead, he suggested, British
competition to supply the Mexican market would drive down British prices
and generate a commercial deficit vis-à-vis Mexico. As a result, specie would
flow from Britain to Mexico, Arrillaga emphasized, not away from Mexico,
as Covarrubias feared.[27] Of course, the idea that Mexico, a small market,
could exercise much power over the price of its imports, much less attract
specie when it historically exported silver to the rest of the world, was a
bit unorthodox, not to say flatly improbable. But this was a situation in
which fiscal imperatives – the need for funds – drove policy, not correct
economic analysis. The resolution to authorize negotiation of a foreign
loan thus passed, but only after further intervention by Lorenzo de Zavala
and Carlos María Bustamante. The only substantive condition attached to
the negotiation was added by Paz, who requested that the *consulados* of
Guadalajara, Puebla, and Veracruz be involved in the negotiation.[28]

And, in fact, the Congreso Constituyente through a circular of June
21, 1823, solicited these *consulados*, advising them that negotiation for a

27 *ACM*, vol. 5: pp. 395–396.
28 *ACM*, vol. 5: p. 391.

foreign loan of 5 million pesos[29] had been authorized and that they were welcome to compete for the business. But just as the *consulado* of Mexico City had done earlier, the merchant communities of Guadalajara, Puebla, and Veracruz showed little interest in participating in such a loan. Indeed, Finance Minister Arrillaga would subsequently complain that it was not until the first Barclay, Herring, Richardson loan was negotiated that the capital market in Mexico City showed much interest in anything involving writing drafts on the London market.[30]

Nevertheless, not everyone in Mexico was entirely indifferent to the prospects of a loan. There were some of the customary "projects" on offer, one of which involved individuals of a certain weight who were or would be involved in Mexico's foreign borrowing. Olazával and Francisco de Borja Migoni floated one of these projects, with Olazával known to us as an unfortunate victim of the failed Barry loan under Iturbide. Migoni was Olazával's brother-in-law and was soon to become a key figure in arranging a loan to Mexico by B. A. Goldschmidt and Company of London.[31]

The *"proyecto"* proposed by Olazával is a strange thing, partly realistic, partly crackpot.[32] It assumed that Mexico could place a loan on the market at no less than 75 (i.e., at 75 percent of par), a figure that turned out to be wildly optimistic in view of what occurred nine months later, when Mexico went into the international market with a loan priced at 50. Moreover, the first year's interest, 400,000 pesos (assuming a 5 percent coupon on an 8-million-peso loan), would be paid out of the proceeds of the loan. So, as Olazával calculated, from an obligation of 8 million pesos, no more than 5.6 million would actually be available (and this seemingly assumed that there would be no fees, commissions, or expenses!).

Olazával then calculated that the government would need 600,000 pesos fast, or as he put it, "as quickly as possible," to deal with the pressing needs of the moment. It would be best to try to find a way to get the money to Veracruz or Mexico City. Another 3 million pesos would be used to cover letters issued on Veracruz "from the moment it is officially known that the loan has been approved," but with the exact amount restricted to the bond issue. It seems quite possible that this was an attempt to clean up the mess

---

29 Less than the amount authorized, perhaps a concession to opponents of the loan. See "Carpeta N° 1 Remitido por el ministerio de Hacienda," *Deuda Exterior*, vol. 12, AGNM.

30 Statement of finance minister, Mexico, April 26, 1825, "Tratado de amistad, navegación y comercio . . . [con] el Reyno de Gran Bretaña" (1825), *Cámara de Senadores*, 1825, vol. 1, Archivo Histórico del Senado, Mexico.

31 See [unknown] to José Javier Olazával, Mexico, June 4, 1823, B. A. Goldschmidt, *Deuda Exterior*, vol. 12, AGNM.

32 "Proyecto que formalizado el préstamo de ocho millones de pesos para que el Gobierno, autorizado por el Congreso nacional, facilita a Dn Francisco de Borja Migoni, residente en Londres, convendría adoptar . . . " Veracruz, May 24, 1823, *Deuda Exterior*, vol. 12, AGNM. The price of the bond is here expressed as a fraction of its face value. So a bond at 75 is priced at a discount of 25 percent from its face value. *"a la mayor brevedad posible"* is translated as "as quickly as possible."

made by Barry, coming as it did hard on the heels of Arrillaga's May 15 circular, reporting Barry's "fraud," and engineered in part by Olazával, who had apparently been left holding the bag.

Yet it was with the remaining 2 million pesos that things took a bizarre turn. Olazával proposed that this sum should find a "mercantile adventure," an attempt to purchase goods in England, France, Germany, and Spain and import them into Mexico in hopes of turning a profit. He believed that the profits of the venture would compensate for the 25 percent discount at which the loan would be priced and that the imports themselves would generate customs revenues that would prove to be of short-term benefit to the government. Carefully, Olazával even specified that 800,000 pesos should be "invested" in English goods "which enjoy the quickest and best sales."

Strangely (or perhaps not so strangely), nothing more was heard of Olazával's (or was it Migoni's?) "project." Perhaps as a second, and presumably better, thought, Olazával communicated to Finance Minister Arrillaga his deep appreciation "for the instruction to . . . Dn Francisco Borja Migoni that he cover with the loan he has been asked to raise the 53,000 pesos with which I guaranteed the letters of the adventurer Barry, as well as Dn Pedro del Paso y Troncoso's 3,000 pesos."[33] Unfortunately, or so it seems for Olazával, this apparently never came to pass. If Arrillaga, once established as a merchant in Veracruz,[34] was trying to do a favor for a fellow *veracruzano*, he did not succeed. Olazával, meanwhile, said he could do nothing more for a government he considered "sober, fair and liberal." Alas, he revealed, he had no money of his own to lend. But he also suggested, and Arrillaga agreed, that once the loan that had been commissioned was raised – and, of this, more momentarily – the funds should be used to negotiate Mexican bills with as much favorable publicity as possible. And, Olazával believed, foreign merchant houses operating in Mexico should be appraised of this loan as well "so that they would not withdraw from negotiating [the government's bills]. The notion that Mexico's ability to raise and service a foreign loan was a sort of fiscal seal of approval from the international financial community informed much of the subsequent history of what came to be known as the London Debt. Well into the 1840s, the Mexican government wanted, and wanted badly, this approval, and it was willing to do what it could (and much that it could not) to gain, maintain, or regain it. Its inability to do so, arguably, gave domestic lenders the chance to dictate the terms of public finance to Mexico's hard-pressed and harried treasury. And its inability to do so would drive Mexican officials to make disastrous choices in refinancing the subsequently defaulted London Debt.

---

33 Josef Javier Olazával to the finance minister, México, May 24, 1823, *Deuda Exterior*, vol. 12, AGNM.
34 "Arrillaga, Francisco," in *Diccionario Porrúa de Historia, Biografía y Geografía de Mexico* (5th ed., 3 vols., Mexico, 1986), vol. 1: p. 194.

Before turning to a detailed analysis of the negotiation and terms of the B. A. Goldschmidt and Barclay, Herring, Richardson loans, it is worth considering foreign proposals that the Mexican government rejected. The B. A. Goldschmidt and Barclay, Herring, Richardson loans may have burdened Mexico with onerous terms, but at the very least, they offered money that actually existed and terms that were by no means the worst. A glance at some alternatives should convince the reader that the Mexican government might have actually made the best of a difficult situation.

For example, the government had financial dealings with a number of foreign merchant houses, among them Hartley, Green and Ruperti of London, from whom it borrowed 30,000 pesos secured on the Mexico City Customhouse in March 1824. Hartley, Green and Ruperti offered to take in payment the government's[35] bills drawn on the Goldschmidt loan, "provided they are given at the same exchange rate as to Roberto Staples and Company." Staples and Company, in turn, had as a principal one Robert P. Staples, a British merchant who had been appointed consul by George Canning.[36] The firm was established in both Mexico City and Veracruz, remaining in business until August 1831.[37] Staples was obviously involved in financing the government. Both Zavala and Finance Minister Arrillaga mention the Staples loan of more than a million pesos, which was, in turn, to be repaid out of the proceeds of the London loans.[38] And in fact, Mora observes that by 1826, the Mexican government had paid Staples more than 174,000 pesos out of the proceeds of the Goldschmidt and Barclay loans, honoring the government's paper out of what was called his "supplementary loan."[39]

The loan that Staples offered the Mexican government in June 1823 contained a number of conditions. Basically it was to be priced at 60, with a 5 percent coupon and a twenty-year maturity in the amount of 20 million pesos. A cash amount of 100,000 pesos would be paid immediately to the Mexican Treasury. The Mexican government would also authorize the firm of Thomas Kinder Jr. to negotiate a loan of £1 million and would revoke "any commission negotiated until now by the government." Staples

---

35 Hartley, Green and Ruperti to the finance minister, México, May 17, 1824, *Hacienda Pública, Sección de Carpetas Azules*, 4ª, 1804–1824, AGNM. Hartley, Green and Ruperti was another casualty of the crash of 1825.

36 Henry McKenzie Johnston, *Mission to Mexico: A tale of British Diplomacy in the 1820s* (London, 1992), p. 74.

37 For Staples, see http://www.pbbooks.com/webfa.htm, or Kenneth Rowe, *The Postal History and Markings of Forwarding Agents* (Louisville, KY, 1996), pp. 175, 251. Also see *Times* (London), January 1, 1833.

38 Lorenzo de Zavala, *Ensayo histórico de las revoluciones de México desde 1800 hasta 1830* (1845; México, 1985 ed.), vol. 1: p. 209; *Memoria sobre el estado de la hacienda pública* (México [1825]), p. 25.

39 José María Luis Mora, *Crédito Público* (1837; México, 1986 ed.), p. 456.

requested that dividends be paid into a sinking fund six months before they fell due, which effectively compelled the Mexican government to remain six months ahead in its payments. Finally, the loan contract provided that in case of untoward occurrences, such as a European war, Kinder would be entitled both to recover the initial cash advances and to sell the bonds at whatever price he could get, not necessarily 60. Clearly the clause was meant to shift some of the risk in the operation to Mexico. Staples would be entitled to an additional 2 percent commission on the dividend payments as well.[40] Some government paper would also be included in the loan.

The reaction to the Staples proposal was general outrage. One commentator, "A Zealous Patriot," called the Staples planned loan "a usurious proposal." Finance Minister Arrillaga, in a letter to "his esteemed friend" Zavala, remarked, "I never could believe he [Staples] could be such a liar however many proofs of his boundless greed I had." Nevertheless, what apparently sunk Staples – more than "boundless greed" – was his inability to deliver the goods as advertised. Arrillaga thought that any potential creditor of the government should be prepared to lend 100,000–150,000 pesos a month in advance as a guarantee of its good faith. Arrillaga accused Staples of "diverting us with vague hopes that were never realized until after two weeks of useless replies [so that] the government decided to commission Migoni with the loan so as to lose no further time." Indeed, José María Bocanegra also makes the connection explicitly: "because a contract could neither be arranged nor concluded [with Staples], Don Francisco Borja Migoni was entrusted with the same duty and with the greatest sense of urgency."

But Arrillaga may well have had other reasons for turning against Staples and to Migoni, including the fear that Migoni was about to turn against him. In a remarkable letter to Arrillaga, both insolent and threatening in tone, Migoni reported that he had gotten wind of the possible Staples loan through the Mexican press – *El Águila Mexicano* (June 21, 1823) and *El Sol* (June 24, 1823) – that he had received on August 20, 1823.[41] Commissioned to negotiate a loan by the Supremo Poder Ejecutivo – and now, as he put it, in an "advanced" negotiation – the word of the Staples project was "disagreeable news." It was, he said, especially disagreeable to those with whom he was negotiating the 8-million-peso loan. There was to be only one loan, Migoni wrote. Having been authorized by Congress to raise the loan at the end of April, why on earth was Arrillaga talking

---

40 *Gaceta Extraordinaria del Gobierno Supremo de México*, August 27, 1823, for the contract and the discussion of the reaction to it that followed.

41 Borja Migoni to the finance minister, London, August 21, 1823, *Deuda Exterior*, vol. 12, AGNM, for this and what follows. "*individuo que debe suponérsele en la clase del mendigo*" is translated as "given that the country was dealing with someone who was basically a beggar."

to Staples by May? "It is just incredible that you would propose another loan of 5 million a month later," he wrote.[42] To make things even worse, Staples would come to the London market "in a flash" to sell the loan that Migoni thought would ruin Mexico's credit entirely, "given that the country was dealing with someone who was basically a beggar." Moreover, Migoni warned, Staples was involved with Kinder, who, he explained, had been involved with the ill-starred Peruvian loans, and was "one of those foreigners with nothing to lose whose only purpose was to suck out the subsistence of the innocent peoples [of America]."

But, in reality, Migoni saved the best for last. "I can't tell you what result the negotiation for the loan will have. I have as yet said nothing to the Houses with which I am dealing . . . but whatever I say must be the truth." The warning was clear. If you do business with Staples, he may turn out to be no better than Barry. If British merchant bankers decide that another loan would be one loan too many, Migoni would surely tell the Supremo Poder Ejecutivo "I told you so." It is hard not to believe that Arrillaga did not get the message and that the message was "Ditch Staples," which he ultimately did.

Migoni repeated his concerns in a much more temperate letter he sent about six weeks later to his friend, associate, and confidant, Alamán, who had recently served as minister of home and foreign relations.[43] "I have spared no effort in trying to make it [i.e., a loan] happen." But, he continued, things had already become difficult enough since he had been commissioned to negotiate the loan in May 1823 – it was now October. The Staples business, Migoni insinuated, had made a difficult business worse. He observed that the "resolution of some provinces to federate" had made things more difficult for him – presumably a reference to the wave of federalist juntas, meetings, and declarations that swept the nation expressing the "overwhelming consensus in support of provincial self-government and autonomy."[44] Presumably what Migoni meant was that a new element of uncertainty had been injected into the picture since he was negotiating on behalf of a *central* government whose precise command over economic resources was now far from clear.

Another complicating factor to which Migoni alluded was the conduct of Antonio López de Santa Anna, which Timothy Anna characterizes as an attempt by Santa Anna to co-opt the federalist movement.[45] Even though Santa Anna's attempt failed, Migoni pointed to it as something else that muddied the financial waters, casting additional uncertainty in the wake of Iturbide's imperial adventures.

---

42 "Y es una cosa increíble ver que V.E. a un mes después propone otro préstamo de Cinco Millones."
43 Borja Migoni to Lucas Alamán, London, October 8, 1823, *Deuda Externa*, vol. 12, AGNM.
44 Timothy E. Anna, *Forging Mexico, 1821–1835* (Lincoln, NE, 1998), pp. 98, 118–120.
45 Anna, *Forging Mexico*, p. 133.

While there were other factors to which Migoni alluded, including the restoration of the Spanish king Ferdinand VII only weeks before in late August 1823, the principal theme of Migoni's discussion was the effect that the ill-starred bond issues of Colombia, Peru, and Chile had on the international capital market. "In 1822," he wrote, "the English were really keen to make loans of this sort, so the obligations of Colombia, Peru and Chile rose to terrifying prices of 96, 90, or 88." But then, he said, "came the Congress of Vienna [October 1822] whose events precipitated an enormous fall of funds in Europe and America. Then the loans of Colombia and Peru were unmasked." As a result, Migoni concluded, "these disasters made the English reluctant to get involved in new loans because of the enormous sacrifices they suffered in the Chilean, Peruvian, and Colombian loans." These loans, Migoni insisted, were tainted by the action of people like Staples, who now resurfaced even as Migoni was trying to arrange for a Mexican loan. Kinder, with whom the Mexican government would also work closely, had been the author of the Peruvian fiasco. "If the government entered into a loan with Staples," Migoni concluded, "it's a good bet that it would have the same result as the Barry loan." Just in case Alamán did not get the message, Migoni spelled it out. "Mexico needs to get serious and no longer deal with a Barry, Smith, Staples or Wavell." Besides, it was best to deal with reputable English houses because the British government would then act as a guarantor of Mexico's independence against the Holy Alliance.[46]

Staples, not surprisingly, saw things differently.[47] It was the *Mexican government* that had come to *him* in 1823 looking for money to pay the army. And it was José Ignacio Esteva as finance minister who "pressed upon him with great urgency" the matter of the loan. Staples, in his own words, "was not much inclined . . . to enter upon such a transaction." But, Staples later asserted, he was assured by the British chargé in Mexico City, Lionel Hervey, that the British government would stand behind Staples should he require support in collecting the loan. Hervey had no right to make such an assurance and he was later sacked for making it by Foreign Secretary George Canning (1822–1827).

The facts seem to be these.[48] Staples claimed that he contracted with Arrillaga on February 9, 1823, for 1.5 million pesos – but not entirely

---

46 It is not clear whom Borja Migoni meant by Smith. "Wavell" was Arthur Goodall Wavell, a secret agent of Iturbide sent to England, possibly to help negotiate a loan, who later resided on picturesque Ladbroke Square in Notting Hill. See Johnston, *Missions to Mexico*, pp. 37–43.

47 *Mexican Justice and British Diplomacy. The Case of Thomas Kinder as Regards the Parras Estate Purchased by Him in Joint Account with Messrs. Baring Bros and Co* (2nd ed., London, 1841), pp. 1–2, 40–41. Johnston, *Missions to Mexico*, pp. 98–99.

48 See "Razón del préstamo supletorio hecho en los años de 1823 y 1824 por D Roberto P. Staples, especies en que lo hizo, letras que giró [1827] *Hacienda Pública, 2ᵈᵃ, Sección de Carpetas Azules*, 1827, AGNM, for this and what follows.

in cash, which comprised but 333,000 pesos. The great bulk of the loan was in government liabilities (*créditos*) and tobacco. Some 237,000 pesos remained undisbursed when in May 1824, Migoni's contract with B. A. Goldschmidt reached Mexico. At that point, "Staples was advised he should draw no further bills and consequently the loan was stopped." According to the same records, Staples was repaid 337,000 from the B. A. Goldschmidt loan, which was earmarked for this purpose. Migoni was also instructed to buy up the notes Staples had issued for the purchase of tobacco and for the purchase of government paper. By 1827, presumably, Staples had nothing to complain of other than lost business.

In light of the view repeated by generations of historians – that the B. A. Goldschmidt and Barclay, Herring, Richardson loans were so onerous in their terms – it is worth considering a telling point. If Goldschmidt was bad, Staples was worse, because the Mexican government deliberately chose to suspend the Staples loan in favor of the terms offered by B. A. Goldschmidt. Onerous the Goldschmidt terms may have been, but they were judged to be an improvement over what Staples had offered. Mexico was, so to speak, free to choose Goldschmidt over Staples. It could have always been worse.

A Tale of Two Agents

Don Francisco de Borja Migoni[49] and Don José Mariano Michelena had little time for each other, but both were instrumental in negotiating loans for Mexico in London. Migoni was a Mexican merchant established in England in 1813 who styled himself a patriot concerned primarily with the finances of the empire. Writing directly to Iturbide,[50] Migoni argued that a foreign loan could compensate for the loss of the revenues of the now-abolished tobacco monopoly and provide the emperor with a respite from the pressures of fiscal reorganization. If the loan were to be contracted in London, it would have the secondary effect of raising the incentive of the British government to recognize the independence of the Americas. Of course, there was something more to Migoni's patriotism. He was best

---

49 Lucas Alamán, *Historia de México*, vol. 5: pp. 667–668; Federico Huth and Company to Lucas Alamán, London, July 21, 1831 Hospital de Jesús, leg. 440, exp. 1. atado 2, AGNM; [Secretaría de Relaciones Exteriores] *Los primeros consulados de México, 1823–1872* (México, 1974), p. 45; Delia Hidalgo, *Representantes de México en Gran Bretaña (1822 – 1980)* (México, 1981), pp. 11–12; Borja Migoni to the finance minister, London, July 21, 1824, *Hacienda Pública, Sección De Carpetas Azules*, 2ª, 1824, AGNM.

Borja Migoni was ostensibly notified on March 9, 1824, that Michelena had replaced the original nominee, Don Pedro de la Llave, as minister. Why it took until July for Borja Migoni to get news of the change is unclear. There is a memo of the notification in *Deuda Exterior*, vol. 12, AGNM.

50 Borja Migoni to the emperor of Mexico, London, March 26, 1822, HD 15–2.1744, BLAC, UT.

situated to carry out the negotiation because of his intimate connections with the mercantile community and his knowledge of American affairs: "no one could do a better job of negotiating than me."

In 1824, he was named consul-general of Mexico in England and authorized to continue negotiations for a foreign loan that Guadalupe Victoria had begun in Guadalajara.[51] Migoni was also associated with Don Pedro de la Quintana, for a time (1836) Mexico's vice-consul in England, and a member of the merchant bank of Lizardi and Company. Migoni actively speculated in the bonds of the Spanish-American republics. He surely realized that a loan for Mexico would have a favorable impact on the prices of the bonds of the other republics. When he died in 1831, his house, with much of its capital tied up in American bonds and in shares of mining companies, was forced to suspend operations. When Migoni received word in July 1824 that Michelena had been appointed Envoy Extraordinary and Minister Plenipotentiary to Britain, Migoni called the news "terrible" and went off to Brighton to sulk. Migoni professed great surprise that he had been relieved of his responsibilities at a moment when "I was covered in glory for having served my country with neither salary nor emolument whatsoever." He was, he admitted, "offended" by what had taken place. Michelena, according to Migoni, was both "arrogant" and "rude," and the language Migoni used to express these sentiments was strong indeed.[52]

Of the two men, Michelena is by far the better known.[53] Alamán portrays Michelena as a moving force, perhaps *the* moving force, in the Valladolid conspiracy in 1808. Arrested once more when the Hidalgo revolt began, Michelena was imprisoned in San Juan de Ulúa and then sent to Spain to fight the French invasion. He later served as an alternate member (*suplente*) in the Spanish Cortes, returning to Mexico in 1822, where he was closely associated with Freemasonry and with the opposition to Iturbide, who had him proscribed. In 1824, Michelena too was sent to England to negotiate a loan.[54]

Michelena was highly critical of Migoni. On June 24, 1824, Michelena arrived at Portsmouth, continuing on immediately to London.[55] That

---

51 Esposición del C. Francisco de Borja Migoni, consul general de México en Londres, sobre el empréstito de que fue encargado," *El Amigo del Pueblo*, September 12, 1827, p. 9.

52 Borja Migoni to the finance minister, London, July 13, 1824, *Deuda Exterior*, vol. 12, AGNM; Esposición del C. Francisco de Borja Migoni, consul general de México en Londres, sobre el empréstito de que fue encargado," p. 22.

53 Alamán, *Historia de México*, vol. 1: pp. 314–317; vol. 5: pp. 646, 711.

54 "Nombramiento de Don Mariano Michelena como Enviado Extraordinario y Ministro Pleipotenciario de México en la Gran Bretaña, México March 2, 1824," in María Eugenia López de Roux, ed., *El reconocimiento de la independencia de México* (México, 1995), pp. 96–97.

55 Michelena to the minister of home and foreign relations, London, June 26, 1824, AGNM, *Gobernación*, leg. 61, exp. 38.

evening, Michelena and his secretary inquired after Migoni "so that he could brief us in detail." "But," Michelena continued, "I've had the disagreeable experience of being unable to find him or even his residence because he made off with everything including his desk, leaving no one, not even a representative, to tell anyone anything." Michelena continued, "Yesterday I learned that under cover of great secrecy that he had dispatched a secret agent to pick up his mail and to forward it to Brussels. So I've written him – how did Michelena know where to write? – without sending on my instructions. Let's see how he replies."

Apparently, Migoni's replies did not satisfy Michelena. "Migoni has handled the duties entrusted to him with indifference. Whenever he is asked to clarify anything, especially some doubtful aspect of the contract he negotiated with the House of Goldschmidt, his answers are quite unsatisfactory. In official or even in ordinary contact with me, he has not treated me with the decency my position demands."[56]

While elements of this rivalry were purely personal – these two men disliked each other intensely – or the reflection of competing financial interests, for both stood to profit handsomely from the loans they made,[57] their clash also discloses something of the political context in which the London loans were negotiated. For negotiating the loans was not only about money, but was also about national politics. And in particular, if Migoni was associated with Iturbide, Alamán, or monarchists, Michelena was probably an ally of Arrillaga and Esteva, called by Michael Costeloe "a convinced federalist."[58] As an introduction to the political circumstances attending the historic loans negotiated for Mexico in London with the merchant banks of B. A. Goldschmidt and Barclay, Herring, Richardson, some account of their interaction is simply indispensable. Indeed, since Michelena arrived in London only months after the republican Congress had formally declared Iturbide a traitor (April 28, 1824), we might usefully regard the early history of the loans, if not the loans themselves, as exemplifying the tension between republicans and monarchists during the first federal republic. The loans were, in other words, a partisan touchstone, and some of the controversy surrounding them surely reflects that, as well as whether or not their terms were objectively disadvantageous or onerous.[59]

---

56 Michelena to the Ministry of Home and Foreign Relations, London, July 16, 1824, *Gobernación*, leg. 61, exp. 38, AGNM.

57 According to Michelena's Instructions, he was to receive 1.5 percent on any loan he negotiated. That alone would have been 300,000 pesos, and his commission on arms and materiel was a further 3 percent. See Juan Guzmán to the minister of Great Britain in México, México, March 7, 1824, Clause 9, in Roux, *El reconocimiento de la independencia de México*, p. 98.

58 Michael P. Costeloe, *La primera república federal de México (1824–1835)* (México, 1975), p. 48.

59 This observation is in the spirit of Rafael Rojas, "Iturbide: La primera traición," *Nexos*, 285 (September 2001), pp. 74–76.

For example, Michelena wrote,[60]

Don Francisco Migoni has no commitment (*compromiso*) to the revolution. Neither has he done the slightest thing for our country. To the contrary, I have facts that suggest that, whatever the case, he has avoided doing anything that would commit the country in opposition to the Spanish party. When he was named the Republic's agent, in his correspondence he did everything he could to encourage the formation of a monarchical party that would favor a Prince from the House [of Bourbon]. Letters written in his hand to well-recommended citizens confirm this. The government has seen two of them. It was from that time that Migoni got the reputation he deserved, and had it not been for the imminent arrival of the Envoy [i.e., Michelena himself] which had been delayed for various reasons, he [Borja Migoni] would have been relieved at once.

So as Michelena saw it, Migoni had not only misused his position, but also botched his mission. "It was at that time that Migoni had been authorized to negotiate a loan," Michelena wrote. And what did Migoni do in return?

He did not meet with those who showed any interest. He solicited no offers. I don't know that he spoke with anyone other than the Banker to the Holy Alliance.[61] He got tangled up with [B. A.] Goldschmidt on October 1 [1823] making an agreement whereby he was obliged to work through Goldschmidt, all the while leaving Goldschmidt free to think about things for three months and then doing what he pleased at the end of that time.[62]

In the meanwhile, Michelena complained, Migoni had spoken with another merchant bank, Barclay, Herring, Richardson, which indicated an immediate willingness to lend to Mexico.[63] But when B. A. Goldschmidt got wind of a possible deal with Barclay, Herring, Richardson, Goldschmidt reminded Migoni that Goldschmidt had already negotiated a Mexican loan and that Barclay, Herring, Richardson must withdraw, "which is what happened." Migoni, according to Michelena, then tried to cover his tracks and did so until February 1824, when the agreement with B. A. Goldschmidt was made public. Meanwhile, Michelena added, Migoni passed on to the Mexican government a series of "lies and contradictions," blaming the Holy

---

60 For what follows, see Michelena to the secretary of home and foreign relations, London, July 24, 1824, *Gobernación*, leg. 61, exp. 38, AGNM, except where as noted.
61 Nathan Rothschild. See Ferguson, *House of Rothschild*, pp. 132–133. With the exception of Brazil, the Rothschilds avoided Latin America in the 1820s.
62 Borja Migoni put the agreement on October 10. See "Esposición del C. Francisco de Borja Migoni, consul general de México en Londres," p. 6.
63 Barclay, Herring, Richardson first appear as merchants of Old South Sea House in London in 1823 and failed in 1826. There seems to be no evidence of their operating after 1829. The firm was not related to Barclay and Company, an ancestor of the modern Barclays. I am grateful to Dr. John Orbell of ING-Barings and to Ms. Jessie Campbell of Barclays for providing me with this information.

Alliance for Mexico's disadvantageous loan terms on the one hand and then blaming the actions of the Mexican government on the other.

And to some degree, Michelena was correct or, at least, Migoni *was* defensive about the terms he had negotiated with B. A. Goldschmidt for Mexico as opposed to, say, those of the contemporaneous Chilean and Colombian loans. "Circumstances forbid comparisons of any sort between those operations and our own. The biggest difference is the change in political circumstances . . . [In 1822, at the time of the Chilean and Colombian loans] the independence of America was not seriously opposed by any, save the constitutional government of Spain. . . . " But since Ferdinand VII had been restored to power as monarch in late 1823, Spain was now reconciled to the Holy Alliance, and had the support of the continental powers "whose influence permits us to have no illusions."[64] In fact, Migoni maintained, he had tried to interest Rothschilds, Baring Brothers, and Reid Irving, among others, but that these houses were convinced that the support of the Holy Alliance made Mexican independence an unlikely outcome.[65]

But Migoni, said Michelena, had been playing for time and trying to hide the entanglement with Goldschmidt. In fact, before February, Michelena said, Migoni had even denied that there was *any* agreement with Goldschmidt.[66] But on February 9, 1824, the contract was made public – "the scandalous contract" – which Migoni had rendered even more odious by praising it. "That's when I came," said Michelena. "Migoni took off in a show of disapproval."

When Migoni finally returned to London after receiving instructions from Mexico to do so, Michelena explained that Migoni spoke to him using "indecent words, not those of a gentleman, arrogant and intolerably insensitive, the result of his disdain for a government that he calls revolutionary."

Michelena laid even more partisan charges against Migoni, some of them patently false. "How can you deny that he failed to monitor [Iturbide's movements] and even though he had every occasion to know his most secret steps, he didn't follow him. He was warned about the preparations [Iturbide] made to flee by the agent assigned to watch [Iturbide], but he did nothing."[67] But Michelena's most damning accusations were yet to come.

---

64 Borja Migoni to the finance minister, London, March 22, 1824, *Deuda Exterior*, vol. 12, AGNM.

65 "Esposición del C. Francisco de Borja Migoni, consul general de Mexico en Londres," pp. 4–5.

66 Which may have been true. Borja Migoni claimed that the restoration of Ferdinand VII caused B. A. Goldschmidt to back off its initial agreement with him. "Esposición del C. Francisco de Borja Migoni, consul general de México en Londres," p. 6. *"entretener el tiempo"* is translated as "playing for time."

67 Not so! Borja Migoni had kept Lucas Alamán aware of Iturbide's European travels, at least to the extent he was informed of them. See Borja Migoni to the minister of home and foreign relations, London, December 29, 1823 in López de Roux, *Independencia de México*, p. 95.

Migoni feigned ignorance about everything and deceived the government by the assurances he gave about Iturbide's intentions. Once Iturbide had departed [for Mexico] [Borja Migoni] would not assist . . . nor did he take every measure possible to frustrate the attack [that Iturbide] had undertaken against the Nation, all under the ridiculous pretext that he lacked the orders to do so even though the Agent [Michelena?] offered to show him [the details] of his [own] mission."

Michelena concluded by making an uncompromising judgment about Migoni's actions. He spoke of the Goldschmidt loan as "perhaps unexampled in the history of borrowing." "Never," Michelena concluded, "was a government as beaten down as Mexico's and never was there an excess more prejudicial to the interests of the Nation." "My opinion of Migoni is quite unsatisfactory. Perhaps I am deceived," Michelena minced few words. After examining the documents of the Goldschmidt file that Migoni had given him, Michelena told Finance Minister Arrillaga, "it seems to me that he has no business conducting the affairs of the Republic, and I told him so."[68] Others seemingly concurred. One wrote that "M[igoni's] naming was a big mistake," for he was a committed monarchist, not a committed republican.[69]

Michelena then tried a different tack,[70] asking Migoni about how much of the Goldschmidt loan Michelena might draw on – this prior to fixing the dimensions of the loan to be contracted with Barclay, Herring, Richardson. Migoni responded, as Michelena said, by flatly refusing to hand any of the Goldschmidt funds over to Michelena. Migoni related that his charge from the finance ministry made no provision for his handing funds over to Michelena.[71]

In a letter to Arrillaga, Migoni sought to justify his conduct. "I went to [Michelena's] residence twice to explain that what he wanted was impossible. I hope you will approve of what I did. What agent can ignore the instructions of his government?"[72] "Señor Michelena," Migoni continued,

told me that he had been offered 10,000 rifles and that if I didn't give him the money, he wouldn't buy them. After I repeatedly told him that I had no instructions from you about this, I told him that long before the loan of £3.2 million, people had made me a thousand proposals about boats, arms and uniforms with plans for contracts to be sent to the government.

---

68 Michelena to the finance minister, London, July 16, 1824, *Deuda Exterior*, vol. 12. AGNM.
69 Tomás Murphy to Michelena, Paris, June 6, 1825 (reservada), HD 18–1.4272, BLAC, UT.
70 Michelena to the minister of home and foreign relations, London, July 25, 1824, *Gobernación*, leg. 61, exp. 38, AGNM.
71 Borja Migoni to Michelena, London, July 20, 1824, *Gobernación*, leg. 61, exp. 38, AGNM; "Esposición del C. Francisco de Borja Migoni, consul general de México en Londres," p. 24.
72 Borja Migoni to the finance minister, London, July 21, 1824, *Deuda Exterior*, vol. 12, AGNM. *"plata viva"* is translated as "cold, hard cash."

After the loan was made, Migoni concluded, all he wanted was the proceeds of the loan in "cold, hard cash."

Michelena found himself outflanked. In August 1824 he received a dispatch from the finance minister, Lucas Alamán –Migoni's close friend. In it, Alamán told Michelena that he was to await new instructions and that circumstances had entirely changed. Only Migoni was to have control over the proceeds of the Goldschmidt loan. Remarkably, throughout the summer and early fall of 1824, Migoni denied virtually every request made by Michelena or his superiors to Migoni for funds to be placed at the disposition of the ministry of home and foreign relations, including one for £100,000. It was as if Alamán and Migoni were holding the others' ministries hostage![73]

Migoni, as one might expect, did not share Michelena's opinion of his efforts, and thought rather highly of what he had achieved.[74] He professed satisfaction that compensated for the "great difficulties" he had faced, principally in providing Mexico with "considerable resources" that would solidify its credit in Europe and in Britain, where the approval of "English capitalists" would be a sign of their support for Mexican independence. Indeed, Mexico was now in a better position than Spain, whose efforts to raise capital in the markets had been stymied by the restoration of Ferdinand VII.[75] Mexico, said Migoni, had to overcome not only the opposition of its "enemies" in Europe, but had also been forced to deal with the examples of the Colombian and Peruvian bonds and the issues these uncertainties had created.[76]

But, Migoni concluded, the real problem he faced – "the thing that really encouraged malevolence" – was the "simultaneous" authorization of the 20-million-peso loan, the Barclay, Herring, Richardson loan negotiated by Michelena,[77] one with "onerous conditions" and "contrary to the established customs and usages of European capitalists." He realized, he wrote, that the "law of necessity" had driven Mexico into the market once more. But if he had succeeded in any degree, it was precisely by creating the presumption in

73 Lucas Alamán to Michelena, México, August 14, 1824, *Gobernación*, leg. 61, exp. 38, AGNM; "Expediente sobre que Don Francisco de Borja Migoni facilite los fondos necesarios para concluir varios objetos importantes a la República y encargodos particularmente por su Gobierno," HD 17–4.4084, BLAC, UT.

74 For this and what follows, see Borja Migoni to the finance minister, London, February 9, 1824, *Deuda Exterior*, vol. 12, AGNM. Borja Migoni to the finance minister, London, November 22, 1824, *Hacienda Pública*, 6ª, 1857–1858, AGNM. Also see "Esposición del C. Francisco de Borja Migoni, consul general de México en Londres," pp. 3–4.

75 Ferguson, *House of Rothschild*, p. 358.

76 Dawson, *First Latin American Debt Crisis*, pp. 54–57.

77 Borja Migoni also believed that the Staples and Barclay loan negotiated by Bartholomew Vigors Richards had spooked British merchant bankers. Why, he asked, was Mexico loading up on debt so quickly? "Esposición del C. Francisco de Borja Migoni," p. 6.

Table 1.2. *Consol Yield, Selected Loans*

Loan	Price	Coupon (%)	Yield (%)
Spain (1820)	65	7	10.77
Chile (1822)	70	6	8.57
Goldschmidt (1823)	50	5	10.00
Spain (1824)	44	5	11.36
Barclay (1824)	86¾	6	6.92

Source: "Espocición del C. Francisco de Borja Migoni, consul general de México en Londres, sobre el empréstito de que fue encargado," *El Amigo del Pueblo*, September 12, 1827, p. 9.

the market that the Barclay, Herring, Richardson loan had been thwarted. What purpose, wondered Migoni, had the Barclay, Herring, Richardson loan served? If the idea was to raise capital in the European market, his negotiation had done that. And if he had been as unsuccessful in raising money as Michelena said, how could Mexico have found funds, "contracting for a second loan before the first one had been completed"? Migoni also criticized the 6 percent coupon of the Barclay, Herring, Richardson loan. It violated the British usury ceiling of 5 percent, which, Migoni said, would provide a "pretext" that would, perhaps, "intimidate the public about the legitimacy of the loan." Besides, he added, the trend was for countries to reduce the stock of debt outstanding at rates more than 5 percent. Contracting at any rate more than 5 percent would thus have raised doubts about the means of payment.

Migoni defended "his" loan at some length, comparing its terms favorably with those received by France in 1818, Spain in 1820, and Chile in 1822, writing, "I feel an inexplicable satisfaction in seeing my diligence rewarded with the result I have obtained." Migoni based his "inexplicable satisfaction" on what we might term his calculations of the consol yield of bonds. If the yield of a consol (perpetuity) is

$$P = C/R,$$

where "*P*" is the market price, "*C*" is the coupon expressed as a multiple of £100, and "*R*" is the yield, then here is what Migoni argued; for comparison, I add the Barclay, Herring, Richardson loan (see Table 1.2).

If the yield is a rough measure of what it cost governments to attract funds in the capital market, Migoni could say that he had done better than Spain by anywhere from 77 to 136 basis points.[78] But it is by no means clear why he thought he had done better than the Chileans. And, unfortunately, the yield of the Barclay, Herring, Richardson loan was 6.92 percent

---

78 A basis point is one-hundredth of a percentage point.

or more than 300 basis points lower than the B. A. Goldschmidt loan. Did Migoni understand this? Perhaps this was the impetus for his defensive tone. "Even if we admit something that is not necessarily true: that [the other loans] have been contracted at an apparently higher price [than mine], these in reality have been subject to sharp reductions [in price]." Of course, subsequent declines in the prices of the bonds were irrelevant to the original cost of capital to these governments, but such were the grounds on which Migoni chose to defend himself.

And perhaps there were ample grounds for his choice. Migoni had initially gone to B. A. Goldschmidt for the loan, but had broken off negotiations with the firm when it looked as if a group of capitalists who claimed to represent the British government might make him a better offer. But, at least in Migoni's opinion, this group, which included Sir George Coburn – one of Nelson's officers who rose to become the First Sea Lord in 1828 – was not on the level; Migoni went so far as to accuse the group of seeking to defraud him. Thus, when Migoni reopened negotiations with B. A. Goldschmidt, he did so from a position of weakness – not to say, of foolishness. This could not have helped his bargaining position with the firm, which was well aware of Migoni's failure to strike the alternative deal.[79]

In any event, Migoni then turned directly to the Barclay, Herring, Richardson contract – the first version, apparently, negotiated by Bartholomew Vigors Richards.[80] His initial criticism was sensible. According to Migoni, the Barclay, Herring, Richardson loan – even though it advanced 500,000 pesos to the Mexican government – would disburse the remaining funds in 500,000 peso installments over twenty-four months, which Migoni claimed was "the time set aside to [Barclay] to ratify the contract negotiated by its agent." But, as Migoni emphasized, B. A. Goldschmidt had provided 1 million pesos immediately to Migoni for use by the Mexican government. So, it would seem that Migoni had a point in arguing that his contract had shifted more risk to B. A. Goldschmidt than did Vigors Richards to Barclay, Herring, Richardson. Migoni also pointed to what he regarded as other disadvantages of the Barclay, Herring, Richardson loan. First, its term was twenty years (as opposed to B. A. Goldschmidt's

---

79 "Esposición del C. Francisco de Borja Migoni, consul general de México en Londres," pp. 12–21, contains Borja Migoni's own bizarre account of the events, with a "syndicate" of "lenders" that included Dr. Patrick Mackie, a British resident in Mexico who had been lobbying for British recognition. See Johnston, *Missions to Mexico*, pp. 2–3. For Coburn, a Tory MP, privy councilor, and career naval officer who participated in the burning of Washington, DC, during the War of 1812, see *Dictionary of National Biography*, IV, 640–642. For swindlers and blackmailers, it was an odd collection, and Borja Migoni even claimed that the president of the Board of Trade, George Huskisson, had been reading Borja Migoni's official correspondence to Mexico.

80 For which see next.

thirty years), which raised annual repayment of principal. But – and this is more interesting –Migoni also claimed that the Barclay, Herring, Richardson contract prevented the Mexican government from buying its own debt in the secondary market. From Mexico's standpoint, this meant, as Migoni put it, "[that Mexico would] renounce the advantage that all governments enjoy in negotiating loans, which is to employ the sums intended to amortize debts in buying up the items for retirement at a price lower than the nominal one." In other words, he said, "repayment must take place at par." This, Migoni thought, was to take whatever benefit the government might reap from buying up its own debt and transfer it to whoever else could purchase the bonds below par in the secondary market.[81]

In the B. A. Goldschmidt loan, moreover, he had secured the right, after ten years, for the Mexican government to deal with whichever merchant bank it desired in retiring the debt. In general, Migoni claimed, his contract offered Mexico more freedom in dealing with the market than did the Barclay, Herring, Richardson loan. He had not obligated the Mexican government to work with B. A. Goldschmidt in the event of a subsequent loan. And, he added, although he had acquiesced in allowing B. A. Goldschmidt to retain sufficient proceeds of the loan to pay the first four dividends and to amortize two years (i.e., 6.67 percent) of the principal, Migoni wrote, "the condition was absolutely necessary. Assuming that it is probable, not to say certain, that we will have to come to the European capitalists on the Exchange for another loan, it would have been impossible to complete the loan, let alone another one, without this stipulation." Such stipulation was part of the Chilean loan, Migoni added, and given "the great distance that separates Mexico from England," it was necessary to reduce "even the slightest fear that something might interrupt interest payments." And so, Migoni concluded, Mexico's credit would be strengthened to the extent that the contract he negotiated with B. A. Goldschmidt was punctually and properly observed.

In all of this, Michelena too came under severe criticism, both in the late 1820s and, later, at the hands of one of Mexico's most famous writers and thinkers, José María Luis Mora. Mora, writing in exile in Paris, was only half wrong in his account of why Mexico was compelled to borrow.[82] "The foreign debt," he said in 1837,

was assumed more on the basis of political miscalculation than financial exigency. True enough, given how much money the government wasted, the British loans were needed. However, this was not what they were thinking about when they

---

81 "Y en vez de estipular las ventajas que resultan de la compra de los efectos que han de amortizar no para el gobierno, no para el público, sino para los contratantes solos" is how he put it.

82 José María Luis Mora, *Revista política de las diversas administraciones que ha tenido la república hasta 1837* (1837; México, 1986), p. 173.

went looking for money. What the people governing thought was the loan, by creating and strengthening vested interests [in Mexican independence] would speed [recognition] up.

"Well," Mora observed, "a mistake of that size was unforgivable, even in those inexperienced times. . . ." And, he observed quite shrewdly,

that, however, was why *they wanted* [emphasis in original: *deseo*] to undertake a *loan from Great Britain* [in original]. On the London Stock Exchange [however] they were more *aware* [in original] than the government and people were about how secure the Independence of Mexico was; how Spain was loathe to support it; and about [how Spain] would attempt to bring [Mexico] to heel once more. *They did not have the same confidence in the new nation's capacity to pay given that its resources were unexplored* [emphasis mine]. So the Goldschmidt loan was very disadvantageous to Mexico, both for the desire that the Mexican government had in contracting for it and for the Stock Exchange's lack of confidence when the loan was made.

Mora certainly had a way with words. His analysis of why Mexico's first foreign loans were so "disadvantageous" could hardly be bettered. There was no precedent for lending to Mexico, so the risks were high and the terms on which the loan was made not at all favorable to the borrower. Mora correctly concluded that however unwise the loans might have been from the standpoint of 1837, there was certainly no reason for the stock exchange to have much faith in Mexico's ability to service them.

The Barclay, Herring, Richardson loan, Mora observed, "[w]as undertaken for the same reasons, ends and objectives as the [Goldschmidt] loan and under conditions even more disadvantageous for the Republic." "When things start badly," Mora said, "they are unlikely to end well. The loans were poorly conceived and worse implemented. They were political – they could not have been worse spent [or] invested in equally political ends." Once Mexico's independence was recognized by England, Mora said, the disposition of the funds was also placed at the service of political aims. Mora called the spending "dopey" (*torpe*) and "wasteful" (*despilfarrada*). "Members of the government and [our diplomats] in the European legations spent these costly funds in unlimited amounts on uniforms and on old and useless rifles for the Mexican army – which cost twice as much as new ones should have."

Mora continued at length. Mexico wanted a navy, but had no merchant marine "on which it must be based." Ships were ordered in Great Britain, the United States, and Sweden, all quite expensive, and some of them could not be completely paid for. The ships were never inspected "because none of the buyers had the expertise to conduct [inspections] correctly. Large sums had been advanced to finance the completion of the ships, but we could not take delivery of them, because with the waste and confusion, there was not enough money left." Mora then went on to attack. He called Vicente

Rocafuerte and Michelena "the butt of jokes and the playthings of frauds who compensated themselves for their useless and exaggerated services in the cause of *independence.*" [emphasis in original]

Mora went on to discuss the case of the brig "Guerrero," a matter to which we will return later. But he essentially concluded that Michelena was not dishonest, only incompetent, "his honor and probity vindicated, his reputation as a businessman somewhat diminished." He got the ships, Mora said, but he didn't know what to do with them "because there were neither officers nor sailors to man them." And so, Mora concluded, "that's what happened in Mexico from so many sacrifices made for the sake of having a pedestrian navy that disappeared soon afterward, rendering no other service than the surrender of San Juan de Ulúa, half because of the services of the Mexican squadron, half because of the sheer anger of the forces arrayed against the Spaniards."

Mora's outburst, and an outburst it was, raises a number of issues very squarely. Certainly, the charges Mora pressed against Michelena were as serious as those that Michelena had laid against Migoni. But in 1837, when Mora made them, Michelena had been defending himself against similar attacks for nearly a decade. In many ways, the discussion goes to the heart of the loans, their purposes, methods, and fortunes.

The charges, to repeat, were already old news. In 1827, Michelena found himself under attack for corruption, and had replied in a pamphlet in which he stated that "the various political positions in which I have found myself have necessarily led to hatred of me and prosecution: not only by defeated parties but also by those necessarily hurt by the course of affairs in which I have taken part."[83] The attack, said Michelena, followed the reasoning and conclusions "like those adopted by enemy agents in Europe to beat us down, to maintain the status of the Holy Alliance, to destroy ours, and to introduce among us a lack of confidence in the good faith of England."[84] Michelena attributed his recent career to opposition to Iturbide "by the violence done in his coronation [as Emperor] and by his dissolution of the Congress."[85] And with his colors thus nailed to the mast, Michelena proceeded to defend himself against those charges he regarded as baseless, irresponsible, and false.

Perhaps most relevant was his defense of his role in the purchase and fitting out of the brig "Guerrero." This bizarre incident reflects scant credit on any of the figures involved. Michelena, it seems, had been commissioned

---

83 *Esplicación de la conducta de Michelena en algunos puntos* (México, 1827), p. 2. "*fueron la burla y el juguete de todos los charlatanes*" is translated as "the butt of jokes and the plaything of frauds."

84 *Esplicación de la conducta de Michelena*, p. 4.

85 *Esplicación de la conducta de Michelena*, p. 7.

to use £10,000 of the proceeds of the Barclay, Herring, Richardson loan to have a "submarine" called the "Guerrero" fitted out.[86] The intent behind the plan was to help end the Spanish control of the fort of San Juan de Ulúa that commanded the approach to the vital port of Veracruz. "[It] was really too sad for the government, me, any Mexican, to see Ulúa in the hands of Spain."[87] Who hatched such a plan? Unfortunately, Michelena may have thought this up himself just as Mora more or less openly surmised. The proof is the reproduction of correspondence between war and naval minister Gómez Pedraza and Michelena, in which Gómez Pedraza stated, in response to Michelena, that a submarine "would have been a great obstacle [to the Spanish] in supplying Ulúa."[88] Michelena, however, seems to indicate that the idea originated with Don Manuel Mier y Terán when he held the war and naval portfolio.[89] Whatever the case, Michelena (or someone) had relayed to Mexico an account of Robert Fulton's triumphant demolition of the brig "Dorothea" in 1805, while the "Dorothea" was moored in the Thames. Fulton used one of his newfangled "torpedoes" to do the job, part of a feverish campaign to interest the Royal Navy in the virtues of submarine warfare.[90] The account of what occurred is so garbled that one can only hope that the file prepared by the Mexican legation in London on the matter surfaces someday.

Mora accused Michelena of idiotically advancing Robert Fulton himself £10,000 (or something like a million dollars today) for a submarine or torpedo that Michelena never got.[91] Unfortunately, Mora got most of the details wrong. Michelena could not have advanced Fulton the £10,000, or if he did, Michelena possessed supernatural abilities. Fulton died in 1816, but Michelena, as we know, was not dispatched to London until 1824.[92] A supposed Captain Johnson of "the secret service of submarine navigation" of the Royal Navy took the £10,000, but, apparently, never delivered the goods. In September 1825, Johnson asked the Mexican government for another £6,000, which he did not get, and then another £1,000, which he did not get either. Not surprisingly, when the Mexican government demanded the return of the £10,000, Johnson replied that "the money was tied up in the boat and the machines, and that he had gone into debt

---

86 Referred to by Michelena as a "*bergantín*," which is quite confusing. "Submarines" of that era bore no resemblance to brigs.
87 *Esplicación de la conducta de Michelena*, p. 19.
88 Gómez Pedraza to Michelena, México, March 29, 1827, in *Esplicación de la conducta de Michelena*, p. 48.
89 *Esplicación de la conducta de Michelena*, p. 19.
90 Alex Roland, *Undersea Warfare in the Age of Sail* (Bloomington, IN, 1978), pp. 109–110.
91 Mora, *Revista política*, p. 176.
92 Roland, *Undersea Warfare*, p. 118.

for even larger sums."[93] Poor Captain Johnson seems to have been tossed into debtors' prison, where he languished. According to Mora, the Mexican government never received the submarine or got its money back, which makes his outburst understandable.

On the other hand, Alamán was quite clear in describing the circumstances that attended the fall and evacuation of the Spanish garrison in San Juan de Ulúa.

San Juan de Ulúa necessarily depended for its pay and provisioning on remittances from Havana. . . . [But] the ships from England purchased with the funds of the loan arrived then commanded by English and U.S. officers. . . . They cut off communication with the Castle . . . which was obliged to surrender on November 18, 1825.[94]

Michelena may have squandered money on the "Guerrero," but if Alamán is correct, the rest of his naval purchases do not seem to have done badly at all.[95] Mora's jibe here is quite unfair. Veracruz was Mexico's outlet to the Atlantic economy and the castle of San Juan de Ulúa commanded the entrance to the port. It had been necessary to move the customhouse to Alvarado, about sixty kilometers down the coast in 1823, and it remained there until late 1825.[96] It is very difficult to form any clear idea of how much the Spanish presence in Veracruz affected trade, but the legal export of gold and silver from Veracruz from 1796 through 1823 averaged $8.14 million yearly, falling in 1823 – when the customhouse was moved to Alvarado – to $1.3 million. Similarly, cochineal exports through Veracruz over the same period averaged 350,000 pounds yearly, falling to 288,245 pounds in 1823.[97] Since the Spaniards had shelled the port of Veracruz at will, beginning in September 1823, it is no small wonder that trade suffered. In other words, ending the Spanish presence at the castle was an important step in finally securing independence from Spain, a fact amply recognized at the time.[98]

Michelena also found himself accused of purchasing rifles at exorbitant prices and of buying uniforms that had previously been worn or that were unsuitable for use in Mexico. Michelena had been ordered to obtain a

---

93 Juan José Espinosa de los Monteros to the war and naval minister, México, March 2, 1827, in *Esplicación de la conducta de Michelena*, p. 48. Britain had no submarine corps and Johnson was probably some sort of shady character.

94 Alamán, *Historia de México*, vol. 5: pp. 820–821.

95 Or was Alamán defending Borja Migoni in this instance? Such a reading is equally plausible.

96 Charles T. O'Gorman to the permanent undersecretary at the Foreign Office (Joseph Planta), México, December 4, 1825, FO 203/5.

97 Charles T. O'Gorman, "Exports from the Mexican Republic," México, March 1, 1825, FO 203/4.

98 Alamán, *Historia de México*, vol. 5: pp. 820, 821.

thousand each, spending 36,000 pesos of the Barclay, Herring, Richardson loan.[99] Michelena rejected the charge saying,

I wasn't told to inspect the uniforms or say if they were cheap enough because I've got no shame in saying I'm not a tailor . . . [It] is absolutely false that the uniforms were old when they arrived [and] it is mistaken and untrue – as widely believed – that I had purchased the arms in England and had a substantial financial interest in them.[100]

By and large, Michelena seemed to think that virtually all the charges laid against him were politically motivated. But why Mora would have recycled them a decade later is a bit less clear, unless motivated by a growing realization that the entire loan business had, by then, turned into something of a disaster.

The politics of these issues is not easy to fathom. Timothy Anna characterizes Michelena as "a champion of provincial rights" as distinct from, for example, Alamán, "the most capable and articulate conservative opposed to provincial power."[101] It is quite clear that Michelena did not enjoy Alamán's full support, for Alamán seemingly favored Migoni, with whom he had a close personal and working relationship. But Anna also interprets the work of the Supreme Executive Power (Supremo Poder Ejecutivo) in 1823 and 1824 as expressing "the will of the center . . . to establish a single center that was declared to represent the nation." Michelena, along with Miguel Domínguez and Vicente Guerrero, comprised the Supremo Poder Ejecutivo. Perhaps, best put, Michelena was a proponent of what Anna terms "moderated federalism," while Alamán was more frankly "centralist."[102] But it is also possible to overinterpret these differences in light of subsequent events. In 1824, Michelena and Alamán had a good working relationship, and Michelena was by no means loath to express his disapproval of Migoni to Alamán in relatively blunt terms or his support for Alamán's tenure in the ministry of home and foreign relations in 1824. If anything, Michelena was keen to present a united negotiating face to the British, and perhaps it was Migoni's resistance to his leadership and authority that Michelena resented most of all.

Perhaps the most logical possibility is that under the Constitution of 1824, one of the obligations of the states of the Federation (Título VI, Sección Segunda, Artículo 161, Fracción VII) was "to contribute to the

99 Gómez Pedraza to Michelena, México, October 27, 1824, and copy of contract in *Esplicación de la conducta de Michelena*, pp. 51–52.
100 *Esplicación de la conducta de Michelena*, pp. 22, 23. True only if a 3 percent commission is not "substantial."
101 Anna, *Forging Mexico*, p. 112.
102 Anna, *Forging Mexico*, pp. 147, 152, 158. Or, as Josefina Vázquez precisely situates Alamán in the 1820s in a private communication, "republican liberal centralist."

consolidation and amortization of debts recognized by the general (i.e., national) congress."[103] In other words, the debts of the general government were literally the debts of the state governments, and, as such, would constitute a burden on state finances. In that case, under the Constitution of 1824, strong proponents of state sovereignty would have ample reason to complain about mounting debts of the general government. Yet it seems unlikely that this could have been the source of Mora's animus, especially in 1837, considering that Michelena was, by Anna's lights, at least, a federalist as well.

Migoni, Michelena's antagonist in England, did not escape attack in 1827 either. His tormentor was the deputy Manuel Crecencio Rejón, who mounted a congressional investigation against his actions and ultimately secured a political judgment against him.[104] It marked another episode in the continuing hostility between Rejón and Alamán and his circle, a hostility that nearly produced a catastrophe for Rejón when Alamán had him assaulted by soldiers in 1831.[105]

The question Rejón had raised was whether Migoni had acted improperly in securing a loan of £3.2 million or 16 million pesos, rather than the authorized amount of 8 million. The response of the finance ministry was that Migoni may have well acted in error, but that the only way to raise 8 million when bringing a loan to market at 50 was by doubling the amount for which the government would contract (i.e., $8/(\frac{1}{2}) = 16 = £3.2$). Moreover, the ministry argued that the financial needs of the state, pressing as they were, justified the borrowing. In addition, if the government had repudiated the loan, had it failed to approve it, "terrible consequences . . . would follow from not doing so."[106] Indeed, had Mexico repudiated Migoni, what would have ensued would have followed the example of Colombia in repudiating the loan negotiated by Francisco Antonio Zea.[107] The ministry also went on to defend the Barclay, Herring, Richardson loan as necessary, to the extent that its proceeds were used to pay interest and principal on the B. A. Goldschmidt loan, keeping the sum of both loans contracted under the authorized ceiling of 28 million pesos.[108]

The response of the congressional committee was venomous, characterizing the ministry's reasoning about Migoni's conduct as "less solid than specious." After all, it concluded, the one guarantee that contractors and

---

103 Felipe Tena Ramírez, *Leyes fundamentales de México* (12th ed., 1983, México), p. 192.

104 *Dictamen de la comisión inspectora de la Cámara de Representatantes del Congreso General sobre si el gobierno se arregló o no a las leyes en la empréstito estrangero que contrató* (México, 1827).

105 Anna, *Forging Mexico*, p. 235.

106 *Dictamen de la comisión inspectora*, p. 6.

107 For which see Dawson, *First Latin America Debt Crisis*, pp. 42–43.

108 Lucas Alamán, *Liquidación general de la deuda esterior de la república Mexicana hasta fin de 1841* (México, 1845), p. 12, makes this point as well.

bondholders required was the approval of the government, not the words of the authorizing legislation, which they never saw. In other words, what mattered was what was approved, not what was authorized. Whatever the government did in the Barclay, Herring, Richardson loan, those "proceedings did not justify what occurred in the contract negotiated by Migoni [with B. A. Goldschmidt] nor did it repair the damage caused the excessive issue."[109]

The conclusions of the congressional report are worth summarizing, especially in light of the default that would occur in October 1827. If the B. A. Goldschmidt loan negotiated by Migoni had been restricted to 8 million pesos, as authorized, with 5 million pesos of the Barclay, Herring, Richardson loan reserved contractually for repaying the B. A. Goldschmidt loan, along with that portion of the B. A. Goldschmidt loan that was to be retained for repayment of principal and interest, "perhaps the Goldschmidt [loan] would have been paid off [thus avoiding] all the damages . . . that the nation will feel for many years. And all because the decree of May 1 [1823, which authorized a loan of 8 million pesos] was not followed to the letter."[110] This was tantamount to holding Migoni responsible for the ensuing financial disasters of the nineteenth century. What Migoni thought of the charges, his response was not recorded here.

Negotiation and Conclusion of the Loans

On August 18, 1823, Finance Minister Arrillaga signed a loan contract with Bartholomew Vigors Richards. The contract was contingent on its acceptance by both the Mexican Congress and the parent firm of Barclay, Herring, Richardson, for Richards had acted on his own "daring" (Table 1.3).[111] Coming as it did within a month of Congress' formal authorization of a foreign loan (July 27, 1823), the proceedings emphasized the initiative of the Supremo Poder Ejecutivo (of which Michelena, of course, was a quondam supplementary member). Negotiations continued and it was not until early December that Richards and Arrillaga agreed on a revised contract that the Congress accepted as well.

On December 9, Arrillaga informed the Congress that Barclay, Herring, Richardson's agent, Richards, had already advanced the government more than 250,000 pesos before obtaining the full approval of Barclay, Herring, Richardson itself.[112] It was precisely at this point that things began to go bad for Barclay, Herring, Richardson – and bad in a major way – for

---

109 *Dictamen de la comisión inspectora*, p. 11.
110 *Dictamen de la comisión inspectora*, p. 12.
111 "Esposición del C. Francisco de Borja Migoni," p. 7.
112 Arrillaga to the Supremo Poder Ejecutivo, December 8, 1823, *Deuda Exterior*, vol. 12. AGNM.

Table 1.3. *Chronology of the Barclay, Herring, Richardson Loan*

1823	
August 18	Arrillaga signs contract subject to revision with Bartholomew Vigors Richards, the first agent of Barclay, Herring, Richardson
August 27	Mexican Congress authorizes loan
December 6	Arrillaga and Richards agree on revised contract
December 9	Mexican Congress recognizes contract. Six-month deadline for ratification
1824	
February 10	Barclay, Herring, Richardson ratifies contract subject to its approval of clauses (contract had not yet arrived)
March 20	Barclay, Herring, Richardson receives "ratification" by Congress
May 20	Barclay, Herring, Richardson receives contract. Delay caused by "accidents about which we are not informed"
June 9	Deadline for Barclay, Herring, Richardson ratification
August 25	Second Barclay, Herring, Richardson loan approved by Mexican government
1825	
January	B. A. Goldschmidt ban expires

it seems as if Richards had been operating as a free agent and had kept Barclay, Herring, Richardson largely in the dark.

In early February 1824, Barclay, Herring, Richardson wrote to the finance minister reminding him of Barclay, Herring, Richardson's willingness to lend to Mexico, "when no native capitalist would assist the government nor any foreigner resident in Mexico except with conditions that could not have been admitted."[113] And as of that moment, Bartolomew Vigors Richards – Barclay, Herring, Richardson's agent – had not yet returned to London, nor kept Barclay, Herring, Richardson advised of the conditions of the contract negotiated with Arrillaga and ratified by the Mexican Congress. But even so, Barclay, Herring, Richardson signaled its willingness to accede to the contract subject to whatever modifications might be needed "both to harmonize this transaction with another engagement of a similar nature recently entered into by Don Francisco de Borja Migoni with the House of Messrs. B. A. Goldschmidt and Company and to make it [illegible] conformable to the usages of and custom by which all contracts for loans are regulated" (Table 1.4). Barclay, Herring, Richardson also agreed to honor drafts against Mexico presented to it in the interim. But Barclay, Herring, Richardson was primarily apprehensive about the

---

113 Barclay, Herring, Richardson to the finance minister, London, February 10, 1824, *Deuda Exterior*, vol. 12, AGNM, for this and what follows.

Table 1.4. *Chronology of the B. A. Goldschmidt Loan*

1823	
May 14	Migoni authorized by Supremo Poder Ejecutivo
1824	
January 12	Migoni contracts with B. A. Goldschmidt
February 7	First seven articles of contract agreed to and deposited in Bank of England
February 9	(Approximate) George O'Gorman, Henry Robert Tute, and James Dillon, commissioned by B. A. Goldschmidt to deliver agreement to Arrillaga, set sail from London

fate of its advances to the Mexican government in light of Migoni's negotiation of the loan with B. A. Goldschmidt. The Mexican government, wrote Barclay, Herring, Richardson, must understand "how injurious to our negotiations with your Excellency must be the issue of bonds by [B. A. Goldschmidt] to so large an amount occupying by these means the funds of those parties which would otherwise have been disposed to advance them upon the Mexican securities we were about to offer them." In other words, Barclay, Herring, Richardson considered that the market for Mexican bonds was only so large and that the B. A. Goldschmidt loan had spoiled it. But if this were true, then why had Barclay, Herring, Richardson negotiated a loan at all?

The answer to this question is complicated, but it seems to come down to the fact that Richards had presented Barclay, Herring, Richardson with a fait accompli. As we have seen, Migoni was authorized to negotiate for a loan on May 14, 1823. Barclay, Herring, Richardson's agent – Richards – signed a contract with Mexico on August 18, 1823. In early October 1823, Migoni reported that he was "on the verge of concluding a contract for a loan of 8 million pesos."[114] "Doing a loan right is not something you can do in four days," Migoni added, "especially if you're dealing with a first-class house, as I am."[115] But between October and the beginning of December, Migoni apparently ran into a formidable snag. Writing to Finance Minister Arrillaga, Migoni said, "Misfortune dogs the 8 million peso loan."[116] The collapse of the constitutional regime in Spain and the restoration of Ferdinand VII, "sowed a lack of confidence, wounding all the foreign funds . . . [and] the announcement that expeditions were to set sail from Spain to reconquer its foreign colonies made it impossible to sell any American loan." And although Foreign Secretary George Canning had

---

114 Borja Migoni to the finance minister, London, October 8, 1823, *Deuda Exterior*, vol. 12, AGNM.
115 Borja Migoni to Lucas Alamán, London, October 8, 1823, *Deuda Exterior*, vol. 12, AGNM.
116 Borja Migoni to the finance minister, London, December 6, 1823, *Deuda Exterior*, vol. 12, AGNM, for this and what follows.

reassured the merchant community in Great Britain about the prospect for the former Spanish colonies' continuing independence, the Barclay, Herring, Richardson loan presented a problem. In the same way that Migoni had railed against the government's concluding a loan with Staples four months earlier, he now turned his fire on the news of the Barclay, Herring, Richardson loan. "You can have no idea of the great disorder the news caused in the market since the announcement of the 8 million peso loan with B. A. Goldschmidt was virtually concluded." Goldschmidt, Migoni went on to say, was the house with which he had been negotiating – "a house of the first rank" – which had even beaten the Rothschilds to the punch in making a loan to Portugal.[117] But now, it seems, Goldschmidt was having second thoughts and the agreement, virtually concluded, held in abeyance.[118]

Barclay, Herring, Richardson, according to Migoni, had sullied itself in the 1822 Colombian loan fiasco, and was trendy (*moderno*), but largely clueless (*no tiene concepto*). He also warned that the contract into which Mexico had entered with Barclay, Herring, Richardson placed that house under no obligation to the Mexican government – "They lose nothing if the contract is not ratified" – a statement that was flatly incorrect, although Migoni may well have known nothing about Barclay, Herring, Richardson's advances to the Mexican government.

One caution that Migoni proposed was well considered. Observing that the Barclay, Herring, Richardson loan was "payable" in Mexico, Migoni suggested that on a 20-million-peso loan, the Treasury might lose as much as 5 million pesos because of exchange fluctuations. While his meaning is not completely clear, he may have been saying that to the extent that funds would actually be transferred to Mexico City from London, sterling would be driven down. If sterling depreciated (because the demand for pesos would rise), the proceeds of the loan in pesos would fall (i.e., it would require fewer pesos to purchase a pound sterling; hence, a pound sterling would convert to fewer pesos). And as we will subsequently see, sterling fell dramatically in Mexico in 1824, indeed, by more than 25 percent! Not surprisingly, Migoni recommended that the Barclay, Herring, Richardson loan be cancelled.

---

117 Borja Migoni had a penchant for exaggeration. Goldschmidt had a reputation, to be sure, but whether it was a house of the first rank in the City of London in 1823 is another matter. Nor did its loan to Portugal – if it actually made one – prevent the Rothschilds from making one on their own account in 1823. See Ferguson, *House of Rothschild*, p. 132. In terms of capitalization, in 1826, Goldschmidt was about 5 percent of the size of Rothschilds. See Marc Flandreau and Juan Flores, "Resources and Reputations: Historical Precedents for Recent Banking Crises," *Annual Review* (Rothschild Archive), http://www.rothschildarchive.org/ib/articles/AR2007BankingCrises. pdf (accessed May 21, 2008).

118 "Esposición del C. Francisco de Borja Migoni," p. 6.

Migoni reiterated his opposition to the Barclay, Herring, Richardson loan (and to Staples as well) in early January 1824.[119] At this point, he announced that he had almost concluded negotiations with B. A. Goldschmidt for a £3 million loan at 55, with 5 percent commission, or at 50, with 5 percent. Migoni thus figured out that the loan would yield £1.5 million. At 48 pence per pound, this meant 7.5 million pesos. Had it not been for the Barclay, Herring, Richardson and Staples loans – the publicity that they generated – and the state of war between Spain and Mexico, Migoni thought he might have done no worse than 60.

Migoni also planned to forward bills to the Mexican government, amounting to £200,000 – or a million pesos – drawn on B. A. Goldschmidt, a kind of down payment on the loan he had negotiated. Remarkably, even at this late date, Migoni was under the impression that the Barclay, Herring, Richardson loan was *not* a fait accompli. He told Arrillaga that the difficulties that the Barclay, Herring, Richardson loan had created for his negotiations with B. A. Goldschmidt were "unimaginable." Indeed, he alleged that if the Barclay, Herring, Richardson loan were to come into effect, B. A. Goldschmidt would have never been able to put *its* contract into effect. Little did he know.

Arrillaga, of course, did not intend to cancel the Barclay, Herring, Richardson loan. It had afforded him breathing room. Indeed, Arrillaga's reply to Migoni suggests that Arrillaga had used his negotiation with Barclay, Herring, Richardson to get the upper hand with Migoni.[120]

Circumstances are not what they were in the past year at the time of the demise of the former Congress authorizing the government to negotiate the loan which was entrusted to you . . . As you will have seen in the summary I gave in my *Memoria* of 3 November of all the income and outgo of the Public Treasury, our situation is perhaps not as deplorable as one might have thought.[121]

Arrillaga also defended the Barclay, Herring, Richardson loan and its associated advances as "a generous help of half a million pesos at 0.5 percent interest a month that has served us well because its conditions are quite fair and don't present the great evils you bemoan (*lamenta*) in case it's approved [or even if it's rejected]." By February of 1824, of course, Arrillaga would have known that he had Barclay, Herring, Richardson deeply committed. And Migoni could have only read Arrillaga's words with chagrin. The

---

119 Borja Migoni to the finance minister, London, January 17, 1824, *Deuda Exterior*, vol. 12, AGNM, for this and what follows.
120 Arrillaga to Borja Migoni, México, February 25, 1824, *Deuda Exterior*, vol. 12, AGNM, for this and what follows.
121 Probably Arrillaga's *Memoria que el secretario de estado del despacho de hacienda presenta al Congreso constituyente. . . del día 12 de noviembre de 1823* [(México, 1823)]. Arrillaga got the date wrong, obviously.

Barclay, Herring, Richardson loan would have gone through and Migoni would be unable to stop it. Not that he didn't try. He actually wrote that he "understood" that Barclay, Herring, Richardson was seeking a year's delay on its loan, which may or may not have been true. If Mexico were to wait for diplomatic recognition (presumably Britain's), its credit would soar, aided by the "credit established by my loan." In this Monte Cristo–like vein, he argued that Mexico could negotiate a loan at "80, 85, or 90." This would be "very interesting for the Finances of the Republic," particularly if the Barclay, Herring, Richardson loan were cancelled, but Arrillaga obviously had no interest in doing so.

On February 7, 1824, B. A. Goldschmidt and Migoni agreed to the first seven articles of the contract and it appears that the remaining eight articles were negotiated around February 5. Given this, it is clear why Barclay, Herring, Richardson wrote to Arrillaga on February 10 1824. Barclay, Herring, Richardson had gotten wind of Migoni's deal with B. A. Goldschmidt and now with its agreement in Mexico in limbo, and with 500,000 pesos in play, it found itself outflanked by B. A. Goldschmidt. As we shall see, the B. A. Goldschmidt contract contained a clause (Article 12) that read, "The aforementioned Don Francisco de Borja Migoni in the name and in consideration of the Mexican government, pledges not to undertake, in Europe or elsewhere, another loan on behalf of the Mexican state for a period of one year, commencing with the date of this agreement."[122] This, in essence, meant that Barclay, Herring, Richardson could issue no bonds until January 1825. And B. A. Goldschmidt did not view this condition as a mere formality. B. A. Goldschmidt's agent in Mexico, George O'Gorman, referred specifically to the condition during a dispute with the Mexican government in September 1824.[123] Panicked, Barclay, Herring, Richardson wrote, this "clause, which entirely prevents us from reimbursing ourselves in the manner . . . intended for the advances we already made . . . exposes us to the risk which may attend the issues of political events during the period stipulated."[124] In other words, once Barclay, Herring, Richardson could issue bonds, events might have conspired to render them worthless. In the complex dance taking place between Mexico; Barclay, Herring, Richardson; B. A. Goldschmidt; Michelena; and Borja Migoni; Borja Migoni and B. A. Goldschmidt sandbagged Barclay, Herring, Richardson, which – quite obviously – had been used by Arrillaga for liquidity and leverage and by its agent, Richards, to make a killing on his commission.

122 Mora, *Crédito público*, p. 440.

123 O'Gorman to the minister of finance, México, September 14, 1824, *Hacienda Pública, Carpetas Azules*, 2da, 1824, AGNM.

124 Barclay, Herring, Richardson to the finance minister, London, February 10, 1824, *Deuda Exterior*, vol. 12, AGNM.

Barclay, Herring, Richardson tried to put the best face on things by claiming that it understood and supported what B. A. Goldschmidt had done. "[We] reflected on the extreme importance of avoiding any act which, however advantageous to ourselves, might in any degree compromise the rising credit of a government newly established." Or even, "[We] are persuaded if we had not taken the part, the said loan would have been negotiated with great difficulty." However, in a more candid moment, Barclay, Herring, Richardson admitted that its own interests were related to B. A. Goldschmidt's in a more complex way. Perhaps it would have been better for Barclay, Herring, Richardson if B. A. Goldschmidt had not also issued bonds, but given that the bonds were there, Barclay, Herring, Richardson wanted to do nothing that "would have prejudiced in any substantive way the credit of [Mexico] in which our own House is involved."[125] In other words, Barclay, Herring, Richardson feared that opposing the B. A. Goldschmidt loan might impair Mexico's credit. With its own bonds yet to come to market, it would do nothing that might damage its ability to recover the substantial amounts it had already advanced. Even if Barclay, Herring, Richardson would rather have avoided involvement with Mexico – and it is far from obvious that it did – the firm was now committed.

The reality was that Barclay, Herring, Richardson now faced a very serious problem. "[You] place us in an extremely difficult situation," the firm wrote.[126] "The difficulties . . . stem, for the most part, from the lack of a general obligation that would authorize us to sell bonds to the public and from the clause . . . that prohibits us from undertaking our loan before January 1825."

As if all this were not bad enough, Barclay, Herring, Richardson soon found itself in an even more nightmarish situation. Legally, Barclay, Herring, Richardson had obligated itself to ratify the final version of its contract with the Mexican government within six months of the date that the Congress ratified the contract, which was December 9 1823.[127] But Barclay, Herring, Richardson did not hear of the Congress' ratification until *March 20, 1824*. Even more bizarrely, it did not receive a copy of the contract that the Congress had accepted until May 20, 1824. Barclay, Herring, Richardson could offer no explanation for the delay which it attributed to "accidents about which we are not informed." William Marshall (of Manning and Marshall fame) thought he knew. He accused Bartholomew Vigors Richards – Barclay, Herring, Richardson's erstwhile agent in Mexico – of

125 Manning and Marshall to the finance minister, México, July 17, 1824, *Deuda Exterior*, vol. 12, AGNM.

126 Barclay, Herring, Richardson to the finance minister, London, April 10, 1824, *Deuda Exterior*, vol. 12. AGNM.

127 I have seen a copy of this contract dated 1827 that puts the original as December 5, 1823.

retaining the loan contract in his power long after Congress had ratified it. But Richards vigorously denied the accusation and it is not obvious why he would have wanted to do so in any event, since the delay was to ultimately cost him his position as the agent for Barclay, Herring, Richardson.[128]

Acutely aware of a potential disaster in the making, Barclay, Herring, Richardson approached Migoni to see if the Goldschmidt loan could be modified in any way. In particular, the house "suggested in consequence that some arrangement should be made by which we should be secured against any want of the necessary funds."[129] Specifically, Barclay, Herring, Richardson proposed that a reserve fund be created out of the Goldschmidt loan "should any unforeseen circumstance deprive us of our loan in the next year." Migoni dismissed the request out of hand, saying that "[he] considered the matter but could not interfere in it as he [had] no instructions from his Government on the subject."

Barclay, Herring, Richardson was clearly stunned by Migoni's reply. In particular, it questioned how "your Government, not being aware of the clauses introduced into the contract with Messrs Goldschmidt and Company, could . . . anticipate any delays with the negotiation of the loans contracted with us . . . [and] . . . deemed it unnecessary to convey any instructions to remove the difficulty to which we are exposed?" But Migoni remained intransigent, replying, "I explained to you that having no instructions from my government on the subject . . . I could not interfere. As such, I must request you [to] suspend further communication to me either directly or indirectly on the subject."[130] It is difficult to know what Migoni hoped to accomplish by his obstinacy. If the purpose was to promote foreign lending to his government, the ostensible goal of Mexico's financial representation in Europe, his actions would have accomplished precisely the opposite. If he were trying to discredit Michelena, however, Migoni was rather more successful. What is clear is that the idea that Mexico's lenders enjoyed a royal road to profit, one independent of or free from serious risk, is simply mistaken. The panicky tone of Barclay, Herring, Richardson's correspondence at this moment makes the point most graphically. Its business with Mexico was *potentially* very lucrative, carrying a 10 percent commission,

---

128 *Contestación a la carta de Don Guillermo Marshall inserta en el suplemento al Sol núm 490 del sábado 16 de octubre*, México, October 25, 1824, p. 3. In a later protest, Barclay, Herring, Richardson claimed that the contract had been held up by a two-month delay of H. M. S. Thetis in Veracruz, something beyond the firm's control. See the protest directed to the president of Mexico, September 30, 1826, *Gobernación*, leg. 91, caja 151, exp. 1, AGNM.

129 David Barclay and Charles Herring to Francisco Borja Migoni, London, March 30, 1824, *Deuda Exterior*, vol. 12, AGNM.

130 David Barclay and Charles Herring to Francisco Borja Migoni, London, March 31, 1824, and Borja Migoni to David Barclay and Charles Herring, London, April 3, 1824, both in *Deuda Exterior*, vol. 12. AGNM.

worth some 1.4 million pesos. But the Mexican government had yet to guarantee anything.[131]

At the same time, the signals to Barclay, Herring, Richardson from the Mexican government could have seemed only mixed, not to say confused. The Supremo Poder Ejecutivo professed "its most express thanks" and offered "all consideration and recognition . . . [of] your just reimbursements." Having come to the assistance of Mexico in its time of extreme need, Barclay, Herring, Richardson would enjoy "the broadest and most agreeable field for the substantial Capital" it offered to Mexico, especially in "the most profitable undertakings of political economy." In particular, because Barclay, Herring, Richardson was negotiating for ships and weapons for Mexico, "the means of defense required to consolidate the political existence of the Republic . . . and the recognition of our independence," Mexico would show Barclay, Herring, Richardson "gratitude and benevolence" as well as "a decided preference" for finding other projects that were of great interest to Mexico. And, as a clincher, the Supremo Poder Ejecutivo informed Barclay, Herring, Richardson that it planned to discard "other offers extended to it both before and after said contract as his Excellency Señor Don José Mariano Michelena . . . will have informed you." However, the Supremo Poder Ejecutivo continued, it was awaiting Barclay, Herring, Richardson's "speeding up the purchase and shipment of those military goods which we have so badly needed."[132]

However, there was another reason for the Supremo Poder Ejecutivo's growing insistence with Barclay, Herring, Richardson. By late May, Finance Minister Arrillaga had become embroiled in a nasty dispute with B. A. Goldschmidt over the first tranche of its loan. According to B. A. Goldschmidt's agent in Mexico, George O'Gorman (brother of British consul-general Charles T. O'Gorman), new bills drawn against the first tranche of £200,000 would not be paid since £200,000 in bills had already been made over to Migoni, but placed in escrow for B. A. Goldschmidt in the event the loan fell through. As O'Gorman put it, "they would not give two undertakings for one and the same installment."[133] Arrillaga, in turn, professed the "greatest amazement" that B. A. Goldschmidt would negotiate no further bills on the first tranche of the loan.[134] Small wonder that the Supremo Poder Ejecutivo awaited Barclay, Herring, Richardson's action

131 "Esposición del C. Francisco de Borja Migoni," pp. 7–8.

132 [Arrillaga?] to Barclay, Herring, Richardson, México, May 20, 1824, *Deuda Exterior*, vol. 12, AGNM.

133 George O'Gorman to the finance minister, México, May 26, 1824, *Hacienda Pública, Carpetas Azules*, 2ª, 1824, AGNM. On this point, also see Lucas Alamán, *Liquidación general de la deuda esterior de la República Méxicana hasta fin de Diciembre de 1841* (México, 1845), pp. 7–8.

134 Arrillaga to George O'Gorman, México, May 27, 1824, *Hacienda Pública, Carpetas Azules*, 2ª, 1824. AGNM.

"with great impatience." It needed fresh funds. By late summer, this issue too would have become critical.

Nevertheless, the tone of the Mexican government's reply – its coquettish offer to give Barclay, Herring, Richardson preference in its most attractive deals if only the firm would see to it that its forthcoming aid arrived – makes one wonder whether or not there was a strategy behind Mexico's actions, a kind of holding out the prospect of better things if Barclay, Herring, Richardson would simply cooperate this time. Were it not for the fact that Migoni and Michelena cordially detested each other, it would be easy to conclude that they were in cahoots. But it is more realistic to think that this state of affairs suited the Supremo Poder Ejecutivo's purposes. With shrewd players like Arrillaga, Alamán, and Esteva within its ministerial ranks, it is hard to believe that a policy of divide and conquer its foreign creditors never occurred to any of them. At the very least, the image of an impotent Mexico in 1823 and 1824, prostrate and supplicant at the feet of its lenders, is an inaccurate one indeed.

At all odds, and perhaps not wishing to overplay its hand or frighten off other potential lenders by sticking rigidly to a technicality, the Mexican government showed itself "disposed to concede" to Barclay, Herring, Richardson the right to issue bonds "at the best price it could obtain on the London market for its own benefit, to which end it could approach [the Finance] Ministry for instruction about the conditions that ought to obtain."[135] Of course, Barclay, Herring, Richardson would still be unable to issue bonds before January 1825, so that its principal concern went unaddressed. But at the very least, Barclay, Herring, Richardson did not face the nightmarish prospect of losing 500,000 pesos; with interest, the amount was more like 560,000.

Still, the offer to compose differences was not made out of the kindness of the Mexican government's heart. In an *acuerdo* summarizing the Finance Ministry's position on the matter, Arrillaga admitted that after the first four dividend payments on the B. A. Goldschmidt loan had been made, "only a scant six million pesos" of the loan remained. Of that, two million were required to pay the Staples loan. With 4 million left, the ministry listed outstanding obligations that were due – and these totaled 9.3 million pesos, in which were included debts to the tobacco planters; to creditors whose funds had been seized by supporters of independence during the civil war from the silver *conductas*; and from interest on the public debt. These were politically powerful interests whose demand could not be ignored. Indeed, the tobacco planters must have taken some solace in the fact that the finance ministers

---

135 Arrillaga to Robert Manning and William Skinner Marshall, July 7, 1824, *Deuda Exterior*, vol. 12. AGNM.

in 1823 and 1824, Arrillaga and Esteva, were Veracruzanos both.[136] The Supremo Poder Ejecutivo had no choice: the show must go on. As Michelena observed in 1824, Barclay, Herring, Richardson had acted with "generosity" in affording the Mexican government an advance of 500,000 pesos when, as Barclay, Herring, Richardson put it, "neither patriot nor foreigner wanted to assist the government." It wasn't so much the amount that Barclay, Herring, Richardson had advanced as it was its "timeliness" (*ocasión*) and "opportunity." The person to whom Michelena's observation was pointedly directed was Don Francisco Migoni.[137]

The abrogation of the original contract, negotiated by Bartholomew Vigors Richards – Barclay, Herring, Richardson's original agent in Mexico – led to an acrimonious dispute between Richards and William Marshall.[138] Marshall, here making an initial appearance in Mexican financial history as a junior representative of Barclay, Herring, Richardson, had previously represented the firm in its dealings with the Colombian government, but the amount of money was relatively small – some 500,000 pesos. This time, he and his associate, Robert Manning, were after bigger fish, and the new loan they negotiated with the Mexican government was 16 million pesos (rather than the 20 million that Richards had negotiated). Their commission, presumably shared with Barclay, Herring, Richardson, amounted to 1,040,000 pesos and probably formed the capital with which Manning and Marshall created their partnership in 1824. Richards also insinuated that Barclay, Herring, Richardson failed to recover at least 100,000 pesos of the 500,000 that had been at risk because of Manning and Marshall's maneuvering. Richards' unhappiness knew no bounds, and he soon found himself elbowed out of the way by Manning and Marshall, whom he regarded as interlopers who had no authority to do anything as long as Richards remained in Mexico City. Yet, all of this was to no avail since Richards lost the loan and his commission on it. By November 1824, Manning and Marshall were firmly ensconced in Mexico as Barclay, Herring, Richardson's representatives, a position that Richards had held as recently as June. When the Mexican government formally abrogated the first Barclay loan in September 1824, it gave as its reasons the loan negotiated by Migoni with B. A. Goldschmidt and the failure of Barclay, Herring, Richardson to meet the specified deadline for ratification of its initial contract. But Barclay, Herring, Richardson was not free of the Mexican government,

---

136 Barbara Tenenbaum, *The Politics of Penury. Debts and Taxes in Mexico, 1821–1856* (Albuquerque, 1986), pp. 112, 156.

137 Michelena to Borja Migoni, México, May 27, 1824, *Deuda Exterior*, vol. 12, AGNM.

138 *Sol: suplemento al número 490 del sábado 16 de octubre de 1824*; *Sol: suplemento al número 479 del martes 5 de octubre de 1824*; and *Sol: suplemento al número 509 del jueves 4 de noviembre de 1824*.

for to recover anything, it would have to contract once more, this time, through the agency of Manning and Marshall. Since the first Barclay loan seems to have been negotiated on better terms than the B. A. Goldschmidt loan, it seems reasonable to ask precisely what's going on here?

Analysis of the Loan Agreements

Barclay, Herring, Richardson's reason for undertaking a second contract with the Mexican government is clear enough. In so doing, the Mexican government agreed to recognize the outstanding obligation it had already incurred to the house, but whose legal status remained in limbo as the first contract went unratified. But why would the Mexican government undertake a second agreement with Barclay, Herring, Richardson if it had the B. A. Goldschmidt loan in hand? One reason, perhaps, was the pressure that the credit market placed on Mexico. As the lengthy and unedifying bickering between Migoni, Michelena, and various ministers of the central government unfolded, Mexico's credit rating suffered severely. Between April and August of 1824, the relative price on the Goldschmidt loan trading on the London Stock Exchange fell by 29 percent. In September 1824, when the new contract with Barclay, Herring, and Richardson was signed, the Goldschmidt loan rose by some 23 percent.[139] Thus the market judged the central government not *more* but *less* likely to default *in the short run* when it signed the second contract. In part, this was now because the initial capital disbursed by Barclay, Herring, Richardson gained a measure of security that it had hitherto not enjoyed, an effect that spilled over on to *all* Mexico's international financial obligations. But there was another reason as well, one that makes discussing the contracts in detail of some value.

There seems to have been a vast difference between the first and second Barclay, Herring, Richardson contracts. In the first contract, Bartholomew Vigors Richards promised to deliver more than a million pesos in armaments within eight months, including seventy thousand rifles, ten thousand carbines, four thousand shotguns, five thousand brace of pistols, twenty thousand swords, and, not least, four new frigates of war, with forty-four cannon "equal to those of the British Navy and kitted out according to the regulations of that fleet." If brigs or corvettes were available, that would be better, and the ships were to be provided with crews, "American, if possible," as well as with half a complement of officers.[140] The second Barclay,

---

139 These are prices relative to British 21.5 percent consols.
140 "Contract Celebrated by Dn Bartolomé Vigors Richards in the Name of Barclay, Herring and Compañía of London with Supremo Poder Ejecutivo of Mexico," December 5, 1823 (copy, México, April 1827), *Hacienda Pública, Carpetas Azules*, 1827, AGNM.

Herring, Richardson contract,[141] however, simply provides, in its eighth article, to deduct the cost of whatever materiel Barclay, Herring, Richardson had furnished under the first contract from the proceeds of the second. Of greater interest, and a key to understanding Mexico's subsequent default, was the seventh article of the second contract, which dedicated fully 25 percent of the proceeds of the Barclay, Herring, Richardson loan to the repayment of B. A. Goldschmidt, thus raising the price of Goldschmidt's bonds and reducing their yield. In retrospect, it was simply courting disaster to make servicing a significant part of one loan contingent on raising another, but that is precisely what the Mexican government did, and established a precedent for paying dividends only when fresh funds were available. The Barclay, Herring, Richardson loan also arranged for the repayment of its first six quarterly dividends from its own proceeds! Likewise, the repayment of its principal – or the first year and a half, at least – was deducted from the loan proceeds and placed in a sinking fund. While it is certainly true that money is fungible, the idea that repayment could occur only by increasing savings (or reducing) consumption was hardly encouraged by such a strategy, with what effect on the probability of default *in the long run* one can only speculate.

By and large, Barclay, Herring, Richardson (and their original agent, Richards, probably) made good on the first contract with the Mexican government. An accounting of the disposition of the funds of Mexico's London loans published in the *Times* (London) on August 17, 1827, reveals that the value of the military and naval stores delivered (whatever their condition or suitability for Mexican conditions) corresponds almost precisely to what the Mexican government contracted for in 1823. The only case in which this was not true was in the matter of fighting ships, for here the government received the frigate *Liberty* and the brig *Victory* for roughly £75,000, which was £20,000 more than the contracted sum for four ships. Yet no one, as far as the documents reveal, complained about this,[142] and Barclay, Herring, Richardson was compensated for the 500,000 pesos it had advanced the Mexican government in 1824 with interest as of February 1825, suggesting that William Marshall's charge against his rival Richards

---

141 Mora, *Crédito Público*, pp. 443–450, for the second contract, London, dated August 25, 1824.

142 Other than a baffled government auditor in Mexico. Because there had been two contracts, two distinct orders for naval vessels had been placed: the first in Sweden and the second in London. Interestingly, Manning and Marshall swung the contract in favor of ships purchased in Britain that were retired from service in the Royal Navy. The Swedish order, placed by none other than Michelena, was cancelled. It is hard to suppress the thought that enduring tales of México's ending up with a couple of battered British ships in return for good money had more to do with lost commissions than defective ordnance. See José Ignacio Esteva, *Contestación á las observaciones del señor contador de crédito público sobre la cuenta y memoria del ramo referente á los ocho primeros meses del año de 1825* (México, 1828), pp. 33–34, for the details.

was untrue. But Marshall (and his partner, Manning) were able to elbow
Richards aside because, as the *Times* (London) accounting reveals, they were
acting as agents not only for Barclay, Herring, Richardson, but also for
themselves. Independently of Barclay, Herring, Richardson, Manning and
Marshall had lent the Mexican government 500,000 pesos in what was
presumably a private placement – no bonds were involved – and made a
success of it. Small wonder that Mexico was willing to do business with
Manning and Marshall at the same time it dangled the prospect of future
profits in front of Barclay, Herring, Richardson. Indeed, that firm *committed*
itself, albeit vaguely, by Article 11, to fund the Mexican government at
more than the £200,000 monthly (Article 6) that the contract stipulated,
provided sixty days' notice was given. One wonders, indeed, how Barclay,
Herring, Richardson would have responded had it not been ill-used by the
Mexican government! The remainder of the contract was taken up with
the administrative details. The loan was to be secured on a third of the
customs revenues of the Atlantic and Pacific ports, which were judged to
be a sufficient source of revenue, with whatever interim funding measures
to be taken as Congress saw fit. The bonds carried a 6 percent coupon, with
16,000 bonds denominated £150 and 8,000 denominated £100. As usual,
these were bearer bonds. The issue was brought to market at 86.75 percent
and was to be retired by 1865.

If the Barclay, Herring, Richardson contract was relatively straightforward, the B. A. Goldschmidt loan was not. Its complexity is often belied
by the simple and, indeed, simplistic terms in which it is discussed. Even
Tomás Murphy's distinguished history dispenses with the agreement in
twelve lines.[143] Yet it seems clear that the contract itself was an exercise in
studied ambiguity or, at least, in an attempted assessment of risk. Judging
the creditworthiness of a newly independent nation was no easy thing,
especially in a market in which the issues of imaginary nations, however
briefly, found a willing reception among investors.[144] Moreover, the pressure of circumstance, economic and political, is evident in the language of
the contract.

The contract specified (Article 4) that the loan would be for a term
of thirty years, ending in 1853, and would be priced at 55, but with
a 5 percentage point commission, thus being brought to market at 50.
Eighteen thousand bonds were to be issued (with sixty coupons, or two
each year). The first dividend was due on April 1, 1824, and the last on
October 10 1853. The contracted amount was £3.2 million.

But B. A. Goldschmidt did not immediately commit itself to issuing
the full £3.2 million, at least on its own account. The initial obligation

143 Murphy, *Memoria sobre la deuda*, p. 5.
144 Dawson, *First Latin American Debt Crisis*, pp. 41, 60.

(Article 2) was £1.2 million of which B. A. Goldschmidt was obliged to pay half by January 1825: of the £600,000, the first payment of £200,000 would accompany three agents of B. A. Goldschmidt who had set sail for Mexico. While Arrillaga asked Migoni that the £200,000 be paid over in gold specie, Migoni demurred, instead investing these monies in exchequer bills from February 7, 1824, when the loan was funded until April 1 and when the first dividends were due. Thus the £200,000 was more than sufficient to cover the first half year's interest of £80,000, provided it was not spent on something else. Surely, this was what Migoni had in mind when he admonished Arrillaga not to draw on the proceeds of the loan before they were available – the protested Barry bills of over £10,000 were yet to be reckoned with and would constitute a major drain on the funds Goldschmidt provided.[145]

Yet Goldschmidt may have also been unwilling to commit itself to a country whose future political nature or even existence was by no means certain. A set of supplementary articles (perhaps sent to Mexico with Goldschmidt's agents) to the loan observes that

if a change should take place in the form and essence of the state of Mexico either by convulsions occurring there or the tie to which unites the different provinces of which it is composed being broken, it rests with the said B. A. Goldschmidt and Company and under no circumstances with the Mexican nation or its Government to cancel the said purchase of Three Million two hundred thousand pounds of Mexico stock and to consider the present Contract as null and void.

On the other hand, B. A. Goldschmidt recognized as

distinctly understood and agreed that the right of the said B. A. Goldschmidt and Company to cancel the contract . . . is not applicable in case the republic of Mexico should on the arrival of the before mentioned agents in the City of Mexico be changed to a Federative State in as much as all the Provinces comprising such a Federative State are jointly and severally (*in solidum*) engaged for the amount of said Loan of Three Million two hundred thousand pounds.[146]

The phraseology clearly reflects the political currents of 1823–1824 and their implications for international lending. On the one hand, B. A. Goldschmidt was hedging its bets, paying out the loan by monthly tranches, and then only if some sovereign entity called the "state of Mexico" or the "Mexican nation" continued to exist in some recognizable form. But what

---

145 Borja Migoni to the finance minister, London, February 9, 1824, *Deuda Exterior*, vol. 12, AGNM, and "Mexican Finance," *Times* (London), August 17, 1827.

146 "Loan of Three Million Two Hundred Thousand Pounds Sterling for the Service of the State of Mexico . . ." (Special Bond marked "B" offered by the annexed contract), *Deuda Exterior*, vol. 12, AGNM.

form? Migoni did well in inducing B. A. Goldschmidt to recognize that the "Republic of Mexico" could well become a "federative state" (no one seems to have assumed that they were, ipso facto, one and the same thing) and that in the event that the provinces recognized the debt contracted, the contract would remain valid whatever else B. A. Goldschmidt's preferences might be. It is not obvious that this principle, which would be embodied in the Constitution of 1824, was clearly perceived in late 1823, much less in the *Acta Constitutiva de la Federación* (January 31, 1824), which appeared almost simultaneously with the contract.[147] Migoni, whatever his own political views were, knew which way the political winds were blowing and anticipated them well. At the very least, what this addendum to the contract suggests is that B. A. Goldschmidt engaged in *risky* lending, but not *reckless* lending. By the same token, the Mexican government needed to borrow, wanted to borrow, and would ultimately pay dearly in order to borrow. But its borrowing in 1823 and 1824 should not be judged, anachronistically, by subsequent events in 1825 and 1826. And Mexico was by no means unable to affect the terms on which it borrowed. Indeed, as we shall see, its very borrowing roiled the international markets of which Mexico is usually assumed mostly a passive victim.

Financial Crosscurrents

While it would be an exaggeration to call the financial currents that buffeted Mexico in 1824 and 1825 unprecedented – one thinks of the expropriation of savings from New Spain at the end of the eighteenth century – they were certainly substantial. How substantial? Well, large enough to produce very large gyrations in the peso–sterling exchange rate. Indeed, one of the most knowledgeable observers of Mexican affairs in the middle 1820s, British consul-general Charles T. O'Gorman, called the swings in the exchange rate "extraordinary." How extraordinary? From Table 1.5, it is apparent that between January and November 1824, sterling fell by nearly 30 percent against the peso. From July through November alone, it fell by nearly 20 percent. An even more revealing way of judging what occurred is to examine Figure 1.1, which shows the depreciation as a nearly headlong fall in sterling, followed by an equally sharp rise after November 1824 and another appreciation of the peso after April 1825.

Why did sterling fall? O'Gorman asserted that "the extraordinary rise in the exchange is to be exclusively attributed to the markets having been forced by the use of bills on London . . . in consequence of the Loans to the Mexican government and of provision made by the agents of foreign

---

147 Tena Ramírez, *Leyes fundamentales de Mexico*, pp. 154–161.

Table 1.5. *The Exchange Rate of Mexico on London, 1824–1826*

		Par = 48 pence/peso			
1824		*1825*		*1826*	
January	44	January	55	January	51
February	44	February	50		
March	45	March	47		
April	46	April	47		
May	46	May	49		
June	47	June	51		
July	48	July	54		
August	49	August	53		
September	62	September	53		
October	55	October			
November	57	November	52		
December	56	December	52		

Sources: 1824–1825: Charles T. O'Gorman, "General Summary of Various Rates of Exchange in Mexico on London," México, March 1, 1825, FO203/3 and 1825–1826; "El Cambio en esta Plaza," México, September 2, 1825, *Hacienda Pública, Carpetas Azules*, AGNM 2ª, 1825, and "Noticia exacta de las alteraciones que ha tenido en esta plaza el cambio de letras sobre Londres..." México, March 10, 1826, *Hacienda Pública, Carpetas Azules*, AGNM 2ª, 1825.

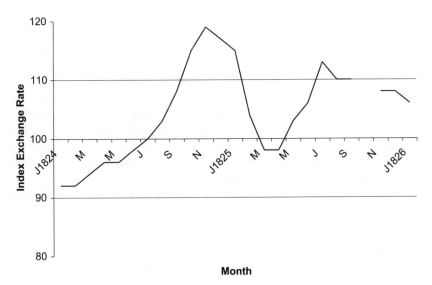

Figure 1.1. Exchange Rate of Mexico on London, 1824–1826 (see Table 1.5).

mining companies for establishment and outlay in the mining districts."[148]
What O'Gorman meant by this probably requires some comment.[149]

The equilibrium exchange between sterling and the peso was roughly 5
pesos (or dollars) to the pound. Since there were 240 pence to the pound,
the "par" of exchange was 48 pence to the peso (240/5 = 48). One way
funds could be transferred was, for instance, for the Mexican government to
write ("draw") bills of exchange against Goldschmidt on London. The bill
would then presumably be purchased by a broker in Mexico City who could
resell the bill to a third party who could use the bill to make payment on
some outstanding debt in England. The broker's willingness to buy the bill
was a product of many factors, but it all came down to supply and demand.
A flood of bills on London naturally made it more difficult to dispose of
such bills without discounting them further, which is to say, by offering
fewer pesos for sterling. In the event, the peso rose against sterling because
fewer pesos were required to purchase a pound and the state of the Mexican
exchanges was said to be "favorable."

O'Gorman was certain that British lending had affected the exchange.
Between February 1824 and the year's end, O'Gorman calculated the bills
drawn on B. A. Goldschmidt and Company ($4 million), R. P. Staples
and Company ($1 million), and the mining companies ($1 million) totaled
some $6 million (at a time when Mexican GDP was around $240 million).
These bills rather than "the natural operations of trade" explained the fall
of sterling. In October 1824, sterling hit an unprecedented low of 60 pence
to the peso.[150] But at the same time, other factors operated in a contrary
direction. According to Nicholas Biddle, elected president of the Second
Bank of the United States in 1823, funds had been flowing out of Mexico
because there were many persons there who were "desirous of placing their
property out of reach of revolutions, who by this [occasioned] a more than
ordinary demand for bills on foreign countries," and Biddle reported that
the Mexican government was actively selling exchange in February 1825.[151]
Given how valuable the peso had become, this made sense and effectively
pushed the peso back toward a parity of 48 pence.

All sorts of anomalies were occasioned by these gyrations of the exchange.
For example, the firm of Manning and Marshall became involved in a
nasty spat with Don Pablo Obregón, the Mexican minister to the United

148 "General Summary of the Various Rates of Exchange." Finance Minister Arrillaga gave an identical
explanation on July 20, 1824, just as the rise of the peso got seriously under way. See *Gaceta del
Gobierno Supremo de la Federación Mexicana*, July 24, 1824.

149 A classic guide is George J. Goschen, *The Theory of the Foreign Exchanges* (16th ed., London, 1894).

150 "El Cambio en esta Plaza," México, September 2, 1825, *Hacienda Pública, Carpetas Azules*, 1825,
2ª, AGNM.

151 Walter Buckingham Smith, *Economic Aspects of the Second Bank of the United States* (Cambridge, MA,
1953), pp. 137, 138.

States, over the disposition of funds for the use of the Mexican legation there.[152] The amount in dispute, 16,000 pesos, was seemingly trivial. But Obregón went all the way to Alamán with his complaint. It seemed that Manning and Marshall, finding itself with surplus funds on the account of the Mexican government, had dispatched them from New York on board a frigate, "Hussar," bound for Mexico. Obregón was irate. He insinuated that Manning and Marshall made only desultory efforts to contact him. Obregón believed that the problem stemmed from the firm's need to ship the funds to Mexico "to fulfill the contract they had celebrated with the government of Mexico."[153] Obregón's position was that he could have made use of the money and that, besides, shipping specie to Mexico cost money in freight and insurance.

Marshall's reply, even if patronizing, was revealing. After protesting that he had made an effort to contact Obregón, Marshall explained that

I cannot agree with your opinion that sending specie to Mexico is disadvantageous for the government. In fact, these days, the best remission to Mexico is *in specie* (*dinero efectivo*) [italics in original], and for the following reasons. The advices I received from Mexico yesterday gave an exchange rate of 57 [pence to the peso]. Sr. Semiat, in business here, showed me an advice from his brother that he took from [George?] O'Gorman against Goldschmidt and Company of London at an exchange of 58 pence per peso!!! [And]... he is sure that at some point he may get 60 or 62! You will see that if pesos in Mexico are worth that exorbitant exchange, the best speculation is to send pesos. With them, you buy bills of exchange and send them here [i.e., New York] where they command a 7 or 8 percent premium. So the best thing for the government is pesos and I haven't the slightest doubt that they will be glad I sent them.[154]

Nor was this an isolated instance. Robert Manning had negotiated Mexico's bills drawn on B. A. Goldschmidt, outbidding the Bank of the United States in the process. Whereas the Bank willingly offered Obregón a premium of 5 percent on the bills, Manning offered 8 percent (this was precisely why the peso receded from its highs in October 1824 to somewhat lower levels in November) plus 4 percent annual interest on the funds from bills that he had purchased, but had not yet cleared! In all, Obregón believed that Manning was offering a premium of about 11 percent, "the best available here [i.e.,

---

152 Based on an unclassified nineteenth-century expediente, AGNM.

153 Lucas Alamán to the finance minister, México, January 21, 1825, in unclassified expediente, AGNM.

154 Copy of Marshall's letter of December 3, 1824, to Obregón, dated January 19, 1825, in unclassified expediente, AGNM. These substantial deviations from the par of exchange are very unusual and may be evidence of financial pressure on the Mexican government, which was literally willing to sell its bills for what it could get.

Philadelphia]." Obregón ultimately negotiated £19,000 with Manning, and he clearly would have done more had he had the bills available.[155]

This was not just a matter of Obregón's personal pique with Marshall. Michelena made virtually the same observation from his post in London in early December 1824 – "negotiating bills of exchange on the United States of the North will yield advantages in view of the rapid rise of the peso in London" – and we may be sure that "speculation" on the peso was standard practice at this point.[156] As Ferguson emphasizes, the Rothschilds made arbitrage transactions into something of an art form in their government lending. By their standards, Manning and Marshall were small potatoes.[157]

The Mexican government itself got into the act. In May 1824, a directive of the Supremo Poder Ejecutivo provided that "in order to cover some urgent needs, bills will be drawn against the 8 million [i.e., B. A. Goldschmidt] loan at $45\frac{1}{2}$ pence at 3 days sight and at 46 pence at 60 days sight in [Mexico City], with the funds to be delivered on the coast of Veracruz less the [illegible] costs of transportation, as was announced on 15 [May, 1824]."

The funds were available, the Supremo Poder Ejecutivo maintained, in Jalapa and Alvarado and the government would either draw bills or endorse bills payable on sight to whoever would take them at the premium agreed on with the finance minister. The Supremo Poder Ejecutivo felt certain that given an ounce of silver would bring 47 pence in London, anyone who took Mexican bills at 45.5 stood to make 1.5 pence per peso, or about 2.7 percent. Given a nominal yield on consols of 3 percent, with a market yield somewhat above that, the return promised by such a speculation was by no means insignificant.[158]

To repeat, these operations themselves were perhaps not so unusual. What is more disquieting is the clear impression that one gathers from the documents that a firm like Manning and Marshall had a clearer idea of exactly what was going on with the government's money than the government did itself. In this regard, an accounting for a 500,000-peso payment from the Barclay, Herring, Richardson loan is instructive.[159] It was possible to account for 363,089 pesos of this payment, but of the remainder – 136,910 pesos – it was necessary to secure "various reports that have been requested." Indeed, it turned out that 30,000 pesos of this amount "belonged to the first loan contracted with Goldschmidt."

155 Pablo Obregón to the secretary of home and foreign relations, Philadelphia, November 26, 1824 (copy of February 7, 1825), *Hacienda Pública, Carpetas Azules*, 1824, 2ª, AGNM.

156 Michelena to the finance minister, London, December 8, 1824, *Hacienda Pública, Carpetas Azules*, 1824, 2ª, AGNM.

157 Ferguson, *House of Rothschild*, pp. 92–93.

158 See memorandum of May 18, 1824, "Para *El Sol*," *Deuda Exterior*, vol. 12, AGNM.

159 The information appears in a draft document dated September 25, 1826, in the unclassified documents to which I have alluded.

While such a remark does not point to fraud or dishonesty, it does raise an issue to which we will later return: did the Mexican government have the *administrative* capacity needed to supervise the funds it had borrowed? Unfortunately, the evidence on this score is not reassuring.

It is hard to avoid the impression of loose ends. While Migoni expressed the common sentiment in 1824 that "Europe" would soon recognize Mexican independence "and [that] when this happens, Mexico's credit, now established by my loan, will rise to 80, 85 or 90 percent, by which the Republic will be able to borrow 'however much it wants' at these prices."[160] But how wrong he turned out to be. Indeed, by December of 1824, even with the exchanges still favorable to Mexico, a quite striking dispatch from Michelena discussed the active intervention of the Second Bank of the United States on behalf of Mexican credit.

As we have seen, the Bank took an active interest in Mexican affairs. For one thing, the Bank had an agent operating in Mexico; for another, in his correspondence with Pablo Obregón, Marshall refers to "the President of the Bank (Mr. Bidale [*sic*], whom you know)."[161] But he observed that Biddle had refused to honor the drafts of a certain Mr. Robinson, whom Obregón wished to employ as a source of funds for his use, "because he did not know if that gentleman was authorized to draw bills of exchange." Biddle had reason to be concerned. According to Obregón, by the end of 1825, when the financial crisis that shook the London money market had unfolded, Mexico's drafts and bills suffered from "a considerable loss in markets in the United States," which could only mean they were now heavily discounted. But according to Obregón, "Mr. Biddle, President of the Bank of the United States, was kind enough to write me that, even though Mexico's credit was in the doldrums (*entorpecimiento*), he had honored Mexico's drafts without the market's loss. I sent him a letter thanking him for his good offices, a proof of the generous interest he takes in our affairs."[162] In light of Mexico's extensive borrowing and Migoni's wildly mistaken prediction, how could Mexico's credit have fallen into the doldrums? Unfortunately, loans or no, the Federation's treasury was running dangerously close to empty. Remarkably, its available balance of funds in early 1825 was around 50,000–60,000 pesos – a hand-to-mouth operation if there ever was one.[163]

160 Borja Migoni to the finance minister, London, February 13, 1824 (muy reservado), AGNM, *Hacienda Pública, Carpetas Azules*, 2ª, 1824. "*la cantidad que quiera*" is translated as "however much it wants."

161 Marshall to Obregón, [New York], December 3, 1824 (copy, México, January 19, 1825), unclassified documents, AGNM.

162 Michelena to the finance minister, London, December 8, 1825, *Hacienda Pública, Carpetas Azules*, 1824, 2ª, AGNM.

163 *Gaceta Extraordinaria del Gobierno Supremo de la Federación Mexicana*, 5: 23 (February 17, 1825), pp. 121–127, cited in Carlos María de Bustamante, *Diario histórico de México*, T. III, vol. 2, Anexos (México, 1984), pp. 203–205.

Yet there was another reason for the Federation's problems, a situation that could have well invited the intervention of Nicholas Biddle. It probably developed as a result of the competing claims made by B. A. Goldschmidt and Barclay, Herring, Richardson, or simply reflected deepening financial problems. Some of the details are murky, and given the nature of the dispute, may never be clear. But, again, the ability of the government to administer the loans and control the funds seems somewhat hazy. Around May 1824, George O'Gorman, B. A. Goldschmidt's agent in Mexico City, publicly refused to authorize the negotiation of any further bills of the first tranche of the loan. The consequences of O'Gorman's action were extremely serious for the credit of the government: the price of Mexican 6 percents (the Goldschmidt loan) fell from 68 to 42.5 between April and August 1824. Michelena became terribly concerned. He wrote from London that the Goldschmidt loan, Iturbide's departure from London, and problems with the Peruvian loan had driven down the American funds. He implored Finance Minister Arrillaga to write as quickly as possible "to deny the falsehoods that intrigue here is spreading." And so "our credit will rise to the level it deserves to be."[164] And from New York, Obregón wrote that he could not purchase artillery and munitions because the bills drawn on B. A. Goldschmidt had been protested – they lacked O'Gorman's signature.[165]

A memo, apparently written subsequently by Finance Minister Esteva, accused O'Gorman of having a "heart . . . metallized [*sic*] and blindly determined to increase the open financial distress [*quebranto*] that the Nation suffers."

Indeed, Esteva alleged that O'Gorman had determined to establish a bill brokerage [*banco de cambio*] with undeserved and illicit profits. The reason for Esteva's ire – ostensibly – was O'Gorman's supposed attempt to extract a fee of from 1 to 3 percent on bills drawn against B. A. Goldschmidt, supposedly his fee for his authorized signature.[166]

To say that a campaign was mounted against O'Gorman, and a vicious one at that, is an understatement.[167] The campaign involved the intervention of his brother, Charles; marginal notes on the documents concerning the case refer repeatedly to President Victoria's desire to be kept abreast of events as they occurred. Accused of advising correspondents in New York and Philadelphia to avoid negotiating Mexican bills drawn against

---

164 Michelena to the finance minister, London, July 16, 1824, *Deuda Exterior*, vol. 12, AGNM.

165 Obregón to the minister of home and foreign relations, New York, October 29, 1824, *Hacienda Pública, Carpetas Azules*, 2ª, 1824, AGNM.

166 Undated, unsigned memorandum, México, *Hacienda Pública, Carpetas Azules*, 1824, 2ª, AGNM.

167 *Documentos que comprueban la conducta de D Jorge O'Gorman en el giro de letras del Gobierno de México sobre el préstamo contratado por esta República con la casa de B.A. Goldschmidt y Compañía de Londres* (México, 1825). "*un espediente instructivo o informativo*" is translated "an instructive and informative proceeding."

B. A. Goldschmidt, O'Gorman was arrested, not for any formal trial, "but as an instructive and informative proceeding" (see p. 7 of the document cited next) that had the distinct air of a Star Chamber proceeding. The tone adopted against O'Gorman was positively ugly and very nearly hysterical. By November 1824, at least, word of the affair reached London, and the firm of Barclay, Herring, Richardson was said to have explicitly prohibited its own Mexican agents from similar operations in Mexican bills of exchange.[168] Michelena, in turn, went directly to B. A. Goldschmidt in an effort to reassure the markets that O'Gorman was freelancing, rather than acting on the house's orders.[169]

What exactly had O'Gorman done?

According to O'Gorman, he was doing nothing more than enforcing the contract between the Federation and B. A. Goldschmidt. According to Articles 6 and 7, the first £200,000 tranche was due immediately on signing. At that point, nothing more would be due until June 20, 1824, at which point another £50,000 would become available. If, as O'Gorman maintained, the Federation was attempting to draw on the proceeds of the loan before June 20 by drawing bills beyond those already delivered to Migoni in London, he was justified in refusing to proceed further. Given that the correspondence began on or around May 26, it is hard to see how O'Gorman was violating the agreement, and even Migoni had cautioned against drawing more in bills than was available in liquid funds.[170]

What seems more likely is that O'Gorman had run afoul of the Federation by his hard line and that he had gotten snared in Mexican political divisions as well. Even though by September 20, 1824, another £200,000 should have been available to the Federation, O'Gorman was refusing to honor bills drawn by Finance Minister Esteva on B. A. Goldschmidt. His motive seems to have been the Barclay, Herring, Richardson loan, whose very existence he regarded as a "positive violation" of the twelfth article of the contract between the Federation and B. A. Goldschmidt, adding that "Messrs B. A. Goldschmidt will hold the government responsible . . . for all damages, prejudices and losses that may ensue."[171] So, quite possibly, O'Gorman was maneuvering, simply trying to protect the interests of B. A. Goldschmidt as he saw them – pressing the finance minister to avoid committing scarce resource to Barclay, Herring, Richardson. On the other hand, it is easy to

---

168 *Times* (London), November 18, 1824.

169 Michelena to Obregón, London, December 4, 1824, HD 17–7. 697, BLAC, UT.

170 Borja Migoni to the finance minister, London, February 9, 1824, *Deuda Exterior*, vol. 12. AGNM. Johnston, *Missions to Mexico*, pp. 116–117, suggests that O'Gorman was charging for rewriting the original bills in denominations different from those specified in Article 7. If so, the dispute took place in a gray area, but one that was by no means inconsistent with contemporary practice.

171 O'Gorman to the finance minister, México, September 14, 1824, *Hacienda Pública, Carpetas Azules*, 1824, 2ª, AGNM, for this and what follows.

understand why the finance ministry, desperate to secure adequate funding, would entertain and accept Barclay, Herring, Richardson's offer; however, it might impair its future capacity to service to B. A. Goldschmidt loan. It is speculation, of course, but George O'Gorman's pressure on the Federation may have forced its hand with Barclay, Herring, Richardson, for when that loan was renegotiated, as we saw, a substantial portion of its capital was dedicated to paying off the Goldschmidt loan.

And to make things more complicated, O'Gorman may have stumbled, inadvertently perhaps, into the sharpening rivalry between the Yorkino and Escocés factions in the nascent cabinet of Victoria. It is hard to prove – but difficult to avoid the impression – that O'Gorman may have been too closely identified with Alamán for his own good or may even have been "guilty" of doing Alamán's partisan dirty work. O'Gorman made this connection all too clear by placing himself squarely under Alamán's patronage when the struggle with the finance ministry erupted. As early as May 1824, O'Gorman had begun to dispute Finance Minister Arrillaga's right to draw further bills on the B. A. Goldschmidt loan (just as Alamán's ally Migoni was doing in London), and within two weeks, open warfare had broken out.

O'Gorman emphasized again that Arrillaga had no right to issue further bills on the first tranche of the loan, stating that he had no right to draw "as many other bills as he may wish upon the persons who have accepted the original bill merely because he was the possessor of the original bill." In very intemperate language, O'Gorman told Arrillaga that his "intimating in no very measured language our incapacity or want of good faith as contrasted with that of our own Principles . . . must . . . have been studiously intended by Y[our] E[xcellency] as a bar to all further intercourse." After further ranting, O'Gorman concluded, "in all future communication . . . it may be necessary for us therefore to . . . avail ourselves of the mediation of the Secretary of State for Home and Foreign Relations [Lucas Alamán]." Alamán had held the portfolio only since May 15, so O'Gorman's action must have seemed precipitous, at best. Arrillaga, in turn, was succeeded by Esteva, who was the Grand Master of the York Rite. Within a year, Alamán would be forced out of government until 1830 – the victim of what Anna has called "a well-organized conspiracy" mounted by the Yorkinos.[172] And when O'Gorman was detained – he was later permitted to leave the country – one of his principal tormentors was Esteva. Circumstantial evidence, to be sure, but the British loans were nothing, if not political, and may justifiably be said to have been something of a *cause célèbre*. In the United States, the *Saturday Evening Post* reported that the loans to the Mexican government were said to occupy public attention almost entirely.[173] In the end, the

172 Anna, *Forging Mexico*, p. 198.
173 June 19, 1824.

business was settled on by the direct intervention of Michelena with "the Messrs Goldschmidt," who assured him that measures necessary to put a stop to any "unfounded rumors" about Mexican credit would be taken immediately.[174]

The Camacho Mission

In January 1826, President Victoria authorized José Ignacio Esteva and Sebastián Camacho to sign a Treaty of Friendship and Commerce between the United Kingdom and Mexico. Certain commercial issues remained unresolved, however, and Victoria determined to send Camacho to London to iron them out.[175] Camacho, a *jarocho* like Esteva, nevertheless had another duty as well, receiving "surest instructions . . . [regarding] the accurate settlement (*acertada liquidación*) of the foreign loans." To do the job properly, he was given access to all the files of the finance ministry regarding the loan, and assigned the assistance of Don Guillermo O'Brien, who occupied the foreign loan desk at the ministry and who would travel to London with Camacho.[176]

What the "settlement" turned out to be was a series of instructions that reveal Esteva's preoccupation with the loans. In the broadest sense, Camacho's instructions again suggest that the Federation was *not* supine in the face of foreign lenders. It did what it could to minimize costs, to control its agents, and to supervise the performance of the lenders and its agents. It did not always succeed because it could not always have succeeded. But, at the very least, the Federation was aware of the more problematic aspects of the loans, what we have called "loose ends."

One of the most serious of Camacho's instructions concerned the behavior of Migoni, Vicente Rocafuerte, and Barclay, Herring, Richardson. While simple politics cannot be ruled out, Camacho was asked "with the greatest reserve" to determine if news of the surrender of Ulúa had given any of these parties the opportunity to profit from their position. The news had gone out from Veracruz in two ships and, presumably, would have pushed up the price of Mexican bonds on its arrival in Britain. Suspicions of insider trading had been raised, for the instruction speaks of "possible losses our

---

174 Michelena to the Mexican minister to the United States, London, December 4, 1824, HD 17–7.697, BLAC, UT.

175 Delia Hidalgo, *Representantes de México en Gran Bretaña (1827–1980)* (México, 1981), p. 14, and Johnston, *Missions to Mexico,* pp. 190–216.

176 Esteva to Camacho, México, June 23–24, 1826, *Deuda Exterior,* vol. 5, AGNM. His charge is contained in "*Instrucciones para el Exmo Sr Ministro Plenipotenciario Dn Sebastián Camacho . . .* in the same place. "*el quebranto que nuestro Erario podría acaso sufrir . . . de la noticia de la rendición de Ulúa para la compra de acciones*" – quotation rearranged slightly – is translated as "possible losses our Treasury would have suffered."

Treasury would have suffered," – an accusation that makes sense if an agent of the government waited to purchase debt in the secondary market only after informing a confederate to hold off selling at a previously lower price. Since the government had explicitly reserved the right to repurchase its debt in the secondary market, some such arrangement was a real possibility, but whether the suspicion was simply politically motivated is impossible to tell.

Of equal moment, perhaps, was Camacho's instruction to verify the prices at which the relevant portion of the Barclay, Herring, Richardson loan (25 percent) had been used to retire the B. A. Goldschmidt obligation between April and September 1825, according to Rocafuerte. Camacho was told to verify prices quoted by Migoni as well: "You will secretly determine if the prices at which the purchase of bonds for retirement were those current on the Exchange on the days at which they took place and if they took place as stipulated in the contract." Camacho was to make legal claims in the event that irregularities were detected. And if purchases had not been made at prices that most favored the Federation, this would constitute "a stockpile of opportune claims and arguments" that could be used to contest other expenses that the Mexican government had born as well as "to publicly air whether or not those sums should be paid." In other words, Camacho was being sent to England to aggressively represent and defend the financial interests of the Federation, in public, if need be.[177]

A second area of concern for Camacho was the behavior of the houses of B. A. Goldschmidt and Barclay, Herring, Richardson. The news of the failure of the House of Goldschmidt, the anecdote with which this chapter opened, reached Mexico only on the eve of Camacho's departure for Britain around May 1, 1826. By his own account, Esteva was taken completely by surprise. His irritation with Migoni was palpable.[178] Amid uncertainty of what suspension of payments might mean for Mexico, Camacho was told to determine what balance of the proceeds of the loan had yet to be disbursed. Since he was told that one of B. A. Goldschmidt's agents in Mexico City, Henry Robert Tute, was managing 70,000 pesos of Goldschmidt's funds in Mexico City, "[i]t would be quite opportune to reject any pretext in London whatsoever to attach these funds to those subject to the disposition [of B. A. Goldschmidt's] creditors." Moreover, Camacho was told to recover

---

177 I have found no evidence to support any wrongdoing on the part of anyone. There is nothing in the press, and nothing in the archives (to the extent that it is possible to search them systematically). And perhaps most importantly, there is no quantitative evidence of anything unusual or unexpected happening during these months. The relative price of Mexican bonds remained basically unchanged and, indeed, rose by some 16 percent (relative to April 1824) in the run up to the recognition of Mexican independence in January 1825.

178 See Esteva to Borja Migoni, México, May 1, 1826, in *Esteva*, Contestacion á las observaciones del señor contador de crédito público, *Supporting Documents*, No. 32.

the 1 percent commission charged by Barclay, Herring, Richardson for honoring bills drawn against the proceeds of the B. A. Goldschmidt loan because a portion of that loan had already been remitted to Mexico in gold bullion. Some bills drawn on the full amount had apparently been dishonored.[179] These charges amounted to £2,352, which the government rejected. "[I]t is unfair for the Republic to bear the charges, which Your Excellency should avoid by all means, because the last two remissions have been made without the authorization of the government." In general, there seems to have been considerable unhappiness with Migoni's handling of the B. A. Goldschmidt loan, including the exchange rate for gold shipped to Mexico. Indeed, Camacho was even instructed to reject the charges accruing to the Federation when one of the gold shipments to Mexico was transferred (on the high seas?) from the cutter "Lion" to a warship of the Royal Navy, "supposedly because of the fear of pirates." At the very least, the whole business was considered suspicious because the Finance Ministry had determined "albeit extrajudicially" that the transfer had occurred to leave the cutter "Lion" free to transport papers concerning B. A. Goldschmidt's business affairs "unimpeded" (*espedito*).

The results of Camacho's inquiry are enlightening. In his report of April 10, 1827, Camacho confessed to finding little substance to the Federation's claims. In fact, his sympathies lay more with B. A. Goldschmidt, which, he said, argued against the government's claims "with reasons that were not ill founded." Given the huge swings in the exchange rate that had occurred, Goldschmidt had actually ended up with a balance in its favor of some 15,000 pesos after all was said and done, and this according to an accounting provided by Camacho himself. Within a month, the claims of the Federation against B. A. Goldschmidt were submitted to arbitration and decided in B. A. Goldschmidt's favor, a result with which Mexico concurred. It may well be that B. A. Goldschmidt did Mexico few favors with the terms of its loan, but there is no evidence that it failed to comply with them. If anything, the Mexican authorities appear to have lost track of the money. In 1824 and 1825, when the loans were first negotiated, there appears to have been literally *no one* responsible for accounting for the disposition of their proceeds at the finance ministry. The bureaucracy of the Federation was in a state of flux, offices were as yet unfilled, and conflicting administrative jurisdictions had yet to be clarified. The ensuring mess may have been everyone's responsibility, but in reality, it was probably nobody's fault.

179 About $1.6 million in 396 bars of gold and 4,261 doubloons. "*Mexican Finances*," *Times* (London), August 17, 1827. Camacho was unsuccessful in this. This same accounting showed that these charges, and more, were applied. "*con razones no desnudas de fundamento*" is translated as "with reasons that were not ill founded."

Nevertheless, much the same happened with Barclay, Herring, Richardson. Ostensibly, the firm went bankrupt, owing Mexico more than $700,000 in undisbursed proceeds of the loan.[180] Through their agents Manning and Marshall, Barclay, Herring, Richardson tried to arrive at a settlement with the Mexican government and proposed various combinations of cash and credits, all of which were ultimately deemed inadequate. Part of the problem was that the finance ministry claimed to lack "very essential" data with which to make a decision, while Sebastián Camacho characterized Barclay, Herring, Richardson's accounting as deficient. "We do not know how much this company *legitimately* owes the Republic" [italics in original]. Is there a better word than *mess* to describe a country's defaulting on what was, essentially, an unknown sum?

Toward a Model of Bond Prices, Fiscal Factors, and Politics

It is one thing, perhaps, to speak about Mexican bonds and the events that affected them in anecdotal terms. Doing so comes naturally as well. For a variety of reasons, a systematic account of the effect of events on Mexican bond prices, an "event study," appears difficult. There are technical considerations – for instance, the absence of an appropriate index with which to compute the excess returns necessary for such an exercise – to keep in mind. Moreover, Mexico was repeatedly struck by nearly simultaneous disturbances: news of the expulsion of the Spaniards and of Spain's planned reconquest of Mexico, for example, reached London within a six-week interval in 1829.[181] Disentangling their effects using a standard moving "event window" must inevitably include both and thus "contaminate" the results of the analysis. Still, there is something to be said for making an effort, albeit informal, to identify the general factors that affected the twists and turns of bond prices. At the very least, we may have a clearer idea of the multiple constraints Mexico faced as it sought to maintain its credit in London. For it was the presence of multiple, simultaneous, and not always mutually consistent constraints that make for the complex interplay of domestic and foreign factors in the history of early national Mexico. It is this complex interplay that sometimes creates the impression that there is little or no stable structure for understanding what occurred. Thus the effort is useful.

In the absence of a formal model, it might prove helpful to consider some of the ways in which contemporaries thought about what affected Mexican bond prices on the London Stock Exchange. As the diplomat

---

180 See *Dictamen de la Primera Comisión de Hacienda sobre la propuesta de los socios de la estinguida casa de Barclay, Herring, Richardson y compañía* (México, 1828) for this and what follows.
181 *Times* (London), June 18 and July 30, 1829.

Manuel Eduardo Gorostiza succinctly put it during his time in London, "uncertainty [in the means of payment] is really one of the reasons our bond prices rise sluggishly."[182] As we will see, uncertainty surrounding Mexican debt service in 1827 resulted in a wild gyration of prices. The same occurred in early 1828 and in early 1829, when dividends fell due.[183] So, presumably, we could begin with the reasonable (and historical) assumption that the price of a bond reflected the income it produced. There are a variety of procedures for testing such a relationship, the simplest being ordinary least squares (OLS) regression. Using annualized data for the period 1825 through 1846, a choice of dates dictated strictly by the data available, we regress dividend and principal payments made by Mexico on the price of bonds.[184] The result is

$$\text{Mexican bond price} = 30 + (7.4/10^6) \text{ payments,}$$

where the estimated coefficient on *payments* is significant at the 99 percent level. Payments also explain (*r*-squared) about half the variance in the level of bond prices. Unfortunately, this common sense result suffers from a technical problem in estimation, but there is no great danger involved in assuming that bond prices and payments are positively related. In fact, payments appear to be the one variable that remains significant no matter what specification we select.

For Mexico's central government, the reality of early nineteenth-century finance was bleak scarcity. Scarcity imposed difficult choices, none of which were made easier by the political consequences they entailed. The basic notion of opportunity cost is quite relevant: to pay one creditor or set of creditors was to deny competing claims. That one of the choices that involved servicing foreign claims was especially fraught, for Mexican decisions would involve the country's future access to the international capital market and also the possibility of foreign intervention. At the same time, powerful domestic interest groups ultimately comprised the creditors that fashioned the ways and means of the political game at home. A regime chose to alienate domestic financiers at its peril, for domestic financiers might well be suppliers of arms and war materiel.

The puzzling issue is how to capture the essence of this choice. Obviously, the remissions of principal and dividends that Mexico mattered, but it is far more difficult to find a well-specified statistic that measures the payments

---

182 Manuel Eduardo Gorostiza to the finance minister, London, June 16, 1831, unclassified Hacienda papers, AGNM.

183 *Times* (London), January 6 and February 20, 1828; and January 9, 1829.

184 The regression is not spurious because the data series are cointegrating. Payments include principal and interest, but exclude the value of certificates issued on Mexican customs. Calculating an average yearly bond price is, unfortunately, dictated by the best data available on payments, which is annual.

Mexico made to its *domestic* creditors. Figures for fluid sums, like the unfunded or floating debt, are not easy to locate: even the most expert of students, Manuel Payno, demonstrated that few of the commonly cited figures are secure, and certainly none are available on an annual basis.[185] For that reason, I have employed data on domestic loans as a crude proxy for payments made to domestic creditors. It is, of course, possible to argue that Mexican public finance before 1870 was a kind of Ponzi scheme in which borrowing from one set of lenders effectively permitted the repayment of others. But it should be possible to find some evidence of this and none is forthcoming.[186] What is clear is that there was essentially one source of funds to finance the government – the maritime customs – and that the use of these funds to pay the internal debt reduced Mexico's ability to service the London Debt. Our expectation, then, is that introducing domestic loans in a model should depress the price of bonds on London. That is, the coefficient on a term for loans would have a negative sign.

Before testing to see if this is so, we might consider one more dimension of the question. Both Mexican payments and domestic loans are absolute sums and really mean little unless measured in relation to capacity to pay. While there are a variety of standard measures of capacity to pay, we employ the maritime customs – and specifically, the Veracruz customs – as a relevant measure. While hardly perfect and increasingly less so as the outports developed – until the mid-nineteenth century, if not later – the Veracruz collections counted most. The London market could be assumed to have reasonable knowledge of the customs and prospective payments,[187] and even more importantly, every regime prior to the French Intervention used the customs as a basis for funding government obligations to the extent they could be funded at all. Thus, we employ this series as a factor by which to rescale or normalize Mexican payments and domestic loans. Basically, then, the price of Mexican bonds is hypothesized to be a function of Mexican payments and Mexican domestic loans when both are measured in relation to the Veracruz customs revenues.

There is an intuitive interpretation of these measures. From the standpoint of the London Stock Exchange, the ratio of Mexican payments (dividend and principal) to Veracruz customs revenue could be interpreted as a measure of how serious a particular government was about satisfying the demands of the London bondholders. Not just an absolute increase in payments, but the remission of a greater share of the customs revenue was

---

185 See especially Manuel Payno, *La deuda interior de Mexico* (México, 1865).

186 For instance, by introducing a lag structure into the model and observing if the sign of a relevant coefficient changes. It does not.

187 An excellent example of just such a disclosure was given by Tomás Murphy in the *Times* (London), October 21, 1846.

an effective measure of Mexico's willingness to satisfy the London bond-holders. By the same token, an increase in the fraction of the customs that financed domestic lenders conveyed the opposite message – that lenders at home held the upper hand and that the London bondholders would suffer. We estimate the model (with a stochastic error)

$$\text{Mexican bond price} = a + b(\text{Payments to London/Veracruz customs})$$
$$+ c(\text{Domestic loans/Veracruz customs})$$

by OLS for 1825–1845. The relevant parameters are $a = 39.92$, $b = 2.5$ (significant at 99 percent), and $c = -4.13$ (significant at 96 percent). The adjusted r-squared is .58 and the Durbin–Watson statistic is 1.55. The F-statistic is 14.7 (significant at 99 percent). We might consider the constant "a" the predicted value of bonds in the absence of payments to London or domestic loans. This is a little like the situation in the late 1820s, when the annualized average price of bonds was, in fact, about 40. The parameters "b" and "c" have the expected signs: ($b > 0$) and ($c < 0$). Together, the right-hand variables explain 58 percent of the variance in Mexican bond prices in 1825–1845. The Durbin–Watson statistic gives no evidence of positive first-order serial correlation, which is conventionally interpreted as indicating a "complete" model. One very interesting feature of the results is the very large errors in 1827 and 1829, here displayed in standardized form in Figure 1.2.

We have already alluded to such volatility, and in the next chapter, we will examine what significance we might attach to these seemingly abnormal spikes. For now, it is enough to note that in the period up to the Mexican War, the greatest volatility in the market occurs *before* 1830; after that date, the reactions of the London Stock Exchange are considerably less extreme.

To summarize then, the model we employ suggests that the behavior of the London bondholders should be broadly affected by three factors. The first, most obviously, were the payments made by the Mexican government. In and of itself, anything that affected its capacity to make these affected the wealth of the London bondholders through the price of bonds. Anything that interfered with payments – factors both political and economic – then possessed a broader significance. Occurrences within Mexico that diverted funds, especially to military ends, inevitably affected bond prices, although it is debatable whether the London bondholders cared about Mexican politics per se. By the same token, purely economic or fiscal shocks that affected the ability to service the debt, albeit indirectly, became matters of bondholder (and foreign) concern. Variations in the structure of the Mexican political system that systematically affected the ability of the central government to meet its obligations, such as the running dispute between advocates of centralism and federalism, were then also of concern to

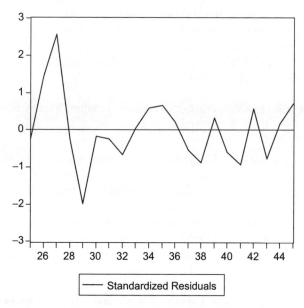

Figure 1.2. Standardized Residuals of Fitted Mexican Bond
Prices, 1825–1845 (see text).

the London bondholders. Similarly, since they affected the capacity to pay, Mexican policies involving seigniorage, the real exchange rate, tax regimes, the government balance sheet – even the disposition of war indemnities – affected the bond market and even broader macroeconomic aggregates. Not surprisingly, the role of this "peripheral" state, Mexico, in the Atlantic economy was indeed crucial in the Panic of 1837 and, perhaps, in the Indian Mutiny of 1857 as well.

By the same token, the position of Mexican interest groups that placed demands on public finance through the avenue of the domestic debt was critical. The emergence of a class of government financiers or *agiotistas* in the 1830s paralleled to some extent another moratorium on payments to the London bondholders because it was impossible to satisfy both sets of creditors at once. As we will see, the characterization of the *agiotistas* as "vampires of the Treasury" owed something, if not the epithet itself, to the enmity of the British bondholders, whose interests were threatened by these powerful insiders. Again, this was simply a matter of opportunity cost, but the choice of whom to pay would be dictated by the sharpening internal conflicts of the 1830s. The course of Mexican bond prices would thus reflect the loss of credibility of a state that was to fall increasingly into the hands of a competing financial and commercial oligarchy, one not to the London bondholders' liking. All this will be explored in subsequent chapters.

Finally, the model suggests that bond prices reflected both exogenous economic factors and the political economy of commercial policy. Since the maritime customs reflected factors as diverse as international economic cycles and the vagaries of Mexican silver mining, Mexico and its London bondholders were, to an extent, hostages to fortune. But it would be wrong to suppose that they were no more than hostages to fortune. Again, subsequent discussion will demonstrate that nascent industrial interests in Mexico shaped commercial policy and the volume of maritime customs. Thus the drive to modernize the textile industry after 1837 had a direct bearing on Mexico's foreign creditors, bringing the British Foreign Office to bear on multiple facets of the domestic economy seemingly unrelated to the London Debt. Similarly, the manipulation of the customs to finance military campaigns that began with – but were by no means limited to – Texas also traced an indirect line from the Alamo to Whitehall. The connections and pressures were generally subtle, but they existed nonetheless and will be taken up later as well.

The Loans: How Big, How Bad?

The questions of how large the loans to Mexico were and how much they ended up costing Mexico should not be confused. One involves capacity to pay: could Mexico have generated the resources needed to make timely repayment of interest and principal? The other involves a rate of discount: how much would the country sacrifice in the future to consume more now? A third consideration is how the money was used: whether for productive investment or as a substitute for tax revenue. We should treat each of these questions in turn.

There are a number of standard measures of a country's capacity to pay.[188] One, the ratio of net external debt to gross domestic product (GDP), would be calculated for Mexico over an interval that would depend on GDP, which was somewhere in the neighborhood of 200–240 million pesos around 1800. Since the loan indentures specified a nominal total of £6.4 million, or 32 million pesos, we obtain an interval estimate of 13 percent $< x <$ 16 percent. This was well below the level that Mexico reached during the debt crisis of the 1990s (i.e., 78 percent in 1986).

A second measure is the rate of net external debt to the export of goods and services. I would estimate this for the mid-1820s as 119 percent $< x <$ 139 percent. Again, this is well below the levels observed in Mexico in the 1980s (i.e., 435 percent in 1986).

The final measure is the ratio of net interest payments to the export of goods and nonfactor services. I would estimate this (before default in 1827)

188 William R. Cline, *International Debt Reexamined* (Washington, DC, 1995), pp. 39–57.

as 6.7 percent $< x <$ 7.8 percent. Again, this is low compared to the debt crisis, where it reached 30.6 percent in 1986.

If each of these indicators seems low in contemporary terms, the issue of why Mexico defaulted is no clearer, or at least, does not fit the classic criteria of an external transfer problem. Interestingly, Carmen Reinhart, Kenneth Rogoff, and Miguel Savastano reach a similar conclusion about Mexico (and a larger group of mostly Latin American economies), terming it "debt intolerant" (i.e., liable to default at atypically low levels of indebtedness) and speculating that debt intolerance may have something to do with weak systems of public finance.[189] Contemporaries understood this and said as much. "Of the means of the Mexican people to pay the interest of their debt there can be no question. The great difficulty seems to be – owing to the imperfect machinery of the government – in forcing from the pockets of the people a just contribution toward the national expenditure and national burdens."[190] Still, the confusing way in which the data are reported makes drawing any firm conclusions difficult. The early republic reported deficits, but whether they include or exclude debt service is not always clear. In other words, it is hard to tell whether what is reported is a *primary* budget deficit (i.e., one that excludes interest on the foreign debt). If Robert Wyllie's[191] contemporary analysis was correct, the Federation was probably running small primary budget *surpluses* in the mid-1820s, since the reported deficits are smaller than the 1.8 million pesos that would have represented debt service. This could explain why the early republic felt itself under such intense pressure – it was attempting to save enough to service the foreign debt.

What did Mexico pay for the money it borrowed from Britain? There is no simple answer to this question, and at this point, I would limit myself to the years 1825–1850 – the years that roughly bracket the first era in the history of the debt, ending with the close of the War of 1847 and the attempted fiscal reorganization that took place thereafter. The almost universal tendency in the historiography is to assume that the loans were very expensive, but there are virtually no efforts to fix magnitudes. One interesting and surely pioneering attempt was made by Alamán, who focused on the nominal size of the loans and what Mexico actually took from them, concluding that "each peso that Mexico got cost it five."[192] But even if Alamán was correct in his calculations, his focus was on the original cost

189 Carmen Reinhart, Kenneth Rogoff and Miguel Savastano, "Debt Intolerance," in William Brainard and George Perry, eds., *Brookings Papers on Economic Activity*, 1 (2003), pp. 1–74.

190 Excerpted from a letter to W. Parish Robertson in Robertson, *The Foreign Debt of Mexico* (México, 1850), p. 38.

191 Robert Crichton Wyllie, *México: Noticia sobre su hacienda pública* (1845; México, 1977), tables A and B, note 2, believes these sums are generally included.

192 *El Universal*, March 11, 1853, or a compound rate of about 8.4 percent over twenty years.

of the loans, not on what we might imagine as the cost of funds over time. This, instead, would be a matter of determining what Mexico paid, say, twenty-five years, not a trivial matter in view of the various suspensions, conversions, and moratoria that took place.

Murphy also made an attempt to measure something like the cost of the loans as of 1848.[193] His argument is, at first sight, a bit puzzling. "As of July 1827, the debt stood at near 26 and $\frac{1}{2}$ million pesos. If nothing had been done, if not a red cent in interest had been paid, the debt in July 1847 would not have stood at more than 56 million pesos." That is a compound rate of increase of less than 4 percent per year, or something less than the unweighted average coupon rate of the two loans. This seems impossible until one examines the way in which Murphy reached his conclusion. There is no point in reproducing it, for it is misleading. Murphy simply took to be what he calculated as the outstanding principal in July 1827 and then assumed equal payments of simple interest of 5 or 6 percent for twenty years. In other words, he assumed that no compounding on arrears would have taken place in the absence of any payment whatsoever. That makes for ease of calculation, but hardly constitutes a reasonable counterfactual, whatever else one thinks of the exercise!

As a very preliminary matter, I would argue that Mexico actually received about 11 million pesos in proceeds from the Goldschmidt and Barclay loans. *On average*, during the twenty-five-year period through 1850, Mexico paid about 750,000 pesos per year. And in 1850, having paid that much for twenty-five years, Mexico was believed to owe approximately 50 million pesos. *If these figures have any validity at all, they imply that interest effectively accrued on the loans at a rate of about 10.5 percent per year.* This is higher than Murphy imagined, but not all that far from what Alamán guessed. Interestingly, these calculations come very close to fitting the overall totals for the London Debt reported by Guillermo Prieto in 1850. Prieto also reported, without indicating how he arrived at the conclusion, that the market rate for the loans was *not* 5 and 6 percent, but 7 and 10 percent.[194] But perhaps more importantly, my estimates are virtually identical to those presented by Francis Falconnet, the bondholders' commissioner in Mexico, to the Chamber of Deputies in 1852.[195] Falconnet had worked for Baring Brothers; his calculations for this period are the clearest available, and I am inclined to regard them as definitive, as did the Cámara de Diputados.

193 Murphy, *Deuda esterior*, pp. 139–140.

194 [Guillermo Prieto?], *Dictamen de la Comisión de Crédito Público de la Cámara de Diputados sobre el Arreglo de la Deuda Inglesa* (México, 1850), pp. 5, 6.

195 Francis Falconnet to the Commision de Crédito Público, October 28, 1852, *Gobernación*, unclassified documents, AGNM.

The actual returns that a representative bondholder received are, of course, nearly impossible to determine. It is no great accomplishment to show that, for example, someone who purchased a Mexican bond at the beginning of the Mexican War and sold it at the end would have realized a capital loss of about 50 percent over two years – the bonds fell by roughly 50 percent and no dividends were paid during the conflict. Assumptions and examples could be multiplied to "prove" that anything could have happened over any particular interval. There was, however, at least one contemporary accounting that can be crudely interpreted as a rate of return. W. Parish Robertson, who went to Mexico as a special agent of the bondholders after the Mexican War, determined that between 1837 and 1849, the bondholders in the aggregate received £1,026,802 in cash and certificates.[196] Assuming that this reflects the market value of everything received, we might make the following calculation: In 1837, the average price of a bond was about 20. In 1849, bonds stood at about 18. Thus, if a bondholder had received no income, but merely purchased the bond in 1837 and sold it in 1849, he or she would have suffered a capital loss of 10 percent. In 1846, the conversion ("Mexican Five Percent New Consolidated Debt") consisted of an issue of 50,000[197] bonds, so we might surmise that a bond's share of the total income would be £20. To compute the return, we employ the formula ((End-of-period wealth less beginning-of-period wealth)/(Beginning-of-period wealth)), or $(38 - 20)/20 = 90$ percent. This 90 percent, however, would have been realized only over thirteen years, so the compound return is a little more than 5 percent per year.[198]

Obviously, if interest accrued on the London Debt at 10.5 percent yearly while an investor might expect a compound return of 5 percent, the spread between the two rates represents something of an opportunity cost, what we might term the "economic" as opposed to the "financial return" of purchasing Mexican bonds. On average, the economic return from 1837 to 1849 to holding Mexican bonds was −5.5 percent per year. A British investor would have been far better served by holding consols, which yielded 3.35 percent over the same period. Ex post, British investors lost about 8.3 percent a year from not holding the riskless security.[199]

---

196 Robertson, *The Foreign Debt of Mexico*, p. 24.

197 According to a specimen of the Series A bond in AGNM.

198 The bondholders' committee calculated the average dividend between 1837 and 1846 at 1.75 percent per year. *Statement of Proceedings in Relation to the Mexican Debt Published by the Committee of Spanish American Bondholders* (London, 1850), pp. 54–55. Also see G. R. Robinson to the foreign secretary, London, October 14, 1848, FO 97/273, PRO.

199 Robertson and Francisco de Paula Arangoiz offered his own illustrative calculations in their *Pieza justificativa del arreglo de la Deuda esterna de México* (México, 1849), pp. 84–89, but they are a bit bizarre, assuming, for instance, that debt service continue uninterrupted between 1827 and 1849. Nevertheless, the best that Robertson could do was a return of about 1 percent per year, *without*

As an alternative, one might draw on Manuel Payno's remarkable study published at the time of the French Intervention.[200] By 1862, Payno calculated that the British bondholders had been paid 29.5 million pesos. The original issues had been brought to market at a discount, for 21.8 million pesos. Interest payments had commenced in 1824, so someone who bought and held the bonds for thirty-seven years – a mythical first-generation investor – would have earned 0.8 percent per year (or less than 1 percent). The average yield on British consols over the same period was 3.28 percent. So, ex post, our mythical first-generation investor would have *lost* about 2.5 percent per year by not holding the riskless security. This is a highly stylized example, for it ignores the costs of the intervening conversions that occurred, but for anyone who had bought a Mexican bond in the early 1820s and persisted in holding on through 1862, the results were, to put it mildly, very disappointing.

The Goldschmidt and Barclay loans are good examples of what Albert Fishlow has called "revenue finance," or borrowing to balance government accounts rather than to undertake productive investment. "While national debt grew as a liability, on the asset side, there was nothing."[201] Of the 11 million pesos that Mexico received, something in the neighborhood of 1.7 million pesos alone was spent on ships and armament – about 15 percent.[202] While the brigantines "Libertad" and "Bravo" were certainly national assets in the military circumstances of their day, they produced no income to service the loans, and were thus by no means self-liquidating expenditures. Remarkably, the costs and charges of remitting 396 bars of gold and 4,263 doubloons to Mexico came to nearly as much, 1.6 million pesos.[203] Whether this was money well spent is hard to say, but a charge of 15 percent simply to move the loan proceeds to Mexico seems like a very bad idea. As it stands, one gets the distinct impression that much of the remainder of the original loans was used for debt service. And as we shall see, enormous expenditures for debt service seem to have been a strong thread in the history of Mexican public finance through the Second Empire. As Fishlow emphasized, the distance from revenue finance to debt

allowing for substantial capital losses. His notion of opportunity cost is a little different from ours, but even he assumes that there was some relatively stable rent to be gained from lending directly in Mexico. In other words, Robertson also concluded that a typical investor lost money in Mexican bonds between 1825 and 1849, and his "typical" investor was a long-term holder.

200 Manuel Payno, *México y sus Cuestiones Financieras con La Inglaterra, La España y La Francia* (1862; México, 1982), p. 301.

201 Albert Fishlow, "Lessons from the Past: Capital Markets during the Nineteenth Century and the Interwar Period," *International Organization*, 39:3 (1985), p. 400.

202 *Dictamen de la Comisión de Crédito Público de la Cámara de Diputados sobre el arreglo de la Deuda Inglesa* (México, 1850), p. 66.

203 *Times* (London), "Mexican Finances," August 17, 1827.

crisis is short indeed, and the early Mexican republic traversed it with ease.

Conclusions

When H. G. Ward, who was appointed chargé d'affaires to Mexico in 1825 by George Canning, considered the impact of British lending on Mexico, his judgment was largely favorable. There was, he thought, no question that the loans had proved expensive and that some of the proceeds had been wasted. Yet without the loans, Ward averred, the lengthy economic depression into which Mexico had fallen because of the civil wars would have continued unabated. British investment in Mexican mines and the proceeds of the loans had been used to reactivate some of the resources of the Mexican economy. And so it was that Ward, who returned to Britain in 1827 and who ultimately brought his concerns about Mexico's future to Parliament, regarded the subject of the loans rather benignly.[204]

Was Ward correct? Was his optimism justified? Certainly, there were others who saw matters as Ward did. Writing to the *Times* (London), a certain "HM" made the case for British lending about as well as anyone could. "[T]he merchants of Great Britain saw no likelihood of reaping the advantages of a free commercial intercourse with the ci-devant Spanish colonies unless their independence were securely established." But the only way to effect this was by "recourse . . . to loans of money in order . . . to secure to Great Britain the early and uninterrupted benefits of commerce with those extensive regions." The result, thought HM, was that "so important a branch of trade was secured to [Great Britain that] our merchants and men of trade were enabled to cause to be circulated immense sums of money through Great Britain by the purchase of arms and other warlike stores and consequently to give a very considerable stimulus to trade." Indeed, concluded HM, "the greatest portion of these loans was immediately employed for legitimate purposes in the country in which they were raised."[205]

That this view was not precisely the Mexican one should come as no surprise. In 1825, *El Pensador Mexicano* reproduced criticisms of Pablo de Villavicencio, the so-called Payo de Rosario, who agreed that the English loans were valuable – but only to the English – and were of a piece with the destruction of the Mexican artisan textile industry whose destruction was hastened by a wave of British cottons imported in the 1820s. Ironically, as we have seen, the appreciation of the real exchange rate in Mexico associated with that wave of imports was almost certainly a consequence of British lending.

204 Henry George Ward, *México en 1827* (1828; México, 1981), pp. 258–259.
205 Letter of December 17, 1839, in the *Times* (London), December 20, 1839.

Another variant of the British view appeared in *El Pensador Mexicano* in 1824. Yes, it was certain that British lending had created no small interest there in the independence of Mexico. But it was hardly an interest that was in itself benign. The British contractors had put a great deal of money into play in Mexico. And they would do what it took to see that their interests were preserved. So consider the fate of poor Iturbide as an object lesson. Harried in London and watched by Michelena, by the British government, and by the merchant banks themselves, Iturbide represented a threat to their interests. Were he to return to Mexico, there would be a Second Empire and "they would not recognize our independence, or they would have to make war to get their money back, with the resulting paralysis of their trade." This they could not want, and so it was "quite natural that they would never permit in any way [Iturbide's] return to America." A small change in perspective, but a substantial change in judgment.

Modern historians have generally been divided in their evaluation of Mexico's first ventures into the international capital markets. A quasi-official history[206] succinctly terms them "costly" and "creating problems almost from the very beginning." Jan Bazant[207] concurs that the loans were expensive, considers that their proceeds were wastefully spent, but nevertheless concludes that the injection of funds provided some breathing room to the nascent republican government. A more recent effort finds in the first British loans the origins of a new sort of dependency, one involving Britain rather than Spain.[208]

It is not so much that these views — and others could be cited — are wrong as they are oversimplified. The emerging republic went to the London market of its own volition, but with the distinct assistance of domestic capitalists, whose response to the government's calls for capital was unenthusiastic, to say the least. Not all choices are good choices, but that does not make them choices any less. The B. A. Goldschmidt and Barclay, Herring, Richardson loans were hardly generous in their terms but the Staples loan was worse and the Barry loan verged on outright fraud. Moreover, it is hard to avoid the impression that the Mexicans played B. A. Goldschmidt and Barclay, Herring, Richardson off against each other, even though the existence of two loans may have been dictated as much by political considerations as by anything else, with the partisans of republican centralist Alamán promoting the B. A. Goldschmidt loan, while liberal federalists like Arrillaga and Esteva "supported" Barclay, Herring, Richardson. One has only to read the latter firm's panicked correspondence to realize that the Mexican government had it over a barrel, rather than the

---

206 [Secretaría de Hacienda y Crédito Público], *Deuda externa pública mexicana* (México, 1988), p. 12.

207 Jan Bazant, *Historia de la deuda exterior de México (1823–1946)* (2nd ed., México, 1981), pp. 24–40.

208 José Zaragoza, *Historia de la deuda externa de México, 1823–1861* (México, 1996), p. 14.

other way around. As for the Goldschmidt loan, it was bad, but there were worse, including some of the contemporary Spanish loans. And then, of course, both houses went bust, with Barclay, Herring, Richardson directly inculpating Mexico for its fate. Much the same was said about the collapse of B. A. Goldschmidt. One can only conclude that if the lenders were thieves, they were inept ones, at best.

As to the mishandling or misuse of the loan proceeds, the Mexicans *were* at war with when the loans were made: their spending money on rifles, ships, and uniforms was, perhaps, not so strange a thing.[209] It is so difficult to separate the charges of maladministration from the partisan context in which they were made – especially given the vituperation surrounding the presidential election of 1828 – that one is tempted to observe that the commentary was hardly disinterested on either side. It is always absurdly easy to ridicule weapons (literally) worth their weight in gold.

There does seem to have been a problem that might require more consideration later: the administrative ability of the Mexican government to manage and account for the funds it got, or literally, to keep track of them. The disordered state of the archives and the documents may give a false impression of the chaotic conditions in the ministries concerned with the loans, especially at the time of their inception, for there were specific officials entrusted with the supervision of the loans. Yet the tenor of Camacho's official charge in 1826 lends weight to the evidence that even rudimentary accounting controls were never systematically applied and that much took place behind the scenes. This would not be the last time that charges of insider trader and malversation were leveled against Mexican officials entrusted with handling loan funds, but it is one thing to charge and another to prove. I have found no solid evidence of corruption of this sort and nothing untoward in the movement of bond prices, at least for the interval when the accusations were made. Government ministries in Mexico operated on a shoestring and this as much as anything else, including honest incompetence, may account for the persistent feeling that "something strange is going on here." Perhaps so. Perhaps not. At least no one could find much proof at the time.

As to the direct economic effects of the loans, these could not have been anything more than modest. Much of the money received was spent abroad rather than at home, and could have added little to aggregate demand in Mexico. But more to the point, the B. A. Goldschmidt and Barclay, Herring, Richardson loans produced, in round numbers, something like $22 million at most, not all of it discretionary. The GDP of Mexico at the time was somewhere in the neighborhood of $240 million. Just on the basis of crude numbers, it is hard to see how the loans could have had much

---

209 See Bazant, *Deuda Exterior*, pp. 37–38, for just this point.

of an effect on production and employment, for here was an open economy with a high propensity to import and a presumably high propensity to withdraw savings in the form of landownership. There is, in other words, no presumption of a high multiplier, or one whose dynamic effects were quickly realized. What *is* indisputable is that British lending had a dramatic effect on the real exchange rate, causing an appreciation of the peso that coincided with the surge of imports in 1825 – a yet another blow to New Spain's once-thriving textile industry. Perhaps *El Pensador Mexicano* got it right. The British loans helped finish off the *obrajes*.

As to whether or not the Mexican loans helped finish off Goldschmidt, the matter was more controversial. As one observer, a certain J. Y. C., put it, "it is entirely false that [the crisis in the City] was caused by the sums that passed from England to the Mexican Republic." As far as Goldschmidt was concerned, J. Y. C. wrote, the house would have suffered far worse losses if "it hadn't have made a million pesos off the Mexican loan." The Mexican bonds ruined no house, J. Y. C. concluded. "It's all confined to matters arising from and limited to the London Stock Exchange" (*todo nace y todo queda dentro de la Bolsa de Londres*).[210] L. A. Goldschmidt, in the grave two months, was in no position to reply. Barclay, Herring, Richardson thought otherwise.

All these, however, were merely the proverbial "first steps." Yet more portentous events were to follow on this "twisted path full of dangers and obstacles." The twisted path would lead to default in 1827, protracted negotiations with the London bondholders, war with Texas, a collapse in domestic finances in 1837, and a regrettable commitment of the northern territories to the British bondholders as a guarantee of their acquiescence: Cry "Havoc!" and let slip the dogs of war.

210 J. Y. C., "Variedades: México y Londres," reproduced in Bustamante, *Diario Histórico de México*, Anexos, May 1826.

2

Default

If John Bull has not hitherto purchased experience at a very dear rate in placing confidence in the prospects held out by the Republics of the New World
in relation to the regular liquidation of the interest on money he was a few
years since so ready to advance, we should imagine that the operations in the
Foreign Stock Exchange this week will completely satisfy him on this point.

–*Times* (London) February 10, 1828

Enter the Sixth Great Power

In early January 1827, Consul-General Charles T. O'Gorman seemed relatively optimistic about Mexican finances. "The dividends due in London
will be punctually provided for," O'Gorman predicted. Moreover, "there is
in my opinion sufficient [revenue] left to prove that the country can readily
support its expenditure without the aid of foreign loans and without imposing any new contributions." And finally, "[i]f the proposed reduction in
the Army and Navy is carried, as well as a further reform in the Finance
Department and a proper modification of the Customs House Tariff on a
large scale, a large surplus may be safely counted upon."[1] Prophecy was not
O'Gorman's strong suit. It was not possible to do much of what O'Gorman
had hoped. For one thing, the sharp increase in the number of prohibited
goods in the tariff of 1827 produced a sharp decline in tariff revenues
through Veracruz, and hence, a fall in government income. For another,
military spending, driven by deteriorating domestic political conditions,
rose sharply in 1827; it did not fall. O'Gorman could not have foreseen
these events or, at least, anticipated them in any detail. Hence the fiscal
balance of the Federation deteriorated between January and July 1827.[2]

But by late July 1827, O'Gorman had begun to fear that the government
would be unable to service the London Debt because of what he called its

---

1 Charles T. O'Gorman to the foreign secretary, México, January 12, 1827, FO 50/37, PRO.
2 Michael P. Costeloe, *La primera república federal de México*, p. 231, who ties default directly to military
 spending.

"pecuniary embarrassments." His conversations with the finance minister and other officials had been unsatisfactory. While they insisted that Mexico would meet its obligations, O'Gorman thought, albeit incorrectly, that the government was not "fully aware of the disastrous consequences to [its] credit which would result from the postponement of the dividend for a single day." Specifically, O'Gorman worried that no provision had been made for the remission of the October dividend even though the government knew that without extraordinary measures, the Treasury would not have the resources required to do so.

When Barclay, Herring, Richardson wound up its affairs, the agency for the Mexican government was assumed by Baring Brothers. The involvement of Barings with Mexico had begun some time in early 1825, when Alexander Baring offered the house's services to Mariano Michelena.[3] By drawing on funds advanced by Baring Bothers, O'Gorman wrote, "the Government relied too much from the interest which they supposed Messrs Baring to have in keeping up the price of Mexican stock in London." The plan was to have Baring Brothers draw bills on London that would make payment on the October 1827 dividend and be reimbursed for a prior debt the Mexican government had with the house. But O'Gorman believed that Barings would not cooperate, since the firm had declared that it would not pay the dividend until an actual remittance of specie occurred or that information regarding a pending shipment of silver was received.[4] The implications of such a stand were disastrous.

Our discussion of the loan contracts in Chapter 1 indicated that both loans included provisions for setting aside interest and principal payments out of the proceeds of the loans.[5] The B. A. Goldschmidt loan included setting aside two years of dividend (£320,000) and principal payments (£96,000). The Barclay, Herring, Richardson loan included setting aside six quarters of interest (£288,000) and principal (£48,000) *plus* a quarter of its proceeds (£694,000) toward retirement of the B. A. Goldschmidt loan. In effect, the dividends on both loans were prepaid until 1826. But beginning in October 1826, Mexico would have been servicing *both* loans out of current resources. In theory, the interest payments or dividends alone amounted to £352,000 per year. That was an enormous sum, nearly 1.8 million pesos yearly. And, indeed, in 1826–1827, Mexico remitted 1.4 million pesos to Great Britain. This represented more than expenses for

---

The tariff of 1827 was associated with reduced customs collections, a pattern that would hold true through to the tariff of 1853. A regression of the number of prohibited and duty-free goods on Veracruz customhouse revenue yields the correct sign, albeit at a 70 percent significance level.

3 Michelena to the secretary of home and foreign relations, London, March 31, 1825, HD, BLAC, UT.

4 Charles T. O'Gorman to [unknown], México, August 15, 1827, FO 50/35, PRO.

5 The following is based on "Mexican Finance," *Times* (London), August 17, 1827; *Memoria de Hacienda, 1828*, pp. 2, 12; and Murphy, *Deuda Esterior*, p. 6.

the active militia (1,144,565 pesos) and for the ministry of home and foreign relations (222,399 pesos) combined. It even exceeded the *contingente* or payment of the states to the Federation (979,145 pesos). In addition, in 1824 and 1825, the government retired about £1.1 million in principal, of which about £850,000 came from the loan proceeds; the remainder, £250,000, could have come only from current revenues. So, late in 1826, Mexico effectively assumed servicing the loans on its own. It was able to do so for less than a year. Absent fresh resources, which meant the assistance of Baring Brothers, default was not exactly inevitable, but very likely. For without fresh resources, there was nothing to squeeze and nowhere to go. Baring Brothers had effectively made the decision for Mexico. As a committee of the Mexican Congress put things with deadly accuracy, "[the budget surplus was] occasioned by the loans and not by the produce of the revenue."[6]

As October approached, O'Gorman became increasingly worried. He contacted the commanding admiral of the Jamaica squadron to secure a warship that could be dispatched to Veracruz to pick up the dividend payment. He reminded the finance minister that "the period is at hand." O'Gorman discussed the matter with President Guadalupe Victoria, who had in 1826 staked his government's reputation on repayment of the loans,[7] and with the minister of home and foreign relations. He observed that the government had been forced to borrow $40,000 from a British merchant house so as to pay the troops of the Mexico City garrison.[8] By October 13, with the government technically in default, O'Gorman saw no way out. Barings had withdrawn its offer to pay the dividend and the only other avenue open was, as he had put it, by going "to the Capitalists."[9]

About the time when O'Gorman had begun to sound the alarm, the news began to roil the London market. The *Times* (London) reported that "a severe decline was experienced in Mexican bonds . . . fears being entertained that . . . the Mexican government had failed in its attempts to raise a loan on the Republic . . . [and that] the dividends which fell due [i.e., October 1] will not be forthcoming."[10] All hell broke loose on the London market. August 1827 witnessed the worst one-month decline in Mexican bonds until the 1860s as they fell nearly 30 percent relative to British consols. The *Times* (London) reported that the fluctuations in Mexican bond "have been almost unprecedented."[11] *Unprecedented* was the word. Between September 10 and September 16 alone, Mexican 6 percents fell 16 percent.

6 *Analysis of the Memorial Presented by the Secretary of the Treasury to the First Constitutional Congress of the United Mexican States . . .*, p. 45.

7 See Victoria's message on the closing of Congress in 1826 in *Aguila Mejicana*, May 26, 1826, reproduced in Bustamante, *Diario Histórico de México*, Anexos, May 1826.

8 O'Gorman to [unknown], México, September 18, 1827, FO 50/35, PRO.

9 O'Gorman to Viscount Dudly, México, October 13, 1827, FO 50/35, PRO.

10 August 19, 1827.

11 September 16, 1827.

On the evening of September 14, 1827, Minister Vicente Rocafuerte announced that "he had no funds in hand to pay the dividends due." By September 25, discussion in the Chamber of Deputies had turned to why the funds to pay the dividends were not at hand and the disastrous impact that default would have on Mexican credit abroad.[12] Even though speculators moved in hoping that funds from Mexico would arrive, the stock exchange was said to be in a state of "agitation." The prospect of default had taken 20 percent off Mexican bonds in a single week.[13] So, as a result, the actual default was a nonevent in the sense that October 1 brought no news. "It was expected by many that some notification of the payment of the dividends would be made public today, but nothing whatever has transpired."[14] For the remainder of the year, the bonds rose and fell on rumors, plausible and otherwise, of the prospect of payment. But none was made. By early December, the dividend due on January 1, 1828, no longer seemed likely to materialize. Rocafuerte, who had previously informed Victoria that a default would have caused him "to die of shame," tried to talk Mexico's credit up, and succeeded, albeit briefly.[15] In the event, no payment was made until April 16, 1828. And even then, resumption lasted only until October 27, 1828. By June 1829, the "arrears" of dividend payments missed amounted to more than 4 million pesos, and relative to the price of consols in 1824, Mexican bonds had lost 70 percent of their value.[16]

In light of these facts, some of the behind-the-scenes maneuvering was distinctly odd, and the huge collapse that occurred just prior to default suggests that the market had been taken by some surprise. This included some people who should have known better, or may have had reasons for wishing otherwise. For example, Robert Manning reported that neither Victoria nor his ministers seemed much disturbed at Baring Brothers' refusal to pay the dividends, the proximate cause of the Mexican default, although one inevitably wonders how much of this apparent insouciance was really quite studied. "Such is the sense," Manning wrote, "they entertain of the importance of their credit abroad!" Manning continued "that the Minister of Finance" – no longer José Ignacio Esteva, but Francisco García – "should have received the intelligence with such sang froid to me is not surprising." "I confidentially knew," said Manning, "he was determined to send in his resignation and consequently cared little for the future." "What

12 Carlos María de Bustamante, *Diario Histórico de México, 1822–1848*, Anexos, Octubre de 1827.
13 *Times* (London), September 16, 1827.
14 *Times* (London), September 30, 1827.
15 Rocafuerte to the president of Mexico, London, September 4, 1826, in Esteva, *Contestación á las observaciones del señor contador de crédito público sobre la cuenta y memoria del ramo referente a los ocho primeros meses del año de 1825*, pp. 37–38.
16 *Memoria de Hacienda, 1830* (México, 1831), p. 13.

can I say," he concluded, "in defense of persons so indifferent to the interests of their country?"[17]

But it may also be that the Federation thought it could find some way out. Manning and Marshall themselves alluded to such a possibility in September 1827, reporting to Baring Brothers that the Mexican government would be able to pay Barings for the dividends already furnished by getting a loan from a certain "Mr. Wilson." "If this is the case," they reported, "our joint [venture] will turn out very profitable." It is hard to imagine that such a venture involved anything other than speculation in Mexican bonds.[18] Indeed, Manning and Marshall had spent August in warning Mexico of the consequences of default. "We reminded [then Finance Minister Tomás Salgado] of the discredit that would accrue to this government if a house of [Baring's] standing and character were to break off connections with [Mexico]." Or even more bluntly, "We very distinctly pointed out to him the serious results which would follow the non-payment of the dividends." As a result, Manning and Marshall said, "[Salgado] appeared to be sensible of our arguments and immediately assured us that there was money to be shipped by the first man of war." Satisfied that they had "frightened" Salgado, Manning and Marshall concluded that "[we] cannot imagine that any serious disturbance can take place so as to materially affect the prosperity of the Republic."[19] It would be easy to conclude that Manning and Marshall were out to make money by convincing Barings to keep the tap open, but it is also important to remember that optimism (or greed) can get in the way of common sense.

If Salgado possessed no real sense of urgency about default, it may well have been because he had other colleagues in government who also minimized its importance. The congressional deputy from Michoacán, Francisco Manuel Sánchez de Tagle, saw no reason to panic either. Commenting on a proposed short-term loan from the "House of Wilson" to provide the resources to avoid default, Sánchez de Tagle pronounced himself skeptical of any such plan. There were no unanticipated shortfalls in revenue, he commented – just the plain reluctance of the states to pay their share of the *contingente* and the apparent inability of the Federation to do much about it. But even if there had been a problem, Sánchez de Tagle complained, borrowing to make up the shortfall would have been a bad idea. The British, he argued, were not so stupid. They would have seen the extraordinary means to which Mexico had been pushed to make its October payments, and this would have redounded to Mexico's credit not a whit. If the idea of creditworthiness was to ensure the future availability of funds, paying off the British this way was not likely to have the desired result. Besides,

17 Manning to Baring Brothers, México, November 28, 1827, HC 4.5.2 10a, BBA.
18 Manning and Marshall to Baring Brothers, México, September 22, 1827, HC 4.5.2 5ᵃ, BBA.
19 Manning and Marshall to Baring Brothers, México, August 11, 1827, HC4.5.2. 3ᵃ, BBA.

Sánchez de Tagle concluded, if Mexico didn't pay, it could end up buying its bonds in the secondary market for 20 or 25 rather than the prevailing price in the 50s. "Let the market open and see how many millions they'll sell us at this price." While this hardly smacks of fiscal prudence, Sánchez de Tagle's intuition that "they need us as much as we need them" has the distinct air of Keynes' famous jibe more than a century later about whose problem a defaulted loan really was, the borrower's or the lender's.[20]

The 1820s were, of course, a time when investors and statesmen were nothing, if not bullish on Mexico, even to the point, perhaps, of assuming, in modern terms, that countries do not go broke or are simply too important to fail. One senses as much in the words and writings of well-connected British political figures who could have had no idea of what the future would bring and who did not regard the default teleologically as one of a chain of inevitable events that would bring Mexico to grief. H. G. Ward, as astute an observer of the economy as one could hope for, thought the default had ruined Mexico's credit in European markets. Yet he regarded its financial embarrassments of 1827 as "temporary"; the simple consequence of pressures abroad in the Finance Ministry in 1826 makes things look good for foreign investors, to overestimate revenues and underestimate expenditures. Here was a wealthy country whose silver mines were far from exhausted and whose output would be back to prewar levels by 1835, a prediction that was not far wrong.[21] When William Huskisson, Member of Parliament for Liverpool, addressed Parliament about Mexico in May 1830, he made no mention of the default whatsoever. Mexico was important for Britain, indeed for Europe as a whole, because it offered a potentially ample market for manufactures and, in return, supplied silver, whose monetary importance could hardly be understated. After a decade of deflation and suffering from an outbreak of rural violence and artisan radicalism in 1830, Britain needed Mexican silver to arrest the fall in the price level. Hence, Huskisson reasoned, Britain needed Mexico, in whose recovery it had a vital interest.[22] Finance was too important to be left to bankers and bondholders.

What Now?

To have said that the Mexican government evinced no concern over default was, however, at best an exaggeration. By early December, the secretary

---

20 Sánchez de Tagle's congressional speech of September 25, 1827, is reproduced in Bustamante, *Diario histórico de México*, Anexos, October 1827.

21 *México en 1827*, pp. 256–259, 294, 383, 405–406, 408.

22 William Huskisson, *The Speeches of the Right Honourable William Huskisson with a Biographical Memoir Supplied to the Editor from Authentic Sources* (3 vols.; London, 1831), vol. 3: pp. 569–587. Also see E. J. Hobsbawm and G. F. E. Rudé, *Captain Swing* (Hammondswoth, 1973); and W. S. Jevons, "On the Variation of Prices and the Value of Currency Since 1782," in E. M. Carus-Wilson, ed., *Essays in Economic History* (3 vols.; London, 1962), vol. 3: pp. 1–28.

of the British legation, Richard Pakenham, had reported that the Mexican Congress had on November 21 passed a law authorizing the finance minister to raise a loan of $4 million "for the purpose of paying the dividend on the public debt and other urgent demands upon the Treasury."[23] Unfortunately, added Pakenham, "no person has been found to supply the money." "I fear," he concluded, "there is little prospect of any remittance being made to the English Creditors." Pakenham had urged both Victoria and the finance minister to avoid temporizing and, if necessary, to state that the government faced payment problems. Anything, Pakenham thought, was preferable to letting the matter simply cause increasing uncertainty.

And it did act. On May 23, 1828, the government promulgated a decree by which one-eighth of the customs revenue would be set aside for payments on the London Debt, since Mexico "wished to restore its credit at any cost . . . the impoverishment which affects it notwithstanding." A law of October 2, 1830, raised the payment to one-sixth of the available revenues from the customs at both Veracruz and Tampico.[24] Under the insistent prodding of the British minister, the Federation had come to institute the policy of earmarking customs revenue that would become known as "the funds."

Yet it was one thing to specify that part of the customs revenue should be earmarked to pay the foreign debt. Collecting it – especially, collecting it in cash – proved quite another matter. One official complained that very little cash was actually collected in Veracruz. Instead, merchants who incurred duties on shipments used government obligations endorsed in their favor to discharge their debts. These were the various and sundry "credits" of the Federation that circulated at large discounts; to the extent that they could be used to satisfy customs duties (or even fund loans!) instead of cash, the nominal duties collected and liquid funds available were very different. This official complained that he didn't get much that could be sent on to the Treasury. "You can't segregate the funds when what resources there are keep shrinking. I have warned the authorities about the very serious consequences of their policies."[25]

These policies effectively turned gold into dross, because, for example, a government IOU written against the customs might be worth little in cash, but much more when negotiable for duties payable on imports. One critic claimed that the practice reduced the nominal level of duties on foreign goods to half of what the tariff schedules demanded.[26] Lest one

---

23 Pakenham to [unknown], México, December 3, 1827, FO 50/36, PRO.

24 *Memoria de Hacienda, 1830*, p. 14, and *Memoria de Hacienda, 1831* (México, 1832), p. 18.

25 Fausto Aceves to the finance minister, Veracruz, July 2, 1828 (*corte cantidad* translated as "he didn't get much").

26 M. F. A., *Reflecsiones sobre el tesoro público de México por un verdadero amante y colaborador de su independencia* (Puebla, 1836), p. 9.

think that this estimate be wildly biased (published in Puebla, perhaps, by a disgruntled industrialist for whom nothing short of prohibition was adequate protection), a committee to reform the treasury published a series of revealing estimates for 1833 through 1840 which show that the actual reduction was 48 percent. After deducting payments on contracts to the *agiotistas*, or private government financiers, the Federation was left with derisory sums: as little as 2.3 million pesos in cash in 1836–1837, or "as much" as 12.1 million pesos in 1838.[27] Shortage begot shortage. Because the government's rate of discount was high, it placed a low value on future income, preferring to anticipate revenues in this way. Defaulting on dividend payments was one result.

Not that there were no choices to be made. As Lucas Alamán was to remark, the law of May 23, 1828, "was not enforced because while a part of the receipts from customs was pledged for [this] purpose, the whole of those receipts were in fact employed to cover the expenses of the government."[28] What expenses? Manning and Marshall informed Baring Brothers in Spring 1828 that "there is no money in the Treasury and the Minister [i.e., José Ignacio Pavón] in order to secure sufficient to pay the troops will submit to anything provided the day of payment be distant."[29] By early 1829, the story had changed not a whit: "[T]he Government finds itself unable to pay the troops [and] remittances to England are at present out of the question."[30] Events such as the Spanish reinvasion of 1829 drained resources and simply raised the opportunity cost of servicing the debt to unacceptable levels. So, added to the unavailability of fresh external funds, there were important – indeed, vital – questions of domestic politics that involved competing constituencies. What now, indeed?

To resolve a problem, it is first necessary to understand it, to ascertain its dimensions, and to identify the range of causes and possible remedies. And this the Federation now set out to do, with the added complication that the situation was unprecedented and its analysis uncertain. Much would depend on the abilities, commitments, loyalties, and personalities of the ministers involved. Manning called the finance minister who assumed the portfolio in the beginning of November 1827 (i.e., García) "a straightforward and honorable man." "[T]he few attentions he has already adopted in his department has [*sic*] given general satisfaction."[31] Within three weeks, Manning had changed his mind about García, arguing that García had been

27 [J. Espinosa] *Bases del Plan de Hacienda Pública que... Deben Fijar a Marcha de Desarrollo* (México, 1841), Table "Estado que demuestra el juego de todos los valores que han compuesto las cuentas del ministerio...."
28 Lucas Alamán to the minister of the Mexican Republic in England, March 5, 1830, in *Proceedings of the Committee of the Holders of Mexican Bonds... the 26th of May, 1830* (London, 1830), pp. 3–4.
29 Manning and Marshall to Baring Brothers, México, March 4, 1828, HC 4.5.2. 22, BBA.
30 Manning and Marshall to Baring Brothers, México, January 31, 1829, HC 4.5.2. 21ª, BBA.
31 Robert Manning to Baring Brothers, México, November 7, 1827, HC 4.5.2.8, BBA.

the beneficiary of party factionalism that had resulted in the resignation of Esteva. When Esteva did resume the position in 1828, Manning was much cheered, calling Esteva a partisan of War Minister Manuel Gómez Pedraza, whom Manning judged sympathetic to merchant banks such as Baring Brothers.[32] This was quite important, since the finance minister had control over which syndicate of lenders would be deemed successful in bidding for the right to finance the internal debt, a lucrative prize as well as a competing demand for financial resources when repayment fell due.[33] O'Gorman too praised Esteva as finance minister, saying that he had administered the Treasury well, something O'Gorman never thought about Esteva's predecessor.[34] As finance minister, Esteva monitored the performance of Mexico's bonds on the London Stock Exchange with great care. In the aftermath of the horrific crash of the London market in December 1825, foreign bonds would fluctuate wildly for most of 1826. Esteva viewed the fall in price of Mexican bonds with considerable alarm. Writing to Rocafuerte, Esteva observed that "some of the bonds had fallen to an unbelievably low price, one scarcely credible."[35] Esteva's use of "credible" is an interesting one, quite modern in its implications. For Barclay, Herring, Richardson had put the matter plainly: "The price of the foreign funds [i.e., bonds and equities most generally] on the London Stock Exchange is the index that serves as a political barometer; and in the Europe, the credit of the state is an indication of the stability of the government."[36] Esteva was only too aware that the credibility of the Federation – perhaps of Mexico more generally – was the issue in default and that the movements of bond prices *could*, albeit not necessarily *should*, be read as a commentary on the twists and turns of Mexican political affairs. Blamed by a group of Spanish expatriates in London for the decline in Mexican bond prices because of his 1825 *Memoria de Hacienda*, Esteva argued that their fall in no way signaled a lack of faith in Mexico's credit in general, but was driven by specific events such as various barracks revolts in Mexico, the arrival of Spanish frigates in Havana harbor, or even "combinations of Jewish bankers" that had brought down all the funds, including British consols.[37] So it had fallen to Esteva to define and interpret the issues involved for the international financial community, something that would presumably provide one of the bases on which the Mexican government would make policy and decide what to do,

---

32 Robert Manning to Baring Brothers, México, September 20, 1828, HC 4.5.2.18, BBA.

33 See *El Sol*, December 19, 1829, supplement to number 172.

34 Charles T. O'Gorman to [unknown], México, January 15, 1827, FO 50/37, PRO.

35 Esteva to the Mexican chargé d'affaires in London, México, January 15, 1827, FO 50/37, PRO.

36 Barclay, Herring, Richardson to the finance minister, London [1824?], *Deuda Exterior*, vol. 12, AGNM.

37 *A los Españoles Ociosos en Londres. Un Mexicano Ocupado Contestando al Número 20 de su Periódico* (México, 1826).

for some things could be controlled (dividend payments) and some things (Spanish frigates, Semitic combinations) could not be.

Rocafuerte, too, in London demonstrated his desire to find some expedient way out of default. In Rocafuerte's view, the way out involved jettisoning Baring's financial agency for the patronage of Rothschild. Writing Esteva's successor in 1829, he said,

> you know that Señor Rothschild is the most powerful capitalist in the world, a man with great influence in the mercantile sphere . . . [If Rothschild were to become Mexico's financial agent in Europe], it would be necessary to resolve to send by packet out of Veracruz 20, 30, 40, or 50 thousand pesos, but never less than 20 thousand. It will also be necessary to give every shipment we send to Señor Rothschild as much publicity as possible in English newspapers as well as our own. We should avail ourselves of the prestige that Rothschild's name brings to reconcile ourselves with our European creditors to strengthen our own credit. Observing strict regularity is more important than the amount we send.[38]

In the event, this turned out to be remarkably close to the strategy that, by design or default, most governments in Mexico would observe until the outbreak of the War of 1847 put paid to any chance at all of continuing payments of any sort.

A similar desire motivated Rafael Mangino, a fiscal bureaucrat who succeeded Esteva as finance minister in the 1830s. Mangino was nothing if not knowledgeable. His pedigree in office went back to the Bourbon monarchy.[39] His position might be characterized as one of cautious optimism. O'Gorman reported a conversation with Mangino in which Mangino "candidly confessed to me that he does not see the remotest chance for some years to come of the Mexican nation being able to pay the arrears of the dividends now due." But, O'Gorman continued, "[h]e is confident in case no fresh [Spanish] invasion occurs and that good order and tranquility are maintained that next year's [i.e., 1832] dividend will be paid and also the interest upon the amount of the arrears if the Bondholders agree to the prospect of capitalizing them."[40] So by 1830 or so, officials of the Federation were discussing elements of a plan that included paying something, paying consistently, and trying to induce the London bondholders to accept capitalization of the arrears or missed dividend payments. Mangino shared in the sentiment that it was important to rehabilitate Mexico's credit in the international market. "The present government [of Anastasio Bustamante]

---

38 Rocafuerte to the finance minister, June 4, 1829, *Hacienda Pública, Carpetas Azules*, 1828–1839, 2da, AGNM.

39 "Rafael Mangino y Mendivil," in Linda Arnold, ed., *Directorio de Burócratas en la Ciudad de México, 1761–1832* (México, 1980), p. 161.

40 O'Gorman to Percy Bidwell, México, June 10, 1830, FO 50/62, PRO.

desires at all costs to recover its credit by adhering to the law, its poverty notwithstanding." For "once lost, [its] credit [can only be reestablished] with time, good faith, and considerable effort."[41]

Mangino had considerable incentive to take the problem seriously. Another element of the emerging response was contributed by Manning and Marshall, who reported to Baring Brothers that

we lose no opportunity of pressing [Mangino] . . . on remittances on account of the dividends. We must do the Minister this justice to say that he is exerting himself for the accomplishment of that objective, and that on the last packet an order was sent to Mr. Gorostiza [i.e., Manuel Eduardo Gorostiza, appointed chargé d'affaires in London in 1829] desiring him to call a meeting of the principal Bondholders in order that they may appoint an agent properly and duly authorized to secure here one-eighth part of the Customs house.

Gorostiza did just this, but when his instructions arrived, they came from Alamán. Clearly, the subject had come up for discussion in Bustamante's cabinet, where the initial plan was undoubtedly formulated.[42]

The final piece of the puzzle was figuring out exactly how much was owed, a difficult subject under the best of circumstances, when the amount of interest accrued normally changed every day. But what we have referred to in our previous chapter as administrative incapacity and "loose ends" in Mexico made the matter of resolving on a course of action even more complex. For example, in March 1827, a report to the *oficial mayor* of the finance ministry observed that

there should be some account of the sums delivered to Michelena in London, but I am given to understand that the accounts of the loans coming from London are not what they should be and the government has made a number of claims in the matter. But according to our best intelligence, it isn't possible to give an account as clear and updated as one might expect.[43]

Another report admitted that "in the Ministry we should find some account of the exchange rate [from May 1824 through June 1825]."[44] It was nowhere to be found.

These issues were also raised by Lorenzo de Zavala as finance minister in 1829, when he complained bitterly about the administrative chaos that ruled the finance ministry, with its "inextricable confusion of debts,

41 *Memoria de Hacienda, 1830*, p. 14, and *Memoria de Hacienda, 1832*, p. 14.
42 Manning and Marshall to Baring Brothers, México, March 25, 1830, HC 4.5.2 29, BBA.
43 See the report by Ildefonso Maniau, México, March 29, 1827, *Hacienda Pública, Carpetas Azules*, 2da, AGNM.
44 Report to the *oficial mayor* of Hacienda, México, June 7, 1828, *Hacienda Pública, 1827, Carpetas Azules*, 2da, AGNM.

borrowings, salary arrears, advances and more." "A merchant house," he concluded, "is better administered than our public fisc: commissaries, customs houses, treasuries, all obscured by an enveloping chaos."[45] As late as 1870, Matías Romero remained scandalized by the records of the era. In matters of foreign borrowing, he said, "you have to be as precise as possible." Unfortunately, Romero continued, because of inexperience, mistakes were made. "The data is so incomplete as to make it impossible to understand by reading the annual reports of the Finance Ministers alone!" It would eventually reach the point, in 1842, that Alamán would be commissioned to determine how accounts with the bondholders stood. According to Romero, Alamán's report was the "first understandable report about the negotiations for the loans, their proceeds and disbursement, and about how these brought about the ruin of public finance."[46] This inevitably raises the issue of how much of the dispute between the bondholders and Mexico was a consequence of confusion, rather than substantive disagreement – or perhaps, of substantive disagreement largely born of confusion?

The Bondholders (and Mexico) Reply

In 1827, William Fletcher, an erstwhile ship's surgeon, was appointed hospital assistant at Sierra Leone by the British Army Medical Board. Shortly after arriving, the unfortunate Fletcher took ill with a fever and died. Poor Fletcher. After a career that had taken him to Gibraltar, India, and Spain – and which visited him with cholera and a host of other ailments – Fletcher had managed to accumulate a little money. He did this, it seems, by doing a little moneylending himself, especially while in India. When Fletcher's brother – Joseph, an unemployed clerk – learned of his death, he immediately made inquiries about William's belongings. He was especially interested in Mexican bonds of which he believed William to have been in possession of.

William's stockbroker confirmed that he had indeed purchased Mexican bonds in January 1827. In particular, the stockbroker documented William's market activity in early 1827. On January 9, 1827, William sold five hundred "New Fours" at 94.75. He then invested the proceeds in seven hundred Mexican bonds at 65.5. It was these bonds, their disposition, that so keenly interested William's brother, Joseph. The bonds had apparently vanished or, worse, been stolen, since as bearer bonds, they were valuable to anyone in their possession. Joseph obviously thought these to be the most valuable (or only) part of William's estate. Unfortunately, it is not clear how

---

45 Lorenzo de Zavala, *Esposición del secretario del despacho de hacienda . . . a las cámaras de la unión a su ingreso al despacho del ramo* (México, 1829), p. 7.

46 *Memoria de Hacienda, 1870*, par. 322.

the story ends. Baring Brothers, in whose employ William's stockbroker was, had advanced the claim as far as Mexico, where the trail goes cold in the archives.[47]

Fletcher, of course, was a person of modest means. His capital, some £450 of it, could hardly compare to the £70,000 that Miss Crawley had in consols in Thackeray's *Vanity Fair* or to the more substantial accumulations of Mexican bonds found throughout the British Isles, in France, Holland, and Germany. There were bondholders in the East Indies as well.[48] What exactly did the British bondholders learn of the fate of their purchases in the 1820s and 1830s? At first, not much good news. In January 1828, the *Times* (London) reported that "it [is] understood that a small quantity of dollars was on its way." But no such payment appeared, which meant that "the Bondholders have so often been hoaxed that until the dollars arrive in this country their bonds will not be fully made up." During the week of January 20, 1828, letters from Veracruz stated that none of the silver arriving in Veracruz was destined to pay interest or principal on the Mexican debt, and the bonds fell 5 percent on the London Stock Exchange as a result. On February 2, the Mexican packet arrived, but it held no specie to pay the dividends.[49] On February 10, the *Times* (London) sarcastically referred to the Mexican bonds as the "crack stock of the South American states [that] have sunk to 35 and $\frac{1}{2}$, about 10 percent under their value a fortnight since. Around May 25, they underwent still another wild ride, closing at 28 and $\frac{3}{4}$." The cause, once again, was said to be "advices received from Mexico through the United States as to the shipment of dollars . . . [It] appears that not a single dollar has been received . . . [W]hat is worse, no prospect is held out of any remittances." Two weeks later, the bonds closed at 26 "in a terrible plight from the knowledge of the fact that the Government does not possess one-fourth of the sum due to the holders for dividends." On June 29, "the Bondholders have again been duped by favorable news from Mexico." But here a new theme emerged, one that would also prove quite relevant to the situation: "Until the revenues of the Mexican Government should have so far improved as to enable it to pay its domestic debts, it is certain that foreign claimants must wait."[50] The rumors and cold realities were so often repeated that by August 1828, the whole business of there is money, there is not, prices rise, and prices fall was simply called "a repetition of the old story 'that the most strenuous exertions were making by the Finance Minister of Mexico to raise money that the Bondholders be paid'."[51]

---

47 See *Gobernación*, leg. 91, caja 151, exp. 1, fs. 381–398, AGNM.
48 *Proceedings of the Committee of the Holders of Mexican Bonds . . . the 26th of May, 1830*, p. 24.
49 See variously January 6, January 20, February 3, 1828.
50 See variously February 10, May 25, June 8, June 29, 1828.
51 *Times* (London), August. 31, 1828.

Yet, as we have seen, there was *something* to the "old story" of "strenuous efforts," at least by early 1830. At the time of the default, the Federation had offered to capitalize the arrears of the loans (i.e., add the unpaid interest to the outstanding principal), issuing new bonds at 5 or 6 percent, depending on in which loan the bondholders had participated. A similar arrangement was floated on June 5, 1829, offering to capitalize the arrears through January 1830 with 5 percent bonds. Finally, on October 2, 1830, the Federation announced once more that it would capitalize any interest payment, current or otherwise, which fell due until April 1, 1831, and half of those that fell due between that date and April 1, 1836. The arrears would be capitalized at 62.5 percent on the 5 percent loan and at 75 percent on the 6 percent loan. Both would be repaid by a lien of 16 percent on the maritime customs of Veracruz and Tampico.[52]

What was remarkable about these arrangements is that, by and large, they represented almost entirely the substance of the proposals made by the Committee of the Holders of Mexicans Bonds to the Mexican government. It took three years for the bondholders to come around, three years of the "old story" of "strenuous efforts" and disappointed hopes, and of surging and falling bond prices, but when they did, they accommodated themselves to the Mexican position and made it their own. How and why did this happen? How did an arrangement seemingly unacceptable in 1827 become acceptable in 1830?

The first reason, perhaps, is to recognize the gradual accommodation of markets to the inevitable. In January 1829, when the capitalization of arrears seemed all but certain, Mexican bonds lost 26 percent of their value in one month. When the proposal to capitalize the arrears was announced in June 1829, the relative price of Mexican bonds stood at 28. But by October 1830, it had risen to 47 – an improvement of 67 percent! The uncertainty around Mexican bonds simply grew until a concrete proposal was made. After the initial shock wore off, Mexican bonds rose thereafter, almost as if the bondholders, given sufficient time to absorb the news, slowly priced the proposal into their expectations, especially once the Committee of Bondholders had assented. The committee met – publicly, at least – on May 26, 1830 to explain its position on the payment of arrears and their capitalization in a new issue of bonds.

Indeed, the unusual reduction of interest accruing between 1831 and 1836 was presented by the committee as a way of staving off a further period of default by insisting on a close compliance to the terms of the original issue. Yet the committee's flexibility was hardly the product of altruism. The published proceedings state that the arrangement was intended to "prevent the Bondholders from being subject to those injurious and violent

---

52 *Memoria de Hacienda, 1830,* p. 13, and *Memoria de Hacienda,* 1870, par. 337.

fluctuations in the price of the bonds, which are sure to arise, if when the quarterly payments of interest shall recommence, they be not regularly continued."[53] In other words, having experienced default – its swings of rumor, hope, and fear – the bondholders had adjusted to reality. They would take what Mexico offered if Mexico offered anything reasonable. And what seemed reasonable in 1830 was different from what seemed reasonable in 1827. More cynically, the bondholders could always sell new paper for something, which was better than waiting around for the republic to send nothing. In the short run, then, the capitalization of arrears made some sense. In the long run, it led Mexico, at least, to catastrophe.

Times, of course, had changed as well. With the revolt of Bustamante against the government of Vicente Guerrero, a new regime – centralist *avant la lettre* – came to power.[54] This government, which had as its éminence grise Alamán, proved more sympathetic to the British bondholders than its predecessors. It was concerned with strengthening the federal government and the national executive, limiting the franchise and reducing the power of the civic militias. With such "developmental" innovations as Alamán's Banco de Avío as its centerpiece, the government would remain in place until the liberal reaction of 1832. In a pattern that was to subsequently reassert itself, the London Stock Exchange enthused over its financial prospects and Mexican bond prices rose from 26 in January 1830 to a high of 39 in June 1831. The shift that produced the increase was readily discernable.[55]

Accordingly, in March 1830, Gorostiza had received instructions from this government to call the meeting of the bondholders to effect a settlement of their claims.[56] Gorostiza watched the London market carefully. He was especially sensitive to the impact of events on bond prices and, presumably, their effects on investors and speculators. In the popular unrest leading up to the passage of the Reform Law (1832) in Great Britain, Gorostiza perceived some opportunity. On the one hand, he wrote,

the popular movements that occurred in [London] on the opening of Parliament, although no serious thing in themselves, nevertheless had an effect on the English funds. Consols – which were most solid – fell 7 percent in 2 days, what a scandal, something unseen since 1815. It should come as no surprise that the foreign funds, which follow the consols, fell in proportion to them – [Mexican bonds] dropped to 30.

53 *Proceedings of the Committee of the Holders of Mexican Bonds . . . the 26th of May, 1830*, p. 28.
54 Costeloe, *La Primera República Federal*, pp. 249–327.
55 Will Fowler, "Joseph Welsh: A British Santanista (Mexico, 1832)," *Journal of Latin American Studies*, 36 (2004), esp. pp. 43–44.
56 Manning and Marshall to Baring Brothers, México, March 25, 1830, HC 4.5.2.29, BBA.

However, and here Gorostiza saw the silver lining, the Mexicans could seize the opportunity so offered. He wrote, "Lucky for us, the good news that the packet ship from Mexico brought regarding the state of the country and the Bondholders' hopes that their proposals (i.e., those made in May 1830) might be realized coincided exactly to the benefit of our credit." "On that very day," he continued, "the consols continued to fall while ours went up by more than 2." Gorostiza fairly exulted,

There couldn't be better circumstances. [Our bonds] will go up by 8 to 10 percent. Yesterday they closed at 36 and $\frac{1}{2}$ and there they'll stay with some bouncing around until the next packet arrives. So we'll hope that the law (i.e., segregating customs funds) will have been approved and the news that the vice-consuls in Veracruz and Tampico have gotten the agreed on 16 percent. May God grant this because if we continue faithfully to pay what is owed, *it's virtually certain that we'll get whatever we want in the market.*[57] [italics mine]

In other words, the receptiveness of the bondholders to a compromise was itself heavily influenced by conditions in Britain and Mexico, and in early 1830, political and financial conditions there, and elsewhere on the Continent, were more likely than not to produce a flexible approach to the issues raised by default.[58] Moreover, in February 1830, the threat of further Spanish military action in Cuba appeared to recede, something that could only secure the commercial activity and customs revenues of Veracruz and Tampico from the previous disturbances to which they had been subject.[59] As if to emphasize this point, Huskisson, Member of Parliament for Liverpool, spoke to Parliament on May 20, 1830, of Britain being "deeply interested in the tranquility, welfare, and prosperity of Mexico." As a result, Huskisson added, "Cuba ought not to be allowed to become the point from which expeditions attack Mexico."[60] Thus, in Spring 1830, both Mexico and the bondholders were able to contemplate a financial arrangement with much greater confidence, if not certainty, than previously and even though the outbreak of the war of the South in mid-March 1830 would place the Federation under severe financial strain.

New adjustments in Mexican commercial policy abetted these circumstances. The (nominal) maritime customs from July 1, 1830, to June 30, 1831, were 8.3 million pesos, an enormous increase in the 4.8 million registered from July 1, 1829, to June 30, 1830. The increase occurred because

---

57 Gorostiza to the finance minister, London, November 20, 1830, *Hacienda Pública, Carpetas Azules*, 4ª, 1820–1824, AGNM.

58 Ferguson, *House of Rothschild*, pp. 227–228.

59 *Times* (London), February 20, 1830, and C. T. O'Gorman [?] to the British vice-consul in Tampico, México, July 8, 1829, FO 203/14, PRO.

60 *Speeches of the Right Honourable William Huskisson*, vol. 3: pp. 570, 575.

relaxation in prohibitions specified by the tariff allowed a larger volume of imports and, hence, duties collected.[61] Mexico's capacity to pay thus increased.

At this point, it appears that minister of home and foreign relations, Alamán, managed to convince the London bondholders that they were the recipients of the Federation's especial largess. On March 5, 1830, through Gorostiza, Alamán reported that previous domestic loans contracted in 1827 and 1828 for 4 million pesos had been suspended "with the consent of the creditors," thereby releasing funds that would have serviced the domestic debt. In reality, the suspension was a rescheduling (through laws of March 4 and September 4, 1830) that raised 1.2 million pesos in anticipation of customs revenues. While later analysts such as Romero were ultimately skeptical of the long-run consequences of these measures, Alamán's gestures were viewed as eminently pro-British, and O'Gorman observed that "nothing can be more friendly and cordial than [Mexico's] disposition toward Great Britain." Indeed, the British Foreign Office would later claim that the Mexican expedient of setting aside customs revenues in favor of servicing the London Debt had been pressed on the Finance Ministry by the British minister in Mexico. As a result, Mexican finances were reported in the British press "to be in a better state than for some time past and [Alamán] is said to have a considerable amount due from mercantile houses on account of duties."[62] Alamán, on the other hand, had his own sources in Great Britain and monitored the financial and political situation quite carefully, so he knew what he was doing. His informant was none other than Francisco Borja Migoni.[63]

Everybody Wants to Be Played

Gorostiza was a distinguished littérateur, diplomat, and indeed, heir to a portion of the estate of Viceroy Revillagigedo the Younger.[64] He had a hand in organizing Mexico's first commercial consulates abroad in 1824.[65] In June 1829, he had been requested to negotiate a settlement with

61 *Cuestión del Día. Reflecsiones Sobre la Hacienda Pública, el Crédito . . .* (México, 1853), table 2, "Aduanas Marítimas," and notes.

62 *Memoria de Hacienda, 1870*, par. 386; Charles T. O'Gorman to the commander-in-chief of the Jamaica Station, México, May 5, 1830, FO 203/16, PRO; *Memorandum Relative to the Relations Existing between Great Britain and Mexico with Regard to the Claims of the British Bondholders* ([London], 1869), p. 4, which misdates the action to 1833; *Times* (London), April 1, 1831.

63 Borja Migoni to Lucas Alamán, London, October 20, 1831, *Hospital de Jesús*, vol. 440, exp. 2, AGNM.

64 For a brief profile, see Ángela Moyano Pahissa, "Manuel Eduardo de Gorostiza," *Cancilleres De México* (2 vols.; México, 1992), vol. 1: pp. 191–197.

65 *Los primeros consulados de México*, p. 17, and *Representantes diplomáticos de México en Washington, 1822–1973* (México, 1974), pp. 16–17.

Barclay, Herring, Richardson stemming from the considerable monies due to Mexico that remained undistributed when the firm suspended operations.[66] In the view of Baring Brothers, Gorostiza had been given full power to handle financial affairs of the Mexican government in London.[67] In 1836, he would be named Envoy Extraordinaire to the United States. He presented his credentials to President Andrew Jackson scarcely three weeks after the Battle of the Alamo.

In late 1829, Gorostiza revealed that he had been contacted by a merchant bank named Marcos Crespo and Company whose principal was a native of Guayaquil.[68] It was a small firm, he observed, but he was confident that he could draw on the resources of a couple of larger firms as well. Crespo and Company's timing was hardly a coincidence. The capitulation of the Spaniards at Tampico had brought "another new house of the first rank" into the picture. It, too, wanted to lend, or so it was said. Presumably, acting as Mexico's financial agent was one of the things Crespo and Company wanted.[69] Gorostiza characterized the firm's proposal as "a great financial operation that would reduce interest payments by means of a conversion loan." Gorostiza suggested that the operation might be carried out by another partner – he suggested Baring Brothers, an unlikely choice – presumably to keep the cost of the conversion down. It was, he observed, a matter of robbing Peter to pay Paul, for speculators would now lose the opportunity to profit from swings in the price of the defaulted issues. In return, there would be a steady flow of dividends. "It's a play," he concluded, "but everybody wants to be played." Mexico could conceivably end up owing more, but its credit would be the better for the conversion. Gorostiza also insisted that any firm involved in the conversion should own enough of the defaulted issues to be able to make a market for the new issues: "there's no doubt that if a sixth of the bonds are converted in the early stages [by the bankers] then the other Bondholders will be brought along by their example." He also sounded the voice of experience. The funds realized by the conversion should be deposited immediately or should be used to purchase bills of exchange. He wanted no repeat of the Barclay, Herring, Richardson fiasco in which the Mexican government had become an unwilling creditor.

66 Lorenzo de Zavala to Gorostiza, México, June 5, 1829, HC 4.5.4.3, BBA. For more detail, see Chapter 1.

67 Baring Brothers to the finance minister, London, April 20, 1831, *Hacienda Pública*, unclassified papers, 1831, AGNM.

68 Gorostiza to the finance minister, London, November 19, 1829, *Gobernación*, leg. 91, caja 151, exp. 1, fs. 26–31. (*todo el mundo quiere que se le engañe* is translated as "everyone wants to be played.") (*en el acto* is translated as "immediately.")

69 Marcos Crespo and Company to Gorostiza, London, December 10, 1829, *Gobernación*, leg. 91, caja 151, exp. 1, AGNM.

Table 2.1. *Five Percent Loan of February 7, 1824, Amortized
According to the Loan Agreement of 1825*

Principal	3.2 million
Less	0.8 million
Balance of loan	2.4 million
Plus 6 percent loan, 1825	3.2 million
Funds available	5.6 million
Memo Items	
Arrears of interest on 5 percent loan through July 1, 1830	330,000
Plus Arrears of interest on 6 percent loan	528,000
Total Arrears	858,000
Contracted interest on both loans per year	312,000

Note: All values are in pounds sterling.

The actual arrangement that Marcos Crespo and Company proposed was presented by the bank as an act of financial selflessness, Gorostiza demurred. What is particularly interesting about the proposal is that it alludes to a few merchant banks that held positions in Mexican bonds. This suggests that another pressure for settlement was coming from bigger actors than even the Committee of Bondholders. Gorostiza summarized the proposal in a haphazard and somewhat orotund document that he sent back to Mexico City in December 1829. The Mexican government, the proposal read, would save £88,000 per year (440,000 pesos) in interest costs and even the underwriters' commissions would be paid through the issue of the conversion bonds – a dubious economy, but one proposal all the same. Moreover, the Mexican government would pay off at once some 429,000 pesos of accrued interest then in arrears. "The Mexican government will do what is most difficult in treasury operations, the reduction of interest and debt, difficult even for Great Britain," and it would do this "without advancing a red cent." All of this, it was argued, would give Mexico advantages that not even the various European debtors shared.[70]

Marcos Crespo gave an account of the status of the loans (see Table 2.1). According to Marcos Crespo, the 5 *percents* would be converted into a new bond issued at 5 percent; the 6 *percents* would similarly be converted at 6 percent. But Marcos Crespo envisioned a settlement in which, on the 5 *percents*, only 75 percent of the face value of the bonds would be converted into new consolidated bonds on a cash basis. The remainder was to be paid in "propiedades nacionales." The bondholders would be compensated "as

70 As in note 60, but see "Bentajas Económicas." ("*sin tener que hacer abanze pecuniario*" is translated as "without having to advance a red cent.")

an indemnity" by receiving fully a payment of a third on their holdings (i.e., a claim of $30 would be paid at $40). Thirty dollars of the claim would be in new consolidated bonds. The remainder, $10, would be paid in "propiedades nacionales." A similar arrangement was to hold for the *6 percents*. So, hypothetically, $40 in *5 percents* would be converted into $30 of new consolidated 5 percents plus $10 in "propiedades nacionales."

Obviously, Gorostiza was enthusiastic about Marcos Crespo's proposed settlement, pausing only at the prospect of gaining a write-down in principal by using "propiedades nacionales." They might not be worth much at the moment, Gorostiza observed, but with the growth of population and agriculture, national lands, for instance, could be worth a lot. There was nothing very specific about which lands would be used, and in any event, there were laws against the ownership of real property by foreigners. Yet this particular idea, which did not feature in the Conversion of 1830, was an important aspect of the Conversion of 1837. One suspects that it figured prominently in the dynamics of Mexican foreign policy down through the annexation of Texas, for this peculiar form of "lands for bonds" inextricably bound the solution to the foreign debt to the retention of national territory.

It also seems as if the Federation had not ruled out attempting to borrow fresh funds in Great Britain or the United States, and allocating part of the new money to the arrears on the first loans. Joel Poinsett reported that President Guerrero wanted to float a loan in Great Britain and the United States, both in the amount of £5 million. But Poinsett made it clear that he would offer no support for the loans unless the arrears of the previous loans were funded. To be secured on the maritime customs, the loan would be disbursed at $200,000 monthly to the Mexican government: "It would prevent extravagances."[71]

I can find no evidence that such a loan ever took place, although its provisions did not differ from a number of other schemes floating around.[72] A loan for £1.2 million would raise £400,000 in cash and £800,000 in government debts as provided for by Congress. The arrears of the earlier loans would be paid and dividends guaranteed until October 1829. Deposits would be made in the Bank of England and the Bank of the United States, on which Mexico would draw. At the rate of $200,000 per month, the cash would be exhausted in less than a year's time. The underwriters would be given up to two years to deliver the credits so as not to drive up the price

---

71 Manning and Marshall to Baring Brothers, México, March 4, 1829, HC 4.5.2 22, BBA.

72 See, for example, "Propuesta que se hace de un préstamo a la Hacienda Pública," México, November 17, 1829, *Gobernación*, unclassified, leg. 22, exp. 13, AGNM. This proposal envisioned the use of the bonds themselves as part of a fresh loan, along with the customary component of "qualified credit." (*"a cualquier otro modo"* is translated as "or some other means.")

of the paper by chasing the notes. The proposed bond issue would carry a 6 percent coupon with interest payable every six months.

The Federation was explicitly prohibited from altering commercial policy since in so doing, tariff revenues would be affected. Half of its customs revenue would be applied to repayment of the present loan and half to past loans. The contractors' commission was 2.5 percent, while the payment of dividends and the redemption of principal carried a commission of 1.5 percent.

In short, there was a flurry of activity surrounding the foreign debt in late 1829 and early 1830. Gorostiza's point was well taken, for Mexico seemed poised to reenter the international capital markets and fresh funds were available – at a price. Was it that everyone wanted to be played or that everyone, now, wanted to play?

Gorostiza, for his part, wanted to play. Confident that he could rely on Baring Brothers "or some other means" to make up whatever shortfall Mexico experienced in the forthcoming 1832 dividend payments on the original 5 and 6 percent bonds, Gorostiza turned to the prospect of entering the secondary market in an effort to shore up Mexico's credit and support bond prices. Moreover, Gorostiza recommended that the Federation spend 10,000 pesos a month to buy up deferred bonds (see below) as a way of amortizing the arrears the deferred bonds represented at a fraction, say a third, of its nominal value.[73] Sensitive to the charge that the original contractors had fleeced Mexico, Gorostiza saw this as a way of evening things up. But the finance minister, Mangino, vetoed the idea. "[P]resent circumstances don't permit the Treasury to spend additional funds on this."[74]

Capitalization or Conversion?

The actual "Conversion" of 1830 was, in fact, a capitalization of the arrears from default through April 1, 1831. Bonds, the so-called deferred bonds, were to be issued in place of the unpaid interest on the B. A. Goldschmidt and Barclay, Herring, Richardson loans. The bonds were "deferred" in the sense that they would pay no interest (on the capitalized amount of the unpaid interest) until 1836. The original 5 and 6 percent issues, of which about £5.3 million were outstanding, continued to trade and were liable

---

73 Gorostiza to the finance minister, London, November 17, 1831 (reservada), *Hacienda Pública*, unclassified papers, AGNM. Gorostiza had already persuaded Baring Brothers to make up the shortfall in the half-dividend payment of July 1831, but Barings told Mangino that this would not happen again. Hence Gorostiza's insistence in advising Mangino to commit a substantial quantity of Mexican resources as evidence of his bona fides. See Baring Brothers to the finance minister, London, July 21, 1831, *Hacienda Pública*, unclassified papers, AGNM.

74 Mangino to the Mexican minister in London, February 16, 1832, *Hacienda Pública*, unclassified papers, AGNM.

for the resumption of dividend payments in 1831. But they were now accompanied in the market by 5 and 6 percent deferred bonds as well. The relevant decree of Finance Minister Mangino was dated October 2, 1830.[75] In any event, another act of May 20, 1831, was required to approve the agreement made with the bondholders.[76]

An obvious reason for the immediate issue of the deferred bonds was liquidity. An unhappy owner of the original issue could now sell rights to the defaulted interest at whatever discount the market dictated, thus getting out from Mexican bonds completely. Manning pressed hard for the immediate issue of the deferred bonds by Baring Brothers, holding daily meetings with Mangino in an effort to persuade him of the advantages to Mexico, not to mention Barings, of doing so. It was a propitious moment, Manning argued, "particularly as appearances are now in favor of a probability of [Mexico's] being able to redeem a part of that debt for . . . new bonds." Mangino, according to Manning, was willing enough to go along, "provided a clause be inserted in [the bonds] that their amount will be paid in 1836 if before that period the Mexican nation has not paid the original bond from which the new ones originate." Manning clinched the argument by emphasizing that the bondholders had been gravely damaged by what he bluntly called "the malfeasance on the part of the Mexican nation on the original contract."

Mangino understood Manning's argument very well, but feared that he would be unable to gain the support of the Senate and the Chamber of Deputies. In early May 1831, Manning reported to Baring Brothers that he was lobbying the Senate and the Chamber of Deputies vigorously on the issue of the deferred bonds.[77] Mangino patiently explained the details of the conversion to the Chamber of Deputies. He concluded by saying that "the decree authorizing the said funding in the term proposed is a measure to which the government would not be compelled by necessity if it possessed sufficient [funds] to meet the arrears, but in the present case we actually obtain advantages which in other circumstances would not be conceded to us after all."[78] The advantage, presumably, was that Mexico reserved the right to prepay interest on the deferred bonds, in which case they would be cancelled. A similar proviso held for principal payments as well.[79] These conditions, imposed by the Chamber of Deputies, were perhaps what President Bustamante had in mind when he announced, albeit prematurely,

75 HC 4.5.4 5/2, BBA.

76 *Memoria de Hacienda, 1870,* par. 390.

77 Robert Manning to H. S. J. Mildmay, México, April 2, 1831, HC 4.5.2.31, and Robert Manning to Baring Brothers, México, May 2, 1831, HC 4.5.2.32 BBA.

78 Mangino to the Chamber of Deputies, undated, HC 4.5.4.5.1, BBA.

79 Juan Antonio Mateos, *Historia Parlamentaria del os Congresos Mexicanos* (13 vols.; México, 1997), vol. 7: p. 420.

that "the public treasury improves day by day. Our credit in foreign markets is stronger because of our faithful observance of our duties."[80]

When any negotiation is concluded, it is worth asking *cui bono*, or who profited from the arrangement. Certainly the bondholders got something substantial, but not everything. On the one hand, the device of the "deferred bond" and capitalization of arrears was almost precisely what had been agreed to by the Committee of Bondholders in its negotiations with Gorostiza, and Baring Brothers happily termed the scheme "the plan we have adopted." Indeed, Baring Brothers had every reason to be pleased. One of the key figures in the London negotiations was Alexander Baring, whom Gorostiza characterized as participating in talks "out of deference to me." The house wanted guarantees that the arrears would be capitalized before it released any funds, which it got.[81]

Gorostiza also lobbied the bondholders, working closely with John Diston Powles – whom Gorostiza termed "the most influential of the Committee" – a merchant with wide (if shady) Latin American experience and connections to Manning and Mackintosh as well.[82] In fact, Gorostiza used Powles' authority to intimidate other members of the committee, especially Sir Robert Wilson, into agreeing to certain technical points of the conversion, notably, whether subsequent dividends would be paid twice or thrice yearly. At one point, Gorostiza effectively threatened to scuttle the whole deal if Wilson failed to cooperate in the bondholders' name, but without their explicit consent. "Frightened," Gorostiza bragged, "Sir Robert surrendered." "Once we got this last *triumph* [italics mine]," said Gorostiza, "everything else was easy."[83]

Well, maybe not quite that easy. Alamán – who, as minister for home and foreign affairs, was stage-managing the negotiation – had offered to pay a million dollars a year in dividends, a sum rejected by the bondholders as "entirely inadequate." Instead, the Committee of Bondholders pushed for $1.6 million per year – a sum the committee regarded as a show of good faith on Mexico's part, but in reality, about what Mexico owed anyway.[84] Still, this was far in excess of what Mexico could have paid: if Mexico had

---

80 Mateos, *Historia Parlamentaria*, vol. 7: p. 433.

81 Baring Brothers to the finance minister, London, October 20, 1831, *Hacienda Pública*, unclassified papers, AGNM; Gorostiza to the finance minister, London, July 21, 1831, *Deuda Exterior*, vol. 13, AGNM.

82 Gorostiza to the finance minister, London, July 21, 1831, *Deuda Exterior*, vol. 13, AGNM. For biographical information on Powles, see Michael P. Costeloe, *Bonds and Bondholders. British Investors and Mexico's Foreign Debt, 1824–1888* (Westport, CT, 2003), pp. 168–169; and Malcolm Deas, "Powles, John Diston (1787/8–1867)," in H. C. G. Matthew and Brian Harrison, eds., *Oxford Dictionary of National Biography* (Oxford: OUP, 2004). http://www.oxforddnb.com/view/article/57749 (accessed September 28, 2007).

83 Gorostiza to the finance minister, London, July 21, 1831, *Deuda Exterior*, vol. 13, AGNM.

84 John Marshall to the chargé d'affaires in Mexico [London, June 1830], FO 50/64, PRO.

1.6 million, it would not have defaulted. Even the most careful analysis of the public finances of the era, one characterized by utter realism, estimated that Mexico could pay out 1.1 million pesos per year on the London Debt.[85]

Finance Minister, Mangino, for one, was saturnine about fiscal prospects, and O'Gorman claimed that Mangino did not want to publish the required annual report on the condition of public finance and the Treasury.[86] Hence, perhaps, this is why O'Gorman told the Foreign Office that "I am afraid . . . that 6th of the duties [i.e., 16 percent of maritime customs] will be far from yielding sufficient to pay the half dividend from the 1st of April [1831]."[87] O'Gorman did say that Mangino was confident that barring yet another Spanish invasion and "assuming that good order and tranquility are maintained that the dividends [for 1831] will be paid as well as the arrears, should they be capitalized."[88]

Mixed messages, to be sure. Deliberately so? Were Alamán and Mangino pursuing a well-known negotiating strategy, or was there simply confusion at the top? It is difficult to see how anyone could have been confused. Gorostiza, who worked for Alamán, was in communication with Baring Brothers, Finance Minister Mangino, and the Committee of Bondholders – everyone that mattered. It seems, instead, the Federation had managed to "play" or browbeat the representatives of the bondholders, just as Gorostiza had claimed. Besides, the terms of the capitalization were by no means completely unattractive, and *ex ante*, at least, there was a real possibility that the bondholders could become wealthier by raising the present value of their holdings. This was because the period of deferral was not long, interest rates were not especially high at 5 or 6 percent, and the capitalization of interest at between 62 and 75 percent was reasonable. The Mexican government bought some time to deal with the arrears, but it was obligated, for the most part, to continue current interest payments, and this proved troublesome – hence the differing assessments of Alamán and Mangino. Alamán was not the finance minister and could live in the long run. Mangino had no such luxury. As long as he remained in the government (basically, when Bustamante was in power), until May 20, 1832, the remissions of silver to Britain remained substantial. In principal (and in public), the bondholders and Mexico had struck a very reasonable compromise. Yet the arrangement

85 [J. Espinosa] *Bases del Plan de Hacienda*, notes to table "La deuda pública puede considerarse. . . . "
86 O'Gorman to Percy Bidwell, México, June 10, 1830, FO 50/62, PRO.
87 O'Gorman to the Foreign Office, México, October 7, 1830, FO 50/63, PRO. The so-called 16 percent fund did *not* include all customs revenues. For example, the duty on the export of silver was excluded from funding the dividend (as unaffordable for Mexico) and, even more importantly, so were the duties on ordinary cottons – a major item in Mexico's import bill. This may go some way to explaining O'Gorman's diffidence. See "Dividends" Veracruz, August 20, 1831, HC 4.5.4.6. 7, BBA.
88 O'Gorman to Percy Bidwell, México, June 10, 1830, FO 50/62, PRO.

may have proved all too accommodating as far as Mexico was concerned. The brief period of financial optimism that prevailed would, quite literally, go up in smoke.

The English Have Gone Crazy

As a result of the Conversion of 1830, dividend payments flowed once more to Great Britain, some 1.5 million pesos from 1831 through 1835. Well did Manuel Payno complain in 1862[89] that Mexico deserved much better of the intervening European states, since as a matter of justice, Mexico had made a concerted effort to pay its debts when it could least afford to do so. This was especially so in 1830–1831 and 1831–1832. Indeed, as late as January 1832, Antonio López de Santa Anna himself claimed to be very solicitous in seeing that regular dividend payments take place "being particularly zealous in everything that contributes to the honor or credit of my country."[90] The results of the new arrangements were visible in the financial markets, and through the first half of 1830, the price of Mexican bonds relative to consuls increased by nearly 50 percent. Gorostiza and Alamán launched an offensive designed to reassure the London bondholders that Mexico was serious about servicing the London Debt.[91] For a while the results were impressive.

Yet the sources of funding soon dried up. The law of October 2, 1830, specified that 16 percent of the maritime customs of Veracruz and Tampico should be deposited with the British consuls resident acting as collection agents for the bondholders. The Federation had seemingly every intention of carrying out this agreement, and indeed, it had become a preoccupation bordering on obsession for both Mexico and its financial agent, Baring Brothers. For example, in late 1831, Bustamante decided that if what was available for debt service was insufficient, as Baring Brothers was now warning, the funds to make up the difference should come from elsewhere in the Federation's budget if the resources could be diverted "without prejudice" and replaced later. All the relevant officials in Mexico City, Tampico, and Veracruz were apprised of the situation.[92]

But as Gorostiza noted in June 1831, matters had already gotten complicated, because no one knew exactly how much Tampico was prepared to send. What had been sent was "inadequate," and so "I have been unable to

---

89 Manuel Payno, *México y sus Cuestiones Financieras con La Inglaterra, La España y La Francia* (1862; México, 1982).

90 Santa Anna to the British consul-general, Veracruz, January 18, 1832, FO 50/74, PRO.

91 *Times* (London), May 7, 1830.

92 Memo from the Finance Ministry to the customs administrator of Veracruz, México, October 26, 1831, *Hacienda Pública*, unclassified papers; and Baring Brothers to the finance minister, London, December 22, 1831, *Hacienda Pública*, unclassified papers, AGNM.

calm the Bondholders. . . . This uncertainty is really one of the reasons our bond prices rise sluggishly."[93] Gorostiza hammered away at the effect that uncertainty had on the bondholders. It was not simply a question of paying what was owed. A government had to make payment on the precise day it was due, or all its sacrifices would come to naught. "Our bonds today are between 31 and 32; the players (*jugadores*) give as a reason that we are 160,000 pesos short of the half dividend due January 1 [1832] and it is almost impossible that the three packets that will arrive by then should bring so much." If compliance with the conversion were to start out badly, Gorostiza thought, was it any wonder that the bondholders might soon – and justifiably – question the credibility of the entire arrangement.[94]

The British bondholders were, to say the least, upset by the turn of events, and the state of affairs produced a sense of "great dissatisfaction."[95] The British minister, Pakenham, reported that he had closely questioned Finance Minister José María Bocanegra, but was told that the expenses of the "Revolution" against the government of Bustamante, then engulfing central Mexico, ruled any scheduled payments to Britain out of the question. Some, such as Zavala, had long argued against putting Mexico on any predetermined schedule of payments, commenting that Guerrero, in his brief period as president, thought it "unwise to promise payment when the government hasn't the means – or attention to detail – required to make such a pledge."[96]

Exactly how matters stood by 1833 is not completely clear. Bocanegra, who served then as finance minister, produced an insightful but ultimately defensive account of the Federation's credit, which is enlightening, but not persuasive.[97] From the standpoint of the bondholders, the middle 1830s proved disappointing as the Conversion of 1830 quickly unraveled. From 1835 through 1839, there was an effective moratorium; from 1836 through 1839, absolutely no payments were made, at least according to Payno. Indeed, in October 1831, Alamán was informed,

the English have gone crazy wondering why there has been no money for the sixth part from Tampico, or how it could be that the customs house of Veracruz, that produced $460,000 in July, could send only $28,000 by the packet *Sphynx* when it

93 Gorostiza to the finance minister, London, June 16, 1831, *Hacienda Pública*, unclassified papers, AGNM. The exact amount that arrived was 23,000 pesos. Gorostiza to the finance minister, London, July 21, 1831, *Deuda Exterior*, vol. 13, AGNM. ("*es de ruin cuantía*" is translated as "inadequate.") ("*es una de las causas que más entorpece la subida gradual de nuestros fondos*" is translated as " . . . our bond prices rise sluggishly.")

94 Gorostiza to the finance minister, London, October 20, 1831, *Hacienda Pública*, unclassified papers, AGNM; Gorostiza to the finance minister, London, July 21, 1831, *Deuda Exterior*, vol. 13, AGNM.

95 Pakenham to the foreign secretary, México, August 9, 1833, FO 50/80 A, PRO.

96 Lorenzo de Zavala to Manning and Marshall, México, May 2, 1829, HC 4.5.4–14, BBA.

97 Bocanegra, *Memorias*, vol. 2: pp. 513–525.

should be $76,000 . . . The English believe that for the January 1 (1832) dividend there won't be enough money, which is why the Mexican funds are falling every day . . . [T]he public is so irritated that it curses the independence of the new states of the Americas.[98]

One of the leaders of the Committee of Bondholders in London, Wilson — whom, as we recall, Gorostiza had previously managed to bluff — thus reported that the moratorium had created serious difficulties. The Mexican government, Wilson wrote, needed to do something to demonstrate its bona fides. The silence of the authorities was a "grave injustice" to the bondholders, but up until late 1835, they had "stifled their resentment." Wilson complained that the Mexican government's pleading poverty offered no justification for seizing the funds that had been set aside to pay dividends. Mexico should find the funds elsewhere. Still, something or anything was better than nothing, and Wilson signaled the bondholders' readiness to enter into a new agreement (*convenio*) in which the bondholders would receive 3 percent rather than the 6 percent to which the fund had subsequently been reduced in 1833. Wilson added (quite accurately) that the 6 percent sinking fund had never really operated and that the bondholders had become victims of what Wilson termed "civil discord." In high dudgeon, Wilson complained that Mexico would never have gained its independence without the loans made to it. The bondholders, he wrote, could no longer wait patiently. And here any semblance of decorum or diplomacy went out the window, for Wilson's tone became menacing. He is worth quoting in full:

I always foresaw that Mexico could value the goodwill of the English nation. If Mexico had done so and thus exercised due respect in meeting its obligations, it would probably not find itself insulted by a neighboring State and forced to spend hefty sums to destroy a rebellion undertaken by a bunch of bandits and their allies. But I digress. This is politics (*Pero esta es una digresión política*).[99]

Indeed it was. Yet it fairly indicates the growing frustration of the bondholders. Miguel Santa María, Mexico's Special Envoy to Madrid, wrote that it was impossible to quiet the bondholders since the issue of suspended dividends was making Mexico's foreign relations difficult. Santa María, who seems to have been a party to debt negotiations in London, was nearly apoplectic at the state of affairs, and wrote in frustration that he had tried to keep the president of Mexico (most likely Santa Anna's surrogate Miguel Barragán) apprised of the situation. In particular, he said that he had tried to keep the bondholders from meeting and petitioning the British government for assistance. The minimal dividends paid in late 1835 had made

---

98 Francisco Borja Migoni to Lucas Alamán, London, October 20, 1831, *Hospital de Jesús*, vol. 440, exp. 2, AGNM.

99 Robert Wilson to Miguel Santa María, London, November 27, 1835, *Hacienda Pública, Carpetas Azules, 1835–1836*, 2da, AGNM.

things worse, not better, and Santa María had asked José Justo Corro – an interim president who followed Barragán – to intervene and pay the arrears plus whatever else was then falling due. It was hard to keep the bondholders quiet and Santa María feared that by spreading "bitter invective against our country," they would further impair Mexico's credit.

The continuous change in Finance Ministers, the reasons for their resignations, the lack of order in the organization of that ministry are thrown in the face of the Minister of the Republic (i.e., Santa María) whose good name is besmirched if we fail to take extraordinary and immediate steps to pay the arrears and meet our current obligations religiously, our country's credit will be ignominiously lost and our government will receive neither consideration nor respect.[100]

By July 1836, Santa María had framed an elaborate statement about the debt, its causes, and its consequences. It is a remarkable document, a sort of jeremiad in which the political and economic questions of the moment were linked. In it, Santa María termed the foreign debt "important," "urgent," and "grave" and warned that if the debt did not receive "preferential action," "Mexico's nationality may be threatened with moral extinction in the opinion of other nations in the political world." No doubt intimately familiar with the details of Foreign Secretary Viscount Palmerston's maneuvers in Spain, Santa María likewise feared the intervention of Palmerston in the Mexican debt question, all the while arguing that the Texas revolution was ultimately responsible for the financial disorder that had stopped dividend payments. Not coincidentally, the Mexican government had redirected its resources into the domestic public debt for purposes of war finance – an action that had angered the London bondholders even further. The bondholders, Santa María alleged, complained "about the management of the public funds, the absence of economies, and the continuous oscillations and civil wars, saying that these were the reason why a bunch of adventurers had dared to rebel against a nation of 8 million inhabitants." He continued,

Had the Mexican government, it is said, met its obligations as far as credit was concerned, things might never have happened, or if they had, turned out differently. [Mexico would have had] numerous and powerful allies in Great Britain and the British government would have assumed an active role in building a strong and permanent barrier against the ambitious gaze against that rich and extensive territory [i.e., Texas] which the government in Washington and the greedy states of the Union have had for many years.

---

100 Miguel Santa María to [unknown], Madrid, March 25, 1836, *Hacienda Pública, Carpetas Azules, 1835–1836*, 2da, AGNM. (*"cuyo carácter es así humillado"* is translated as "whose good name is besmirched.")

Forgive me if I indicate how unfortunate the position you have left me in as far as my mission is concerned. The daily newspapers have confirmed what happened in Texas on April 21 (i.e., the Battle of San Jacinto).[101]

Public discussion of where events were leading could be found in *extenso* in the British press. One piece opined that there was little chance of an internal political settlement in Mexico in 1836. "The army cannot be reduced and it absorbs all the country's resources and more. Anyone in power has to pay the army first, so where are we to find the money to pay the foreign Bondholders."[102] Or finally, and very ominously, José María Ortiz Monasterio – the acting minister of home and foreign relations between 1835 and 1837 – reported the following summary of an interview he had with the British minister.

Inform the government of Mexico that the way in which the states of Hispanoamerica continued to retain interest payments on their debt has produced a strong sense of indignation in England, and this might oblige the English government, in the not too distant future, to act on its own, if in the interim, the American states do not, of their own accord, do justice to the English creditors. There was recently a deputation of the Mexican Bondholders to His Majesty's first Secretary of State and Foreign Affairs to renew their complaints about the noncompliance of [the Mexican] government and demanding the effective protection of His Majesty's government to obtain the satisfaction of their just demands. The protection of His Majesty's government will be conceded before long if the motive for complaint is not removed. Allow me to assure you, Sir, that the subject is one which merits the closest and most serious attention of the Mexican government.

Ortiz Monasterio then added his own words: "The President Himself has asked me to ask you [Finance Minister Rafael Mangino] what reply should be given to His Majesty's Minister?"[103] A good question, even as the London bondholders were threatening, "fitting out armed vessels to make reprisals on the Mexican government" for sequestering the funds on which the debt was to have been secured.[104]

The answer, when it came, was no surprise. The minister of finance wanted to satisfy the claims of the bondholders, but was thwarted, "much to his disappointment, by the late political occurrences which completely

---

101 Miguel Santa María to the secretary of home and foreign relations, Madrid, July 17, 1836, *Hacienda Pública, Carpetas Azules*, 2da, AGNM. For Palmerston, see Kenneth Bourne, *Palmerston: The Early Years, 1784–1841* (New York, 1982), pp. 553–554.

102 *Times* (London), January 7, 1836.

103 Ortiz Monasterio to the finance minister, México, September 18, 1836, *Hacienda Pública, Carpetas Azules*, 2da, AGNM.

104 *Correspondence... and Communications from the British Government Relative to Loans Made by British Subjects, 1823–1847*, Mr. Backhouse to Mr. Warrington, London, February 24, 1836.

[drained] the national treasury."[105] Such evasions worried thoughtful Mexicans. "Have no illusions about it, England is the country that most positively and efficiently protects its subjects and their interests anywhere in the world," observed José María Luis Mora.[106] Why, Mora continued, would Mexico wish to alienate Britain at precisely the moment that British international support was most valuable? "Do we want to increase our difficulties and the number of our enemies, making England one of them?" A fair question.

Investors or Traders?

The talk of animosity toward Mexico, of the possibility of British intervention – Palmerston's famous memorandum regarding the private risk of British investors in foreign securities lay well in the future – and of the great damage suffered by the Mexican bondholders raises the questions of who was hurt by default, how badly, and why. It is not clear that *everyone* who purchased Mexican bonds lost money, something the representatives of the bondholders were understandably quick to suggest in the 1830s. Of course, any owner of the bonds who expected to receive a secure income was badly deceived because Mexico paid, at most, about half of the interest due on the bonds through 1850 (see Chapter 1). Even worse off were the purchasers of the bonds at original issue, because if they held them through the 1830s, they would have suffered severe capital losses as well. As one correspondent pointed out in 1839, the Mexican 5 percents were issued at 58 and the 6 percents at 85. In late 1839, they were selling at 23 and 29, respectively. "To these transactions," wrote one disgruntled investor, "is to be attributed . . . the ruin of hundreds of hardworking persons and their families."[107] These persons were what another correspondent called "bona fide bondholders," or "those who hold as permanent investors."[108]

Yet there was another group of bondholders, "those who hold merely for sale" and whose interests were "directly opposed" to the permanent investors. The permanent investors "need a steady state of things," while those who held for sale "require events tending to produce fluctuations in prices." The permanent investors "are scattered all over the world and cannot attend meetings in the city." The speculators "are always minding their business in the neighborhood of their market, the Stock Exchange,

105 *Correspondence . . . and Communications from the British Government Relative to Loans Made by British Subjects, 1823–1847*, Minister of finance to minister of foreign affairs, México, December 19, 1836.
106 Mora to Bernardo Couto, Paris, July 14, 1838, in "Papeles Inéditos y Obras Selectas del Doctor Mora" in Genaro García, ed., *Documentos inéditos o muy raros para la historia de México* (México, 2004), p. 530.
107 "Foreign Loans Contracted in 1824 and 1825," *Times* (London), December 17, 1839.
108 "Mexican Bonds," *Times* (London), June 29, 1843, for this and what follows.

and are always ready to attend meetings at the shortest moment." These were, it was said, the principal members of the Committee of Bondholders in London, at least by the early 1840s. Some evidence presented later (Chapter 4) strongly suggests that the speculators were parties like Barings, who could accumulate vast amounts of depreciated paper on their own account. Between 1830 and the outbreak of the Mexican War, there were at least half a dozen occasions when the monthly jump in Mexican bond prices exceeded an arbitrary threshold of 16 percent. In June and July 1843, the total rise in bond prices was 40 percent.[109] Speculators, in other words, were not necessarily interested in a settlement, or at least the sort of settlement that attracted investors. From this it would also follow that the speculators would have no particular interest in political stability in Mexico – quite to the contrary, perhaps. One could almost wonder, instead, if they were speculating on instability! And if in the course of things, speculators were to form ties to political figures in Mexico or Britain, it becomes an open question whether or not the supposition that bondholders crave stability was necessarily true. It may be that buy-and-hold investors craved regular dividends rather than Toad's Wild Ride, but big investors had regular contact with Mexico's ministers. Ordinary investors very rarely make their presence felt in the archives.

The point is that not everyone lost money on Mexican bonds.[110] It is all too easy to imagine situations in which short-term holders, speculators, or traders (the historian's perspective on arbitrage is very different from the economist's) could make a great deal of money. This would be particularly true of speculators who had access to inside information: "Consider how desirable it must be to a dealer in stock to be a member of a committee which receives the earliest information of events, certain to produce fluctuation." The rumors of these opportunities coincided with the arrival of Santa Anna on the national political scene and, if anything, strengthened during the early 1840s. One very concrete example is the jump in Mexican bond prices on the London Stock Exchange that occurred in June 1833, when the inauguration of Santa Anna was reported in the "Money Market and City Intelligence" column of the *Times* (London).[111] It was one of the larger movements of the 1830s. O'Gorman characterized the agent for the Committee of Bondholders in Veracruz in 1832, acting British vice-consul Joseph Welsh, of being a Santanista who openly supported the General.[112] The relation between Santa Anna, the Committee of Bondholders, and Mexico's financial agent in London would become most fraught

109 These are my calculations.
110 Compare with Dawson, *First Latin American Debt Crisis*.
111 June 14, 1833.
112 Charles T. O'Gorman to Welsh, Santa Fe, January 19, 1832, FO 50/74, PRO.

and complex in the 1840s, and it is difficult to disentangle rumor from mere allegation, let alone substantive finding. Still, as late as 1845, some in and around the Committee of Bondholders in London held Santa Anna in high esteem, or, at least, claimed to.[113]

At the time of the Conversion of 1830, we can identify, at least nominally, the leadership of the Committee of Bondholders in London. It seems to have been an assemblage of the great and the good, and it is obvious why the Mexicans were concerned about alienating them: Alderman Thompson, William Ward, Sir Robert Wilson, Alexander Baring (later Lord Ashburton), and George Robinson. All were Members of Parliament, and Baring, Ward, and Thompson were considered especially prominent.[114] Alexander Baring, first Baron Ashburton, was a member of the merchant bank Baring Brothers and a financier with other extensive connections to America, particularly to the United States. William Ward was elected a director of the Bank of England in 1817 and distinguished "by his accurate knowledge of foreign exchange." Or if one wants to find an even more familiar example of a figure who speculated in Mexican shares, although, to be sure, in mines rather than in the public debt, there was a certain Benjamin Disraeli – a chronic victim of financial malaise who was burned in the bubble of 1824–1825.[115] These were not the sort of people a government bent on rehabilitating its credit would want to alienate, and in view of the failure of the Conversion of 1830 and its subsequent adjustments, some effort had to be made to mollify them. Or relations would continue to worsen. As they did.

The Conversion of 1837

At one time or another during his tenure in Mexico, Percy Doyle (1806–1887) would serve as secretary of legation (1842), chargé d'affaires (1843, 1847, 1851), and minister plenipotentiary (1851–1856). Astoundingly, as late as 1884, Doyle – then 78, his eyesight failing, but his faculties intact – would continue to advise the Foreign Office about Mexico, drawing on his knowledge of events there half a century earlier. Doyle had also served

---

113 See, for instance, Robert Crichton Wyllie, *México. Noticia sobre su Hacienda Pública Bajo el Gobierno Español y Después de la Independencia* (México, 1845), especially "Estado de la Hacienda Pública de México en 1843."

114 John Orbell, "Baring, Alexander, First Baron Ashburton (1773–1848)," in H. C. G. Matthew and Brian Harrison, eds., *Oxford Dictionary of National Biography* (Oxford: OUP, 2004), http://www. oxforddnb.com/view/article/1380 (accessed September 28, 2007); E. I. Carlyle, "Ward, William (1787–1849)," rev. Robert Brown, in H. C. G. Matthew and Brian Harrison, eds., *Oxford Dictionary of National Biography* (Oxford: OUP, 2004), http://www.oxforddnb.com/view/article/28712 (accessed September 28, 2007; and "Mexican Bonds," *Times* (London), June 29, 1843.

115 Robert Blake, *Benjamin Disraeli* ([1966] London, 1998), pp. 24–25.

with British missions in Washington (1825), Madrid (1829), and Belgium (1832). He was, in other words, a diplomat of considerable standing and experience.[116] It is therefore of some interest to read of the relations he described between Antonio López de Santa Anna and Francisco de Lizardi, a London-based merchant who had assumed Mexico's financial agency from Baring Brothers in 1835. The circumstances of Lizardi's links with Santa Anna were intriguing. Doyle reported that Santa Anna had demanded $20,000 (at least half a million dollars in contemporary terms) as the price of giving Lizardi the agency. Lizardi, in turn, had offered $15,000. Santa Anna "eventually received" $18,000. General Valentín Canalizo, one of Santa Anna's cronies and president for a time, received $8,000. The finance minister, Ignacio Trigueros, got $12,000. Manuel Baranda, at justice, received $7,000. Bocanegra, at home and foreign relations, received $3,000. José María Tornel, at the war office, got $2,000. Scurrilous rumors, perhaps? To the contrary, Doyle concluded, "This will prove to your Lordship [Aberdeen, the Foreign Secretary] the extreme difficulty of getting any measure of justice for the Bondholders carried through, that is, as long as Lizardi and Company can afford to continue that system of bribery and Santa Anna remains in power."[117]

Santa Anna was a busy man. Doyle reported that Santa Anna had been offered $200,000 (at least $5 million in contemporary terms) as a "present" for the recognition of the independence of Texas aside from $5,000,000 offered the government.[118] What had seemed possible in 1830, an equitable and largely amicable resolution to the debt problem in which the bondholders got much of what they wanted, had apparently disappeared by 1842. There were, as we have said, signs – straws in the wind, perhaps – that Great Britain's official patience had begun to wane. In late 1839, Mexico had imposed new *consumo* duties on foreign manufactures, a step that deeply concerned British manufacturing interests. Pakenham had advised Mexico that "Her Majesty's government might be compelled in retaliation of such unfriendly measures to recognize the independence of Texas and to adopt effective means to recover the vast sums which the

116 *The Foreign Office List for 1852 . . .* (London, 1852), p. 35; Percy Doyle to the foreign secretary, London, August 16, 1884, in *Further Correspondence Respecting the Renewal of Diplomatic Relations with México.* Confidential Print No. 5109 (May, 1885), p. 29; Edgar Sheppard, ed., *George, Duke of Cambridge, a Memoir of His Private Life* (2 vols.; London, 1906), vol. 2: p. 162; Raymond A. Jones, *The British Diplomatic Service, 1815–1914* (Waterloo, ON, 1983), p. 20.

117 Percy Doyle to the foreign secretary, México, January 29, 1844, British Museum, Add. Ms. 13126. The merchant firm of F. de Lizardi and Company is listed in *The Post Office London Directory for 1836* (37th ed.; London [1836]), p. 335, at 4 Barge Yard, Bucklersbury.

118 February 1842, British Museum, Add. Ms. 43170. Doyle was reporting on an offer made to Santa Anna in writing by General Hamilton, the plenipotentiary in England for the Republic of Texas as reported by Pakenham to the foreign secretary, México, February 17, 1842, FO 50/153, PRO.

Mexican government owes to England in the shape of interest on the public debt." "This language," Pakenham observed, "has induced the Mexican government to withdraw the objectionable project of law."[119]

With default, the failure of the Conversion of 1830, the end of the federal republic, and the new moratorium on payments after 1835, relations between Mexico and the bondholders – the bona fide ones, at least – had begun to deteriorate, and with them, relations between Mexico and Great Britain. In part, the problem was nothing more than the magic of compound interest. Payno described it well. "The London debt," he wrote,

like the other foreign debts we have, instead of diminishing, grow steadily larger year by year. The funds set aside from the customs, the many sacrifices made, the Treasury's lack of money, itself the fruit of civil disturbances, all of it every year leads down a blind alley. Since the interest and principal aren't paid, the credit of the country is impaired, the creditors can count on nothing, and the following year, as time goes by, the arrears grow worse and worse.[120]

The initial London principal of £6,400,000 had been reduced to £5,281,750 by 1827 by both the sinking fund and payments, but had climbed to £6,020,697 in 1830. By 1832, the total was £6,857,550, and by 1837, £9,247,937. This meant that after 1832, the debt was compounding at a rate of about 6 percent per year at a time in which economic growth was stagnant, or at best, not much above zero. Things could not continue in this way indefinitely, and they did not, for at that rate, accrued interest on the London Debt would at some future point consume national income.

In the late summer of 1837, discussions between the bondholders and the Mexican government were renewed. "The present administration under Bustamante is so far conducting itself to the entire satisfaction of all moderate peoples . . . The ruinous loans to the government (i.e., the short term internal debt) will be gradually paid off. As to revolutions, we consider them at an end for the present."[121] The initial proposal to resolve the debt problem was published in Mexico City on April 12, 1837. The letter as quoted before was published on September 12. The Conversion of 1837 was agreed to and published on September 14, 1837 – all told, an interval of five months. But the short period between the proposal and its subsequent ratification is a little misleading – for much had transpired behind the scenes in 1835 and 1836 and more was to follow between 1837 and 1840.

119 "Memorandum on the Heavy Additional Duty Levied on Foreign Manufactures in Mexico with Regard to Which a Deputation from Liverpool, Glasgow and Belfast Have Requested an Interview with Lord Palmerston," March 9, 1841, FO50/150, PRO. "Project of law" should be understood as a literal translation of *proyecto de ley,* or more commonly, "bill."

120 Payno, *México y sus cuestiones financieras,* p. 11.

121 *Times* (London), September 12, 1837.

The acting minister of home and foreign relations, Ortiz Monasterio, openly doubted that Mexico would have the money to produce a settlement. Arguing that the Federation had a deficit that exceeded $10 million, Ortiz Monasterio thought that the system of *agiotaje* was the decisive obstacle to repayment since at least some of the loans the *agiotistas* made were funded in depreciated government paper. In an aside, Ortiz Monasterio quoted the administrator of the Customs House of Veracruz, who said that he would be delighted to pay the bondholders' agent, but that "he had no money." If the agent would take paper (depreciated government notes), well, "everything would go smoothly." The state of the Federation's finances was "sad" according to Ortiz Monasterio – everywhere you looked was sad. "The powerful states of the North," he observed, were under the control of Santa Anna's regular units "and were kept that way only by force." Texas, in the north, was in open rebellion and Tamaulipas, through which the army had to travel, "supposedly refuses to recognize the authority of the central government." Chiapas was in rebellion, and in Acapulco, "General Alvarez maintains his position." And so, Ortiz Monasterio observed, "there is little chance of any permanent settlement." As a consequence, "the army cannot be reduced in size, which absorbs all the country's resources."[122] His conclusions followed logically: "Whoever takes power has to attend to the army first. In these circumstances, *there is no way of figuring out how to pay the foreign Bondholders* [emphasis mine]. We have always paid them with fine words. Money is another matter."

And it continued to be. Problems multiplied as Baring Brothers with-drew from the Mexico's financial agency in Europe. Aside from Baring's having played a critical role in underwriting dividend payments and in structuring the capitalization of the arrears, the firm had also undertaken to pay Mexico's diplomats abroad when the government was unable to do so. Between July 1835 and March 1836, for example, the Mexican minister at London had drawn nearly $100,000 to cover diplomatic expenses. With the effective suspension of dividend payments in 1835, Barings became alarmed and pressed Manning and Marshall, its agent in Mexico, for repayment "to compensate in some way for the harm done to the house."[123] At the same time, the secretary of the Mexican legation in London, Agustín Iturbide Jr. reported that he had had no guidance from Mexico on how to proceed.[124] Relations between Mexico and Barings became quite tense,

122 A report by Ortiz Monasterio, March 28, 1836, *Hacienda Pública, Carpetas Azules*, 2da, 1835–1836, AGNM.

123 Manning and Marshall to the finance minister, México, December 4, 1835, and Antonio Vallejo to Manning and Marshall, November 19, 1835, both in *Hacienda Pública, Carpetas Azules, 1835–1836*, 2da, AGNM.

124 Baring Brothers to the Mexican minister in London, London, March 1, 1836, and Iturbide to Baring Brothers, London, March 4, 1836, *Hacienda Pública, Carpetas Azules, 1835–1836*, 2da, AGNM.

and in an act of desperation, given how tight funds in Mexico were, the Mexicans authorized a $10,000 payment to Barings in 1836 and twice that in November 1837. The 1836 payment had been authorized by the interim president himself, José Justo Corro.[125]

But by July 1836, Barings had frankly refused to advance any additional monies to the Mexican legations in Europe. It was at this point that Santa María, who had been involved in the London negotiations, instructed Iturbide Jr. to regard a new merchant bank as the official financial agent for Mexico in England and France, the house of Lizardi and Company, pending approval in Mexico. Santa María had the connections to make the arrangement work, because General Barragán, interim president and Santanista, approved the appointment. Indeed, so closely was Santa María identified with Lizardi and Company that Baring Brothers claimed that it had been advised by the Mexican government that the agency would be held by [Lizardi and Company] "in conjunction with His Excellency Mr. Santa María."[126]

Santa María worked tirelessly to bring the Lizardi house into the debt negotiations. He enthused as to how Lizardi had stepped into the breech when Baring Brothers refused to advance Mexican diplomats in Europe any further funds, calling their position "an intemperate announcement." The Lizardi firm had offered to finance Mexico's diplomats "spontaneously in support of our national honor in such affecting circumstances."[127] Santa María argued that Barings saw Mexico only as a business proposition but that Lizardi was a Mexican firm guided by "national interest." As a "Mexican" firm, Lizardi's own interests would coincide with Mexico's interests and in its wide circle of mercantile contacts. Moreover, Santa María argued that Baring suffered from a conflict of interest. The Mexican government had brought suit against Barclay's, but Barings could scarcely be expected to work diligently against another merchant bank.[128] Lizardi, on the other

Iturbide (1807–1866) was the "Prince Imperial" and son of the emperor, Agustín I. He was reportedly educated at Ampleforth Abbey in Yorkshire for two years, leaving in 1826. For biographical data, see http://www.geocities.com/Athens/Column/7292/gene.html (accessed September 28, 2007). Also see "Ampleforth Old Boys, 1802–1830," http://www.archive. zenwebhosting.com/sites/students/list1803.htm (accessed September 28, 2007). One suspects that Iturbide's interest in all of this was purely financial. Even his signature on a bond (which was required) provided fee income. I am grateful to Father Anselm Cramer OSB, archivist at Ampleforth Abbey, for his assistance. There is a reference to Iturbide's presence at Ampleforth in *Ampleforth Journal* 1 (1896), 230–231.

125 Rafael Mangino to [unknown], México, March 11, 1836, and Mangino to the finance minister, *Hacienda Pública, Carpetas Azules, 1835–1836*, 2da, AGNM.

126 Barragán to Santa María, México, October 24, 1836, *Carpetas Azules, 1835–1836*, 2da, AGNM, and Baring Brothers to Lizardi and Company, February 14, 1837, *Deuda Exterior*, vol. 12, AGNM.

127 Santa María to the finance minister, Madrid, July 17, 1836, *Carpetas Azules, 1835–1836*, 2da, AGNM.

128 A doubtful conclusion, since Baring Brothers had recommended against a settlement that Barclay, Herring, Richardson offered to Mexico in 1828.

hand, had handled the complicated probate case of Migoni, and could be relied on to handle Mexican interests.[129] Indeed, it had an extended history of financial dealings with the Mexican government going back to 1829, when D. Manuel de Lizardi was involved in a huge 400,000-peso funding operation with the Federation.[130]

Baring Brothers, then, "had caused a grievous wound to the [Mexican] government's credit at precisely the very delicate moment at which Mexico finds itself. When negotiating the terms of recognition from the Court of Spain [Mexico] needs ministers and diplomatic agents to represent with dignity its rights and interests." Moreover, continued Santa María, "add to this the war our country finds itself in Texas, an enemy for whom the United States has sympathy; the Republic is threatened with both dismemberment and foreign war. In such circumstances, it is critical to choose [agents] who will support our legations and consulates." But most importantly, "if the future capitalization [of the debt] were to be undertaken with the participation of Baring Brothers, the house of Lizardi could not in all fairness and with respect to its good name in Europe, continue providing the [cash] supplements [to the diplomatic corps] that it had been supplying since February [1836]. I have obligated myself," said Santa María, "to defer the process of capitalization [i.e., the new debt conversion] until [Barragán] knows about the problem I face." "Please," he advised the finance minister, "let [Barragán] know what arrangements I think proper." Santa María got what he wanted, as did the firm of Lizardi and Company. Or to put it another way, Lizardi's money and Santa María's influence helped determine the timing of the Conversion of 1837.

Mexico's fiscal situation was a matter of greatest concern to Santa María. There was no way for the government to service the debt as things stood;

---

129 Santa María to the finance minister (secret), Madrid, July 17, 1836, *Hacienda Pública, Carpetas Azules, 1835–1836*, 2ᵈᵃ.

130 *Razón de los préstamos que ha negociado el Supremo Gobierno de la Federación . . . con autorización del Escmo. Sr. Ministro de Hacienda Ciudadano Lorenzo de Zavala* (México, 1829), p. 4.

   Francisco de Lizardi and Company was established in London and Liverpool in 1835, based in part on the liquidation of Quintana, Brothers, and Alexander Gordon. Lizardi was a big firm in the 1830s, big enough to be mentioned in the financial press in the same league as Barings and Rothschilds, at least in its dealing with the Americas. See, for example, *Bankers Circular and Monetary Times, 1837–1838* (London, 1837–38), p. 173. For the announcement of the establishment of the house, see RAL/XI/112/124, TRA.

   For the Lizardi, like the Rothschilds, nationality was a matter of convenience. After the death of "Mexican" Manuel J. de Lizardi, one family member, Miguel A. (de) Lizardi (the "de" seems to have come and gone as well) claimed that Manuel J. did not consider himself a Mexican and "cannot have claimed the right of a Mexican citizen." This when filing a claim in Manuel J. *against* Mexico under the auspices of a United States Claims Commission, for which he claimed U.S. citizenship. See M. A. de Lizardi to Low Smith & Watkins, New Orleans, March 15, 1872. Box 7, Folder 40, Skilton Family Papers, 1798–1917, Institute Archives and Special Collections, Rensellaer Polytechnic Institute.

nor did he think there was much immediate prospect of doing so, "without greatly diminishing the resources to sustain the civil and military administration of the Republic or to provide internal improvements that are so greatly needed." The time had come, Santa María said, to take measures that would restore Mexico's public credit and that "having had occasion to deal with Sr. Don Francisco de Lizardi and his brothers, I recognized in them a fund of honesty as well as a vast acquaintance with mercantile matters and questions of the public debt."[131] From 1835 through 1845, Francisco de Lizardi and Company was to act as the financial agent for Mexico in London. What Lizardi was proposing, according to Santa María, was an immediate conversion of the London Debt that would reduce it to 40 percent of the capital and 50 percent of the interest pending in October 1837 while gradually amortizing the remainder. This would, it was said, result in an approximate annual savings of 1.5 million pesos, perhaps not so coincidentally, equivalent to the annual dividend payments under the original issues of the bonds. It was for this reason that Santa María wanted that Lizardi and Company be awarded the agency. Acting minister Ortiz Monasterio, to whom Santa María had directed his correspondence, passed it on to finance minister Ignacio Alas with a recommendation from interim president Corro "to take whatever steps necessary to satisfy the Republic's Bondholders." Even so, Corro allowed, "recent political events had emptied a national treasury already exhausted by previous divisions."[132]

Looking at the complex interplay of proposals, resolutions and reports would indicate that the Conversion of 1837 emerged in the following way:[133] First, Pedro de la Quintana, of Lizardi and Company, went to Mexico *before* April 1837 to present the conversion proposal crafted in London by Lizardi and Company. The proposal went to the *Consejo de Gobierno*, which reviewed and altered it, assenting to some of Lizardi and Company's requirements while rejecting others. The Mexican government then issued a "decree," dated April 12, 1837, embodying its counteroffer. (Some related legislation regarding lands in the public domain appeared on April 4.)[134] The intervening months witnessed intense negotiation in London between Lizardi and Company, Iturbide Jr. – the chargé d'affaires – and the Committee of Mexican Bondholders.

Perhaps just as important was the reemergence of Bustamante as president in January 1837. Bustamante, prudent as ever, was anxious for Palmerston to understand that "a new order of things would be

131 Santa María to [the Minister of Home and Foreign Relations], Madrid, July 17, 1836, and appended note of December 19, 1836, *Hacienda Pública, Carpetas Azules, 1835–1836*, 2da, AGNM.
132 See the appended note, given before, signed by the oficial mayor of home and foreign relations.
133 This account is based largely on "Préstamos Extranjeros, 1837," *Deuda Exterior*, vol. 5, AGNM.
134 *Leyes, decretos y convenios relativos a la deuda extranjera* [México 1848?], pp. 10–15.

consolidated."[135] Centralism, "the new order of things," would induce Mexico "to reestablish its credit and cover its foreign obligations." "Nothing would be neglected," wrote Bustamante to Santa María, "in making the exact payment of the dividends." The reason was to induce Palmerston to use his good offices in the service of maintaining Mexican sovereignty over Texas. "[I]f the laws and regulations on the conversion and amortization of the foreign debt have the results you [i.e, Santa María] expect, both the Bondholders and Mexico would benefit." Bustamante urged Santa María "to see to it that Lord Palmerston knows [what is being done] to assume the payment of the foreign debt, which, he added, was closely linked to the 'important business of Texas'." No Texas, in other words, no conversion.

It was in precisely such fraught circumstances that the bondholders met at the City of London Tavern at Austin Friars on August 9, 1837, to consider the provisions of the newly contemplated conversion. The proposal they heard, made on behalf of the Mexican government by Lizardi and Company, was not entirely to their liking. Lizardi and Company communicated this accurately enough to the finance ministry, reporting that the only thing the meeting accomplished was the formation of a subcommittee to look into the matter.[136] Subsequently the subcommittee met and recommended that the proposed consolidation of half of the existing debt into one new bond should be accepted. The second recommendation concerned the land warrants, a proposal to which no debtors' group warmed. Rather than issue land warrants, the subcommittee recommended that Mexico issue "deferred" bonds that would pay no interest through an indefinite period (possibly through 1866). The bonds *could* be converted into land at a specified rate, with the Mexican government pledging 25–30 million contiguous acres to be reserved solely for the use of the bondholders. In turn, the bondholders could form colonization firms to bring "Irishmen, Scots, Swiss and Polish Catholics who presently and in such numbers populate the deserts of [the United States]."

In a sense, the arrangement remedied the deficiencies of the Conversion of 1830, but the new proposal was *both* a conversion and a consolidation in which an outstanding bond and its arrears would be exchanged for a new bond plus a land warrant. Five percent bonds would exchange at par and 6 percents at a 12.5 percent premium, that is, 112.5. The arrears dating to 1831, which involved a substantial amount, would be added as well. The sum would then be apportioned as follows: 50 percent to a new 5 percent

---

135 For this and what follows, see Anastasio Bustamante to Miguel Santa María, México, June 2, 1837, Archivo Genero Estrada, Legajos Encuadernados, 1064. Secretaría de Relaciones Exteriores, México (SREM).

136 Treasury report, México, November 29, 1837, *Deuda Exterior*, AGNM, for this and what follows. Also see Murphy, *Deuda Exterior*, pp. 9–10.

Table 2.2. *Conversion of 1837 Including Land Warrants Illustration Using 6 Percent Issue*

	Pounds Sterling (£)	Shillings (s)	Pence (d)
£100 bond	112	10	0
23 and ½ coupons to October 1	35	5	
	147	15	
One half in bonds at 5 percent	73	17	5
Remainder land warrants	73	17	5

Source: Times (London), August 10, 1837.

bond and 50 percent in land warrants. An example that appeared in the *Times* (London) illustrates the operation (see Table 2.2).

The idea of land warrants, which was floated at the time of the 1830 conversion (and in the Marcos Crespo proposal), now became a crucial part of the conversion – the lands, "vacant government lands" in the departments of Texas, Chihuahua, New Mexico, Sonora, and California, "a portion of the most valuable and . . . only disposable property which the nation possesses." The attraction of the scheme is easily grasped. If, as the Mexican government believed, its current and accumulated debt was $48,000,000 (which is about where Alamán put it) and its annual interest at $2,500,000 (roughly 5 percent), this was "an amount beyond the present resources of Mexico to meet." The statement was true enough, for Mexico had sent so much to Britain only once – in 1826 – prior to defaulting in October 1827.

If one argues, and there seems no cogent reason not to, that the opportunity cost to Mexico of ceding ostensibly vacant lands to foreign bondholders was zero, the proposed consolidation and conversion would have reduced Mexico's foreign indebtedness by 50 percent at a stroke. For Mexico, one supposes, this was a very attractive prospect. Indeed, the Chamber of Deputies subsequently concluded in 1850,

this operation presented the nation with great advantages. First, two funds were consolidated into one, which made accounting and payment simpler. Second, the 6 percent fund was reduced to 5 percent, saving the Republic 1 percentage point in the future. Third, half the debt would accrue no interest for 10 years. And fourth, the amortization of the deferred debt would involve no monies from the ordinary revenues of the government, aside from nourishing the hopes that the empty [*sic*] lands of New Mexico, California and Sonora would in no time be populated by hard-working folk. This involved nothing less than the important political belief of settling the frontier to avoid the separation of all the lands of New Mexico, Texas and Upper California that occurred in 1848.[137]

137 *Dictamen de la commission de crédito público de la Cámara de Diputados sobre el arreglo de la deuda inglesa*, pp. 8–9.

Similarly, Alexander Forbes (d. 1863) – a founding partner of Barron Forbes & Company of Tepic – wrote in his history of California, "there had been some thoughts of proposing to the Mexican government that it should cancel the English debt – which now exceeds fifty millions of dollars – by a transfer of California to the creditors." This would be a "wise measure" for Mexico because "in no case can [California] ever be profitable to [Mexico], nor can it possibly remain united to it." By ceding California, Forbes concluded, Mexico would be "getting rid of [the debt] for nothing." If California were ceded to pay off the debt, Forbes thought, "it would certainly bring a revenue in time."[138]

Putting the best face on things, Lizardi and Robinson, the president of the Committee of Bondholders, argued that a new day had dawned for Mexico. Spain had now recognized the independence of Mexico, so there was no danger of reinvasion. Once the Texas question was "settled," the Mexican army would be reduced by two-thirds, "which for many years past had alone consumed a very large portion of the whole revenue collected." Population was growing and a "state of order and security" had returned to the country. If any of the dividends went unpaid, the customhouses of Veracruz and Tampico were to honor the bonds' coupons as orders for payment to the extent of one-sixth of customs duties. This expedient alone was designed to maintain the market in coupons at 70–75 percent of their face value.

The land warrants, however, were the centerpiece of the scheme. Robinson and Lizardi and Company claimed that the agreement would effectively place a lien on all Mexico's vacant lands. The particular parcels on which they focused would come to occupy a central position in subsequent difficulties between Mexico and the United States. Aside from Texas, a province that was mildly characterized as a province that "resists the authority of Mexico," the prize was

a tract of country between the Río del Norte and Río Nueces, fronting 100 miles on the Mexican gulf and extending back to the mountains, containing about 30,000,000 of acres and being still vacant could be appropriated to the Bondholders and must in the course of a very few years become of great value, the soil and climate being admirably adopted to the production of cotton, rice, tobacco, wool and all

138 Alexander Forbes, *California. A History of Upper & Lower California . . .* ([1839] San Francisco, 1919), pp. 152–153. A useful account of this and related schemes is Lester G. Engelson, "Proposals for the Colonization of California by England in Connection with the Mexican Debt to British Bondholders, 1837–1846," *California Historical Society Quarterly*, 18: 2 (1939), pp. 136–148. Forbes's proposal, when published in the British press in 1839, provoked a very negative reaction on the London Stock Exchange. This may have something to do with the fact that the net revenue to Mexico from Upper California around 1839 was $32,000. See Forbes, *California*, p. 307. The bondholders obviously discounted future income substantially.

kinds of grain and cattle, and the climate being temperate and the country very healthy, so soon as good titles could be given, applicants would be found for the purchase of the lands with little trouble for the Bondholders.

"Within five years after the Texian question is settled," the analysis continued "that country will have a settled population and its land will be held at high price." Very interestingly, Lizardi pointed to the "present unsettled state of affairs between Mexico and Texas." Which was "one of the strong reasons why the [plan] should be taken as it is without delay." The implication was only too clear. If British bondholders took legal possession of lands in Texas, then the British government would be placed, one way or another, in the position of guaranteeing Mexican sovereignty over Texas in the course of safeguarding its nationals' claims to land title. The reasoning was perfect: Great Britain would administer and enforce the Conversion of 1837, while Mexico would discharge half the London Debt and involve Britain in the defense of its sovereignty. Such an arrangement was appealing to the Mexicans, for as Juan Almonte put it, "the consequences of this measure will be immense: with it we prevent Texas from carrying out its independence because we will have created an interest against it."[139] But what of the British government and the bondholders, and presumably, the Texans? The "tract" of land under consideration as security for the bondholders would ultimately become the "disputed" boundary between Mexico and the United States, the ostensible casus belli in 1846. No land could serve two proprietors.

Texas Two-Step

The Texans clearly understood what was afoot and the "Private and Confidential Agent for the Government of Texas in Mexico," James Treat, called the discussion "very important." Treat, writing to Mirabeau Lamar, president of the Republic of Texas, thought a guarantee of 100,000,000 acres to be ambiguous in the sense that it could be located in any of five departments. But, he concluded, "my impression is that the [Mexican] Government had in view the lands between the Nueces and the Rio Grande to locate the 25,000,000 [specially hypothecated areas specified in Art. 7, Clause 2 of the Conversion of 1837]." In an attempt to head off any effort by Britain to guarantee Texas' continuing subjugation to Mexico, the Texans pressed England for outright recognition of independence. Palmerston, the foreign secretary, went so far as to say that "the Government of Great Britain [was] perfectly satisfied that the people of Texas had attained their independence

139 Almonte to Luis G. Cuevas, quoted in Faustino A. Aquino Sánchez, *Intervención Francesa, 1838–1839. La diplomacia Mexicana y el imperialismo de libre comercio* (México, 1997), p. 209.

and were entitled to its acknowledgment."[140] At the same time, the Texans
had learned that "Mexico had actually assigned to the Mexican Bondholders
as a security for their debt the public lands in the 'Department of Texas,'
something the Texans' agent in London, General J. P. Hamilton, called
an 'absurd mockery'." "I need not insist," Hamilton observed, "upon the
absolute nullity of this convention as far as Texas in concerned."[141] Nevertheless, in a meeting with the bondholders, the Texans admitted that such
an arrangement would entitle the bondholders to a claim "on the whole
indemnity to which Texas may be willing to pay for the quiet possession
of the Country." While Texas might well attribute its willingness to make
such an arrangement as a matter of honor and magnanimity, one could see
where the prospect of a payment of some $5 million might also induce
the bondholders to lobby Palmerston energetically in favor of the independence of Texas. Hamilton thought that precisely this had transpired: "The
Mexican Bondholders ardently desire this [and] they will endeavor at once
to have it effected."[142] Or was this beneath the honor of President Lamar
to consider?

Apparently not. Texas' agent admitted quite openly that this would
obtain "the aid of an influential class of individuals in London . . . [so that]
the Mexican Bondholders would thus . . . be enabled under the protection
of . . . [the British] Government *to take care of their own interests*" [italics in
original]. The bondholders were understandably enthused about such a
possibility: "They seemed to regard this as a great boon paid on account
of the interest on their bonds." No doubt. Within a year, of course, Great
Britain had recognized the independence of the Republic of Texas (treaties
signed 1840; July 28, 1842).[143] How much the British bondholders had
to do with this is unknown. Yet Pakenham observed that if Mexico were
to come to an amicable settlement with Texas, Texas, in turn, would give

---

140 Treat to the president of the Republic of Texas, México, February 1 and 8, 1840, *Annual Report
   of the American Historical Association, 1908* (2 vols.; Washington, DC, 1911), vol. 2(1): pp. 542,
   559–560. General Hamilton to the British minister at México, New Orleans, November 20,
   1839, FO 50/134, PRO, for most of what subsequently follows.
       The full diplomatic history of the Texas Republic is thoroughly discussed in Joseph William
   Schmitz, *Texan Statecraft, 1836–1845* (San Antonio, 1941).

141 Hamilton to the foreign secretary, London, November 5, 1840, *Annual Report of the American
   Historical Association, 1908*, vol. 2(2): p. 909. On Hamilton, see Robert Tinkler, *James Hamilton of
   South Carolina* (Baton Rouge, 2004), pp. 170–205.

142 Hamilton to the secretary of state of the Republic of Texas, London, December 3, 1840, *Annual
   Report of the American Historical Association, 1908*, vol. 2(2): p. 918.

143 "Diplomatic Relations of the Republic of Texas," *The Handbook of Texas Online*,
   http://www.thsa.utexas.edu/handbook/online/articles/view/DD/mgd1.html (accessed September
   28, 2007). The treaties embodying recognition were actually signed in November 1840. For
   details see J. L. Worley, "The Diplomatic Relations of England and the Republic of Texas," *The
   Quarterly of the Texas State Historical Association*, 9: 1 (1906), pp. 1–40.

Mexico "the prospect of getting rid of a large portion of [its] debt by the concession which the Bondholders hope to obtain from the Texian government."[144]

According to James Webb, minister plenipotentiary from Texas to Mexico, concession involved an agreement between the Republic of Texas and Great Britain, a convention entered into on November 14, 1840. By the terms of the convention, Texas agreed to pay £1 million of the Mexican foreign debt, provided a treaty of peace was signed between Texas and Mexico through the mediation of Great Britain. "We now present ourselves," Webb ironically concluded, "rather in the character of purchasers of the country, rather than as conquerors."[145] As a result, Ashbel Smith, the chargé d' affaires of the Republic of Texas in London concluded unequivocally, "The Mexican Bondholders and persons engaged in Mexican trade, two important interests, are now decidedly in favor of establishing peace between Texas and Mexico."[146]

In any event, Lizardi and Company warmly recommended accepting the Conversion of 1837 to the bondholders. "[We] consider the present unsettled state of affairs between Mexico and Texas to be one of the strong reasons why the decree should be taken as it is without delay." Moreover, once Britain recognized the independence of Texas, the rights of the holders of land warrants there would have to be recognized by the government in Texas. Make hay, so to speak, while the sun shines.[147] At the same time, Lizardi and Company pressured Iturbide Jr. in London to accept revisions to the April 12 document that the bondholders desired. The firm reported that it had "worked hard to get the decree of April 12 accepted without any changes." However, "they saw, to the extent they were allowed to participate in the Bondholders' meetings, that everything might fall apart and for sure, that the decree [of April 12] would go out the window if the parties involved didn't get the changes they wanted." If Iturbide thought he lacked the authority to accept proposed changes in the decree, then he "should take the responsibility on his own."[148] Iturbide, in turn, contacted his government,

---

144 Pakenham to the foreign secretary, México, February 26, 1841, FO 50/144, PRO.

145 James Webb to Pakenham, on board Texas schooner *San Bernard*, Harbor of Sacrificios near Veracruz, June 1, 1841, *Annual Report of the American Historical Association, 1908*, vol. 2(1): pp. 753–754.

146 Ashbel Smith to the secretary of state, Republic of Texas, London, July 3, 1842, *Annual Report of the American Historical Association, 1908*, vol. 2(2): p. 972. The best recent survey of these matters is Lelia M. Roeckell, "Bonds Over Bondage: British Opposition to The Annexation of Texas," *Journal of the Early Republic*, 19: 2 (1999), pp. 257–278, who flatly attributes British recognition of Texas in large part to the interest of the bondholders.

147 *Correspondence . . . and Communications from the British Government Relative to Loans Made by British Subjects, 1823–1847*, Backhouse to [George] Robinson, London, November 6, 1839.

148 Lucas Alamán, *Liquidación de la deuda*, pp. 30, and following.

desperate for news about Texas, whose status would largely determine the viability of the proposed conversion.[149] And finally, as if all this were not enough, Lizardi and Company had lobbied the British minister in Mexico – Pakenham – directly on behalf of the bondholders, urging him to impress the virtues of the conversion on the Mexican government itself.[150] Self-interested or not, it was some performance, a deal orchestrated in London, Mexico City, and New Orleans, where the firm was also established. Only the Rothschilds could have done much better.

A Denouement . . . of Sorts

The formal agreement was made public on September 14, 1837. The reaction recorded by the London Stock Exchange was, on the whole, quite mixed. It was almost as if no one quite knew what to make of the proposal. There was little euphoria; what there was of it did not last. Over the next year, relative bond prices bounced around, but there was nothing so pronounced as a trend.

The *Times* (London) reported, probably truthfully, "At the termination of the perusal of this document an animated discussion ensued indiscriminately among the shareholders," which sounds like a polite way of describing a riot that occurred at a bondholder's meeting.[151] "Some were of the opinion that the proposition ought to be rejected in toto." Others, we are told, "[i]magined the better plan would be to accept the proposal as far as the moiety of the interest would be paid in money, but refuse the tender of the grant of lands." A third group "would give the decree more deliberate consideration." Robinson, who chaired the meeting, pointed out that the bondholders could not adopt a piecemeal approach to the settlement. "They must either surrender the original security, the bonds, and receive for them new bonds for the one half and land warrants for the other, or else they must retain their former security." One bondholder suggested – to the cries of "Hear, hear" – that the matter be referred to the Committee of Spanish-American Bondholders "who had throughout exhibited such great ability in the management of the affairs of the Bondholders."

What did the bondholders want? Clearly, they wanted money rather than public lands. Or as one bondholder put it, "Mexico offers us grants in Texas, and we all know they might as well offer grants in Yorkshire or Burgundy." The land warrants in which they were to receive half the conversion were gone. In their place were, again, "deferred bonds," the deferred referring to the condition that the bonds would accrue no interest

---

149 Agustín Iturbide, Jr., to the *oficial mayor* of home and foreign relations, London, March 15, 1837, Archivo Histórico Genero Estrada, Legajos Encuadernados, 1064, SREM.
150 Schmitz, *Texas Statecraft*, pp. 92–93.
151 *Times* (London), August 7, 1837, for this and what follows.

until 1847. Yet the warrants idea did not disappear. The bondholders were now given the *option* of converting the deferred bonds into "vacant public lands" in Texas, Chihuahua, New Mexico, California, and Sonora. The bonds would convert at £4 per acre and accrued interest at 5 percent beginning October 1, 1837, to the date of taking possession of the land as well. Lizardi and Company gave the Committee of Mexican Bondholders substantially what it wanted, or perhaps, we should say what Iturbide Jr. did. Iturbide seemed particularly proud of his handiwork. Writing to the Finance Ministry, he observed that between January and February 1838, Mexico 6 percents had risen by 2 percent – actually it was 2 percentage points or 8 percent – "surely due to the Bondholders anticipating that the project pending (i.e., the conversion) will be approved [in Mexico and they will receive word of it soon]." "But, Iturbide continued, however much prices may rise, it won't last if the agreement for sending cash (i.e., the dividends) isn't carried out."[152] Exactly no cash was sent forward to Great Britain until 1840, so the bondholders' hopes for a quick rectification of the situation would ultimately come to naught.[153]

Lizardi and Company and Iturbide tried to sell the authorities in Mexico on the deal.[154] The deferred bonds would save half the interest on the foreign debt, and the deferred bonds would be worth nothing if foreign investors did not strive to bring the underlying lands to which the bonds were linked into production. Lizardi and Company also took credit for keeping the segregation of customs revenues to pay dividends down to 6 percent when the bondholders were actually demanding 20 percent. Of course, Lizardi and Company had plenty of its own incentives to want to see the arrangement succeed. Lizardi and Company's agent in Mexico, Quintana, asked the Mexican government to grant 10 million acres to "the principal commercial houses in Europe for success in this business."[155] It is true that Rothschilds had some interest in Mexico a decade earlier; some Rothschilds money had made its way into supporting Mexico's European legations. But their interest in Mexico could scarcely have been more than marginal and their interest in Mexican bonds smaller still. Could Mexico have seemed so much different to them from Spain, whose civil wars and deferred bonds raised red flags within the family's inner circle?[156] One wonders whether Lizardi and Company may simply have seen the consolidation of the Mexican debt as a way of buying access to a circle of contacts to which the house had been excluded?

152 Agustín Iturbide, Jr., to the finance minister, London, February 15, 1838, *Deuda Exterior*, vol. 5, AGNM.

153 Undated report (Año de 1843), *Deuda Exterior*, vol. 5, AGNM.

154 Alamán, *Liquidación de la deuda*, pp. 30 and ff.

155 "Prestamos Extranjeros," *Deuda Exterior*, vol. 5, AGNM.

156 Ferguson, *House of Rothschild*, pp. 356–367.

Finally, there was the matter of Lizardi's direct financial interest in brokering a deal. The firm began by asking for a 6 percent commission on the value of the land warrants to be paid by a further bond issue. This was serious money, nearly 1.4 million pesos in cash commissions, but when the proposal went forward to the Consejo de Gobierno, it offered a 2 percent commission in land warrants or cash commission of 1 percent "if and when circumstances allowed."[157] There were other matters that did not go the firm's way either. The bondholders demanded that the original bonds be placed on deposit with the Bank of England; "otherwise [they] would have thought we were trying to deceive them," presumably by continuing to trade in the original bonds. Nor was Lizardi and Company able to postpone the date from which interest would accrue until 1866. But the firm concluded, "We flatter ourselves that the Supreme Government will approve what we have negotiated. If we hadn't done what we did, we would have lost the great benefits to the nation that the agreement celebrated with the Bondholders brought." Iturbide added that he had negotiated in good faith as well, and was resigned to whatever the government in Mexico would do.[158]

In Mexico, the agreement did not prosper. On December 28 and 29, 1837, the Consejo de Gobierno rejected the agreement of September 14, 1837, saying, in effect, that it had no authority to reach such an agreement and that the executive power had no authority to sanction what had been negotiated either. Only the Congress could authorize any such negotiation and the document the Congress had authorized was that of April 12, 1837. Historians have become increasingly aware of the substantial power that the Congress in its various incarnations exercised in the early nineteenth century and of the corresponding debility that sometimes afflicted executive authority.[159] In this matter, the result was no different. Even if Lizardi and Company owned Santa Anna, Congress was another matter, and to this agreement, the Mexican Senate was a particular obstacle.[160] And so matters stood until the spring of 1838. At this point, Colonel Almonte was sent to London "for the opening of fresh negotiations with the Holders of Mexican Bonds for the acceptance of some middle term between the project first proposed to them and that to which the Mexican chargé d'affaires [i.e., Agustín Iturbide, Jr] was induced to assent without the necessary authorization of his government."[161]

157 Murphy, *Memoria sobre la deuda exterior*, p. 9.
158 Alamán, *Liquidación de la deuda*, pp. 30, 31.
159 Reynaldo Sordo Cedeño, *El Congreso en la Primera República Centralista* (México, 1993), pp. 19–59.
160 Mora to Bernardo Couto, Paris, July 14, 1838, and Couto to Mora, Paris, May 29, 1839, in "Papeles Inéditos y Obras Selectas del Doctor Mora," in Genaro García, ed., *Documentos inéditos*, pp. 530, 532.
161 Pakenham to [Foreign Secretary], México, April 4, 1838, FO 50/113, PRO.

Meanwhile, the bondholders' irritation – already considerable, as we have seen – nearly brought the whole fraught process to grief. On May 9, 1839, a meeting of all the American bondholders in London had occurred. Among the Mexican creditors, several complained bitterly of the neglect of the Mexican government, and demanded return of their original bonds, the cancellation of the Conversion of 1837, and a return to the provisions of the Conversion of 1830, "which was more advantageous to them." The Mexicans in London were able to restrain the hotheads only with difficulty and were under no illusions that they could stall the bondholders indefinitely. Clearly, the agreement of September 15, 1837, had to be ratified, or trouble would ensue.[162]

In the event, the Mexican government would not send word of agreement or instructions to London until the end of July 1839, a long and costly delay that evidenced the disagreement that attended the issue in Mexico, although Lizardi and Company attributed the delay to "political circumstances that afflicted the republic" and prevented congressional ratification.[163] This was more than disingenuous, because the conduct of Lizardi and Company had virtually created the problem. With the French blockade of Veracruz in 1838, available customs revenues had plummeted. Lizardi and Company had "agreeably" managed to channel funds to bondholders who contrived to apply for payment at *Veracruz* via warrants Lizardi issued. As a result, there was nothing left to send to the bondholders in London, "placing different Bondholders on an unequal footing." There is no indication of how this "evil" transpired, but the erstwhile admirer of Santa Anna, Robert Crichton Wyllie, reported the fiasco with such equanimity that one can only wonder who profited, for more than the required 16 percent of customs from Tampico and Veracruz were required to "fund" it. The principal modification demanded in Mexico stipulated that to the extent that bonds were traded for land, the territory should remain firmly under Mexican control, should not be located in frontier regions, and should consist of settlements that were too small and scattered for foreign immigrants to make any trouble.[164]

A jubilant Tomás Murphy, who received much credit for brokering the final agreement, wrote Finance Minister José Echeverría that word of the government's acceptance of the Conversion of 1837 had been well received. So the Conversion of 1837 was finally settled in 1839, although there was

162 [Unknown] to the finance minister, London, May 10, 1839, *Deuda Externa*, vol. 5, AGNM.
163 See Tomás Murphy, *Memoria sobre la deuda esterior de la Republica Mexicana desde su creacion hasta fines de 1847* (Paris, 1848), p. 11, for reference to opposition to the agreement of September 15, 1837. For the Lizardi statement, see *El Siglo XIX*, May 24, 1842.
164 Alamán, *Liquidación de la deuda*, pp. 33–35; Robert Crichton Wyllie, *A Letter to G. R. Robinson, Esq., Chairman of the Committee of Spanish American Bondholders, on the Present State and Prospects of the Spanish American Loans* (London [1840]), p. 10.

still no peace between Texas and Mexico and the Texans presumably owed the bondholders nothing. Nevertheless, "our bonds traded at 33 today, evidence of the favorable opinion here regarding what the government has done lately in regard [to the debt]."[165] With the drafts drawn on the customs, Murphy thought that "we will soon have the pleasure of seeing our credit, which has been viewed with disdain for so long, reestablished." Murphy reported that there had been a well-attended bondholders' meeting on October 14, 1839, in which they had shown "full agreement" with the results of the negotiation.[166] The evidence from relative bond prices was rather more mixed, although there was some obvious improvement in late 1839 and in early 1840. But then 1839 had been something of a roller coaster anyway, with the London market welcoming news of the defeat of the federalist forces under Urrea and Mejia in June, "as the federal party has for a long time impeded the march of commercial affairs," and just as violently reacting against the publication of Forbes' proposal (mentioned previously) that California be turned over to the bondholders "as a set off against their debt."[167]

It is, perhaps, oddly appropriate that the Pakenham, the British minister to Mexico, captured the mercurial nature of the financial markets in late 1839 with a most remarkable dispatch to Palmerston, the foreign secretary. While the provision of the Conversion of 1837 that permitted the exchange of unpaid dividends for customs drafts would continue to cause no end of fiscal problems to the government in Mexico City, it was a boon to speculators. Pakenham noted that "some of the Bondholders have taken advantage of the privilege." Moreover, Pakenham continued, "those received by the last and preceding packets have been admitted without hesitation or difficulty at the Customs Houses." If the agreement continued to be honored, Pakenham pointed out, "the speculation of purchasing Mexican stock at its present reduced value in England and making use of the dividend warrants in the payment of duties in this country (i.e., Mexico) *will be very profitable* [italics mine]."[168] That Pakenham could have recommended Mexican "stocks" to Palmerston at roughly the same time that Palmerston famously complained about the disposition of the bondholders' claims concerning the American loans – "Would you have us go to war?" – suggests that the ostensibly private nature of commercial and political pressures in the determination of British policy toward Mexico and its competing factions could not be so clear-cut as some historians have suggested.[169]

165 Murphy to the finance minister, October 15, 1839, *Deuda Exterior*, vol. 5, AGNM.
166 Murphy to the finance minister, October 15, 1839, *Deuda Exterior*, vol. 5, AGNM.
167 *Times* (London), June 24 and September 6, 1839.
168 Pakenham to the foreign secretary, México, February 9, 1840, FO 50/134, PRO.
169 See *Mexican Justice and British Diplomacy. The Case of Thomas Kinder*, p. viii.

The Worral Pseudo-Loan

Even as Murphy congratulated the finance minister on the success of the Conversion of 1837, another "loan" controversy loomed on the horizon. The Worral "loan" refers not to another loan per se that Mexico raised on the London market, but rather to the financial transaction that would accompany Mexico's purchase of weapons and ammunition in Great Britain. The nominal amount of the "loan" was to be £130,000 to be raised by issuing stock on the London Exchange. The parties to the loan included a certain Thomas Worral and a British house named McCalmont Brothers. According to an anonymous pamphlet published in Mexico in 1840, a loan of £130,000 was to take place "solely and exclusively to make the other business of arms and ammunition more profitable for the contractor."[170] If a critic of the transaction has described it accurately, its terms were disadvantageous, to put it mildly.

Apparently under pressure from President Bustamante and Congress, the Mexican government, which had already paid 200,000 pesos cash in advance, agreed to "borrow" an additional 650,000 pesos. On the same day as the notional loan was made (*entrega virtual*), the government was to pay 220,000 pesos for 4,000 quintals of gunpowder. Another 330,000 pesos were to be paid for the weapons, as well as for boats and other equipment. Of the remaining 100,000 pesos of the "loan," 50,000 were to be delivered to the government in its outstanding notes. This left 50,000 pesos, which, remarkably, were discounted by 86 percent according to market conditions. The result was that only 7,000 pesos cash was to be received by the Treasury out of the "free" 100,000 pesos of the loan. According to the pamphlet, the Poder Conservador intervened to declare the proposed loan unauthorized on a number of grounds.

Both Tomás Murphy and Lizardi and Company argued forcefully against the loan. For one thing, the interest payments on the original issues were in arrears, and since the Conversion of 1837 was not yet funded, the London Stock Exchange would not allow the new bonds to be listed as "evidently embarrassing for the government." Moreover, Murphy argued (in a lengthy report to Finance Minister Echeverría, written, no less, on the anniversary of Mexican independence, September 16, 1839) that "there are no limits to the hostility and lack of confidence the English public displays to this sort of thing because of the difficulties in which the American Republics have found themselves in meeting their obligations with the original lenders." As far as Mexico was concerned, Murphy continued, the investing public had taken a wait-and-see attitude. It had waited for more than two years for the Mexican government to negotiate the Conversion of 1837 and

---

170 *Ecsamen analítico del préstamo de 130,000 libras esterlinas y vindicación de los Supremos Poderes de la República que intervinieron en la declaración de su nulidad que hizo El Conservador* (México, 1840).

they were, quite naturally, suspicious. Indeed, the British press had called the putative Worral loan a "swindling affair" (*trampa*) whose purpose was simply to find more victims. "There is no doubt," wrote Murphy, "the effect would be disastrous for the credit of the Republic." And, he concluded, "if the Republic's credit is ruined, the new bonds would be worthless." If Lizardi and Company gave no sign of a willingness to be involved in such a venture, Murphy asked, then who else would? Closing, Murphy expressed confidence that the Conversion of 1837 and the implementation of customs certificates would "in a few months have changed the face of everything . . . and a new bond issue would, perhaps, no longer offer difficulties."[171]

At the same time, Lizardi and Company also warned the government of the probable consequences of floating the Worral loan. Naturally, since Lizardi and Company had much invested in the Conversion of 1837, the house declared itself loathe to be a party to anything that could undermine the agreement. The Worral issue would "excite a lack of confidence and impair the foreign credit of the Republic," not to mention the firm that would manage the loan. And, even worse, "it would completely compromise the credit of the Conversion undertaken that brought so many benefits to the Republic." If Mexico's credit were to be damaged by such a loan, "the Bondholders would go to their government pressing it to support the whole of their claims with measures that would bring the most dreadful consequences to the Republic."[172]

Since the loan was intended to facilitate the purchase of weapons and ammunition, Lizardi and Company may have had a vested interest in opposing the loan. The materials were, it is true, to be used in a renewed campaign against Texas. But Lizardi and Company had supplied Mexico with weapons, having built the ironclad "Montezuma" for the Mexican navy, a vessel destroyed by the Texas ship "Invincible" in March 1836. Lizardi would remain involved in trying to have vessels built for Mexico in England armed while not falling afoul of Britain's ostensible neutrality in the hostilities between Mexico and Texas.[173] How much of Lizardi and Company's principled interest was self-interest – in preventing someone else from getting a share in the Mexican arms market is an open question.

171 Tomás Murphy to the finance minister, London, November 23, 1839, *Deuda Exterior*, vol. 12, AGNM. ("*poco decoroso*" is translated as "evidently embarrassing.")
172 Lizardi and Company to the finance minister, London, September 17, 1839, *Deuda Exterior*, vol. 12, AGNM.
173 "Montezuma Affair" and "Pocket," *The Handbook of Texas Online*, http://www.tsha.utexas.edu (accessed September 28, 2007), and Dodson to the Foreign Office, London, May 7, 1842, FO 83/2303, PRO.

Conclusions

It is perhaps fair to conclude that the progress of the Conversion of 1837 was halting because the agreement was itself a mixed blessing. By converting half the principal of the debt to deferred (until 1847) status, the conversion offered breathing room from the press of interest payments. In return, Mexico agreed to convert its 6 percent bonds at a 12.5 percent premium that *added* to, rather than reduced, principal. While Mexican authorities were appropriately sanguine about the results, a modern analyst might, perhaps, be somewhat more skeptical. In 1850, the Chamber of Deputies concluded that the conversion saved Mexico 10 million pesos when the debt stood at about 46 million.[174] But that is misleading, for the calculation is apples and oranges: the gross reduction in interest adjusted for the increase in principal. There is a more meaningful way of looking at this.

The present value (discounted at 4 percent) of the savings in twelve years of interest was approximately 9.4 million pesos. That was what the bondholders gave up to obtain a 2.6-million-peso increase in the value of principal. In essence, they sacrificed 6.8 million pesos or £1.36 million, which is one way of viewing what Mexico saved. But why would anyone make such a disadvantageous trade? Presumably, they did so to realize immediately the gain from the increased principal. At first blush, it appears that they viewed the 2.6 million pesos as certain and the 9.4 million as less so, or to put it another way, if there was no better than a 27 percent chance of collecting the 9.4 million pesos, the bondholders would take the 2.6 million pesos. But even that is an optimistic assessment, because bonds in 1837 were trading around 20, not par. So 2.6 million at par was 520,000 pesos at market, which implies that at the margin, the bondholders saw little better than a 5 percent chance of (.20*.27) ever getting what was originally owed to them.

In other words, by 1837, there was not much cause for optimism. No wonder the bondholders seized on the possibilities offered by the conversion, albeit reluctantly. Nevertheless, while the Conversion of 1837 did not solve the problem of default, it was, in essence, the basis for discussions in the early 1840s and for a subsequent agreement that would resume (or enlarge) the flow of dividends to the bondholders. A number of features that characterized events in the 1830s here require some emphasis, as insights into the political economy of the Mexican debt and as "lessons" to be drawn from the decade.

At one level, the market grew to fear federalism and welcome centralism as a source of possible resolution to the difficulties of the bondholders.

---

174 *Dictamen de la Comisión de Crédito Público de la Cámara de Diputados sobre el arreglo de la Deuda Inglesa*, p. 67.

On average, the relative prices of Mexican bonds on the London market
between October 1841 and August 1846 – Santa Anna's first dictatorship
and the remainder of the central republic – reached levels unseen since the
first republic. This, perhaps, was less a matter of ideology than of sheer
pragmatism. Centralism represented the interests of the old core states
of the viceroyalty of New Spain, and by definition, the interests of the
governmental entity on which the ultimate responsibility for paying the
interest and principal devolved. Federalism, in whatever form it took, was
a geographically diffuse tendency that virtually defined itself by opposition
to the authority and fiscal pretensions of the central government. Provinces
in rebellion in the 1830s, like Texas or Zacatecas, reduced the fiscal base
of the central government and made repayment of the debt less likely. Hence
the welcome the market accorded to the coming of the central republic and
the dictatorship because the probability of repayment rose.[175]

Figures like Valentín Gómez Farías might apparently support a more
ideological view of things, but in reality, his preference for repayment of the
internal debt over satisfying the foreign bondholders reflected fiscal circumstances and his own attempt to solidify a political base. In essence, when
constraints on the budget multiplied because of domestic upheavals, state
rebellions, foreign blockades – all features of the politics of the 1830s – the
interests of domestic financiers were paramount, because foreign bondholders were not inclined to see their funds literally go up in smoke. Domestic
borrowing skyrocketed during the 1830s, doubling by the mid-1830s, and
nearly doubling again by the decade's end. The effect of this accumulation
of debt on Mexican bond prices was palpable, because mushrooming internal debt was incompatible with the repayment of the London bondholders.
There was only so much to go around, so many ways to divide up the maritime customs, the government's principal source of funds. In Table 2.3,
I report the results of an ordinary least squares (OLS) regression of the log of
domestic borrowing on the log of the price of Mexican 6 percents between
1825 and 1844 (at the end of the second quarter, roughly coinciding with
the fiscal year). The results are instructive. More than half the variability

---

175 Sordo Cedeño, *Primera República Cetralista*, p. 108. Also see Josefina Vázquez, *México, Gran Bretaña
    y otros países, 1821–1848* (México, 1990), p. 134, who makes a similar point. There was also some
    tendency for relative bond prices to be more stable under centralism than under federalism, but a
    formal analysis of variance produces an F-statistic (1.9) that is not quite significant at conventional
    levels ($p = .22$). Perhaps it is best to regard this connection as a *tendency*, if not an inescapable
    relation. Certainly, the connection between federalism, centralism, and the financial markets was
    blurred at the margins, especially when fiscal problems beset *all* regimes in the 1830s and 1840s.
    But there is also little doubt that the centralists were associated with cleaning up the disorders
    that federalism, correctly or no, has been seen to produce. See María Laura Solares Robles, *Una
    revolución pacífica. Biografía política de Manuel Gómez Pedraza, 1789–1851* (México, 1996), esp.
    pp. 137–139.

Table 2.3. *Internal Borrowing and Mexican Bond Prices:*
Regression Results

Dependent variable		
Log price of Mexican 6 percents		
Independent variables		
Constant	5.78	$t = 12.6$
Log internal borrowing	−.1513	$t = −4.8$
DW $= 1.98$		
$R^2 = .54$		
SER $= .231$		
Mean dependent variable $= 3.578$		
$F = 23.31$		

Source: Memoria de Hacienda . . . 1845, p. 155, and my data.

in bond prices is explained by changes in domestic borrowing, with the expected (negative) sign on domestic borrowing. In essence, the British bondholders were in competition with the *agiotistas* for resources, and this was not a good place to be. Mexican financiers could inevitably trump a bondholder in matters of repayment, because Mexico's financiers had a direct line to the Treasury. Indeed, in the 1830s, the financiers not only ran the Treasury, to paraphrase Stephen Haber, they *were* the Treasury and often the most senior officials of the finance ministry as well.[176]

These frictions were only part of a more general set of growing tensions that characterized the debt question in the 1830s. Mexico and Britain were at loggerheads, as the very different tenor of the negotiations over the conversions of 1830 and 1837 illustrates, but the divisions were, in reality, far more complex. Large and small bondholders, speculators, and investors by no means shared the same interests or incentives, and by 1837, some bondholders also expressed dissatisfaction with the leaders of the Committee of Bondholders. The Texas question had its own dynamic, making territorial issues less tractable for both the bondholders and the government of Mexico. If the land warrants created by the Conversion of 1837 were to have any value, the territorial integrity of Mexico and the retention of its possessions in the southwest were vital – worth fighting over in the basic sense. But the Texans appealed to the bondholders for a separate peace, one that demanded the independence of Texas, perhaps as a British protectorate. In addition, there were shadowy rumors in the early 1830s of United States interest in California linked to a settlement

176 Laura Suárez de la Torre, "Presentación: El Predominio del Agio y la Bancarrota Nacional, 1835–1850," in Leonor Ludlow, ed., *Los Secretarios de Hacienda y sus Proyectos (1821–1933)* (2 vols.; México, 2002), vol. 1: pp. 165–166.

with the bondholders as well.[177] The foreign debt was then an issue with implications for the survival of the Mexican nation well before the 1860s, for the options on offer presented Hobson's choice. There were no good solutions. The Texans could offer to pay off part of Mexico's debt, but only if Mexico recognized the independence of Texas, which proved to be politically impossible (and, in the event, fiscally unlikely for the Texans). The Mexicans could guarantee the bonds using Texas territory, but the Texans could hardly accede to this. Therefore, in some sense, the Conversion of 1837 was legally concluded but practically impossible.

At the same time, the growing political turmoil within Mexico made coherent policymaking difficult. The ministry of home and foreign relations had stated that "the English matters require considerable activity and *uninterrupted attention*" [emphasis mine].[178] But one glance at the roll call of ministers, agents, representatives, negotiators, and so on who served makes it difficult to believe that much continuity of purpose or discussion could be maintained. In London, the negotiations involved, at one point or another, Miguel Santa María, José María Gutiérrez de Estrada, Máximo Garro, Luis G. Cuevas, and Tomás Murphy as minister plenipotentiary between 1826 and 1842. As chargé d'affaires, Agustín Iturbide Jr., Juan Almonte (interim), Tomás Murphy (interim), and José Murphy (as secretary of legation) were present at the same time. The proliferation of reports and summaries that one finds in this period, valuable as they are as historical sources, underscores what must have been the felt need to bring order to a messy and disorderly process. Mistakes were made that cost Mexico money, time, and credibility, mistakes that emphasize a lack of administrative capacity. Significantly, the one constant presence in these negotiations after 1835 was Lizardi and Company, and ultimately, as we will see, if no one can serve two masters, Lizardi and Company evidently decided early on whose interests it would serve. The "Mexican" firm may have negotiated the Conversion of 1837, but whether it ultimately served the interests of Mexico better than did its British predecessor, Baring Brothers, is not an obvious matter at all, for Baring, at least, was instrumental in maintaining a stream of dividend payments, and not for the last time.

At bottom, the oscillations that characterized the political economy of the 1830s were a product of precisely these tensions: the demands of international versus domestic finance. With the growing demand to finance domestic political contests in the early 1830s, the opportunity cost of servicing the foreign debt was simply too high. As Barbara Tenenbaum has astutely noticed, the rise of the *agiotistas* in the early 1830s paralleled the

---

177 Joaquín Moreno, *Diario de un escrbiente de legación* (México, 1925), p. 23.
178 Hidalgo, *Representantes de México en Gran Bretaña*, p. 23.

increasing neglect of the London Debt.[179] But this was probably less a consequence of the Mexican default – the British were unlikely to finance internal conflict in Mexico even had debt service continued – than it was one of having more than one means of satisfying domestic creditors. By and large, the London bondholders had made it plain they wanted to be paid in sterling, not in lands, speculative notes, or anything else. The *agiotistas* were another matter. They were nothing, if not infamous speculators, in the floating debt, and if the Treasury had no cash, a complaisant finance minister – perhaps, like Echeverría, a speculator himself – could always think of something. Domestic financiers like the Martínez del Río, Cayetano Rubio, and Felipe Neri del Barrio had investments in textile mills, and could be compensated with judicious exemptions on the prohibition of imports of raw cotton. Together with a more restrictive commercial regime, such as prohibitions on such items as cotton sheeting, twist, yarn, and thread, artificially raising returns to capital was another way of settling accounts. So too was access to funding from the Banco de Avío, which represented a *direct* transfer of resources from the London bondholders to domestic interests. Or even the reestablishment of the tobacco monopoly, particularly in the form of the *Empresa del Tabaco*, where the rental income was redistributed to the states.[180] But if the London Debt was sacrificed on the altar of domestic interests, it must have seemed worthwhile. In the early 1820s, the Federation could find no takers when it approached domestic lenders for money. That was, after all, why the London Debt was undertaken. By the early 1830s, in what Tenenbaum ironically (but correctly) terms "invisible stability," domestic finance was available – at a price, not in spite of a foreign default, but *because* of it. All that had been necessary was to turn the machinery of state over to the financiers to be employed in the service of their rent-seeking. Unfortunately, the foreigners were not to be so easily discouraged and Mexico was losing the British support when it needed it most, in the face of aggression from its erstwhile "republican" neighbor.

Finally, we have suggested that the presumption that the bondholders in general craved stability is wrong. Once the Mexican issues went into default – and for the most part, stayed there – there was not much prospect of getting rich through clipping coupons. The dividends were simply not reliable enough. Or so the so-called bona fide investors in Mexican bonds in the 1830s complained. By the time of the Conversion of 1837, history – not

---

179 Tenenbaum, *Politics of Penury*, pp. 58–71. Also see Hilary Heath, "Mexicanos e ingleses: xenophobia y racismo," *Secuencia* (1992), p. 91, who dates, incorrectly I believe, the origins of the division to the end of the 1840s and beginning of the 1850s.

180 Robert A. Potash, *Mexican Government and Industrial Development in the Early Republic: The Banco de Avío* (Amherst, 1983), pp. 44, 152; *Reestablecimiento del Estanco de la Siembra y Cultivo del Tabaco en los Puntos Cosecheros Contrato...* (México, 1839), p. 4.

to say the history of the market, which is written in the numbers – affirms that they were correct. From the later 1830s on, the business of Mexican bonds was more often dominated by large financiers, particularly financiers with access to the rotating cast of Mexican finance ministers and Presidents, who made the decisions that affected the price of Mexican bonds. It is in large part to their story, as well as to the issues of the financial debacle of the War of 1847 and the Carthaginian Peace that followed, that we now turn.

3

Blood from a Stone

¡Cuánto cuesta el enmendar un error!
Si se supiera, más fácil, mil veces fuera
obrar bien, que no faltar!
— Manuel Eduardo Gorostiza,
Indulgencia Para Todos

Panic, Pastry, and the Conversion of 1837

As Lizardi and Company was promoting and directing the Conversion of 1837, its commercial world was falling apart. The affairs of Mexico were hardly the house's only concern. With branches in New Orleans, London, Paris, Veracruz, and Havana, the Lizardi were forced to confront the international economic crisis known as the Panic of 1837 in all its complexity.

We normally think of the Panic of 1837 as an affair that principally concerned the United States and Great Britain. Still, economic historians have long been aware of a Mexican dimension to the crisis as well. Peter Temin alluded to the issue in his classic work on the Jacksonian economy, and monetary historians, such as Hugh Rockoff, are only too aware of the implications of Temin's story.[1] Nevertheless, the precise importance of the link from Mexico to the United States is not the central issue. Instead, we are interested in the consequences that the Panic of 1837 had for the success of the Conversion of 1837 – which is to say, for Mexico's servicing the London Debt. We can summarize our argument: the Panic of 1837 doomed the Conversion of 1837 by imposing fiscal (and real economic) conditions on Mexico that made servicing the debt difficult, if not impossible. Ironically, one of the principal links in the chain of circumstances that foreclosed Mexico's option of paying was the action of Lizardi and Company, the very

---

1 Hugh Rockoff, "Banking and Finance, 1789–1914," in Stanley L. Engerman and Robert E. Gallman, eds., *The Cambridge Economic History of the United States* (3 vols., Cambridge, UK, 2000), vol. 2: p. 656: "Mexico was in the throes of a revolution, and considerable amounts of copper money were being issued to finance government expenditure producing a combination of capital flight and inflation-driven exports of silver."

Spanish Dollar

Mexican Dollar

Figure 3.1. Bullion Office, Bank of England. *Note:* Spanish Dollars and Mexican dollars held in the Bank of England's vaults. *Source:* Courtesy of Illustrated London News Ltd./Mary Evans Picture Library.

architects of the conversion. Let us see briefly how the process played itself out.

"The difficulty of raising money seems to be more pressing in the State of Mississippi even than in New York."[2] The anonymous Southern editorialist who wrote that was referring to one of the key triggers of the Panic of 1837

---

2 *New Orleans Bee*, April 1, 1837, for this and what follows.

in the United States, the Specie Circular of December 1836. The circular stipulated that public lands in the United States could be paid for only in silver or gold of which the coins illustrated in Figure 3.1 are an example. Some of the richest lands in Mississippi had been the subject of a speculative boom, a bubble now collapsing as the debt that fueled it had to be liquidated in "hard" money or specie rather than in banknotes. "If General Jackson is culpable for his conduct [as President] in relation to this much abused circular, it is only because he did not issue it four years ago."

But what did any of this have to do with the Conversion of 1837? The answer is straightforward. As the banking system in the United States seized up for lack of specie reserves, the premium offered for specie in financial markets there rose apace, if unevenly. The Mexican peso, which had been relatively stable in New York markets, rocketed to previously unseen levels in the summer of 1837, and this movement was repeated in other money markets in the United States, such as New Orleans. There the financier Pedro Martínez del Río found the peso trading at premiums of up to 24 percent.[3] For hard-pressed southern and western bankers in the United States, there was a logically efficient source of silver specie close by: "by bills of Exchange and other means they can augment the specie in their vaults by importations from Mexico, to meet all demands."[4] Indeed, "we know that before the first of June [1837] [the specie in bank vaults in New Orleans] will be augmented by the receipt of half a million [dollars] from Mexico."[5] Thus the key idea is that Mexico would provide reserves and liquidity to the banks in the United States. And so it did. Nicholas Biddle, the president of the Second Bank of the United States, personally directed that specie balances accumulated by the New Orleans branch of the Second Bank "be returned to the North with as little delay as may be consistent with safety" in order to stabilize the financial center banks of New York City.[6] Joseph T. Crawford, the British consul in Tampico, observed that "within a few months a scarcity of specie has arisen in the United States and agents from the banks have come here for the negotiation of bills and to facilitate the shipment of dollars to [the United States]."[7] As always, Charles T. O'Gorman managed to get to the essence of things. The exchange through the United States was quite favorable, he said, "arising

3 David W. Walker, *Kinship, Business, and Politics: The Martínez del Río Family in Mexico, 1824–1867* (Austin, TX, 1986) p. 107. Also see Manuel Lizardi to N. M. Rothschild and Sons, New Orleans, September 29, 1837, RAL/XI/112/124, The Rothschild Archive, London.

4 *New Orleans Bee*, April 18, 1837.

5 *New Orleans Bee*, April 19, 1837.

6 Nicholas Biddle to the assistant cashier of the New Orleans branch of the Second Bank of the United States, Philadelphia, May 26, 1836, Dreer Collection, 145: Volume: Nicholas Biddle, Historical Society of Pennsylvania.

7 Joseph T. Crawford to the consul-general, Tampico, January 5, 1837, FO 50/110, PRO.

Table 3.1. *Monetary Data, 1830–1837*

Year	Silver Exported	Silver Coined	Copper Coined
1830	8,782,714	8,457,030	132,912
1831	5,513,629	11,539,539	256,730
1832	9,354,086	12,515,008	191,062
1833	12,940,057	12,276,204	520,061
1834	17,537,686	12,532,147	665,939
1835	12,274,714	11,439,638	1,036,103
1836	14,282,743	11,102,692	1,130,364
1837	14,373,514	11,073,843	875,572

Note: All values are in pesos.

These numbers are, without exception, inexact, but the best we currently have. O'Gorman estimated the total export of bullion from Veracruz and Tampico from 1830 to 1834 at 6 million pesos per year ("Returns of Treasure Shipped at Veracruz...," Mexico, September 22, 1835, FO 50/93, PRO). This suggests that the proportion of bullion flowing to England must have fallen from about 75 percent around 1830 to less than half by the onset of the Panic of 1837. The shift was in favor of the United States.

Sources: Silver and Copper coined, *Estadísticas históricas de México*, vol. 2: pp. 802–803; Silver Exported, *Memoria que sobre el estado de la Hacienda Nacional de la República Mexicana presentó a la Cámara el Ministro de Ramo en Julio de 1845* (México, 1846), pp. 114–118.

from the discussion between the government and the Banks."[8] As the data in Table 3.1 suggest, the disturbance in the United States and the resulting shift were enormous. The shipments of specie from Mexico to Great Britain fell by about a third in the 1830s.

Among the most active of "agents" engaged in shipping silver to the United States was the merchant firm Lizardi and Company.[9] "Perhaps no house in the United States has contributed to the soundness and safety of the paper currency as that of Messrs. Lizardi – Certainly no other house has introduced so much specie into the country." According to the New Orleans customs records, from October 1836 through March 1837, the Lizardi had brought some $1.2 million of specie into the United States – an "astonishing" amount.[10] By any reasonable standard, that was astonishing, alright. The Lizardi probably accounted for about 50 percent of all specie exported into the United States from Mexico in 1837. Indeed, by the standards of

8 Charles T. O'Gorman to [unknown], Mexico, February 12, 1835, FO 50/99.
9 In New Orleans sources, the firm was called Lizardi Brothers. There was another, separate firm listed for F. de Lizardi. Surprisingly, there is no good study of the Lizardi, one of the most important merchant banks of its day.
10 *Niles Weekly Register*, April 15, 1837, for this and what follows.
    I used the *Niles* data to estimate Lizardi's import into the United States through New Orleans at $2.3 million in 1837. Total specie imports from Mexico were about $4.7 million. See *United States Commerce with South America, 1821–1898* (Washington, DC, 1898), p. 3323.

the data presented in Table 3.1, the Lizardi would have accounted for 15 percent of all specie exported from Mexico in 1837. One could be forgiven as seeing Lizardi and Company as something of a one-firm open-market operation.

There are two questions that need to be answered: Why Lizardi and Company? And what does this have to do with servicing the London Debt? The first question is not difficult to answer. Lizardi and Company was at serious risk of failure in England from collapsing security prices, so the pressure on the house to expand one of its core businesses, exchange arbitrage, was enormous.[11] Lizardi – with operations in England, the United States, and Mexico – was the ideal candidate for this business, even if "ideal" is not quite the word when failure was the incentive.

The firm's location in New Orleans was a critical element in its success. New Orleans had become the entrepot for British trade to Mexico because British vessels could bring large quantities of manufactured cottons there and dispose of them easily. On the return trip to Britain, they carried raw cotton from the South. Smaller U.S. ships could then bring reasonable quantities of finished goods from New Orleans to Mexican ports without glutting the Mexican markets or worry overmuch about returning in ballast. It was a sensible arrangement from which Lizardi and Company benefited.[12]

The second question depends on how the export of specie affected the Mexican macroeconomy. We may be certain of one thing: exporting silver was the equivalent of exporting liquid purchasing power – a contractionary fiscal policy. With a fixed exchange rate, demand and national income would stagnate or fall, and tax collections would follow suit – here through the channel of reduced taxes on imports. Of course, this was precisely the way the government serviced the London Debt, so there can really be little question as to why there was little interest in implementing the Conversion of 1837. From this standpoint, the Panic of 1837 rendered the Conversion of 1837 impossible. As late as 1842, merchants in Mexico complained that the economic shocks of 1837 (and 1839) had brought business activity in Mexico City to a standstill.[13]

11 A. E. Feavearyear, *The Pound Sterling: A History of English Money* (London, 1931), p. 236; Michael Collins, "The Langton Papers: Banking and Bank of England Policy in the 1830s," *Economica*, 39: 1 (1972), p. 52n; Ralph W. Hidy, "Cushioning a Crisis in the London Money Market," *Bulletin of the Business Historical Society*, 20: 5 (1946), p. 142.

12 Charles T. O'Gorman to the Foreign Office, México, May 4, 1833, PRO 50/80B.

13 Joseph Smith to Joseph Stokes, México, July 12, 1842, quoted in Item 1169 (Washington W. West vs. Joseph Smith and John Stokes, June Term 1843, Court of Common Pleas, Philadelphia, PA) Stokes–Evans–Cope Papers re: Joseph Smith, 1825–1849, Special Collections, Haverford College Library.

    In an ongoing study, Rosa María Meyer and I are analyzing the market for loans to the government in 1837 and 1838. We find a sharp decline in interest rates from 3 to 1 percent per month, an indicator of how severe the contraction was.

But there were other things that the national government did that were not really consistent with servicing the London Debt. Money creation in Mexico (copper coinage, whose circulation was estimated at around 6 million pesos) produced inflation and caused an appreciation of the real exchange rate. Effectively, this raised the incentive for the Lizardi to export silver, for it was now more valuable in the United States than at home. Impoverished governments will use this tactic, called seigniorage, or an inflation tax, to generate resources, and Mexico in the mid-1830s certainly met the definition of "impoverished." The profits from copper coinage were not insignificant, perhaps a million pesos per year between 1829 and 1837, but seigniorage too made the London Debt harder – not easier – to pay by driving silver abroad.[14]

Finally, the infamous Guerra de Pasteles or Pastry War in 1838 put the final nail in the coffin. When the French blockaded the port of Veracruz, they compromised the public finances of Mexico still further. Daniel Cosío Villegas shows that "*impuestos exteriores*" or taxes on foreign trade accounted for nearly 40 percent of the Federation's total income in the 1820s, and were only slightly less than that in the 1830s. A sharp decline in 1837, 1838, and 1839 – to around 20 percent – plainly demonstrates how tightly squeezed the government was for revenues.[15] And this makes no allowance for the anticipation of customs, which O'Gorman termed "ruinous" and which Finance Minister Javier Echeverría claimed in late September 1840 was fully two-thirds "pledged to pay off the public creditors."[16] Richard Packenham went on to say that "in the year 1839 the Mexican government [was] reduced to a state of insolvency owing to the extent to which the Customs Revenue has been anticipated." And under the circumstances of "panic and pastry," the Convention of 1837 was bound to fail to reestablish debt service to any meaningful degree. And fail it did.

The only way Mexico paid anything between 1838 and 1841 was by a measure of last resort, the issue of drafts against the maritime customs of Veracruz and Tampico. These drafts, which were drawn on Lizardi and Company, fell due within ten days of any unpaid dividend. In theory, the drafts were acceptable in lieu of cash duties, although Lucas Alamán believed that they were worthless to anyone who had no business in Mexico. Nevertheless, someone clearly wanted them, for between 1838 and 1841, $1.5 million of the drafts were accepted in Mexico – nearly six times the

---

14 *El Siglo Diez y Nueve*, November 8, 11, 12 and December 1841 for discussions of copper coinage, its depreciation, the disappearance of silver from Mexican circulation (Gresham's law), and the shipment of silver abroad. José Enrique Covarrubias, *La Moneda de cobre en México, 1760–1842. Un problema administrativo* (México, 2000), p. 140.

15 *La cuestión arancelaria en México* (1932; México, facsimile ed. 1989), pp. 65–65.

16 Echeverría to the foreign secretary, México, September 29, 1840, FO 50/149, and Charles T. O'Gorman to the foreign secretary, México, March 2, 1837, FO 50/110, PRO.

amount remitted to England as cash dividends.[17] A government in a tight corner will do what it thinks is necessary to survive.

Santa Anna: The Bondholders' Friend?

Finally, in October 1841, Santa Anna assumed the presidency, putting an end to the regime of Anastasio Bustamante. Bustamante, who had become president in 1837, was closely linked to one of the core constituencies of centralism, the incipient modernizers of the textile industry, the champions of protection, and indeed, the exclusion of foreign textiles.[18] Santa Anna was cut, so to speak, from different cloth. He was said to have come to power supported by foreign merchants, and particularly by the Englishman, Francisco Morphy, who had paid a visit to Santa Anna while the General was still rusticated at Manga del Clavo in July 1841. Amid rumors that the English had bribed Santa Anna and his cronies to the tune of 80,000 pesos – hard to substantiate – the expectation was that Santa Anna would prove far more hospitable to British interests than his predecessor. Between January and April 1842, the price of Mexican bonds relative to consols rose 25 percent. Someone in London was expecting good things from the new regime, and good things were not long in coming.[19] Indeed, Santa Anna was reputed to have felt "great dissatisfaction" at the "exhausted state of the public Treasury at his return to the seat of government," so something was bound to happen.[20]

What occurred in February 1842 were two related developments of interest to the British bondholders. The first was that Santa Anna (or his ministers) suspended payment on the domestic debt, the so-called *funds* of 15, 17, 8, 10, and 12 percent, over the furious protests of their creditors, on February 19, 1842.[21] Left intact were several groups: the tobacco growers of

---

17 Alamán, *Liquidación de la deuda*, pp. 28, 36–37; Payno, *Cuestiones financieras*, p. 46.

18 Sordo Cedeño, *Primera República Centralista*, p. 118.

19 Cecilia Noriega Elío, *El Constituyente de 1842* (México, 1986), pp. 27–43. Also see Bustamante, *Diario Histórico de México*, November 10, 1844. I am grateful to Dra. Josefina Vázquez for clarification of these events.

20 Richard Pakenham to the foreign secretary, México, April 24, 1843, FO 50/161, PRO.

21 *Representación dirigida al Escmo. Sr. Presidente... por los apoderados de los acreedores que tienen hipotecas sobre las aduanas marítimas* (México, 1842). The petition was dated February 9.
    Included in this suspension was the so-called Second English Convention debt to the firm of Montgomery, Nicod and Company, technically English, but in reality a front for a syndicate of Mexican lenders among whom figured the Martínez del Río brothers. See Payno, *México y sus cuestiones financieras*, pp. 67–68. Claims pending on behalf of U.S. bondholders since the Convention of April 1839 seem to have remained in abeyance until restated in the Convention of 1843 with the United States agreed to by Santa Anna, which remained in effect until he was overthrown in late 1844. Wayne Cutler, ed., *Correspondence of James K. Polk* (10 vols., Nashville, 1969–), vol. X: p. 120. It was necessary for Santa Anna to resort to a forced loan among Mexican merchants to

Veracruz, signatories to the First English Convention (October 15, 1842), and the London bondholders, whose long-pending payments under the Conversion of 1837 were now regularized by an agreement of February 11, 1842.[22] The agreement would be associated with very substantial dividend remissions to London in 1842, 1843, and 1844, payments that led to an extremely favorable characterization of Santa Anna by Robert Crichton Wyllie, a shipping merchant who had resided in Mazatlán between 1825 and 1830 and served as a consultant to the Committee of Bondholders.[23] Indeed, the size of the dividend payments, which averaged about $700,000 per year, could have constituted only a true hardship for the Mexican government.[24]

Obtaining the resources to fund the London Debt once more required an almost complete reversal of the political economy of protection previously adopted, particularly under Bustamante. The series of adjustments that occurred was striking: the readjustment of the tariff of 1837 and the implementation of those of 1842 and 1843; the winding up of the lending activity of the Banco de Avío (1830–1842); the already mentioned suspension of the domestic funds; forced loans and a subtle tilt against the interests of the *agiotistas* and domestic industrialists who were the core interest of centralism; and abolition of the *consumo* duty on imports, which was believed to have discouraged trade and thus reduced the capacity to pay dividends.[25] Santa Anna himself went to the extreme of personally denying his field commanders access to the dividend funds when it was reported that a new engagement with the Texans loomed and there was no other way to pay the troops in the North.[26] And to what end? Presumably, to placate the British (and to a smaller degree U.S. claimants), who had emerged as Mexico's principal foreign ally under the Santanista dictatorship. As Josefina Vázquez notes, Santa Anna took great pains to cement

fund the payments to the United States, out of fear, he said, that the United States would invade otherwise. See Percy Doyle to the foreign secretary, México, April 24, 1843, FO 50/161, PRO. The first instalment of 270,000 pesos was due on April 30, 1843, to be paid from customs revenues. The total U.S. claim was $2.5 million. See *Decreto sobre préstamo forzoso de dos millones y medio para pagar la deuda reconocida al gobierno de los Estados Unidos de América* (México, 1843).

22 Richard Pakenham to the foreign secretary, México, April 7, 1842, FO 50/153, PRO.

23 Payno, *México y sus cuestiones financieras*, p. 46; Wyllie, *México. Noticia sobre su hacienda pública*; "Robert Crichton Wyllie," http://hml.org/mmhc/mdindex/wyllie.html (accessed September 28, 2007).

24 *Observaciones imparciales acerca de la Administración financiera en la época del gobierno provisional* (México, 1845), p. 5. To give some idea of how much this was, the French demand for compensation for claims made to the Mexican government in early 1838 was $600,000, so the opportunity cost of settling with the French was approximately the average yearly dividend payments to the British bondholders! See Faustino A. Aquino Sánchez, *Intervención Francesa, 1838–1839*, p. 135.

25 *Times* (London), February 9, 1842.

26 Santa Anna to the customs administrator of Tamaulipas, May 18, 1843, México, Gobernación, leg. 91, caja 151, exp. 1, AGNM.

an "understanding" with Great Britain, perhaps with the joint concern of keeping the Republic of Texas safely out of the grasp of the United States.[27] The agreement of 1842 with the bondholders was the fruit of that understanding. Santa Anna had, it appears, leaned heavily on his foreign creditors for support. So, it would seem, the British debt exercised a decisive influence on the public finances of Mexico during Santa Anna's first dictatorship. Predictably, when domestic payments were resumed in August 1842, the relative price of Mexican bonds headed down once again. Once again, it appears that foreign concerns and the London Debt were driving the direction of domestic political economy – but in reverse.

The Agreement of 1842

Whatever the case, Mexico tried to secure the best terms possible. In the midst of examining proposals advanced by the Committee of Bondholders and by Lizardi and Company, the Mexican government enjoined Lizardi and Company "by means of a secret maneuver, [to] try to get the Bondholders to reduce the amount owing them." If not, their instructions continued, the government's ability to pay the arrears accrued since 1837 would be endangered. The plan called for raising the amount sequestered from the customs revenue from 16.67 to 20 percent. Yet without a reduction in principal, 20 percent would be itself too much. More certificates would be issued, less cash would flow through customs, "and the bondholders would lose out because more time would be required to place even more certificates." In other words, both sides had to make sacrifices.[28]

By February 10, 1842, agreement had been reached, but not without some controversy. Lizardi and Company informed Finance Minister Ignacio Trigueros that some members of the Committee of Bondholders wanted the debentures that were part of the agreement to carry 5 percent interest. Lizardi and Company agreed only to put the matter to the Mexican government, stipulating that its resolution should have no effect on the agreement one way or another. This stipulation created "strong opposition" among members of the Committee of Bondholders. But Lizardi and Company had done its homework. It had proved unnecessary for the firm to call on one of its principals who had been placed "in the heart of the very Committee (*en el seno del mismo Committee*) to defend the good reputation of the Republic and its Government." So, with the services of its ringer not required, Lizardi and Company would recommend the approval

---

27 See, for instance, Worley, "The Diplomatic Relations of England and the Republic of Texas." The standard Mexican account of Anglo-Mexican relations in this period is Vázquez, *México, Gran Bretaña y otros países, 1821–1848*, esp. pp. 156–165.

28 Alamán, *Liquidación de la deuda*, pp. 41–42.

of the agreement and Mexico's credit would be repaired, so that the republic's fiscal fortunes would be put on a par with Brazil or Chile.[29] Indeed, Lizardi and Company produced a letter from Santa Anna dated the previous December, in which "he heartily concurred in the arrangement in course of progress." After a "stormy debate" of three hours, an "immense majority" of the bondholders meeting at the London Tavern decided to support the agreement.[30]

In a confidential dispatch to the finance minister, Lizardi and Company argued that the agreement was a good one and that it would save Mexico millions of pesos. Moreover, it had not strayed from the lines that Mexico had indicated it wanted to be followed – the lessons of 1837 had been learned. But it was important for Mexico to pay the dividends as they fell due: "from here on all our efforts must be directed toward keeping up with the dividend payments as they come due."[31] The advice, while good, was hardly disinterested. Lizardi and Company participated actively in the market, buying bonds on its own account and hoping to resell the now-paying issue at a profit. By late March 1842, the active bonds were trading around 42, their highest level since 1835, and the most they would command until the outbreak of war with the United States. But having purchased them between 38 and 40, the market moved adversely, and by late summer or early fall of 1845, with war well-nigh inevitable, the bonds were again trading in the range of 32. As a result, Lizardi and Company claimed to have lost 130,000 pesos in the operation.[32]

The actual agreement of 1842 was quite complicated.[33] Perhaps it would be best to summarize its essence: if the bondholders agreed to relinquish 50 percent of the interest then due on their bonds, or some £500,000 ($2.5 million), they should receive for the other half £500,000 in debentures. Twenty percent of the duties collected at Veracruz and Tampico were then to be segregated, as opposed to the existing 16.5 percent, thus leaving a residual balance of 3.5 percent of customs to retire the debentures.[34] As virtually all parties agreed at the time,[35] this was no small concession, the equivalent of two years' arrears of interest. In view of its rather remarkable

---

29 Francisco de Lizardi y Compañía to the finance minister, London, February 15, 1842, *Gobernación*, leg. 91, caja 151, exp. 1, AGNM.

30 *Times* (London), February 12, 1842.

31 Francisco de Lizardi to the finance minister (reservada), February 15, 1842, *Gobernación*, leg. 91, caja 151, exp. 1, AGNM.

32 *El Siglo Diez y Nueve, suplemento al número 1365*, August 25, 1845.

33 For its provisions, see Murphy, *Memoria sobre la deuda exterior*, pp. 15, 42n–44n.

34 See the letter signed H. P. I. in *Morning Herald*, April 15, 1844, a clipping of which is found, with others, in *Gobernación*, leg. 91, caja 151, exp. 1, fs. 40–47, AGNM.

35 See, for instance, Santa Anna's decree of October 10, 1842, published in the *Times* (London), December 21, 1842.

size, it is worth asking how Lizardi and Company was able to secure the bondholders' consent, although not easy to give a precise answer.

As late as February 1842, the Texans had continued their offer to assume part of Mexico's British debt if Mexico, in turn, would recognize the independence of Texas, just as Great Britain had now done.[36] Yet Mexico remained reluctant to recognize any such settlement, and would not even agree to an armistice with Texas until 1843. So Lizardi and Company turned its sights elsewhere. In late spring of 1842, Francisco de Lizardi wrote Finance Minister Trigueros expressing his concern for the depressed price of the deferred bonds created by the Conversion of 1837, bonds that traded between 8 and 10 from 1840 through 1843 (my sample data). Lizardi wondered what would happen when the bonds began to accrue interest, technically beginning October 1, 1847.[37] Lizardi's advice was to encourage "the establishment of Colonies in the territories best suited to it" and thus "obtain payment for the Deferred Bonds or as much as seems possible." Not content to simply express concern, Lizardi had approached "the English minister in this capital "so that in their names (i.e., of possible immigrants) he might petition the [Mexican] government for 15 million acres of land in Alta California near the port of San Francisco."[38] He stated, "You may recall that this department is one designated in the decree [of 1837] for the conversion of the debt with its territory pledged to amortization." Lizardi assured both Finance Minister Trigueros and President Santa Anna that the British had no designs on Mexico. Rather they hoped to sponsor European migration to Mexico, flourishing settlements, and a larger market for British goods. Lizardi suggested that the real threat came from the United States, "those who really lust after the possession [of California] and who are masters of the trade in its ports."[39] The bondholders meant Mexico no harm, for they were motivated "by private interest and by the hope that those involved would gain the same advantages that they might find in similar undertakings in other parts of the globe." Truly, Lizardi said, a third of the debt, perhaps even all of it, could be liquidated if the

36 Pakenham to the foreign secretary, México, February 17, 1842, FO 50/153, PRO.

37 The bonds were worth little with no expectation of their being paid, but with high rates of discount (i.e., present-minded bondholders), they should have risen as their date of earning interest approached. This is precisely what occurred. As late as June 1845, the bonds were trading at 21. When news of the war between Mexico and the United States reached Britain on May 30, 1846, the deferred bonds plunged to 15.5.

38 Manuel de Lizardi to the foreign secretary, London, May 2, 1842, *Gobernación*, leg. 91, caja 151, AGNM, for this and what follows. Francisco de Lizardi died in Paris sometime in late winter 1842. His death notice appears in the *Times* (London) on March 17, 1842. I assume that anything referring to Lizardi after that date is to Manuel de Lizardi, unless clearly specified otherwise. (*como por encanto* is translated as "magically.")

39 See also Lizardi and Company's letter to the *Times* (London), August 7, 1841.

deferred bonds were exchanged for land. With a flourish, Lizardi concluded, Mexico's population would receive

a very considerable increase in industrious and hard-working people accustomed to paying their taxes and other public charges religiously, as well as to respect the laws and to obey its magistrates. Its barren and uncultivated lands will be converted magically into settlements full of life and movement that produced every sort of thing that could be exchanged for foreign goods thus increasing the income of the state.

So, perhaps, it was the prospect of gaining a foothold in California for the bondholders that Lizardi held out in their negotiations with them. Certainly, the prospect of turning the independence of Texas to the advantage of the bondholders was fading quickly, perhaps once and for all. So after 1842, the focus of Mexico's discussion with the British would increasingly turn from Texas, which was all but lost, and to California, where the Mexicans hoped they could encourage the British to take a more active interest. Indeed, as late as 1845, Mexico sought to broker a deal using California lands in an effort to involve the bondholders, Manning and Macintosh, and the British government in an effort to thwart the ambitions of the United States there. Obviously the initiative failed.[40]

Bankers to Santa Anna

Merchant bankers in the nineteenth century were not operating eleemosynary enterprises. They were in business to make money, and in this Lizardi and Company was hardly exceptional. The Rothschilds made 8 percent on the British subsidy to Russia in 1814 during the Napoleonic Wars. They demanded a 2 percent commission on the subsidy to Prussia, but did not get it. Nevertheless, they earned a profit of 3 percent. Moreover, the Rothschilds practiced exchange arbitrage, something that Niall Ferguson judges to be especially lucrative because of "the effects of political uncertainty." Lending to governments, especially troubled ones, was a speculative business that justified commensurate returns.[41]

All of this may serve as a background to the *cause célèbre* in which Lizardi and Company soon found itself involved, the so-called clandestine issue of Mexican securities. As late as November 20, 1842, complaints against Mexico continued for its failure to pay dividends on the debentures.

---

40 See, for example, Josefina Vázquez Knauth, ed., *La Gran Bretaña frente al México amenazado, 1835–1848* (México, 2002), and Piero Gleijeses, "A Brush with Mexico," *Diplomatic History*, 29: 2 (April 2005), pp. 223–254. For the Mexican proposal of 1845, see Tomás Murphy's correspondence with his government in Carlos Bosch García, *Material para la historia diplomática de México (México y los Estados Unidos, 1820–1848)* (México, 1957), pp. 530–531.
41 Ferguson, *Rothschilds*, pp. 91–92.

"The fact is," the *Sunday Times* intoned, "that there is not the slightest difficulty in making up the dividends from the receipts of the Customs-houses of Veracruz and Tampico." But even so, "somehow, it has almost always happened, however, that these remittances did not reach [England] before the time of making up the current dividend, so that they were construed as belonging rightfully to the fund for the following dividend on Mexican Actives."[42] If someone suspected that subtle manipulations of dividend remissions from Mexico had begun to take place, the concern was still rather mildly expressed. Within a week, though, insinuations would grow louder.

On November 22, a committee of the London Stock Exchange submitted a request to Lizardi and Company, asking about the number and amounts of bonds issued in connection with the Conversion of 1837; Tomás Murphy refers to "rumors" about an excess or overissue of bonds.[43] Manuel Julián de Lizardi, who had taken over for his brother Francisco, who had died in March 1842, flatly refused to answer any questions put to him by the stock exchange, stating that the bondholders alone had the right to raise the issue. The stock exchange replied that Lizardi's answer was "highly unsatisfactory." At this point, an exchange of correspondence between Lizardi and the Committee of Bondholders did take place, with the committee questioning Lizardi closely as to the sum of bonds it had issued in connection with the Conversion of 1837. And so things stood on Saturday, November 26, 1842.

The next day, the affair became public.

A long piece in the *Sunday Times* reported that "very injurious and unpleasant rumors in regard to Mexican Bonds" had roiled the market during the previous week. The analysis continued, "Some of the Bear party in the Stock Exchange, finding that whenever good news or a remittance came to hand, and that the price got up a little, it was soon knocked down again by sales, and that this has not happened once or twice, but a dozen times, began to wonder how the circumstances could be accounted for." Rumors swirled about that the Mexican government, their agents, or some private party had somehow managed to issue duplicate bonds or that a surreptitious issue had taken place. As a result, "a regular panic has arisen, and the operators for a fall have had it all their own way." As the report then put it, "but the astonishment of the Stock Exchange was great."[44]

Why, precisely, astonished?

It was not, after all, the first time that someone had claimed that the market was crooked. In a remarkably scurrilous allegation in the New Orleans press, someone – "a highly respectable gentleman, long resident in

42 *Sunday Times*, November 20, 1842.
43 Murphy, *Memoria sobre la deuda exterior*, pp. 17–36, except where otherwise noted.
44 *Sunday Times*, November 27, 1842.

Mexico" – accused Alamán of taking advantage of his position as finance
minister to inflate Mexican bonds by scheduling dividends: "One, two,
three remittances are made – the stock rises above par, and Sr. Don L.
Alamón [*sic*], minister of finance, sells out – and here ends the payment of
interest on this loan." Thus did Alamán "make a large fortune by a stroke
of policy." This "saintly fellow" was a "cunning hypocrite" and "swindler"
who raised as much money as he could and had it "quietly vested in Mexican
bonds." Who could have said such a thing? Well, the informant was said to
have the best possible intelligence of events in Mexico City. He also had easy
access to the New Orleans press, with its sizable Mexican expatriate elite.
Of course, the "Lizardi Brothers" (Lizardi and Company) were among New
Orleans' most powerful financial houses, and they moved back and forth
between Mexico and Louisiana with apparent ease. One wonders, ironically,
whether their pots were well practiced in calling kettles black?[45]

At first, public opinion believed that the clandestine issue of bonds had
been designed to surreptitiously raise funds to fight against Texas. This
possibility was raised by Ashbel Smith, serving as the chargé d'affaires of
Texas in England and France from 1842 to 1844.[46] Smith recalled in 1875
that when he arrived in London in April 1842,

> two war steamers were building in British ports [i.e., Blackwall and Liverpool]
> and nearly completed for Mexico and to be employed against Texas.... These
> war steamers were contracted for by M. Lizardi, Mexican consul [*sic*] at London,
> avowedly for the war against Texas.... A rumor in London gave out that the
> steamers were paid for with money furnished to General Santa Anna by the Mexican
> clergy. I also heard sometime afterwards that the English holders of Mexican bonds
> had enabled Mexico to make an additional loan of £200,000.

Contemptuously, Smith concluded, "it was too unimportant a matter to be
worth enquiring into."[47]

But that was emphatically not how Smith regarded the matter as it
transpired. In January 1843, Smith wrote,

> the British holders of Mexican stocks were the securities of the Mexican consul
> at London for the building of the *Guadalupe* and *Montezuma* steamers. This is a
> *certainly* [italics in original] known fact. Large quantities of Mexican stock were
> issued in London secretly as you have probably seen, and sold, as was believed, to
> furnish Mexico the means to operate against Texas.

45 *New Orleans Bee*, June 9, 1837.
46 "Reminiscences of the Texas Republic," December 15, 1875, http://www.tamu.edu/ccbn/dewitt/
   smithasbel1.htm (accessed September 28, 2007).
47 On this matter, see *Hansard's*, 3rd ser., vol. 55, 1842, cols. 964–965 (Sir Robert Peel). Also see
   Mr. Dodson to the Foreign Office, London, May 7, 1842, FO 83/2303, PRO.

Smith, who nursed a grudge against the British well into senectitude – he thought Britain's opposition to slavery had worked against Texas and the South – believed that the bondholders "are violent *anti slavery* men [italics in original] [and] they would spare no money to subjugate [Texas] as they believed it would be doing God [a] service."[48] Indeed, Smith believed that the warships were to be paid for by "remittances of specie to London from Mexico."

However attractive Smith's theory might seem, it nevertheless has an obvious flaw. No one was more outraged by the clandestine issue of bonds than the existing bondholders, whose claims were thereby diluted and whose market value was thought to have fallen by 10–15 percent as a result.[49] However much they may have detested slavery, they hated their capital losses more. Surely, Smith realized this in later years. One might well wonder how a government that defaulted on its internal debt in February 1842 could afford two heavily armed warships in July 1842, yet Smith's allegation is intriguing, but by no means proved. Of course, there was the relation between Santa Anna and the Lizardi firm to which Percy Doyle adverted, and Santa Anna himself drew a bill against "Lizardi of Veracruz" after his capture by the Texans at San Jacinto and prior to his interview with Andrew Jackson, hoping that "Lizardi would honor it." One informant referred to M. de Lizardi and Company as "agents of Santa Anna" and it was through Lizardi that word of Santa Anna's imprisonment had gotten out.[50] The Lizardi, clearly, were bankers to Santa Anna, if not something more.[51] And in the Lizardis' view, the firm had issued the bonds as compensation for participating in the Conversion of 1837 and for the funds it had advanced to Mexican legations in Europe. The exact amount of the so-called overissue

48 Ashbel Smith to the Texas chargé d'affaires in Washington, DC, Paris, January 25, 1843, *Texian Diplomatic Correspondence* (3 vols., Washington, DC, 1911), vol. II (2): pp. 1107–1108, and Ashbel Smith to the Texas secretary of state, London, July 3, 1842, *Texian Diplomatic Correspondence*, II (2), p. 974.

49 *Times* (London), December 3, 1842.

50 "Santa Anna's Captivity," http://www.tamu.edu/ccbn/dewitt/santaanna5.htm (accessed September 28, 2007); Henry Austin to Asa Brigham et al., [n.p.], March 31, 1836, in John H. Jenkins, ed., *The Papers of the Texas Revolution* (10 vols., Austin, TX, 1973), vol. 5: p. 248; Luis Cuevas to the secretary of home and foreign relations, Paris, July 4, 1836, Archivo Genero Estrado, Legajos Encuadernados 1062, SREM.

51 In October 1853, Alphonse Danó, the French minister to Mexico, called Manuel Lizardi "an intimate friend of Santa Anna" and "one of the most influential people of the day," Lilia Díaz, *Versión Francesa de México* (3 vols., México, 1963–1965), vol. 1: pp. 78–79. For some notice of the Lizardi's involvement in a "plot" to liberate Santa Anna from his captivity at the hands of the Texans, see "Declaration of Don Bartholomé Pages Accused of a Conspiracy to Liberate Santa Anna...," Columbia, Texas, August 23, 1836, in Jenkins, ed., *Papers of the Texas Revolution*, vol. 9: pp. 303–304; for subsidies to Santa Anna and others in captivity, see Francisco Pizarro Martínez to the *oficial mayor* of the ministry of home and foreign relations. New Orleans, August 18, 1836, Archivo Histórico Genaro Estrada, Legajos Encuadernados 1063, SREM.

was in dispute, with initial reports putting the amount "exceeding half million sterling."[52] George White of Baring Brothers, relying on Murphy's account of the Conversion of 1837, set the amount at £876,000, or nearly 10 percent of the outstanding debt. In any case, Lizardi and Company had managed one way or another, to put a lot of paper into circulation.

It may well have been that in 1842, Lizardi and Company was in trouble. F. de Lizardi and Company of New Orleans, at least, was one of the larger firms involved in shipping raw cotton from New Orleans to Liverpool. In 1842, the price of cotton had fallen to a low ebb, and in New Orleans, Lizardi was obliged to issue a public denial that the house had suspended payments.[53] It is hard to suppress the thought that the Lizardi's flooding of the market with phony paper in 1842 coincided with a crisis in one of its core businesses. Certainly, £876,000 would have covered a lot of the firm's outstanding obligations!

As matters progressed, public opinion toward Mexico turned sharply negative. "[W]ith very few exceptions," the *Sunday Times* observed, "unmitigated condemnation is passed upon the conduct of the Mexican government in instructing its ministers and agents to violate the solemn compact entered into with the foreign bondholders." The difficulty, then, was that "the debt of Mexico is therefore greater than it was when the bondholders came to the last arrangement, or when buyers who made certain calculations as to the probability of a regular dividend forthcoming, invested at what they considered a fair price." "It is time," the article continued,

these foreign juggles for raising money from our pockets should be put a stop to, as it may be justly affirmed, that every sixpence received by the sale of a foreign bond, not emitted in the first instance on account of some loan to parties openly subscribing their capital, is a fraud upon the public, who are lending more money without their own wish or knowledge to a state they may consider already sufficiently large.

"The debenture holders would surely have had a dividend from the surplus left after paying the interest on the Active Mexican bonds, but the secret why they have never received any, and which, knowing the remittances that arrived, everyone was surprised at, is now sufficiently explained by the illegal issue of more active bonds." Precisely had the transactions been effected: "[T]he sales . . . were made from time to time under the pretense

52 *Sunday Times*, December 4, 1842. A week later, the amount in dispute had risen to "no less than £600,000."

53 Ralph Hidy, *The House of Baring in American Trade and Finance* (Cambridge, MA, 1949), pp. 302–303.

of being for large holders of deceased, or extensive Quaker firms involved in corn speculation, or bad news. . . . "[54]

One can well imagine the prevailing atmosphere. Murphy, the chargé d'affaires, saw both his reputation and Mexico's sullied over an affair about which he could have had little knowledge. The bondholders felt thoroughly fleeced. The London Stock Exchange was pilloried as a den of thieves, corrupt at worst, ineffectual at best. The *Sunday Times* thought there was but one remedy:

As the committee of Spanish American bondholders regularly receives from its agents at Vera Cruz an account of the money received for duties, it should see that such money, which is the property of its clients, was forwarded direct to the Bank of England, since were this done, no overissue could be attempted without immediate detection, the dividend day being sufficient to show that there was more to provide for than their ought to be.

At the same time that both Mexico and Lizardi were the subject of such acerbic commentary, Murphy was trying to press Lizardi into returning the £600,000 to the Mexican government. While Lizardi stonewalled, Murphy fumed, finally warning Lizardi that "if he insists in turning a deaf ear to my urgings, he would have no one to blame but himself for what would happen."[55] And, in fact, Murphy actually succeeded in getting Manuel de Lizardi to sign a note obligating himself to return £630,532 to the Mexican government, explicitly admitting that Lizardi and Company had no authorization to issue bonds for any purpose other than for the conversion of defaulted issues.[56] Yet Murphy's victory was short-lived. Lizardi signed the note on December 2, 1842, but the *Sunday Times* of December 11 made no mention of it, rather continued the drumbeat against Mexico. "From all we learn," the analysis went,

the members of the Spanish American Bondholders' Committee, whether individually, or as a body, feel both mortified and disgusted at the chicanery and imposition practiced by the Mexican government in its clandestine issue of bonds representing a new debt, and taking from the pockets of John Bull no less than £600,000 when he had not the most remote idea of lending it. Nothing less can be made of it.

As far as the Committee of Bondholders was concerned, "the members are, of course, all large holders. They see their prosperity suddenly depreciated."

54 *Sunday Times*, December 4, 1842, for this and what follows.
55 Murphy, *Deuda esterior*, p. 28.
56 Murphy, *Deuda esterior*, pp. 155–157.

By and large, by December 18, 1842, the dimensions of the Lizardi's actions had become clear.[57]

Yet now things took yet another odd twist. A packet from Veracruz arriving in Southampton would bring two puzzling documents. Both were dated October 10, 1842. The first apparently referred to the decree of June 1, 1839, and regulation of June 29, 1839, on the Conversion of 1837. Here the Mexican government gave Lizardi and Company the right to issue bonds for a commission of 2.5 percent plus expenses on the conversion loan. The second document authorized a commission of 5 percent on the agreement of February 11, 1842, concerning the course of interest from 1838 through 1842, which could be paid with a bond issue or by drawing 3.5 percent of the 4 percent increase in the amount of customs revenue collected in Veracruz and Tampico.[58] Both documents were presidential orders that were issued under the signature of Finance Minister Trigueros. In essence, both provided a cover of legality, if not legitimacy, to the surreptitious issue of bonds that Lizardi and Company had undertaken.

The *Sunday Times* wryly observed that "once again we have to wend our way through the financial affairs of Mexico."[59] Murphy was furious, hardly amused. After reviewing the text of the orders he observed, laconically, "some orders" (*Tales eran estas órdenes*). Murphy added that both orders betrayed public trust and "both gave exorbitant commissions." As if all this were not enough, Murphy was compelled to return the legal agreement that Lizardi and Company had turned over to the Mexican legation back to Lizardi.[60]

Stranger events were to follow. In March 1843, Murphy received a dispatch from José María Bocanegra, dated January 24, telling Murphy that General Nicolás Bravo, interim president, wished to congratulate Murphy on the strong stance he took against Lizardi's actions "since [the House] should not have proceeded without the express authorization of the government." Further,

the Gobierno Supremo declares that at the time that the operation (i.e., bond issue) was undertaken, it was done without the Government's authorization and hence was null and void and the fault (*responsabilidad*) [lay with Lizardi]. However, since said government on October 10 agreed to their undertaking the same operation and fixed commissions of 5 and 2 and $\frac{1}{2}$ percent in the instances specified in the dispatches sent to [Lizardi and Company] on that date, this latter document renders the former bond issue] valid. [Furthermore], the Government rules all its public

57 *Sunday Times*, December 18, 1842.
58 Murphy, *Deuda esterior*, pp. 28–29.
59 *Sunday Times*, December 25, 1842.
60 Murphy, *Deuda esterior*, pp. 30–31.

actions legitimate, although in the specific instance [the Government] expresses its disapproval and warns Lizardi that its continued exercise of the Republic as well as the government's continued confidence [requires] that no action regarding the credit [of the Government] be taken without the previous and express permission of the government.[61]

In other words, they should not have done what they did, and better not do so in the future without asking, but we were of the mind to let them do what they did. This dispatch, whose syntax is tortured even by the standards of financial writings of the day, seems wildly at odds with the dispatches of October 10, 1842. If it was wrong, then why should the operation stand?

At the remove of some 160 years, and with the archival materials of the period in a certain disarray, making sense of the incident once and for all is probably impossible. But a few reasonable speculations about what was going on are possible.

One notices, for instance, that the odd dispatch excoriating and inculpating Lizardi went out under the signature of Home and Foreign Minister, *Bocanegra*, while the dispatches of October 19 authorizing the commissions to Lizardi and effectively sanctioning the bond issue carried the signature of Finance Minister Trigueros. This might seem a trivial matter, but in this context, it perhaps takes on some importance. Bocanegra himself had experience as finance minister (1829, 1833, 1837, 1838) and, in the stylized biographies of the era, was termed "honest" and "hardworking," one who had served under Gómez Farías and Santa Anna "without the slightest complaint against him."[62] But in 1842 and 1843, Bocanegra was not the finance minister, and literally told his subordinate Murphy that his zeal for protecting Mexican interests was praiseworthy, but wrong. "Your job is diplomatic, [not] monkeying with the business of the Finance ministry . . . You are to confine yourself . . . to supervising the destruction of the old bonds."[63]

On the other hand, the finance minister – Trigueros – was, like so many of his predecessors, drawn from the ranks of the Veracruz merchant class and extremely well connected, numbering among his patrons (and relations by marriage) the New York–Veracruz concern, Hargous Brothers as well as Santa Anna himself. Perhaps not surprisingly, the historian of his administration at the finance ministry, María Teresa Bermúdez, openly speculates that Trigueros had a connection with Manuel Lizardi as well,

61 Murphy, *Deuda esterior*, pp. 30–31.
62 Bocanegra, *Memorias para la historia de México independiente, 1822–1846*, vol. 2: p. 592.
63 Murphy, *Deuda esterior*, pp. 59–60.

which would complete the circle of Santanista financial interests profiting by the financial irregularities of Lizardi and Company.[64] Bermúdez was seemingly correct, for a British law officer characterized Manuel Lizardi as acting on behalf "of the Mexican minister of Finance in his private capacity," a formulation that speaks to a certain intimacy in matters of state.[65]

So amid indications that there were serious divisions within the Mexican government and that Lizardi and Company had great influence in financial circles, but was openly at odds with Mexico's diplomats, charges and countercharges continued throughout 1844. On April 11, 1844, a report on the London money market expressed thanks to the Committee of the Stock Exchange for exposing the maneuvers of Lizardi and Company, saying that "the Committee have earned the thanks of every bona fide holder. . . . It will teach a salutary lesson to foreign governments that money to almost any amount cannot henceforth be abstracted without impunity from the purses of British capitalists by the convenient circulation of bits of waste paper called 'bonds'." When Lizardi refused to divulge to the Committee of Bondholders the funds in its possession for the overdue payment of April 1, 1844, the committee fairly exploded:

[We] cannot understand on what principle such refusal can be grounded. These monies from the moment they are set apart in Mexico cease to be the property of the Mexican government and are remitted in trust for the bondholders subject to no other condition than the punctual payment of the dividends; and how, under such circumstances, you can withhold information which the committee have no *official* [italics in original] means of acquiring, they are utterly at a loss to comprehend.[66]

In a final spasm of anger, the committee referred to Lizardi's "cool, deliberate, brazen, effrontery." Lizardi and Company, not to be outdone, replied in order to "observe . . . with concern the acrimonious tone pervading your letter, and to state, as our own opinion, that publishing the same in the daily papers, without affording us time to reply, is rather unusual."[67] And so it continued to the great detriment of Mexico's financial reputation, splashed across the pages of London's daily press. Would it ever end? It did, of course, beginning with what Murphy called the "truly country-wide rebellion" against Santa Anna in December 1844, the so-called Revolution

64 "Meter Orden e Imponer Impuestos. Ignacio Trigueros Olea," in Ludlow and Marichal, eds., *Los Secretarios de Hacienda*, vol. 1: p. 221. Trigueros explicitly denied that he had any connection to Hargous, but Ana Rosa Suárez Argüello, *La batalla por Tehuantepec: El Peso de los Intereses Privados en la Relación México-Estados Unidos 1848–1854* (México, 2003), p. 44, regards it as "public knowledge." Of Lizardi, it is uncertain. See *El Monitor Republicano*, December 29, 1846, for Trigueros' denial.
65 Dodson to the Foreign Office, London, May 7, 1842, FO 83/2303, PRO.
66 *The Globe*, April 11, 1844, clipping found in *Gobernación*, leg. 91, caja 151, exp. 1, AGNM.
67 *Morning Herald*, April 24, 1844, clipping found in *Gobernación*, leg. 91, caja 151, exp. 1, AGNM.

of Three Hours. One consequence of that movement was that Lizardi and Company lost the financial agency of Mexico in Europe to John Schneider and Company on April 5, 1845. Thoroughly discredited, newspaper reports suggested that Lizardi was diverting funds for payment of the bondholders to Santa Anna for his personal usage.[68] Indeed, it is abundantly clear that Lizardi and Company had come out on the losing end of a political battle that saw the appointment of Luis de la Rosa, an "anti-Santanista" to the finance ministry in yet another liberal attempt to rein in the influence of the British in general and the London bondholders in particular.[69]

Lizardi and Company, in turn, alleged that the Mexican government owed it money, prompting interim president Mariano Paredes to round on Lizardi, explaining that the firm could expect nothing from Mexico except further public assaults on its reputation, including yet another suit filed in the vice-chancellors' courts in June 1846.[70] Faced with the threat of a bondholders' suit in Chancery Court, Lizardi and Company relented paying more than £65,651 between 1846 and 1847 to Schneider and Company, prompting Murphy to conclude, somewhat prematurely, that "this business worked out happily for the Republic."[71]

It is, of course, virtually impossible to tell exactly whom Lizardi's fraud injured: bearer bonds tell no tales. But we can derive some idea of who hoped to profit from it, or perhaps, to speculate on the possibility that some future Mexican government would make good on Lizardi's dubious promise. In 1851, one speculator, a certain William ("Guillermo") Musson, brought claims against the Mexican government for £200,000 of the excess that Lizardi Brothers issued, roughly 20 percent of the paper sold.[72] Another list of claimants was prepared by the Mexican Financial Agency in London in 1857, fifteen years after Lizardi's maneuvers occurred, so it is possible to identify who held the very speculative issue in the long run. Nominal claims were £517,554. Of these, more than half were held by just three firms: Baring Brothers; Hope and Company; and Glynn Mills and Company.[73] And of these three, one firm, Glynn Mills and Company, was to play a major role in subsequent events in the 1860s (see Chapter 4). Thus, it is possible that the Lizardi's fraudulent paper essentially ended up in the hands of

68 Murphy, *Memoria sobre la deuda*, p. 81, and *Times* (London), July 2, 1845.

69 Laura Suárez de la Torre, "Luis de la Rosa, Ministro de Hacienda," in Ludlow and Marichal, eds., *Los Secretarios de Hacienda*, vol. 1: p. 276; *Times* (London), June 27, 1846.

70 *Times* (London), July 1, 1846.

71 Murphy, *Memoria sobre la deuda*, pp. 81–86.

72 Memo to the finance minister [México], August 25, 1851, SCJN, *Asuntos Económicos*, 1852, "Autos seguidos contra el Señor don Agustín de Iturbide por haber firmado en unión de los señores Lizardi y compañía, mayor número de bonos activos y diferidos de los que debieron existir," AGNM.

73 Francisco Facio, "Lista de los reclamos de bonos diferidos que se hace presentado en esta Agencia," London, November 1, 1857, *Deuda Exterior*, vol. 15, AGNM.

Table 3.2. *Interest and Commission due to F. de Lizardi and Company, London*

1836	7,527
1837	19,880
1838	20,544
1839	21,356
1840	26,074
1841	31,622
1842	38,738
Total	165,741

Note: All values are in pesos.
Source: "Resumen del Saldo de la Cuenta de los Sres F. de Lizardi y Ca., Londres contra el Supremo Gobierno de México" México, September 1856, *Deuda Externa*, vol. 15, f. 452.

no more than four parties of speculators. Not exactly Scotch widows and orphans, were they?

How profitable was Lizardi and Company's business with Mexico? And how important was the firm to Mexican interests? Until the house's papers surface – if they ever do – historians can only speculate. But the records of the Mexican Finance Ministry leave no doubt that Lizardi were major actors from 1836 onward, if not before. In Table 3.2, we report the statistic that the ministry recorded for Lizardi's "interest and commissions." From 1836 through 1842, roughly the period we have thus far considered, these total $165,741. Of course, interest payments would tend to grow annually, just as they did here, but even capitalizing the sum at 5 percent would yield something in excess of 3.2 million pesos. As we shall see, this put Lizardi in the same league as Manning and Marshall as a creditor to Mexico, and one might justifiably hypothesize that the larger prize that came with financing the London Debt was access to Mexican state finance at the highest and most lucrative levels. It was a high-stakes game. When Santa Anna (and centralism) prospered, Lizardi and Company did as well.

Those "war steamers," for instance, about which Smith openly fretted? After the fall of Santa Anna in 1854, an investigation carried out by Mexican officials in London revealed that little or nothing had been done to complete them – for one steamer, not even the keel had been laid. The Lizardi had received 550,000 pesos from Santa Anna for virtually nothing. Juan Alvarez – Santa Anna's nemesis, who was serving as interim president – wanted the ships delivered or the money returned. As far as the documentary record indicates, Alvarez and Mexico seem to have got nothing back from the bankers to Santa Anna.[74] Meanwhile, the Lizardi,

74 SCJN, *Asuntos Económicos*, 1855, "Consulta que hace el Supremo Gobierno, sobre la conducta que debe observar en el negocio relativo a la contrata que celebró la Administración del Excelentísimo

particularly, Manuel Julían de Lizardi, accumulated millions of pesos in the Mexican *internal* debt, and was also a large shareholder in the state tobacco business under the auspices of his patron. So when Santa Anna finally fell, Manuel Lizardi, albeit thoroughly hedged, went with him.[75]

From June through December 1845, the market moved against Mexico. Continuing uncertainty about the status of Texas, troop movements under Zachary Taylor in South Texas, and the rise of an organized federalist reaction to the Central Republic all contributed to sustained turmoil. As we emphasized in the previous chapter, the prospects for repayment under centralist regimes were better than those under federalism, and the prospect of the reassertion of power by liberal figures such as Gómez Farías, never sympathetic to the bondholders, rendered Mexican bonds even more speculative. The reaction was absolutely correct in light of the contrasting payment histories of Mexico under federalist and centralist regimes. From 1830 to 1835, for example, the last five years of the Federal Republic, payments to the bondholders totaled 1.1 million pesos. From 1840 through 1845, under the Central Republic, payments (including customs certificates) totaled 4.5 million pesos and even José María Luis Mora viewed the conservatives as "the most *consistent* power in Mexico."[76] So there was certainly reason enough to worry about the prospects of the bondholders under a return to federalism, let alone to the prospects of national dissolution that war with the United States over Texas might portend. Even in the most optimistic of outcomes, the initial borrowing to finance another campaign in Texas in 1844, some 4 million pesos, would absorb virtually everything used to pay the British bondholders during the previous four years.[77] Once again, things came down to opportunity cost: the Mexicans would pay the price of Texas liberty. The London market priced Mexican securities accordingly.

General don Antonio López de Santa-Anna, con la casa de don Manuel F. [*sic*] Lizardi, para la construcción de dos buques de guerra," AGNM.

But then again, a recent naval history of the navy of the Republic of Texas places the *Guadalupe* and *Moctezuma* in the middle of combat in the Gulf of Mexico in 1842. The *Guadalupe* is said to have been the largest iron vessel ever built in 1842. Could Santa Anna's liberal enemies have simply denied these ships had ever existed after his fall in 1854 as part of a campaign against him? It would not have been the first time – nor the last – that similar charges about weapons were simply fabricated in the toxic politics of the London Debt. See Jonathan W. Jordan, *Lone Star Navy. Texas, the Fight for the Gulf of Mexico, and the Shaping of the American West* (Washington, DC, 2007), pp. 228–229, 246–247, 253–257.

75 "Memorial of the Executors of the Estate of Manuel J. de Lizardi, Deceased [1870?]," Box 7, Folder 44, Skilton Family Papers, Institute Archives and Special Collections, Rensellaer Polytechnic Institute.

76 Calculated from Payno, *México y sus cuestiones financieras*, pp. 45–46. For Mora's analisis, see Mora to Valentín Gómez Farías, Paris, May 20, 1845, VGF 1182, BLAC, UT.

77 Solares Robles, *Una revolución pacífica*, p. 193.

Arms and Men: The Failed Conversion of 1846

With the bond market in an uproar and its creditors irate, Mexico had little choice but to reorganize its international obligations, or at least to attempt to do so. As Murphy put it, the Finance Ministry had resolved as early as April 29, 1845, to undertake a modified conversion.[78] Yet international issues, such as renewed interest in the status of Texas, Mexico's drive to rearm in a final attempt to bring the rebellious province to heel, and Britain's role as a mediator throughout the affair, made the normalization of the bondholders' claims more imperative still. Under Mirabeau Lamar, hostilities between Texas and Mexico had flared anew in 1841. In 1842, the province was once again invaded and San Antonio reoccupied, albeit briefly.[79] Some of Mexico's largest domestic financiers, including the Anglo-Mexican Manuel Escandón, were given huge contracts for artillery, shells, rifles, and swords in 1842. Escandón was given further contracts in 1843 and 1844. Others, including Cayetano Rubio, were contracted to make purchases of uniforms, horses, and saddles "for the campaign to be undertaken against Texas." Nor were naval forces neglected, for Rubio was authorized to purchase 500,000 pesos in steam vessels.[80] Since the bulk of these arms and munitions were to be purchased in Britain, Mexico could hardly spend large sums on their acquisition there, all the while pleading poverty as far as the bondholders were concerned. Indeed, one government notice explicitly linked the timing of the payment for an arms contract to Don Juan Manuel Lasquetty (346,608 pesos) to the availability of funds to satisfy "preferential" expenses for the conversion of the London Debt (including Lizardi and Company's controversial commissions) – and here it was the financier who was to take a backseat.[81] To raise money to finance, "the current war that the Nation carries on with the rebels in Texas and the dissidents in Yucatán," customs duties were raised 20 percent over the level established in the tariff of 1842.[82] And yet while customs revenues had, until this point, been the almost exclusive source of funding debt payments, growing suspicions that this traditional source would never be equal to the demands placed on it led to mortgaging the revenues of the recently (1837) reconstituted tobacco monopoly. Since Escandón had been one of the central financiers involved in the operation of the business in

---

78 Murphy, *Memoria sobre la deuda*, p. 89. See Dublán and Lozano, *Legislación Mexicana*, N° de disposición 2820, which dates the congressional resolution one day earlier.

79 "Military History," *Handbook of Texas Online*, http://www.tsha.utexas.edu/handbook/online/articles/view/MM/qzmtg.html (accessed September 28, 2007).

80 *El Siglo Diez y Nueve*, June 30, 1845.

81 *El Siglo Diez y Nueve*, December 21, 1844.

82 Hacienda decree of April 7, 1843. See Dublán and Lozano, *Legislación Mexicana*, N° de Disposición 2554.

Mexico,[83] it was perhaps inevitable that he would now make an appearance in the negotiations over the Conversion of 1846, for he was in every way suited to the task. As it was, Escandón unblushingly took credit for the negotiation of the final agreement. In Escandón's own words, "we succeeded completely" and it would have been a "dream" to conclude the negotiations without his presence in London, given that war with the United States over the annexation of Texas and its disputed boundary loomed increasingly larger.[84] Texas, the cost and provenance of arms, and the possibility of war with the United States made the Conversion of 1846 inevitable, but ironically, rendered this conversion impossible as well. By November 1846, with General Taylor established in Monterrey, and another swath of the North effectively isolated by forces under Wool and Doniphan, Mexico claimed that it had no resources to prosecute the war with the United States and that it lacked the ability to raise even a general levy (*derrama general*).[85] Servicing the foreign debt would be out of the question as long as the war continued, or so Manuel Payno was to remark in his authoritative history.[86] Sometime in October or November, Santa Anna, having dismissed Mariano Arista, was now at the head of the Mexican army, and reportedly seized $2,000,000 "intended for English capitalists" on its way to Tampico.[87] But this is getting ahead of the story.

And the story, even by the standards set by conversions, is convoluted. Payno – generally a trustworthy, if not unbiased, guide to these affairs – is almost openly impatient with events, dismissing "the complicated incidents . . . and deals between the government and the house of Mackintosh" and summarizing what transpired between April and December 1845 as "just unbelievable" (*¡Cosa increible!*).[88] Alamán published a supplement to his original study of the previous conversions, calling the story of 1846 "a dry one in itself" a rare admission of frustration from someone whose knowledge was a matter of firsthand experience.[89] Antonio Haro y Tamariz,

83 David W. Walker, "Business as Usual: The Empresa del Tabaco in Mexico, 1837–1844," *HAHR*, 64: 4 (1984), pp. 680, 699.

84 Escandón to Ewen Mackintosh, London, June 28, 1846, Correspondence, Folder 3 (1842–1846), Manning and Mackintosh Papers, BLAC, UT. Notice that Escandón misdated this letter to 1844, but corrected the date to 1846 on its rear cover.

   Also see *El Monitor Republicano*, September 24, 1846, for a reference to "el contrato celebrado en Londres por D. Manuel Escandón."

85 *Préstamo forzoso de dos millones de pesos que se hace por intermedio del venerable clero para ayudar al sostenimiento de la guerra contra los Estados Unidos del Norte* (Toluca, 1846).

86 Payno, *México y sus cuestiones financieras*, p. 16.

87 *Times* (London), December 4, 1846.

88 Payno, *México y sus cuestiones financieras*, pp. 12–16. Payno also pointedly noted that the files dealing with the Conversion of 1846 had inexplicably disappeared from the archives of the finance ministry. See Manuel Payno, *Reseña sobre los principales ramos de la Hacienda Pública* (México, 1851), p. 7.

89 Alamán, p. 12. (*una relación árida por si misma* is translated as "a dry one in itself.")

Table 3.3. *Conversion of 1846*

Included in conversion	
Active bonds, including Lizardi fraudulent issue	5,591,650
Debentures, issued for arrears of interest at 50 percent of the sum due	499,096
Deferred bonds, including fraudulent issues	4,624,000
	10,714,746
Converted at the following rates:	
Active bonds at 90 percent	5,032,485
Deferred debentures at 60 percent	3,073,857
Balance of new bonds to Mexican government	2,135,307
	10,241,650
Memo: Interest relinquished on active bonds for 1 and ¾ years arrears	489,269
Reduction in interest and principal	962,365

Note: All values are in pounds sterling.

one of Santa Anna's erstwhile allies, served briefly as the finance minister in 1846, producing a lengthy apologia for his involvement in the affair because his name was associated "with venality as the only reason for my approval of the conversion."[90] Mariano Otero believed that "the undisclosed history of this incident, perhaps more than any other, abounds in incidents of corruption and shame."[91] There was not one version of the contract but three, and the final one, accepted by the Committee of Bondholders in London, was in the end first rejected and then approved in Mexico City by different ministers. The negotiations between Manning and Mackintosh and Mexico were so fraught that at one point, both Bernardo Couto – an eminent jurist and a Mexican architect of the conversion, as well as Escandón's lawyer – and Valentín Gómez Farías begged off meeting with representatives of the firm at the finance ministry for reasons of ill health, with Gómez Farías, in particular, complaining of a "rheumatic attack" that left him indisposed.[92] Coming as it did in the midst of the U.S. invasion, the debacle was nearly complete.

Perhaps the best way of proceeding in this case is to address three questions: (1) what was the Conversion of 1846, broadly defined, as the bondholders understood it; (2) why was the conversion so contentious, difficult, and controversial; and (3) what, if any, were its results? To define the conversion as it was understood by the financial community, we employ White's summary appearing here as Table 3.3 for the use of Baring Brothers

90 [Antonio Haro y Tamariz], *Estracto del Espediente sobre la conversion de la deuda esterior* (México, 1846).
91 Mariano Otero to the Mexican minister in London, México, December 14, 1848, in Genaro García, ed., *Documentos inéditos o muy raros para la historia de México*, p. 584 [italics in original].
92 [Antonio Haro y Tamariz], *Estracto del Espediente*, pp. 48–49.

in London.[93] White summarized the Conversion of 1846 in the following way: By an arrangement of June 4, 1846, Mexico recognized an outstanding debt of £10,241,650 to be issued in 5 percent bonds bearing interest from July 1, 1846. The sum of the reduction in interest and principal corresponds exactly to Alamán's calculations.

Another way of viewing the operation is to take the sum of the bonds included in the conversion (£10,714,746 + £489,269) plus the interest relinquished less the sum of converted bonds (£5,032,485 + £3,073,857). The residual (£2,135, 307) called "Balance of new bonds to Mexican government" was, in effect, the savings realized by the conversion, the decrease in the value of Mexican liabilities circulating.

But there was a catch. That "reduction" was not really a reduction because it was immediately converted into 5 percent bonds as well. Mexico agreed to hand this sum (£2,135,307) over to Manning and Mackintosh in return for 1.6 million pesos in cash plus 5 million pesos in "papers," which, in reality, meant a heterogeneous collection of tobacco bonds, 26 percent fund bonds, and other interest- and non-interest-bearing government obligations. Using quotations supplied by David Walker,[94] we can estimate that the 1.5 million of tobacco bonds probably cost Manning and Mackintosh about 600,000 cash. The 26 percent fund bonds (500,000 pesos par) had a market value of some 125,000 pesos. By Escandón's own admission, the remaining 3 millions in "papers" were worth no more than 300,000 pesos on the market. In other words, for around 2.6 million pesos cash, Manning and Marshall took bonds with a face value of 10.5 million pesos (£2.1).[95]

Escandón informed Manning and Mackintosh that he planned to bring the bonds to market at 31. If so, they would fetch 3.5 million in cash (i.e., about one-third of 10.5 million). In other words, if the numbers held up, the conversion that Escandón took credit for would produce about 900,000 pesos profit, 30 percent, or more, if the fact that the 1.6 million in cash was very likely to be paid out to Mexico over the span of several months. But the numbers did not hold up somehow, for Escandón, after examining several possible outcomes, concluded that they stood to make 400,000 pesos

93 George White, Summary History of the London Debt (ms.), BBA.

94 Walker, *Kinship, Business, and Politics*, pp. 181, 190.

95 Escandón to Ewen Mackintosh, London, June 28, 1846, Correspondence, Folder 3 (1842–1846), Manning and Mackintosh Papers, BLAC, UT, for this and what follows.

   There is a different computation in *Dictamen de la Comisión de Crédito Público*, p. 30. Here Prieto concludes that for 156,000 pesos cash, Manning and Marshall acquired 5 million pesos in bonds. The computation makes Manning and Marshall's participation in the Conversion of 1846 appear far more profitable than it was: for example, Prieto implicitly compared the real value of cash (100 percent) with the nominal value of bonds (not 100 percent by any means) and simply netted out the nominal value of bonds with different market values in calculating the dimensions of the assets Manning and Mackintosh had acquired. It is an oddly tendentious proceeding in an otherwise balanced account.

"under such poor circumstances." Apparently very little went as planned, particularly the "wretched timing of the war" (*la maldita casualidad de la Guerra*). To some extent, Escandón was insulated by a commission of 241,000 pesos he stood to get by brokering the deal. But the deal did not want to be brokered. Schneider and Company, now Mexico's financial agent, had agreed to take £200,000 of converted bonds and pay Mexico 250,000 pesos cash, but only under pressure from Escandón would the house take the bonds and then with "great repugnance." The reason, certainly, was that the "wretched timing" of the war had thrown the bond market into disarray. Escandón thought that Mexican bonds would have to fall by 20 percent before there would be any takers. The only way he could induce Schneider to cooperate was by making over letters of credit to the firm that could be used to pay the January 1847 dividend. If Schneider agreed, Escandón thought – once word was put out, by October, say – Mexico, although nearly bankrupt, could pay the January dividend, the converted bonds might rise to between 35 and 38, and "we would all profit." Escandón concluded that "this convinced them and they came along."[96]

The pricing of the converted issue, always critical in determining the division of gains and losses in any operation, became particularly acute now, because the ratification of the conversion by the bondholders on June 4, 1846, was carried out under extreme uncertainty. Escandón claimed that he knew about the defeat of the Mexican army in the North, the taking of Matamoros, the blockade of Mexican gulf ports by the U.S. Navy, the suspension of debt payments (May 2, 1846), and the seizure of British dividend payments in Veracruz, but that this was through Manning and Mackintosh rather than by official notification. Once word hit London, he said, "it will raise an alarm and screaming and nobody knows how far the bonds will drop." But by May 30, 1846, nearly five days before the ratification, the *Times* (London) reported that "[Mexico] will stand in need of all the money she can lay hands upon and as far as parting with a single branch of revenue that seems out of the question." Already, according to the *Times* (London), "the decline in Mexican was considerable" and "most of the speculators were sellers." Indeed, in the year following May 1846, Mexican bond prices fell nearly 40 percent.[97] Hence Escandón informed Manning

---

96 Or so Escandón thought. In late 1848, Schneider reported that it had more than £100,000 of Mexican dividends in its possession "for the payment of the first dividend of the new bonds of 1846." Who exactly was hustling whom? See Juan Schneider y Cia., "Cuenta de las cantidades de dinero recibidas... applicable al pago del primero dividendo por los bonos nuevos de 1846," London, September 14, 1848, *Gobernación*, leg. 91, caja 151, exp. 1, AGNM. (*Esta reflexión les hizo mucha fuerza y convinieron con mis deseos* is translated as "this convenced them and they came along.")

97 The exact date that news of the outbreak of fighting reached London is fuzzy. The *Sunday Times* (May 31, 1846) said "Tuesday" or May 26. Given that Mexican bonds had already fallen by Saturday (May 30), this makes sense. If Escandón told Manning and Mackintosh that such was not common knowledge by June 4, he may have been simply trying to overstate his importance (and skill) in the

and Mackintosh of its need to make the plan's Mexican architects, whom Escandón named as Bernardo Couto and Miguel Atristaín,[98] understand that the bondholders were truly giving something up and that it was necessary to persuade Mexico to act accordingly. It was just conceivable, thought Escandón, that Britain might pay all or part of the debt if it mediated a peace, but even half would "really be something."

Yet this was Escándon promoting, not necessarily a realistic or even shared appraisal of events. Others thought that British or French intervention was all but impossible because "they hear nothing other than complaints from merchants and Bondholders" and that both nations lacked faith in Mexico's ability to govern itself, which is to say, to act as an independent nation.[99] Indeed, one observer thought that the real consequence of the debacle of the Conversion of 1846 was that it had decisively alienated the British government, which otherwise would have supported a moratorium on dividend payments and even lent Mexico money in its struggle against the United States.[100] There seems to have been no sympathy for the actions of the United States in Europe – quite the contrary. The United States was viewed as being arrogant and aggressive: its conduct was unacceptable and its president, James Knox Polk, was impulsive. There was talk that Viscount Palmerston (then foreign secretary), Clarendon, and Guizot were all deeply interested in the fate of Mexico. Yet none of this meant that the bondholders would ever again see a penny of what had been invested in 1824 and 1825. Small surprise that brokering an agreement under such "wretched" circumstances would be so difficult.

It was also the case that Escandón's maneuverings excited the jealous opposition of other Mexican financiers. Escandón in particular complained of Ignacio Loperena (then resident in London and a major conduit for foreign arms) and Manuel de Lizardi, but the Martínez del Río were ambivalent as well, a case of what Walker called "squabbling over who should handle the foreign debt and under which terms."[101] The issue with Lizardi was all the more serious because it touched on the status of the fraudulent bonds and also whether they were to be included in the conversion. As Escándon put it, the illegal issue of bonds by Lizardi and Company "has been one of the most difficult issues on which we had to agree," and that

negotiation. The jockeying for position must have been intense: Tomás Murphy ignores Escandón completely, but Haro y Tamariz makes it clear that Escandón was in London on government business. (*una gran cosa* is translated as "really be something.")

98 Ironically, two of the Mexican members of the commission that negotiated the Treaty of Guadalupe Hidalgo (along with Luis Cuevas) that ended the war and partitioned the country.

99 J. D. Powles to Manning and Mackintosh, London, August 4, 1846, Manning and Marshall Papers, Correspondence, Folder 3 (1842–1846), BLAC, UT.

100 *Suplemento al número 674 del Monitor Republicano*, December 26, 1846, "La Deuda Exterior."

101 Walker, *Kinship, Business and Politics*, p. 190. Indeed, Loperena was trying to arrange a foreign loan as well. See *El Monitor Republicano*, November 30, 1846. Also see Manuel Payno, *Reseña sobre el estado de los principales ramos de la Hacienda Pública . . . para Lic. José I Esteva* (México, 1851), p. 42.

Murphy had been adamantly opposed to including the illegal issue in the conversion. Escandón blamed Atristaín for the confusion, claiming that he had worded the conversion agreement so as to make any bond, regardless of its origin, eligible for conversion. Significantly, Escandón predicted – correctly as it turned out – that the government might well disapprove of Murphy's conduct.[102]

At bottom, numerous technical and legal issues aside, was the Lizardi's unauthorized issue had seemingly destroyed what little confidence the bondholders had in the value of any agreement.[103] "What checks are to be imposed in order to prevent the issue of more stock than is actually required for conversion," wondered one observer? "Indeed," the analysis continued, "some parties maintain that the Mexican government decidedly contemplates the issue of as much stock as the bonds out at present nominally stand for." Any resulting savings accruing to Mexico would actually be employed as a basis for further borrowing because "the Mexican government . . . is sadly in want of money." And in any event, the war had injected even more uncertainty into negotiations. When the bondholders did agree to the terms of conversion on June 4, 1846, they were doing little more than taking the best deal they could get and then hoping for the best. One bondholder suggested that the conversion was Mexico's way of trying to induce Great Britain and perhaps France to intervene on Mexico's behalf against the United States.[104]

An upheaval in domestic politics precipitated by the outbreak of the war was yet another cause of difficulty, because, if anything, the shelf life of a finance minister, never long under the best of circumstances, was reduced even further. There could be no presumption that what one minister accepted would be ratified by his successor and in 1846 alone, the ministry, if not the man, changed hands fifteen times: an absurd example was Valentín Canalizo, Santa Anna's sidekick, who held the portfolio as caretaker for two days. But some changes were far more consequential. Murphy's tenacious resistance to the inclusion of Lizardi and Company's fraudulent issue in the conversion ran afoul of Lizardi's allies in Mexico City, just as Escandón had predicted. Murphy cooked up a device – let us call them contingent bonds – that would be converted only if the total presented for redemption exceeded the nominal amount of Mexican bonds in circulation less what Lizardi was known to have issued without authorization.[105] In essence, a

102 Escandón to Ewen Mackintosh, London, June 28, 1846, Correspondence, Folder 3 (1842–1846), Manning and Mackintosh Papers, BLAC, UT.

103 *Sunday Times*, May 31, 1846, for what follows.

104 An account of the June 4 meeting appears in *El Monitor Republicano*, August 25, 1846.

105 Murphy, *Deuda Esterior*, pp. 96–98. Murphy claimed that he was compelled to make such an arrangement by John Schneider and Company's unwillingness to be saddled with the liability for the Lizardi bonds. He seems to have been all too happy to agree.

demand for these bonds would force Lizardi's issue into the open, proving that something underhanded had taken place. But the scheme ran afoul of Finance Minister Valentin Gómez Farías, soon to be joined at the hip with a newly restored Santa Anna, who summarily relieved Murphy of his diplomatic post in London, "for not having acted with the precaution which is generally made use of in matters of this description."[106] Even worse, Gómez Farías annulled the conversion as well. It appeared as if the bankers to Santa Anna would have their way.

But what Gómez Farías did not count on was, at least, the stunned reaction of Manning and Mackintosh (and Escandón, no doubt) to what had he had done. Manning and Mackintosh was not just any firm, but was arguably the central government's biggest financier by the War of 1847, and a stunt like this could well destroy them.[107] As late as July 1847, with Scott's army in Puebla, the house "lent" the government 600,000 pesos for the defense of the capital "without interest." By 1854, Manning and Mackintosh's claims against Mexico exceeded 3 million pesos, more than half (1.7 million) of which were for losses sustained in the Conversion of 1846 when bond prices failed to hold.[108]

The shock of Gómez Farías' actions drove Manning and Mackintosh into a fury, and it pressed the finance ministry, writing that "[it] was inclined to carry out the contract they had celebrated [and] were prepared to appeal to the Supreme Court to defend their rights and those of the bondholders in this grave matter." Nothing similar had ever happened since Mexico became independent, and the house warned that its threat had to be evaluated "in light of how much was riding on this operation, much of the money belonging to others who had honored [Manning and Mackintosh] with their confidence."[109] And, in light, too, of how the firm had pulled the government's chestnuts from the fire "without interest" only three months before! Moreover, Manning and Marshall made one particularly serious

---

106 *Times* (London), October 21, 1846. Gómez Farías' order was dated August 28, but Santa Anna did not actually land in Veracruz until September 12. Rumors that "Santa Anna" would nullify the convention were already abroad in London by October 11, but "there is no reason to believe that there is any just foundation for the innuendo." See the *Sunday Times* for that date.

107 And as Rosa María Meyer Cosío painstakingly demonstrates, it ultimately did. See her remarkable "El difícil equilibrio. Tropiezos de una empresa británica con el Gobierno mexicano," in Reinhard Liehr, ed., *Empresas y modernización en México desde las reformas borbónicas hasta el Porfiriato* (Madrid, 2006), pp. 45–103.

108 Unsigned memo (carries pagination 216–217), México, February 13, 1851, *Gobernación*, leg. 91, caja 151, exp. 1, AGNM; "Nota de los créditos que tiene contra el gobierno la casa de Manning y Mackintosh," México, January 15, 1854, Manning and Mackintosh Papers, Financial Documents, Box 2, Folder 2, BLAC, UT; Payno, *Reseña sobre el estado de los principales ramos de la Hacienda Pública*, p. 45.

109 Manning and Mackintosh to the finance minister [México, October 27, 1846] in Haro y Tamariz, *Estracto del espediente*, p. 46.

allegation: The true impetus for the cancellation of the agreement had come from the house of Lizardi.[110] But Lizardi, in turn, was actively supported by Haro y Tamariz, one of Santa Anna's principal spear-carriers, who was backing Lizardi from a temporary perch in London as well. Indeed, the architect of the cancellation was Haro y Tamariz, who, for political reasons, wanted Escandón, Murphy, and Schneider and Company out of the way and pressed Gómez Farías, through intermediaries such as Juan Almonte and Manuel Crecencio Rejón, to accomplish just that.[111] In theory, the reasons were those given publicly by Gómez Farías: Murphy had exceeded his negotiating authority and Mexico could not afford the annual interest payments on the deal, which Gómez Farías put at 2.5 million pesos (about 5 percent of £10 million).[112] But one suspects considerably less public-spirited motives at work as well. Lizardi, with its close ties to Santa Anna, was actively angling to recover Mexico's financial agency in London from John Schneider and Company and was spreading its largesse around the community of Mexican diplomats in London, including Murphy's successor, Benito Gómez Farías, whose own sister worriedly described him as "compromised" in a letter to her father, Don Valentín. As to Haro y Tamariz one can only wonder: Manuel Lizardi simply refers to Haro as a "friend."[113]

Haro y Tamariz, now back in Mexico, succeeded Gómez Farías in September 1846. He was now faced with a deepening war; an improvised central government removed to Querétaro; a blockade by the U.S. Navy that soon extended to virtually the entire Gulf Coast; and the conviction that "such a course [as repudiation of the conversion] . . . would be fatal to the credit of the Mexican government in [the] future in Europe."[114] Ironically, he had little choice but to reverse the very cancellation that he had engineered, for he needed money, and fast. A request for 300,000 pesos of the stipulated cash payment on October 29 coincided with an agreement to reinstate the conversion on Manning and Marshall's terms. Murphy, in the event, did not get his old post back, and there was still more pulling and

110 Manning and Mackintosh to the finance minister, México, February 13, 1847, GF 2564, BLAC, UT.

111 Domingo Ibarra to the finance minister, Puebla, August 23, 1846, GF 1605, and Domingo Ibarra to [José María Lafragua?], August 23, 1846, GF 1597, BLAC, UT.

112 An undated and incomplete draft of a memo by Gómez Farías [1846], GF 4810, BLAC, UT. There are so many corrections and emendations in this that it appears that Gómez Farías had a good deal of trouble writing it, which – in essence – meant rationalizing his actions.

113 Ignacia Farías de Uhneck to Valentín Gómez Farías, onboard steamship *Dee*, December 14, 1846, GF, BLAC, UT; M. J. Lizardi to Mora, Paris, November 20, 1846, in García, ed., *Documentos inéditos*, p. 556.

114 *Sunday Times*, October 11, 1846.

hauling over whether the conversion would be recognized.[115] Murphy, furious and embittered, went off to France to sulk and plot against Mexico, his monarchism the ostensible source of his demise.[116]

Eventually, the Mexican government responded to British diplomatic pressure. In May 1847, the British minister to Mexico, Charles Bankhead, employed his "good offices" to point out that "the contract thus concluded between Mr. Murphy and the Bondholders was duly ratified by the Mexican government" and that "the succeeding Minister of Finance [Gómez Farías had] committed a breach of public faith" in nullifying it. Bankhead concluded that "Her Majesty's Government is of the opinion that the British Bondholders have been unfairly dealt with in this affair." Within a month, Santa Anna had little choice but to reverse himself and finally to approve the Conversion of 1846. Britain had finally begun to move away from its ostensible policy of nonintervention in Mexican affairs, at least on behalf on the bondholders, if not of its own commercial interests more broadly defined.[117]

Nevertheless, as long as Mexico and the United States remained at war, virtually any agreement, no matter how favorable (or unfavorable) to the bondholders, remained a dead letter. "What guarantees can there be for the due fulfillment of any agreement until Mexico is at peace with the United States?" Or, "it is considered strange that Mexican Bonds should have ruled steady notwithstanding the intelligence of the important success of the Americans; but the fact is, we presume, that the bondholders have very little hope of receiving a dividend while the war lasts, and, consequently, regard its termination with favor, whatever may be the cause of its conclusion."[118]

---

115 Haro y Tamariz, *Estracto del espediente*, pp. 47–49; Murphy, *Deuda Exterior*, p. 136. The crown's attorneys in London almost simultaneously concurred, finding no reason for voiding the agreement on October 31. The text of their opinion is printed in *El Monitor Republicano*, December 29, 1846.

116 [Jose María Luis Mora?] to the president of Mexico (Santa Anna), London, September 30, 1847, GF 2818, BLAC, UT. For an account of Murphy, see Marta Ramos Luna, "Thomas Murphy y Alegría," in *Cancilleres de México*, vol. 1: pp. 539–563. This Thomas (or Tomás, as he is also known) Murphy was apparently the son of the Thomas Murphy who was partner in the famous merchant house of Gordon and Murphy whose heyday was half a century earlier. Murphy would reappear in the Mexican delegation to Miramar that offered the "throne" of Mexico to Maximilian and served as his envoy to Vienna.

There is some hint of partisan divisions around the conversion: Mora, Gómez Farías, and Mariano Otero were all critical and all, to a degree, were left liberals. But these seem somehow less well defined the divisions of the late 1820s, perhaps because of the fluidity of the political situation.

117 Bankhead to the foreign minister, Mexico, May 18, 1847, and Rondero to the British minister in Mexico, México, July 30, 1847, FO 97/203, PRO. There was also concern that commercial shocks propagated by war could damage the British economy. See *Financial and Commercial Record*, 19 (1846), p. 321. Also Edward Deering Mansfield, *Life and Services of General Winfield Scott* (Auburn, 1852), p. 477.

118 *Sunday Times*, May 9, 1847.

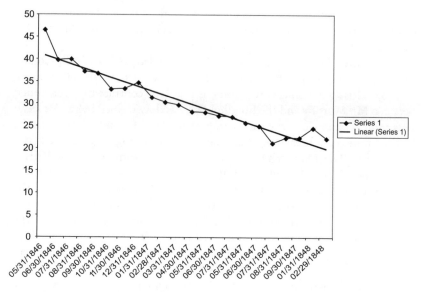

Figure 3.2. Mexican Bond Prices Relative to Consols during Mexican War.

But the price of Mexican bonds relative to consols during the war in Figure 3.2 (May 1846–February 1848) belies the observation, falling by more than 50 percent, from 47 to 22. The longer the war continued, the less confidence the market showed that the bondholders would sooner, if at all later, be paid. This made perfect sense. The United States financed operations against Mexico in part by imposing a war tariff in Mexican ports and seizing the customs. The revenue that could have funded the bondholders' dividends supported the military of the United States instead![119]

The final question is what the conversion accomplished, or what it would have accomplished, in the absence of the war. This is a relevant point because Gómez Farías' disapproval of the conversion that Murphy renegotiated (or was it Escandón) was ostensibly based in part on the concern that it failed to reduce the burden of the London Debt sufficiently. If we return to White's analysis for Baring Brothers, the reduction in principal and interest White calculated was more than £960,000, or about $5 million. That would have been an amount equivalent to nearly 10 percent of the outstanding debt. White's calculations agree with Murphy's for the relevant conversion of June 4, for Murphy too put the "true reduction in the external debt" at more than £960,000.[120] But perhaps the clearest way of looking at the

119 *Financial and Commercial Review*, 21 (1847), p. 86.
120 Murphy, *Deuda esterior*, p. 115.

Table 3.4. *Deuda Exterior*

1825	6.4
1827	5.3
1830	6.0
1832	6.9
1837	9.3
1843	10.9
1847	11.5
1852	10.5

Note: All values are in millions pounds sterling.
Source: Alamán, *Historia de Mexico*, V, "Estado Comparativo de la República mejicana en sus principales ramos entre el año de 1824 ... y el de 1852...."

impact of the conversion is to place it in the context of the overall growth of the foreign debt since 1825, which we do in Table 3.4 and then in Figure 3.3. The debt figures are consistent in the sense that all are supplied by Alamán rather than gleaned from a heterogeneous variety of sources.[121] Graphed logarithmically, it is apparent that their rate of increase is rather steep until 1837, when the conversion was carried out. The rate of increase is noticeably slower thereafter. The notional figure for what the debt in 1846 would have been, £10.3 million, is of course an absolute reduction, but it would have been obtained only if the conversion had actually been observed, which it was not. As things stood, by 1847 the debt had reached £11.5, reflecting two years of arrears that accrued during the war. So, in this sense, the Conversion of 1846 would have represented a very good deal for Mexico and a profitable one for the financiers who effected it. The savings could have come only from those bondholders who suffered the loss of principal and interest, whoever they may have been. Since these were bearer bonds, only those who came forward to identify themselves as aggrieved can be known with certainty.

In an interesting postscript to the matter, Alamán suggests that in the absence of concessions from the bondholders, by 1852, the London Debt would have been approximately £15 million, or about £4.5 million more than it actually was. For Alamán, this was nothing more than the result of the concessions that the bondholders had made since 1832, or put differently, the consequence of Mexico's failure to pay interest routinely. But pay Mexico would, and dearly, in a nineteenth-century version of land

121 Alamán, *Historia de México*, vol. 5: "Estado comparative" foldout at the volume's end for the data and Alamán's commentary on it.

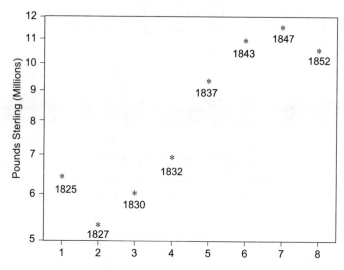

Figure 3.3. Mexico's Foreign Debt According to Alamán.

for peace. What was about to occur would have made the territory for bonds' provisions of the Conversion of 1837 look mild by comparison.

Peace after War

"Weighed down by its enormous debts, the Republic could use up its maritime customs and a few other sources of revenue on payment of the interest of the foreign debt, [on the internal debt, and on back wages to public employees]."[122] Thus, inauspiciously, did Manuel Piña y Cuevas

---

122 *Memoria de Hacienda . . . 1848*, pp. 5, 51.

Robertson, *The Foreign Debt of Mexico*, p. 7, criticized these figures as "concocted for a purpose." The "purpose," presumably, was to minimize Mexico's capacity to pay. But Robertson was merely being dismissive to his own ends. As late as June 24, 1848, the United States had yet to hand over the Veracruz customshouse to Mexican authorities, thus depriving them of a major source of finance. The U.S. invasion had produced administrative chaos within Mexico as federal authorities found themselves at odds with state officials over basic questions of who would pay for the war or, indeed, of who was in control of national resources. It is hard to see how a dismal assessment of the country's fiscal potential in 1848 could have been anything other than plain fact. See, for instance, Mercedes de Vega and María Cecilia Zuletu, *Testimonios de una Guerra: México, 1846–1848* (2 vols., México, 2001), passim. For the specific Veracruz matter, see Mariano Otero to Nathan Clifford, [México, n.d.], vol. 2: p. 442. Otero was serving as minister of home and foreign affairs. Clifford was one of the U.S. commissioners who signed the Protocol of Querétaro to the Treaty of Guadalupe Hidalgo. Nevertheless, it appears that the United States was *not* in violation of Article III of the treaty (failure to deliver the Veracruz accounts to the government in Mexico City within three months of ratification of the treaty), since ratifications had been exchanged at Querétaro on May 30, 1848, or less than a month before Otero's complaint. *United States Statutes at Large, 1789–1875* (18 vols., Washington, DC, 1845–1875), vol. 9: pp. 923–924.

assess the finances of the Mexican republic at the close of the war with the United States. At the moment, Piña y Cuevas calculated stable net revenues of about 5.5 million pesos. Budgeted expenses were estimated at 13.8 million pesos. In other words, Piña y Cuevas was looking at a projected deficit of more than 8 million pesos. The debt to Great Britain, whose resolution had merely been postponed by the war, now stood at nearly 57 million pesos. Such were the facts. Barring the small miracle of putting a fiscal Humpty Dumpty together again, where Mexico's ministers would find the money was not obvious – or, perhaps, it was only too obvious, for certainly they would be reminded repeatedly that the U.S. "indemnity" to Mexico for the damages of the war, $15,000,000, was there.

But not all at once.

By Article XII of the Treaty of Guadalupe Hidalgo, the United States had agreed to make this payment in installments. The first, a flat $3,000,000, would take place at the exchange of ratifications of the treaty, which occurred on May 30, 1848. The subsequent payments, with 6 percent interest, would occur yearly on the anniversary of the first payment. In other words, the remaining payments occurred on May 30 of 1849, 1850, 1851, and 1852 and totaled $16.8 million.[123] These payments were the low-hanging fruit of Mexican finance: everyone came after them. As Guillermo Prieto remarked about Mariano Riva Palacio, who briefly held the portfolio as finance minister, "his only job was to keep the indemnity out of the hands of the agiotistas."[124] The bondholders wasted no time, announcing in early September their intention of sending a representative to Mexico to press their claims in conjunction with Manning and Mackintosh.[125] On September 6, they concluded that "the Bondholders ought to participate in the indemnity fund now in progress of payment by the United States government."[126] The bondholders resolved that the Mexican government was legally obligated to hand over money from the U.S. indemnity and pressed Foreign Secretary Palmerston "to instruct Her Majesty's Minister in Mexico to support the representations of the bondholders to the Mexican government." This seemed to be more than a pious hope. The bondholders reasoned that the territory ceded to the United States included areas specified as collateral for the Conversion of 1837. Thus they had a legal claim on the indemnity ceded in consideration of the loss of territory. But Mora informed his superiors that Palmerston had made no claim on the

---

123 Verified through the appropriation bills (HR 684 (December 20, 1848); HR 388 (September 10, 1850); and HR 46 (January 6, 1852)). These may be consulted through the Library of Congress Web site, "US Congressional Documents and Debates, 1774–1875," http://memory.loc.gov/ammem/amlaw/lawhome.html (accessed August 1, 2007).

124 Guillermo Prieto, *Memorias de Mis Tiempos* (1906; México, 1985), p. 316.

125 *Times* (London), September 1, 1848.

126 *Times* (London), September 7, 1848.

indemnity as far as the bondholders were concerned. Rather, his position was the traditional one. British claimants who had been accorded recognition in diplomatic conventions were entitled to have their claims paid out of indemnity proceeds, no more and no less. The bondholders had been given nothing.[127]

Yet there was some perception that the foreign secretary had slowly become more sympathetic to the position of the bondholders. While Palmerston had reiterated in January 1848 the notion that those who risked their capital abroad were on their own, he allowed that there might be cases in which the nonpayment of interest on foreign loans would be too high a price for Great Britain to countenance.[128] By March, he was taking up Canning's position that the first priority of foreign policy must be the interests of England.[129] By early September, Palmerston made it known to the bondholders that he was instructing Doyle, at this point chargé d'affaires, "to bring [their] claims again before the Mexican government [so that] no effort will be spared on the part of the Mexican Government to fulfill the engagements which they have contracted in regard to the claims of the Bondholders."[130]

Following closely in the wake of the commercial crisis of 1847, Palmerston's position perhaps revealed a growing sensitivity in British official circles to the domestic consequences of severely impaired asset prices, of which the bonds of war-torn Mexico were the outstanding example.[131] In any event, the bondholders had some reason for expecting a more sympathetic hearing from the British government than they heretofore had. By March 1849, Palmerston, suitably instructed by the bondholders' fortunes during the war, had formally stated that whether or not Britain chose to

---

127 Mora to [the Minister of Home and Foreign Relations], London, September 30, 1848, in José María Luis Mora, *Obras Completas* (8 vols., México, 1986–1988), vol. 7: p. 242. Technically, Mora claimed that the U.S. indemnity was a "collateral security" unavailable to the bondholders until ordinary revenues were exhausted. G. R. Robinson to the foreign secretary, London, September 7, 1848, FO 97/273, PRO.

128 D. C. M. Platt, *Finance, Trade, and Politics in British Foreign Policy 1815–1914* (Oxford, 1968), p. 399.

129 John Clarke, *British Diplomacy and Foreign Policy* (London, 1989), p. 232.

130 H. U. Addington to G. R. Robinson, [London], September 2, 1848, *Correspondence between Great Britain and Foreign Powers . . . Relative to Loans Made by British Subjects, 1847–1853* (London, 1853), pp. 32–33.

　　In fact, "short of official interference," Palmerston had already instructed Charles Bankhead – the British minister in Mexico – to "remonstrate" against Mexico's suspension of the Conversion of 1846 as early as March 1847. See Mr. Addington to G. R. Robinson, London, March 31, 1847, in *Correspondence between Great Britain and Foreign Powers . . . Relative to Loans Made by British Subjects, 1823–1847*, p. 112.

131 C. N. Ward-Perkins, "The Commercial Crisis of 1847," in E. M. Carus-Wilson, ed., *Essays in Economic History*, vol. 3: p. 271. W. W. Rostow, *British Economy of the Nineteenth Century* (Oxford, 1948), pp. 124–125.

involve itself in the complaints of the bondholders was simply a matter of "discretion."[132]

It had long been Mora's position that the bondholders were not entitled to any of the indemnity payment and that, indeed, the Conversion of 1846 (unlike the Conversion of 1837) had explicitly ruled out hypothecation of national territory.[133] Thus Mexico had now to abide by the terms of the Conversion of 1846, which was confirmed by the government, once and for all, in 1847.[134] As Mora saw it, the bona fide bondholders should be interested in permanently raising the capitalized value of their assets, something not to be accomplished by merely turning the indemnity over to them.[135] It was simply a question of numbers. The annual interest payment under the Conversion of 1846 was $2.7 million.[136] The yearly payments of the indemnity with interest would be 3 million, 3.72 million, 3.54 million, 3.36 million, and 3.18 million. So turning over a single tranche of the indemnity would simply satisfy one or two dividends without establishing a permanent basis of repayment, the "religious" observance of which had been the mantra of Mexican ministers since the 1830s. The only people to whom one or two dividends were of interest, argued Mora, were speculators interested in temporarily inflating the value of the depreciated bonds, the more profitably to sell them once they had risen. Long-term holders had the classic understanding of bonds as fixed-rent contracts, and were thus not interested in a momentary appreciation. To drive his point home, Mora wrote that the same people behind the push to get at the indemnity payments were the "speculators" behind the Conversion of 1846, by whom he could have meant only players such as Escandón or Manning and Mackintosh.[137] And the market in September 1848 bore out

132 *Circular Addressed by Viscount Palmerston to His Majesty's Representatives in Foreign Status Respecting the Debts Due by Foreign Status to British Subjects* (1849).

133 This was a condition spelled out in the decree of April 28, 1845, which had authorized the conversion: Clause 4, "No podrá enajenar para el pago de ésta, los bienes nacionales, ni hipotecar en todo ó en parte el territorio de la República." See Dublán y Lozano, *Legislación Mexicana*, No. 2820. In addition, Mora argued that certain specific assets had been pledged to the repayments of the bondholders, for instance, customs revenues and silver export duties from Pacific ports. Only if these were insufficient could other sources of funding, such as the indemnity, be contemplated. Presumably, to permit the use of indemnity funds another conversion would have to occur explicitly authorizing their use. Some support for Mora's opinion existed at the Foreign Office as well. See J. D. Harding to the foreign secretary, Doctors Commons, March 28, 1857, FO 83/2305, PRO. Also see *Statement of Proceedings in Relation to the Mexican Debt*, pp. 17–19.

134 Mora to the foreign secretary, London, September 21, 1847, in Mora, *Obras*, vol. 7: p. 127.

135 Mora to [the Minister of Home and Foreign Relations], London, July 28, 1848, in Mora, *Obras*, vol. 7: p. 206.

136 Mora to the foreign secretary, London, September 21, 1847, in Mora, *Obras*, vol. 7: p. 127.

137 Mora to [the Minister of Home and Foreign Relations], London, July 28, 1848, in Mora, *Obras*, vol. 7: p. 206. For corroboration, see Tenenbaum, *Politics of Penury*, pp. 98–99.

precisely what he had predicted a year earlier. There could be no permanent solution to Mexico's history of serial default without a true reduction of the debt, a position that Payno would take as his brief within a few years.[138]

Rory Miller has astutely commented that it was often not clear to Latin American elites in what capacity British diplomats functioned when they held their posts by virtue of mercantile experience.[139] That this was the case with Ewen Mackintosh is beyond doubt, for he was the particular object of Mora's animus. Mora campaigned furiously with Palmerston to have Mackintosh removed as consul-general, initially alleging that Mackintosh had interfered in internal Mexican politics when it suited his business interests. But it soon became clear that Mora regarded Mackintosh as the moving force behind getting access to the indemnity payments. Escandón and Mackintosh had been behind the Conversion of 1846, and we recall that the "wretched timing" of the war had driven down the bonds that Escandón had expected to rise smartly. It was for just this reason, Mora argued, that Mackintosh was mixed up in the indemnity business. This was an attempt to put to right the deal that had collapsed in 1846, for as previously noted, over the course of the war, the bonds had fallen by about half. Mora minced no words: "it was an attempt to work the Mexican government directly by means of pressure or just plain seduction."[140] Getting the indemnity would provide the capital gain that Escandón and Manning and Mackintosh – and even, hinted Mora, Murphy – were counting on before President Polk had disturbed their scheme in May 1846. Indeed, Valentín Gómez Farías explicitly linked Escandón and Murphy and "their interests."[141]

Yet the politics and economics of effecting the transfer of resources were complex and, in a sense, overdetermined. First, Mexico came out of the war with the United States with very little money. The opportunity cost of parting with cash, never trivial, was – if anything – at an historical

---

138 Mora to the foreign secretary, London, September 21, 1847, FO 97/273, PRO.

139 Rory Miller, *Britain and Latin America in the Nineteenth and Twentieth Centuries* (London, 1993).

140 Mora to [the Minister of Home and Foreign Relations], London, October 30, 1848, in Mora, *Obras*, vol. 7: pp. 244–250 [italics in original]. This remarkable dispatch in which Mora chronicles the maneuvering to get the United States to fund the debt issue directly through the Treaty of Guadalupe Hidalgo is the basis for most of this paragraph. Historians such as Tenenbaum and Costeloe have suggested that the pressure the British bondholders placed on peacemaking influenced the whole process. Mora does nothing, if not strengthen and extend their suspicions. See Michael P. Costeloe, "The Extraordinary Case of Mr. Falconnet and 2,500,000 Silver Dollars: London and Mexico, 1850–1853," *Estudios Mexicanos/Mexican Studies*, 15: 2 (1999), p. 289. Mora's sideways slap at Murphy also hints at the solution to another mystery: why Escandón makes virtually no appearance in Murphy's remarkable *Deuda Esterior* around 1846, even though Escandón may have been the central figure behind the conversion. Tomás Murphy may have been in no hurry to publicize the connection for reasons of his own, although Mora has nothing but praise for Murphy's analysis.

141 Valentín Gómez Farías to Benito Gómez Farías [June 1849?], GF 3144, BLAC, UT.

high by 1850. Second, because money was tight, the need to find resources to fund the internal debt was particularly pressing. The conflict between internal and external financial commitments, always sharp, was, a fortiori, sharper still. The external commitments were by no means limited to the London Debt either, as a large number of "conventions" with the nationals of England, France, and Spain required substantial payments as well. Third, with the loss of the territories to the United States, the only thing Mexico had to offer the bondholders was cash, and the only ready cash was the U.S. indemnity. The potential avenues open before 1846 for liquidating the bondholders' claims, especially some variation of offering Texas or California in settlement, were no longer even theoretically possible to any meaningful extent, thus reducing room for maneuver.[142] Finally, the bondholders had found the possibility of a new hearing at British Court and a powerful new ally with an interest in securing access to the indemnity in Baring Brothers. Let us briefly consider these factors in turn.

The U.S. indemnity had created an illusion of public wealth after the war, but it was nothing more than an illusion. "The state of finance here is most deplorable and with every chance of a crash," concluded Doyle.[143] The newly appointed financial agent for the bondholders, Francis Falconnet, offered a similarly glum observation: "The country seems to me in great peril and I do not see the men who are to save it. Providence must intervene to do so."[144] "[A]ttempting to settle claims by charging them upon particular branches of the Mexican Revenue is a very defective and unsatisfactory expedient," the Committee of Bondholders itself objected.[145] One symptom of Mexico's malaise was simply the sheer scarcity of ready money the national government had at its disposal. As of February 1850, there was no cash on hand at the Treasury at all. By April 1850, for example, the median daily cash balance at the Treasury improved to about 12,000 pesos, with a low figure of 1,200 pesos registered on April 5 and ordinary government spending to be cut in half.[146] How precisely does a country with a $50 million debt make interest payments when it has 12,000 pesos in cash on hand – or, as in February, precisely none? More to the point, where had the country's operating revenues gone after the war? Mexico was flat broke.

Since the source of government income was the mostly customs revenues, one assumes that these had fallen at midcentury. And – indeed – they did,

142 G. R. Robinson to the foreign secretary, London, October 14, 1848, FO 97/273, PRO.

143 Doyle to Baring Brothers, México, November 13, 1849, HC 4.5.21, BBA.

144 Falconnet to Baring Brothers [México], March 4, 1851, HC 4.5.25, BBA.

145 "Abstract of M Mora's Note of September 7, 1848 Respecting Claims of the Bondholders and Other British Subjects," FO 97/273, PRO.

146 Calculated from *entrada y salida de caudales*, appearing in *Siglo XIX* on May 1, 14, 22, and 31, 1850. The February figure is found in *Esposición del Secretario del Despacho de Hacienda . . . en 17 de Agosto de 1851* (México, 1850), p. 11.

dropping to under 5 million pesos. Total government revenue was reduced to levels not seen since the early 1820s; in 1852–1853, it was scarcely more than 10 million pesos.[147] There were a number of reasons why the customs had declined, producing "a very serious financial upset to the Republic."[148] The southward displacement of the border with the United States toward central Mexico had, it was said, produced a fall in the cost of and a large increase in smuggling to the detriment of legal imports. In other words, the frontier with the United States was much closer, rendering contraband easier. Moreover, there was also wide agreement that the occupation of Mexico had produced an accompanying glut of imports under the auspices of the occupying army, and as one authority put it, "the new importations since that time have not been and will not perhaps before the close of the year be such as should be in accordance with their usual conditions."[149] But there were others factors that were equally important in driving down government revenue, of which one – the (incomplete) abolition of the internal excise and customs (*alcabala*) by Valentín Gómez Farías in 1846 – was seemingly most important. Finally, income from internal borrowing shrank after the war as the accustomed sources of finance jockeyed for a share of the indemnity business, clearly withholding fresh finance as a means of pressuring the government.[150] In the event, the combined effect of these factors was catastrophic: a state that, if not actually insolvent, was caught in the grip of a liquidity crisis the result of which was near fiscal paralysis.

The tension between meeting domestic and foreign commitments, never far below the surface, had now emerged with some force once more. The fiscal authorities understood that a reduction of payments to the bondholders was intended "to leave more available to attend to public necessities." "Is this a crime?" one anonymous observer asked.[151] "They call the arrangement of the foreign debt terrible (*funesto*)," the author continued. Yet when payments to the bondholders were increased in 1841, Congress "had no other choice." Nevertheless, when Haro y Tamariz raised interest payments, it was observed that "the position [of the government] was very difficult." How difficult? Payno calculated that the unencumbered income of the federal government around 1850–1851 was about 2.65 million pesos yearly,

147 Cosío Villegas, *Cuestión arancelaria en México*, p. 65.

148 *Memoria de Hacienda . . . 1870 . . .*, par. 1091.

149 Mora to the foreign secretary, London, September 7, 1848, *Correspondence between Great Britain and Foreign Powers*, p. 36.

150 Tenenbaum, *Politics of Penury*, pp. 98–109.

151 *Observaciones imparciales acerca de la administración financiera en la época del gobierno provisional*, pp. 50, 51, 55, for this and what follows.

but the dividend payments to London alone now required some 2 million pesos annually.[152] Approximately the same amount was earmarked for the service of the internal debt. But the overall ratio of the principal of the internal to the external debt between 1831 and 1850 had remained roughly in the area of 60 percent. Therefore, from the standpoint of domestic creditors, the service of the London Debt consumed a disproportionate share of available financial resources. Were the U.S. indemnity to be transferred abroad, it would be to the severe discomfort of domestic claimants, and to be done only over "the great opposition to the measure in Congress," who were amply represented there. And who were these domestic claimants? In 1850, the Comisión de Crédito Público declared unequivocally that "Don Gregorio Mier y Terán is the largest holder of the internal debt." He may well have been the wealthiest man in Mexico, so his opposition could make or break a government.[153]

Nor were these domestic claimants alone. Another class of creditors were principally English, French, and Spanish (there were many from the United States as well), who are customarily, if confusingly, known as "convention" creditors. "Convention" has a relatively precise diplomatic meaning, one not always observed in the intricacies of Mexican historical usage of this era: "a less important form of treaty, namely one which is concluded, not between heads of state, but between governments."[154] According to Payno, there were thirteen diplomatic conventions involving Mexico in 1849. As of that date, a number had been completely concluded, including the First (1842) and Second (1844) English Conventions, and the Spanish Convention (1847).[155] Convention debts were different from the bonded debt in a specific way. To repeat, the usual British position on purchasing foreign securities ("funds") had long been that this was undertaken at the risk of the lender, who had foregone the opportunity to employ his or her savings in Great Britain. In the main, "convention" debts were different, although, to be sure, they included foreign lending as well. So, for instance, the First English Convention covered a heterogeneous variety of claims for compensation that had arisen in the course of British subjects doing business in or trading with Mexico. They involved, for instance,

---

152 Payno, *La Deuda Interior de México*, pp. 17–18. The foreign and domestic interest payments are my calculation, as are all others, which draw on pp. 1–17.

153 Jecker Torre to Baring Brothers, México, June 4, 1852, HC 4.5.24, BBA; *El Monitor Republicano*, October 8, 1850.

154 Harold Nicolson, *Diplomacy* (3rd ed., London, 1963), p. 233.

155 Payno, *Deuda Interior de México*, p. 9. The Third English Convention, which famously involved the Martínez del Río and became a *cause célèbre*, did not take place until 1853 (Payno's dating; Walker gives 1851). See Walker, *Kinship and Politics*, pp. 186–216. (*enteramente concluidos* is translated as "completely concluded.")

forced loans imposed on British merchants who believed themselves to be exempted from such impositions. Yet there was also voluntary lending involved, directly with the Mexican Treasury, in what were frequently unsecured or highly risky transactions involving speculative paper in which the claimants were important merchant houses. These, in turn, were able to secure the local intervention of the British minister or chargé d'affaires in coming to terms with the Mexican Treasury.

The major issue, for our purposes, is not the details of the conventions, because, strictly speaking, they had (as of then) nothing to do with the bondholders. What is important is that the "convention" debts represented competing claims against the scarce financial resources of Mexico. They could not be met without depriving the bondholders of income. Yet the implication of suspending payment on a "convention" debt was very different from the implication of defaulting on a bond issue. A "convention" debt had been concluded, at least in the English case, under the authority of a British diplomat that, de facto, made it a diplomatic issue and the official business of the British government. Thus, according to Payno, such debts were privileged, especially regarding funding and payment.[156] Their accumulation and servicing would increasingly take precedence over both the ordinary internal (the so-called floating) debt and the London Debt. It is only in this way that the troubled international history of Mexico in the 1850s and 1860s makes much sense, or why it was that the British bondholders apparently languished for as long as they did without much official encouragement.

The payments required by the "convention" debts after 1841 were sizable. Payno calculated that payments made to England, France, and Spain as of 1861 were $41.5 million. Adjusting for payments made to the British bondholders for principal and interest, the amount was $12 million, or roughly $600,000 per year on average. So, in a sense, by 1862, it was as if 80 percent of the U.S. indemnity could have been paid out in "convention" debts. When we add the amount of the indemnity that was ultimately transferred to the bondholders in the Conversion of 1850 (see later), $2.5 million, debt service virtually exhausted the U.S. indemnity. Money, of course, is fungible, and there are numerous of ways of viewing the "assignment" of the indemnity. They all point in the same direction: debt service.[157] Prieto had anticipated Payno's conclusions as early as 1850, when, as finance minister he wrote, "If you ask what use Mexico made of all the money it got from the United States as a result of its national tragedy, you should answer, without hesitation, that it wasn't in material improvements, defending the borders,

156 Payno, *Deuda Interior de México*, p. 9.
157 Payno, *México y sus cuestiones financieras*, p. 302. Also see *Memoria de Hacienda, 1851*, pp. 29–30, and Tenenbaum, *Politics of Penury*, p. 106.

Table 3.5. *"Assignment" of the U.S. Indemnity, by Class of National Creditors as of November 1850*

French	554,700 pesos	4.4 percent
British$^\alpha$	7,589,447 pesos	61.0 percent
Spanish	371,666 pesos	3.0 percent
United States	599,511 pesos	4.8 percent
German	23,000 pesos	
Unspecified	3,313,257 pesos	26.6 percent
TOTAL	12,451,581 pesos	

Note: Superscript α includes payment both to "convention" and private ("London Debt") bondholders.

Source: [Guillermo Prieto], *Informes Leidos en la Cámara de Diputados por el Secretario de Hacienda* (México, 1852), pp. 41–42.

or for public safety. It went, almost entirely, to our creditors, foreigners mostly"[158] – and as Prieto's breakdown in Table 3.5 demonstrates, mostly British creditors at that, who accounted for 61 percent of the total. The French, later to prove so troublesome, received less than 5 percent of the total. By 1850, Prieto as much as said, the indemnity was "spoken for" – all of it, and more.

Finally, there was at least one other element that made for pressure to transfer a part of the indemnity to the bondholders: the power, money, and influence of Baring Brothers. The story of Barings' involvement in brokering the last two payments (1851, 1852) is a complicated one. It involved accusations of influence peddling, outright bribery, and even venality by the chronically impecunious U.S. secretary of state, Daniel Webster – an unedifying tale not all that different from what was unfolding in Mexico City. We can touch on it only briefly here.[159]

According to Duff Green, a long-time political operator in Washington, he had been contacted directly by the president of Mexico "to make an arrangement with our government, by which, instead of sending specie

---

158 [Guillermo Prieto], *Informes leídos en la Cámara de Diputados por el Secretario de Hacienda*... (México, 1852), p. 40.

159 For a detailed account of the wrangling over the indemnity, see Henry Cohen, *Business and Politics in America from the Age of Jackson to the Civil War. The Career Biography of W. W. Corcoran* (Westport, CT, 1971), pp. 63–101.

For what follows, see "Sobre el pago de los seis millones de pesos y sus réditos que por la indemnización adeudan a México los Estados Unidos," *Hacienda Pública*, 1ª sección, 1850, AGNM; "Memorial to the Senate and House of Representatives of the United States in Congress Assembled," [J. D. Marks, 1851] Td* 1851, vol. 3, Historical Society of Pennsylvania; George Ticknor Curtis, *Life of Daniel Webster* (2 vols., New York, 1870), vol. 2: p. 497n; Daniel Webster to the president of the United States, Boston, August 6, 1851, in Fletcher Webster, ed., *The Private Correspondence of Daniel Webster* (2 vols., Boston, 1857), vol. 2, p. 461.

to Mexico to pay the balance on the Mexican indemnity, our government should accept the bills of exchange of that government [Mexico] payable in New York for the amount."[160] The idea was that Mexico would get a better exchange premium from an outside merchant banker in the United States competing for the indemnity business, but there was another attraction still. The Federation – and presidents Joaquín Herrera and Mariano Arista and their ministers – would control the disposition of the indemnity by writing bills of exchange directly on the U.S. Treasury, which the Mexican finance ministry immediately proceeded to do. They would thus avoid the interference of creditors – Baring Brothers and the bondholders – in determining how the indemnity funds were spent. Besides, the U.S. minister to Mexico, R. P. Letcher, portrayed Arista as frankly pro–United States, revealing that "Genl Arista required me to say to [United States President] Genl Taylor *he loved him very much*" [italics in original].[161]

Whether or not Green was the source of this scheme is irrelevant, for he or his son, Ben E. Green, was certainly involved in it. "Bring them on without delay," he said of the bills of exchange in a letter to Isaac Marks, a Louisianan who was the public face of the proposal.[162] For all intents and purposes, Marks and Green had managed to circumvent Mexico's "long . . . dependence on British capitalists" and induced President Taylor's secretary of state, John M. Clayton, to acquiesce in the idea.[163] Payno, who was in the midst of an exquisitely difficult balancing act between the London and the domestic bondholders – one that collapsed in a storm of domestic recriminations within months – managed to induce Mexico's grandest *agiotistas* to sign off on the deal as well, perhaps softened by the prospect of sharing in a douceur of 70,000 pesos that Marks and Green had discussed spreading around Mexico City.[164] It is hard to suppress the thought that foundations for the Conversion of 1850 had been carefully laid

160 Duff Green, *Facts and Suggestions, Biographical, Historical, Financial and Political Addressed to the People of the United States* (New York, 1866), p. 215.

161 R. P. Letcher to the secretary of the Treasury, México, February 13, 1850, Meredith Family Papers, Collection 1509, ser. 7a, Box 69, Historical Society of Pennsylvania; Prieto, *Memoria de Mis Tiempos*, p. 331, emphasizes that Arista had visited the United States after the war, and had been transformed by the experience.

162 Duff Green to [Isaac D. Marks?], Washington, September 2, 1851, *Hacienda Pública*, 1ª sección, 1850, AGNM.

163 John M. Clayton to H. A. Bullard, New Castle, Delaware, December 19, 1850, in "Memorial to the Senate and House of Representatives of the United States in Congress Assembled," [J. D. Marks, 1851] Td* 1851, vol. 3, Historical Society of Pennsylvania, for this and what follows of Clayton's words.

164 See the (amazing) agreement signed by Payno, Gregorio Mier y Terán, Cayetano Rubio, and Ramón Olarte, Mexico, August 16, 1850, *Hacienda Pública*, 1ª, AGNM; Isaac Marks to [Ben E.] Green, México, July 13, 1850, reproduced in *El Universal*, May 3, 1851.

here, with – as Clayton put it – arrangements with the London bondholders "still pending."

But Baring Brothers and their North American friends had other ideas. When Taylor died in office in 1850, Webster replaced Clayton as secretary of state, and as Clayton put it, "Mr. Webster was not informed of this proposition by me." Webster, publicly at least, admitted that it might be a good moment to "buy off our obligations" of the Treaty of Guadalupe Hidalgo. "There is danger, however, that if this should be done, the money will all go to the creditors of Mexico, leaving her as incapable as she now is of defending her frontiers. Our own territories are interested in this defense against the Indians. Can we trust Mexico?"[165] This certainly was putting an odd twist on things, for Webster was turning what Marks and Green had argued on its head! But when Webster reversed Clayton's decision, he was attacked in Congress as a tool of Baring Brothers, as well as of Corcoran, Riggs and Howland and Aspinwall of New York, who had supposedly set up a slush fund for Webster's personal use in office.[166]

These accusations were roundly denounced by Webster's political allies, of course, but the pressure was pretty clearly on. G. G. Howland wrote to the U.S. secretary of the Treasury "on behalf of commercial friends in Mexico," indicating that he had paper from the Mexican government worth $1.5 million that could be discounted "in anticipation of the arrangement being carried out."[167] This would produce "a handsome commission to Howland and Aspinwall." By March 1851, Corcoran, Riggs was furiously pressuring Mexico to give the business to Barings, which it portrayed as Webster's desire. The problem with this, Finance Minister Mariano Yáñez said, was that

I should tell Your Excellency [President Mariano Arista] that if [we] recognize the House of Barings as agent of the Government of the United States for the payment of the indemnity, I greatly fear that at least the last installment of the indemnity won't get to Mexico and will be retained by [Barings] for the creditors of the English debt.[168]

Barings, need it be said, had its way, although it expected to earn only about 1 percent on the 1852 installment of the indemnity because of delays in getting the money. This was considerably less than the 4 percent it

165 Webster to the president of the United States, Boston, August 6, 1851, in Fletcher Webster, ed., *The Private Correspondence of Daniel Webster*, vol. 2: p. 461.

166 Curtis, *Daniel Webster*, p. 497n; Merrill D. Peterson, *The Great Triumvirate: Webster, Clay and Calhoun* (New York, 1988), p. 479. Corcoran, Riggs of Washington, DC, had been instrumental in arranging financing of the Mexican War by marketing a $16 million loan in Europe.

167 G. G. Howland to the secretary of the Treasury, New York, October 20, 1849, Meredith Family Papers, Collection 1509, ser. 7a, Box 68, Historical Society of Pennsylvania.

168 Mariano Yáñez to the president of Mexico, México, March 3, 1851, *Hacienda Pública*, 1ª, AGNM.

earned on the 1851 installment.[169] Its allies in Mexico, such as Falconnet, were quick to take credit for Barings' success, pointing out the obvious that Arista may have had his own plans for the use of the indemnity and that these did not include the bondholders.[170] Perhaps more to the point, Mexico's "reward" for cooperation was Barings' reemergence as a financier for dividend payments, for it was Barings, through Falconnet's intermediation, who would lend Mexico what it needed to make its January 1, 1852, dividend payment.[171] Under such excruciating financial pressure, Mexico was hardly in a position to alienate Barings, and finding some accommodation with the bondholders was, under the circumstances, only "reasonable."[172] So even though the British did nothing to help Mexico retain Texas, even though the war was over and even though Santa Anna was out of favor (momentarily), British influence continued to make itself felt. As Doyle was to say years later, "our Government assisted them, through me, when all others refused to take any part in the negotiations for peace." Britain, he said, was "[Mexico's] oldest and best friend."[173] Indeed.

In Mexico, nevertheless, strong pressure to act on the internal debt continued.

Rumors have begun to circulate that the settlement of the public debt may perhaps favor certain personages and houses in London, and other powerful ones here. This business demands a public airing, loyal and open . . . in which we trust the interests of the Republic will not again be sacrificed, as is almost always the case in the conventions and conversions of the foreign debt.[174]

Payno wrote that "a Government full of resources and prosperous like that of England punctually pays its debts is nothing strange; but it is remarkable that a country, as has happened in Mexico, has at the same time seen its army without rations and yet paid considerable amounts of money to its domestic creditors and to the bondholders."[175] Payno, of course, knew just

169 Baring Brothers and Company et al. to the secretary of State, Boston, January 14, 1852, in United States, Senate, 32nd Cong., 1st Sess., *Message from the President of the United States . . . urging an early appropriation to pay . . . under the Treaty of Gaudalupe Hidalgo* [sic], pp. 2–3; Cohen, *Business and Politics*, p. 83.

170 *Siglo XIX*, September 11, 1852, and Falconnet to Baring Brothers, México, May 2, 1851, HB 4.5.25, BBA. Also see *Financial and Commercial Review*, 24(1849), p. 469, for the importance of Baring Brothers.

171 [Guillermo Prieto], *Informes leídos en la Cámara de Diputados por el Secretario de Hacienda . . .* , p. 26.

172 Mexico owed Baring Brothers $25,000 as late as 1840. There is no indication that the debt had been settled by the time Barings reemerged as a broker of the indemnity. See "Debe el Sup°Gobierno de México en Cuenta de Dividendos con Baring Hermanos," London, December 31, 1839, *Gobernación*, leg. 91, caja 151, exp. 1, AGNM.

173 Percy Doyle to W. W. Barron, London, July 31, 1868, FO 97/282, PRO.

174 *Siglo XIX*, May 16, 1849.

175 *Times* (London), July 28, 1851.

what he was talking about. He had the unenviable job of appearing to be everyone's ally and the battering he took in the Mexican press for it was tremendous.[176] The assault mounted against him by domestic creditors, industrialists and their political allies, and *agiotistas* such as the Martínez del Río – the core of the centralist coalition – anxious for a larger share of the indemnity, was ferocious.[177] Indeed, as late as April 1850, they had continued to press for as much as 70 percent of the remaining indemnity payments, but as we have seen, they were privately willing to settle for much less by August.[178] Perhaps his was the ultimate accomplishment in the whole sordid business – nobody, perhaps with good reason, wholly trusted Don Manuel Payno.

Back to the Future: The Conversion of 1850

In the midst of all this, the Federation was attempting to resume regular debt service and a postwar conversion of the London Debt after the war had effectively put paid to the Conversion of 1846. There had been an abortive attempt to reach agreement with the bondholders in 1849, but success finally came with the Conversion of 1850. The converted bonds were to carry 3 percent interest, and the bondholders agreed to accept a payment of $2,500,000 in lieu of the arrears of the Conversion of 1846 (eight payments in all). The recognized amount of the principal was £10,241,650. Finally, the consolidated 3 percent bonds were to be funded by customs duties: 25 percent of all import duties, wherever charged; 75 percent of Pacific port export duties; and 5 percent export duties from Gulf ports. In theory, any charge not covered by these sources was to be made up from whatever other source of state revenue possible. The Mexicans were jubilant over the arrangement, calling it "one of the best financial operations we have carried out" and estimating their savings at something around $25 million.[179] The market supported these sentiments, as the relative price of Mexican bonds rose to levels not seen since the outbreak of the war with the United States.

176 According to Valentín Gómez Farías, Payno's predecessor Minister Arrangóiz succeeded in lobbying the Congress to release the indemnity, figuring this would act as the incentive for Britain to reduce interest and principal "as for other nations in London." Valentín Gómez Farías to Benito Gómez Farías [June 1849?], GF 3144, BLAC, UT. Cf. Nicole Giron, "Manuel Payno. El Ir y Venir por la Secretaría de Hacienda," in Ludlow and Marichal, eds., *Los Secretarios de Hacienda*, vol. 1: p. 361, who credits Payno with smoothing matters through Congreso; Payno, *Reseña sobre el estado de los principales ramos de la Hacienda Pública para . . . Lic. D. José I. Esteva*, p. 7.

177 *El Universal*, January 9, February 7, February 12, May 3, May 11, July 11, July 20, 1851, for a sampling.

178 *Historia parlementaria de México*, Session of April 24, 1850, vol. 10, pp. 352–353.

179 [Guillermo Prieto], *Informes Leídos en La Cámara de Diputados sobre el Estado que Guarda el Erario Público*, p. 24; *Mexican National Debt Collected in London* (London, 1860), p. 6.

Figure 3.4. Silver, Perhaps a Dividend Payment, on Its Way to Veracruz.
Source: Courtesy of Illustrated London News Ltd./Mary Evans Picture Library.

Clearly the reduction was thought to increase Mexico's capacity to pay. By November 1852, the physical exchange of bonds was virtually complete, and April 1, 1853, was set as the closing date for the conversion.[180] But others were less sanguine. Falconnet complained,

The new Minister of Finance [José Ignacio Esteva] is at work but no one knows what his plans are. I am afraid he has none ... What they will do to fill up the Treasury is an enigma. They go on notwithstanding making arrangements with their interior creditors and promising large amounts in cash to come God knows where from.[181]

And speaking of optimism, there were the peculiarities of the deal itself and the assumptions embedded in it. In essence, the bondholders were being asked to approve (and approve they did) the sacrifice of 10.2 million pesos in arrears (since the Conversion of 1846) for a payment of $2.5 million "on the indemnity." Since the time period was a short one (July 1,

180 Benito Gómez Farías to Valentín Gómez Farías, London, May 27, 1850, GF3270, BLAC, UT; Francisco Facio to the finance minister, London, December 1, 1852, *Deuda Exterior*, vol. 5, AGNM. Only 751 bonds out of 51,000 remained outstanding as of that date.
181 Falconnet to Baring Brothers, México, March 4, 1851, HC 4.5.25, BBA.

1847–January 1, 1851), there is almost no difference between the actual sum foregone and its present value when discounted at 2 percent – the relevant short-term interest rate. The only way the exchange makes sense is if the bondholders thought there was little better than a 25 percent chance that they would ever see the full value of the arrears, since 2.5 million is, of course, 25 percent of 10 million. Nevertheless, this was – as we have seen – far better than the expectations of the bondholders in 1837, who were looking at a 5 percent chance of payment. The big difference between 1837 and 1851 was, of course, the U.S. indemnity. Knowing that there was some hard cash available ultimately made them more sanguine than they had been earlier, and familiarity with the changing perceptions of the British government gave the bondholders greater reason to feel as if their demands would evoke some form of official support.[182]

Since Payno had carried the draft of the indemnity payment to London and had himself negotiated arrangements for the complete payment of the first dividend payment (July 1, 1851), he correctly or not saw himself as the architect of the Conversion of 1850.[183] His mission, he averred, was nothing less than "to calm the Bondholders" by stabilizing bond prices and "to consolidate the conversion of the English debt by the payment of the dividend and the issue of new bonds." At the very least, Payno's financial liberalism carried the day, for his explicit exclusion of "convention" debts from the Law of November 30 was causing problems. Foreign creditors were now complaining loudly to their governments of the "expropriation" inherent in the law, while Mexican creditors, with no government but their own on which to rely, found themselves increasingly prejudiced. Payno's animus against the "convention" debts was real, for he feared that they turned mere financial disputes into diplomatic questions. Make no mistake, Payno warned Palmerston. Mexico now had its back to the wall. The financial reorganization of 1850 had been undertaken to make payment of both the London bondholders and domestic creditors possible. The budget of the federal government had been pared to 7 million pesos (down from around 20), and 60 percent of the customs were anticipated. Mexico, Payno told Palmerston, was doing all it could. To demand more would be to produce "the breakdown of the Republic and the long-term suspension of debt payments." There was shrinking room for maneuver: either all creditors participated on the same footing or no one could be paid. Within

---

182 "[T]he true policy of the bondholders appears to be secure what they can, and when and how they can, and at whatever cost." *Report of the Committee of Mexican Bondholders* (London, 1855), p. 12. The text of the conversion appears in *Mexican National Debt Collected in London*, pp. 3–5.

183 [Manuel Payno], *Memoria en que Manuel Payno da cuenta al público de su manejo en el desempeño del Ministerio de Hacienda*... (México, 1852), for what follows, which is drawn primarily from pp. 15–16, 29–32, 40–41, 55–60. (*el que durante mucho tiempo no se paguen ni las asignaciones actuales* is translated as "long-term suspension of debt payments.")

Figure 3.5. Arrival of Californian Gold and Mexican Dollars at the Bank of England in 1849. *Source:* Courtesy of Illustrated London News Ltd./Mary Evans Picture Library.

the Mexican Finance Ministry, there were few illusions about how long payments could be continued.[184]

Another indication of changes afoot was the anomalous reaction of the market to Payno's mission to London. When Payno arrived, he brought title to the indemnity funds and negotiated their transfer in May 1851. But the bullion itself did not leave Veracruz until July 1852 and did not reach Southampton until August.[185] Statistically, as one might expect, the bullion's physical arrival was a nonevent, for the transfer of title was what mattered. Yet Payno himself noted that the transfer had no appreciable effect on Mexican bond prices in May 1851, which he attributed to his acumen in negotiating financial affairs.[186] Yet the stability of the bond prices was, strictly speaking, very odd. Barings, understandably, now had more financial credibility than Mexico, at least to judge from the market's reaction, for Barings was once again paying dividends – for the moment! G. R. Robinson of the Committee of Bondholders put it this way: "It is true that the past is no infallible rule for the future; but after the long experience

184 Memo, 2ᵃ Sec de Hacienda (copy), México, August 20, 1852, *Deuda Exterior*, vol. 13, AGNM.

185 The bill of lading of The Royal Mail Steam Packet Company has survived. See *Deuda Exterior*, vol. 13, AGNM, and *Times* (London), August 2, 1852.

186 [Manuel Payno], *Memorial en que Manuel Payno da cuenta al público*, p. 29; *Times* (London), April 2 and 24 1852.

Figure 3.6. Bullion Office, Bank of England. *Note:* Compartment in the bullion vault. Stacking bags of Mexican dollars. *Source:* Courtesy of Illustrated London News Ltd./Mary Evans Picture Library.

which they have had as Mexican bondholders, they cannot possibly place implicit confidence in the punctual performance of the new obligation of the Government to its British creditors."[187]

"The past is no infallible rule for the future"; certainly not. But just as the Conversion of 1830 produced only temporary respite in the face of deteriorating national politics, so too was the Conversion of 1850 to falter. After 1832, one will recall, Mexico imposed a moratorium of payments until the Conversion of 1837, and even then, no significant payment was forthcoming until the 1840s. The Conversion of 1850 produced payments until 1854, whereupon remissions to London essentially stopped. Yet unlike what occurred in the 1830s, the British government would now mobilize resources on behalf of the bondholders, along with its erstwhile partners France and Spain. This was, perhaps, as good an indication of how the

187 G. R. Robinson to the foreign secretary, London, October 14, 1848, FO 97/273, PRO.

international environment changed in the quarter century after the fall of the Alamo, but in reality, many factors shaped the fiscal and financial history of the later 1850s.

First, the bare outline, or what we can make of it: Prieto, repeatedly finance minister in the 1850s and as did Payno, indicated that dividends of 1.5 percent were paid from July 1, 1851, through January 2, 1854, the last dividend to fall due before March 1854 when the revolt that finally toppled Santa Anna began. These totaled about $4.6 million (roughly $2.5 million of which was the U.S. indemnity).[188] After that, things get murkier, and Prieto indicates no payments through 1863. The Committee of Bondholders, for its part, asserted that from 1851 through 1861, only six of twenty-two dividends were paid, worth about 4.6 million pesos.[189] Matías Romero shows that the equivalent of about one payment was made in 1856, but generally implies that no regular service occurred after 1854. With the outbreak of the Reform Wars (1858–1860), nothing further was sent.[190] Both sides, then, agreed that about 4.6 million pesos were paid in the 1850s. Yet under the circumstances, even raising 2.1 million apart from the indemnity was no small feat and required considerable financial sacrifice. Just how much can be gleaned from a survey of the duties segregated in the ports to fund the London Debt?[191] The amounts were collected by private agents (Jecker, Torre and Company in Mazatlán, or Barron, Forbes and Company in Tepic, for instance) in conjunction with customs officials, and if the amounts were modest, they were nevertheless sent regularly. As we shall shortly see, the Federation would come under increasing pressure from the states at just this time to rein in its expenditures and to give preference to the internal debt over the London Debt. And indeed, about 700,000 pesos went to both: the Federation, largely deprived of operating revenues, was now engaged in a delicate balancing act between its creditors. Any shock could destroy the whole arrangement.

188 Guillermo Prieto, *Lecciones elementales de economía política* (2nd ed., 1876; México, 1989), pp. 821–822. Payno may have been Prieto's source, for he too concludes that from July 1851 through July 1862, six dividends amounting to 4.6 million pesos were paid. Manuel Payno to the finance minister, México, October 14, 1868, *Deuda Exterior*, vol. 9, AGNM. It is possible to verify more than 100,000 pesos remitted to England in 1856, but the documentation is woefully incomplete. See Deuda Contraída en Londres, "Comprobantes," 1856, vol. 5, AGNM.

189 "Sacrifices Submitted to by the Bondholders in Favor of Mexico," in Report of the Committee of Mexican Bondholders, London, November 22, 1861, FO 97/280, PRO.

190 *Memoria de Hacienda, 1870*, pars. 1711, 1713.

191 "Comisión de los agentes de los Tenedores de Bonos en los Puertos (1854)," *Deuda Exterior*, vol. 13, AGNM. I recalculated collections from the reports submitted by the customs officers in the ports corresponding to 1850–1853. My total was about 2.3 million pesos – or about 700,000 pesos per year – allowing for considerable differences in the reporting period.

Santa Anna, in his final appearance as "Dictator," was inclined to co-operate, and he has been portrayed in 1853–1854 as virtually desperate to curry favor with the British because of growing pressure from the United States.[192] Doyle reported on the results of an interview in 1853 in which he stressed the importance of continued payment to Santa Anna, with Doyle reporting that "[Santa Anna] gave positive orders on this point to the Minister of Finance." But, Doyle added, "[n]otwithstanding my exertions, I much fear that it cannot be done."[193] Indeed, it could not be done, at least indefinitely, because neither the money nor the political will was there. When Santa Anna needed the British, it made sense to sacrifice to try to keep up the dividends. But now, with Texas and the rest gone, the point was largely moot. Even one of the linchpins of postwar British financial diplomacy, the so-called Doyle–Ramírez Convention (1851) – which included claims and former agreements made with Richard Pakenham, the Martínez del Río, and Montgomery Nicod and Company – proved unequal to its object. It was revised in 1852, and raised from 12 to 16 percent of customs duties in 1852 and then from 3 to 6 percent interest in 1858.[194] With both the bondholders and the "convention" claimants protesting bitterly, the symptoms of fiscal disorder were only too quick to emerge. The first dividend under the Conversion of 1850 (July 1, 1851) required £20,000 to be borrowed from the house of Cristóbal de Murrieta and Company. The 1852 payments were lent in part by Baring Brothers and the firm of Jecker, Torre.[195] Here again was "debt-led debt," the very process that had precipitated default twenty-five years earlier.

The British argued that only financial liberalism could save Mexico from itself, particularly of the sort associated with the liberalization of international trade. While they had delivered this message, more or less consistently, since the 1830s, changing international and domestic circumstances now made the message more palatable. As Doyle put it, "I have

---

192 Marcela Terrazas y Basante, *Inversiones, Especulaciones y Diplomacia. Las Relaciones Entre México y Estados Unidos Durante La Dictadura Santannista* (México, 2000), pp. 180–183. A summary of her principal findings appears in "Los Especuladores y el Debate Parlamentario Norteamericano en Torno al Tratado de la Mesilla," in Marcela Terrazas Basante and Ana Rosa Suárez Argüello, eds., *Política y Negocios: Ensayos sobre la Relación entre México y los Estados Unidos en el Siglo XIX* (México, 1997), pp. 293–378. Also see Paul Neff Garber, *The Gadsden Treaty* (Gloucester, MA, 1959), p. 99.

193 Doyle to the foreign secretary, México, August 2, 1853, FO 97/273, PRO.

194 "British Convention Debt," HC 4.5.36.3i, BBA; and Doyle to the foreign secretary, México, January 20 and February 2, 1854, FO 97/273, PRO. A convenient table of British conventions and their provisions is included in U.S. Congress, House, 37th Cong., 2nd sess., "The Present Condition of Mexico" (Washington, DC, 1862), p. 332.

195 *Memoria de Hacienda*, 1870, pars. 1322, 1715; Jecker, Torre and Company to Baring Brothers, México, October 1, 1852, HC 4.5.59, BBA.

just, after fighting day and night against the manufacturers, who are very powerful . . . had a free trade tariff published which will settle for good and all the principle of taking off prohibitions which we have been trying at here for 20 years." The liberalism of the reform movement was closely associated with a much-changed attitude toward international trade, embodied, as Doyle reported, in the tariffs of 1853 or – as Cosío Villegas argues – of 1856.[196] In the minds of the British, the tariff was an issue of public finance, a way of funding debt service. Prohibitions, of course, yielded nothing: "H. M. Government feels assured that if the rate of duties imposed by the Mexican tariff were considerably lowered, great encouragement would be afforded to foreign commerce [and] the revenue of Mexico would thus be sensibly augmented."[197] It was, and long would remain, the standard liberal capitalist critique of Mexico, but it was now increasingly taken up by Mexican liberals themselves. "[Without] lowering the tariff to the level of the United States', without [a reform] of the Customs, and without introducing economies, it is clear that the State will not . . . and a deficit will be there just as it has always been," wrote Benito Gómez Farías.[198]

The Governors Meet

Moving in the direction of liberalizing commercial policy was itself a reversal of policies of some twenty years' standing. Reducing tariffs and ending prohibitions would strike at the very base on which the political economy of centralism had been constructed, the coalition of industrialists and *agiotistas* for whom prohibitions had been beneficial. These were primarily the holders of the internal debt, the group whose interests would be sacrificed to propitiate an increasingly aggressive British lobby. At the same time, the states would themselves be pressed harder to support the Federation through their payment of the *contingente*, now reestablished with the return of the federal system. Coming at a time when the economy and the mechanisms of public finance were yet to recover from the war with the United States, the pressures were irresistible. An outright fiscal rebellion now broke out, championed by some of the core states of the republic, which adopted a position of "can't pay, won't pay" and sought to maintain – and in some cases to shift – the fiscal burden of foreign debt service once again to the consumers of importable goods.

196 Doyle to Baring Brothers, México, May 30, 1853, HC 4.5.22, BBA; Cosío Villegas, *Cuestión Arancelaria*, pp. 31–32, 91–93. Note some disagreement here between Doyle and Cosío Villegas. Cosío Villegas associates 1853 with Santa Anna, who had a long association with prohibitions, especially on cottons, and high tariffs. Whatever the case, Santa Anna was gone for good by August 1854.

197 Foreign Office, September 3, 1851, draft memo, FO 97/273, PRO.

198 Benito Gómez Farías to Valentín Gómez Farías, London, May 27, 1850, GF 3270, BLAC, UT.

The dimensions of the problem can easily be grasped by examining Maps 3.1 and 3.2. In Map 3.1, the shaded states are those that had paid an average of more than 50 percent of the *contingente* in 1825–1827. Compliance was surprisingly robust and the delinquency of three war-torn states, Michoacán, Querétaro, and Tlaxcala, can easily be understood, if only because their economies had not yet recovered from the damage of the rebellion. Chiapas was hardly a secure member of the Federation and, of course, had not been a part of colonial Mexico. Nuevo León and Tamaulipas did not pay, but it was the usual complaint of the central states that the peripheral ones essentially lacked the capacity to do so. Now contrast this picture with the one that emerges in 1851. By and large, it is the old colonial heartlands of the Meseta Central plus Michoacán that remained the financial core of the Federation, at least on this evidence. Elsewhere, support for the Federation, measured by willingness to pay for it, had largely evaporated. As Prieto tartly put things, "as far as the contingente of the States went, it had become a fairy tale, and not always an amusing one." Paradoxically, the war with the United States may have strengthened support for liberalism in the long run, but it certainly did little to revive the fortunes of federalism.[199]

When Payno was in London negotiating with the British bondholders and handing over an ample tranche of the war indemnity payment to them, the state governors or their deputies met with President Arista and his cabinet to reconsider the fiscal relation between the states and the Federation.[200] "We believe that nothing less than the existence of the Nation is at stake," *El Siglo Diez y Nueve* opined, and the dramatis personae did nothing to belie its opinion: Muñoz Ledo (Guanajuato), Riva Palacios (Mexico), and Verdugo (Sinaloa) were all state governors in attendance – and so too were representatives from Jalisco, Chiapas, Oaxaca, Querétaro, Tamaulipas, and Nuevo León. While the states conceded that "the Congress can tax Mexicans" according to the Constitution of 1824, this admission did not extend to what was deemed the confiscation of private property or income.[201] Yet the reality of the situation was considerably more prosaic. The states were, in effect, holding the Federation hostage and demanding control over its taxing and spending authority, or as contemporary documents put it, "holding a *residencia* without an *audiencia*."[202] At issue, once again, was the

---

199 The only systematic study of the *contingente* is Jorge Castañeda Zavala, "El *Contingente Fiscal en la Nueva Nación Mexicana, 1824–1861*," in Marichal and Moreno, eds., *De Colonia a Nación*, pp. 135–188. Castañeda Zavala calculates that noncompliance with the levy rose from 24 percent on 1824–1837 to about 60 percent in 1846–1851, p. 137; Prieto, *Memorias de Mis Tiempos*, p. 318.

200 *El Siglo Diez y Nueve*, August 19, 1851.

201 *El XIX*, September 7, 1851.

202 *Documentos relativos a la reunión en esta Capital de los Gobernadores de los Estados convocados para proveer a las exigencias del Erario Federal* (México, 1851), p. vi.

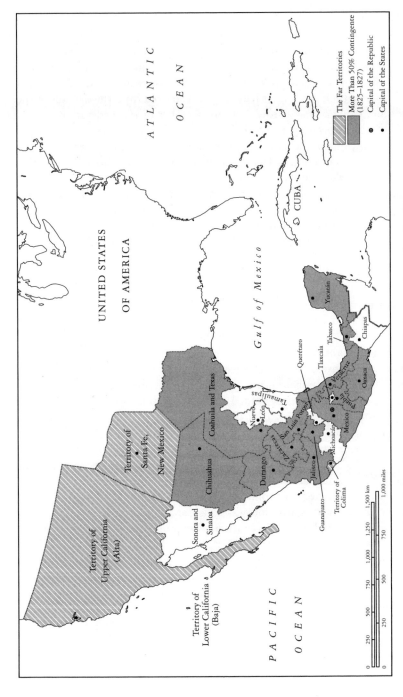

Map 3.1. States Paying More Than 50 Percent of *Contingente*, 1825–1827 (see Chapter 3, note 197).

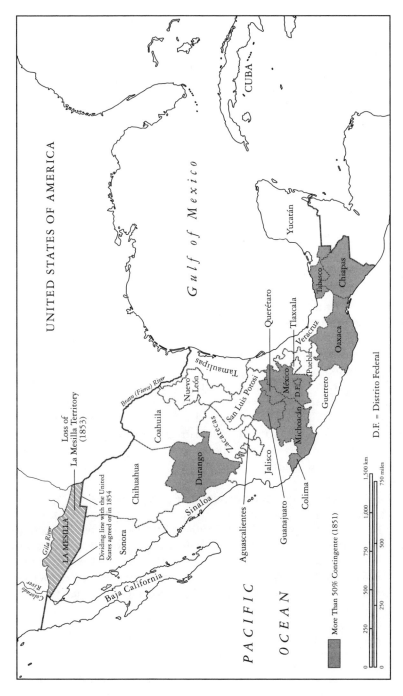

UNITED STATES OF AMERICA

Loss of
La Mesilla Territory
(1853)

LA MESILLA

Gila River

Colorado River

Dividing line with the United
States agreed on in 1854

Baja California

Sonora

Chihuahua

Coahuila

Nuevo
León

Bravo (Fierce) River

Tamaulipas

PACIFIC

OCEAN

Sinaloa

Durango

Zacatecas

Aguascalientes

San Luis Potosí

Jalisco

Guanajuato

Colima

Michoacán

Querétaro

México
D.F.

Tlaxcala

Guerrero

Puebla

Veracruz

Oaxaca

Tabasco

Chiapas

Yucatán

Gulf of Mexico

CUBA

More Than 50% Contingente (1851)

D.F. = Distrito Federal

0   250   500   750   1,000   1,500 km

0   250   500   750 miles

Map 3.2. States Paying More Than 50 Percent of *Contingente*, 1851.

215

balance between funding the internal and external debt in what was, quite literally, a zero-sum game.

Arista's finance minister, Piña y Cuevas, provided a succinct summary of the Federation's position: "Now that the external debt is in order [i.e., by the Conversion of 1850], I can make a commitment to the internal debt insofar as I am able." Piña y Cuevas suggested that he was feeling pressure from Congress to fund the internal debt but that he could do so only within the limits of his resources: public finance and the public debt were a "two-edged sword."[203]

The issue was the operation of the Conversion of 1850. If all of its commitments, domestic and foreign, were honored, Piña y Cuevas calculated that the resulting fiscal deficit would be $20 million – an impossible sum. A blanket suspension was theoretically possible. However, the "conventions" had been included in the Conversion of 1850, ostensibly under diplomatic pressure, and nonpayment could bring immediate confrontation with England, France, and Spain. A blanket suspension, while tempting, would be impossible for domestic creditors to swallow. So, instead, Piña y Cuevas sought to avoid the *Via Crucis* by following the *via media*: a partial suspension of the internal debt, with the resulting deficit of 3.2 million pesos to be financed in part by a consumption tax (*consumo*) on foreign goods. Thus what the Federation took from domestic debtors with one hand, it would return in part through indirect taxes. This was centralist political economy with a federalist face: old wine, used bottles, but a new vineyard. Yet Piña y Cuevas' position was moderation itself when faced with the intransigence of the states, whose representatives resisted paying the *contingente* to permit the Federation to service the foreign debt. It was to be assigned to the internal debt instead. As Prieto put matters with ironic, if penetrating, accuracy, "Piña y Cuevas, with unheard of sagacity, wanted to strengthen the federation and centralize the revenues, but the States would not permit it."[204]

The situation was desperate because the Federation was attempting to spend the same pesos on more than one expense. The presence of the indemnity from the war with the United States had created the perception of greater income than Mexico actually enjoyed, for it was the income for a one-time "sale" of national assets. As this became clear, the various claimants on Mexico's scarce resources became increasingly clamorous. Domestic interests and debtors pressured the Federation through Congress

203 *Documentos relativos a la reunión . . .* , p. 5. (*debo contraerme a la interior, puesto que se halla ya arreglada la esterior, hasta donde lo permitió nuestra posibilidad* is translated as "now that the external debt. . . .") (*doble cuestión* is translated as "two-edged sword.")

204 See Piña y Cuevas' report of June 13, 1851, in *Documentos relativos a la reunión . . .* , pp. 7–22; *Dictamen . . . leído en la sesión de 26 de Junio de 1851* in *Documentos relativos a la reunión . . .* , pp. 41–52. Castañeda Zavala, "El *Contingente* Fiscal," in Marichal and Moreno, eds., *De Colonia a Nación*, p. 154; Prieto, *Memoria de Mis Tiempos*, p. 316.

and the states without much regard for ideology, for the leaders of the revolt, such as Octavio Muñoz Ledo and Vicente Riva Palacio, came from both the conservative and liberal sides of the political spectrum. The British bondholders pressured Mexico through their agent, through their contacts, through Baring Brothers, and increasingly, through their diplomats. The result was stalemate. The final report of the governors' meeting as much as admitted so. The governors and their representatives could not remain in Mexico City indefinitely to press their case. The Federation and the states could not even agree on the dimensions of the problem: it was a case of what would run out first, time, money, or patience.[205] But in the final analysis, Mexico's domestic creditors proved persuasive. They were, after all, numerous and right there: financing arms purchases, tobacco growing, silver mining, and textile production. In the long run, the Convention of 1850 would be undermined by its opponents, mostly domestic. In 1851, payments on the internal debt were about 700,000 pesos, or roughly as much as the London bondholders received exclusive of the U.S. indemnity.[206] By 1854, the London Debt was once more in default, the advantages obtained by the Conversion of 1850 notwithstanding.

Toward Intervention

Default (or renewed moratorium) in 1854, of course, did not bring British intervention in 1855. As matters transpired, a further seven years would pass before British forces reached Veracruz. Ironically, after the excitement of Barings' success in securing the indemnity payment in London had passed, the market became steadily less volatile (if not more favorable) until 1858, when instability began to pick up once more. Yet this emphatically does not mean that finance took a backseat to political upheaval. As Payno eloquently summarized,

the ten years running from 1852 through 1862 were marked by a continuous change of administrations and, hence, by sudden alterations (*trastornos*) in the method of accounting for the debt; by the hypothecating (*empeño*) of various branches of government revenue, and by the issuance of still more bonds, orders for payment and liabilities (*títulos, órdenes, y documentos*), all of which are to be found even now (i.e., 1865) in the market.[207]

Yet the international context in which these "sudden alterations" occurred was quite different from what obtained in 1827, 1830, 1837, 1842, or even

---

205 *El Siglo XIX*, September 12, 1851. By the governors' accounting, the Federation was supposedly running a surplus. Not even the most optimistic finance minister seriously suggested as much.

206 Romero, *Memoria de Hacienda ... 1870*, par. 1320. The calculation for payments to London is mine.

207 Payno, *Deuda interior*, p. 23.

1846. Patience, good manners, and diplomatic niceties – all of these were wearing thin.

Consider, for example, the bondholders' open anger with both Mexico and the house of Jecker, Torre after the dividend of January 1, 1852, had been paid. In 1854, Doyle used some of the bluntest language he had yet employed in complaining about this arrangement to Santa Anna. In a nutshell, Jecker, Torre had advanced Mexico $250,000 to pay the dividend and the firm was repaid out of the customs revenues assigned to the bondholders. The problem, so to speak, was that Jecker, Torre was reimbursed in excess ($8,500) of what they were owed, and had applied the surplus to another government debt rather than return it to the bondholders' fund. Doyle, seemingly overwrought, complained that "[Santa Anna's] good faith had been surprised on this occasion" and so too the good faith of the Mexican government. The bondholders, Doyle wrote, had been "despoiled of what is their own property" by "an act of this nature." Doyle went on in this vein, thoroughly incensed, showing more anger than he had ever displayed during the festivities involving Lizardi and Company in the 1840s, which was a scandal and at least criminally avaricious. The difference was that Doyle was now on the defensive, having been accused by the bondholders of failing to vigilantly guard their interests. At the same time, his eponymous convention had come undone, leaving him in a position in which no one was being reliably paid.[208] When Joaquín María de Castillo y Lanzas was appointed Mexican minister to Great Britain, he felt compelled to send the British foreign secretary (fourth Earl of Clarendon, 1853–1858) a confidential note protesting that "there is nothing in [this case] to justify the imputation of bad faith on the part of the government of Mexico."[209]

But bad faith was obviously a concern of the Committee of Bondholders, and in a sign of worsening relations, Mexico's financial agent in London – Colonel Francisco Facio – wrote repeatedly to his superiors complaining that his position was becoming untenable. Facio claimed that the Committee of Bondholders blamed him for everything: depressed bond prices, a paucity of dividend remissions, notices that never appeared in the London press. Everything. Worse, Facio believed that the committee was going to propose to Mexico that he be replaced as financial agent by Baring Brothers, whom Facio thought would do nothing more than act as a bondholders' agent. He allowed as how his predecessors, such as Lizardi and Company or Schneider and Company, may have given the bondholders something

---

208 Doyle to the minister of home and foreign relations, México, June 15, 1854, FO 97/274, PRO.
209 Castillo y Lanzas to the foreign secretary (private and confidential), London, July 27, 1854, FO 97/274, PRO. Similar sentiments were voiced by Finance Minister Olasagarre, who wondered aloud how a country that suffered from a "backwardness of payments in every branch" could be accused of not doing its utmost to meet its foreign obligations. México, November 30, 1854, FO 97/274, PRO.

to complain about. But clearly exasperated, Facio was looking to Mexico for an expression of support, which he in fact received.[210] Still, it is obvious that the bondholders had entered a new phase of restiveness, for they were holding everyone's feet to the fire, British and Mexican alike. For example, they bitterly criticized Santa Anna's payments of 60,000 pesos to the London branch of Cristóbal de Murrieta and Company out of customs funds, even though, as we noted before, that house had advanced part of the July 1851 dividend![211] When Mexico received the proceeds of the sale of the Mesilla Valley in 1854, the bondholders (and other creditors) pressed for their share of the $10 million. But the outbreak of the Ayutla revolt against Santa Anna in March 1854 put paid to their aspirations. Instead, Santa Anna was compelled to treat with his circle of financiers, who would underwrite his campaign against Alvarez. Manuel Escandón, the Martínez del Río, Manuel Lizardi, Cayetano Rubio, and others received the majority of the indemnity, perhaps 60 percent of it overall. Facio, on the other hand, got a mere 270,000 pesos, supposedly for the bondholders, who had unabashedly petitioned Santa Anna in May 1854 for 3,000,000 pesos only to escalate their demands by June to 4,500,000 pesos – nearly half the proceeds of the Mesilla sale.[212] Their interests had been sacrificed to domestic political exigencies: it was the familiar pattern of domestic opportunity cost. As the Committee of Bondholders pointed out to Lord Clarendon in 1854, "out of seven half yearly dividends which up to the date have become due . . . three only have been paid." As a result, the "market value of Mexican bonds . . . [fell] from 36 percent, at which they actually stood, to 24 percent," whereas had the debt been serviced, "the committee believed the bonds would be quoted at 50." The combined loss in interest and principal the committee put at £3.2 million, a result the committee termed "deplorable."[213]

---

210 For Facio's file, see "Sobre el informe del Comité de tenedores de bonos Méxicanos de Londres y junta general celebrada en 26 de febrero último," 1855, *Deuda Exterior*, vol. 13, AGNM.

211 Memorial to the Mexican financial agent, México, March 30, 1854, *Deuda Exterior*, vol. 13, AGNM. On Murrieta, see Montserrat Gárate Ojanguren, "Financial Circuits in Spain: Merchants and Bankers, 1700–1914," in Alice Teichova, Dieter Ziegler, and Ginette Kurgan–van Hentenryk, eds., *Banking, Trade and Industry. Europe, America and Asia from the Thirteenth to Twentieth Century* (New York, 1997), pp. 80–81. For the amount, Payno, *México y sus Cuestiones Financieras*, p. 48.

212 *Memoria de Hacienda, 1870*, pars. 1538–1548; Percy Doyle to the foreign secretary, México, August 2, 1854, FO 97/274, PRO; Alexis de Gabriac to the minister of foreign affairs, México, June 23, 1855, in Díaz, *Versión Francesa de México*, vol. 1: pp. 185–186; Francis Falconnet to Baring Brothers, México, August 2, 1853, HC 4.5.25, BBA.; *Resolutions at a General Meeting of Mexican Bondholders at the London Tavern, on the 15th May, 1854* ([London], 1854), Sec. IV, p. 2; Francisco Facio to the finance minister, London, June 1, 1854, *Deuda Exterior*, vol. 13, AGNM.

My understanding of the connection between the sale of the Mesilla, the liberal Ayutla movement, and domestic finance has been shaped in large measure by Terrazas y Basante, *Inversiones, Especulaciones y Diplomacia*, pp. 77–87.

213 C. Staniforth to the foreign secretary, London, September 2, 1854, FO 97/274, PRO.

At the end of April 1855, Santa Anna suspended debt service, causing the bondholders to write Clarendon in an appeal against "one of the most flagrant acts of injustice, oppression, and bad faith that is now attempted to be perpetrated in Mexico." Only a year earlier, Santa Anna had told the Committee of Mexican Bondholders that "I certainly consider your claim to have the overdue dividends paid perfectly just . . . [and] am using my best efforts to acquit myself of these sacred obligations."[214] The French minister to Mexico, de Gabriac sheds additional light on the source of their ire, writing that Santa Anna "had a payday" (*cobró*) with whatever funds the Treasury had before heading off to suppress the rebellion.[215] His Serene Highness had double-crossed the bondholders.

In June, Santa Anna attempted to raise a huge forced loan in Mexico City of $655,000, with little success. In July, $25,000 of bondholders' funds were appropriated by General Miguel Blanco, "principally to pay arrears to the Garrison" that had gone unpaid and was becoming restive.[216] In some desperation, the bondholders' agent in Mexico observed that "the only mode which lies open to the Bondholders to get their interest respected is to use their interest with Her Majesty's Government to obtain for their agreement the sanction of a diplomatic Convention." "By it," he pointed out, "[the Mexican government] never could answer to a British Minister . . . that it is a concern in which he [i.e., the Minister] has nothing to do."[217] Indeed. But an official of the French legation doubted that even "convention" debts were secure: either domestic creditors or the United States would command the government's attention. "Against this eventuality, which couldn't be more likely, France and England together must hasten to be on guard."[218] So by the unlikely catalysis of the Liberal Revolution, Britain, France, and, one should add, Spain had begun by late 1855 to define their financial interests in Mexico in opposition to the growing regional power of the United States and the immediacy of domestic Mexican pressures.

The period between the final departure of Santa Anna from power and the effective *autogolpe* of Ignacio Comonfort (August 12, 1855–December 17, 1857) that marked the start of the Three Years' War was one of growing

214 *Times* (London), April 21, 1854.

215 Charles McGarel to the foreign secretary, June 1855, FO 97/274, PRO. Neither Dublán and Lozano nor Romero in the *Memoria de Hacienda, 1870*, makes *any* reference to such a suspension, which is odd. The French minister to Mexico refers to the suspension as one of the "diplomatic conventions," which technically had nothing to do with the London bonds. See Alexis de Gabriac to the minister of foreign affairs, México, May 2, 1855, in Díaz, *Version Francesa de México*, vol. 177: p. 1.

216 Charles McGarel to the foreign secretary, London, July 6, 1855, FO 97/274, PRO.

217 Charles Whitehead to H. M. chargé d'affaires, México, June 27, 1856, FO 97/274, PRO.

218 Note of the first chancellor of the French legation, México, October 19, 1855, in Díaz, *Versión Francesa de México*, vol. 1: pp. 214–215 [emphasis mine].

national and international tension for Mexico. It is hazardous, in modern historical discourse, to use terms such as "unrest," "chaos," or even "rebellion," for they are ideologically loaded, not neutral descriptions of a state of nature. Nevertheless, the sort of people who purchased Mexican bonds or their representatives abroad – be they British, French, or North American – were nearly uniform in their perceptions of growing national dissolution. The United States and its agents, in some sense the proximate root of all evil from a European perspective, were no less impressed with the complex regional, ethnic, and political fissures than other observers. In the eyes of French officials reporting on events in Mexico, imminent absorption by the United States threatened, and with it, commercial consequences of the most desperate sort for the French and their British counterparts. The British, directly concerned with the collapse of payments to the bondholders, were similarly unsettled. It would have been remarkable if the atmosphere of impending national disaster did not affect the market for Mexican bonds, and as one can clearly see in Figure 3.3, it did. But notice, too, that the trend is nonlinear with a point of inflection in late 1857. That is, from roughly 1852 to 1856, the price of Mexican bonds relative to *consols* fell, all of which makes perfect sense. No one who actively doubted the survival of Mexican nationality could have been a sanguine buyer of its outstanding obligations.[219]

Nor should one minimize the role of the gathering liberal pressures that culminated in the Ayutla Revolution in 1854 as a factor depressing the London market. Once again, the market reacted badly to liberalism and, now, to its manifestly pro-American orientation, something that augured poorly for European prospects in Mexico. While there were aspects of Mexican liberalism, especially those advocating freer trade that could ultimately raise Mexico's capacity to pay and redound to the benefit of the bondholders, there was much to fear as well. Amid open speculation that the United States had channeled financial support to Santa Anna's enemies in 1854, there was also the prospect that a liberal rapprochement with the United States would divert more resources in the wrong direction – North. Britain's traditional commercial hegemony in Mexico would be threatened. Analogies to the Eastern Question were freely drawn, with Mexico as the Ottoman Empire of the Western Hemisphere and the United States as Russia. Exactly where this would leave Great Britain (and France) was a matter of some conjecture, but there can be no doubt that such images

219 I base this paragraph on a wide reading of diplomatic correspondence from agents of the United States, Great Britain, and France during this period. For a convenient summary of some of this material, see Salvucci, "Origins and Progress of US-Mexican Trade, 1825–1884," pp. 716–720; Díaz, ed., *Versión Francesa de México*, vol. 1, passim, and FO 97/274, for example, pp. 233–397, PRO.

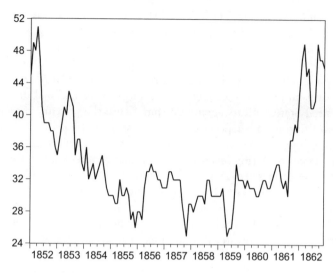

Figure 3.7. Mexican Bonds Relative to Consols, 1852–1862.

also weighed heavily on the market for Mexican bonds, which, measured
by monthly changes, fell nearly 60 percent of the time between 1852 and
1856.[220]

Equally interesting is the overall rise in Mexican bonds after September
1857 and through early 1862 in Figure 3.7. Since this more or less coincides
almost exactly with the outbreak of civil war in Mexico and the final
realization of European intervention, it is worth asking what was occurring.
After all, during the war with the United States, Mexican bonds fell. They
did not rise. During the Three Years' War, the opposite was seemingly true.
Could the London market have welcomed open combat between liberals
and conservatives, or does something else account for the paradoxical result?

One reason why prices began to rise is that the pressure placed on the
authorities in Mexico by the bondholders and their agents to leave the
dividend funds alone was having some effect by late 1857. In a particularly
striking instance of this phenomenon, the inability of the representatives
of Lizardi and Company to collect a very substantial debt showed that
some politicians were unwilling to violate previous agreements with the
bondholders.[221] In this case, ordered to pay out $38,000 pesos to an agent

220 See Donathon C. Olliff, *Reforma Mexico and the United States: A Search for Alternatives to Annexation,
   1854–1861* (University, AL, 1981), pp. 2–56, esp. 46–47.
221 These materials are found in papers covering the years 1855 through 1865 in *Deuda Externa*,
   vol. 15, fs. 413–438, 449–452, and 527–531. Revealingly, several of the regional customshouse
   administrators complain of being unable to locate material in their archives because, as one in
   Tepic put it, "the files in this office are beyond incomplete, in the worst disorder, because of the

for Lizardi, the administrator of the customshouse of Manzanillo complained that the agent, Don Pedro del Valle, was pressuring him to use bondholder and convention funds. "Please tell me if I should make such a dispersal of monies (*aplicación*)?" The finance minister, pressed to take responsibility, turned the matter over to Comonfort,[222] acting as president of the republic. Comonfort, who never said "no" directly, and instead ordered that the funds should come from the taxes levied on the next conducta of silver dispatched for shipment abroad from Veracruz. A notation at the foot of the document minutes "Posts notified 26 Oct. 1857." So, in effect, Comonfort's directive went out to all the customshouses in late October 1857: Don't touch the bondholders and convention funds. Remarkably – or coincidentally, depending on one's faith in the ability of markets to gather information – Comonfort's indirect decision fits the timing of the beginning of the rise in relative bond prices almost exactly.

The bondholders also received a more sympathetic hearing from the conservative interim president, Félix Zuloaga (1858), than they had from his predecessor, Comonfort. Zuloaga fired their long-time antagonist, Don Francisco Facio as Mexican financial agent, replacing him with Baring Brothers, just as Facio had predicted would occur some years earlier. The conservative government also seemed receptive to the idea of allowing the bondholders to have specially designated private agents in the ports, or "interventors" collecting the monies due them, under the dubious theory that Mexican military officers would be less likely to violate private property rights than they would the public property of an embassy.[223] Then too the bondholders received energetic support from the commander of the British squadron in the Gulf of Mexico, Captain Hugh Dunlop, who was determined to see British financial interests respected, even though he frankly admitted that he knew little about their workings. Dunlop, not yet forty years old, and the British Minister, Loftus C. Otway, enjoyed an unusually good working relationship. Otway too was uncharacteristically aggressive in pursuing the bondholders' interests, writing that "once and for all, what we demand, and what we are determined to obtain, is a just fulfillment of our

revolution." Wisely blaming the liberals (it was 1865), he complained that "they destroy whatever documents they find at hand whenever they occupy this place." For the quotations in the text, see Ricardo Palacios to the finance minister, Colima, February 23, 1857.

222 In August 1856, the bondholders' committee attacked Comonfort, claiming that "under General Comonfort's Government the Bondholders have been treated with even less consideration of their rights than under any preceding government." That was certainly an exaggeration, but few senior Mexican politicians were in the habit of simply ignoring such charges. *Report of the Committee of Mexican Bondholders* (London, 1856), p. 11. (*Informaron los asientos en 26 de Oct de 57* is translated as "Posts notified. . . .")

223 See Loftus C. Otway to the (Mexican) minister of foreign relations, México, July 24, 1858, and Otway to the foreign secretary, México, August 5, 1858, FO 97/275, PRO.

unquestionable rights."[224] So British officials on the scene agreed on the
measures required to get the bondholders paid, if possible. This favorable
convergence of public and private sentiments, evolving in Mexico out of
direct control of the Foreign Office in London, was a genuine novelty.[225]
The energetic British legation in Mexico had, for once, seized the initiative.

Another explanation, equally intriguing and wholly consistent with the
London market's long-term support for conservative regimes, was provided by the *Times* (London). In February 1859, the following observation
appeared in the paper's "Money Market and City Intelligence" column.

As far as [Mexico City] is concerned, even the semblance of authority has ceased
to exist. Happily the process of exhaustion seems within a few months of completion... With regard to the prospects of the Bondholders, they are of course
improved by every step that hastens the extinction of the Republic as an independent State and it is to be remarked that their immediate position appears
likewise to have been benefited by the arrival of a British squadron which will
fulfil [*sic*] the duty of seeing that their portion of the Customs dues is no longer
misappropriated.[226]

Indeed, 1858 was in general a very bad year for the liberals. The conservatives effectively held power throughout the year. The liberals were able to
hold on to the port of Veracruz only with very great difficulty, even as the
conservatives occupied Córdoba and Orizaba. Since the control of Veracruz
was very much the principal object of the civil war, the growing likelihood that the conservatives might seize it confirmed the prediction in the
Times (London) and corresponded to the strengthening of the market.[227]
Nevertheless, from February through April 1859, bond prices again fell,
seemingly contradicting the analysis in the *Times* (London). Yet it is worth
looking a little farther, for the fear that British observers expressed as the
civil war heated up (and the port of Veracruz itself fell under siege) was
that the intervention of the United States would be inevitable and that
the provinces of Sonora and Chihuahua would be lost to Mexico. Since
"the whole Mexican territory is mortgaged for the payment of the English

---

224 Loftus C. Otway to the commander of the British squadron in the Gulf of Mexico, México, Jan-
    uary 23, 1859, FO 97/275, PRO; for Dunlop, see http://www.pdavis.nl/SeaOfficers.php?page=2
    (accessed July 25, 2007). For biographical data on Otway, see *The Annual Register 1861* (London,
    1862), p. 479.

225 See Hugh Dunlop to the British minister in México, aboard the H. M. S. Tartar, January 12, 1859,
    FO 97/275, PRO.

226 February 3, 1859, for this and what follows.

227 Carmen Blázquez Domínguez, *Veracruz Liberal, 1858–1860* (México, 1986), pp. 70–97, 114–
    130. For the circumstances of U.S. recognition of the liberals at Veracruz in April 1859, see
    pp. 129–130.

debt . . . it cannot be periodically diminished without trampling upon the rights of the bondholders at home."

In general, British markets typically supported the conservatives and moved against the liberals during the Three Years' War. The determined efforts of the liberals to raise funds in the United States provided an even more compelling justification. Loans raised in the United States would divert debt service from the London bondholders, reducing the value of the bonds. Greater involvement by the United States in Mexico, championed by a substantial group of liberal politicians, raised U.S. influence in Mexico and held out the prospect that scarce Mexican assets (territorial concessions, nationalized church properties, additional customs receipts) would be liquidated in an effort to gain U.S. support or to compensate it for assistance rendered against the conservative faction.[228]

Conclusions

What mattered then, at least in this period, was whether or not bondholders thought they were going to get paid. To the extent that events conduced to a different fiscal regime, one more or less likely to produce dividends, then events and politics mattered. But stability per se seems not to have generated much of a premium, and a large class of bondholders – usually called "speculators" as opposed to bona fide investors or traders rather than investors – stood to benefit from substantial swings in prices. The long-term holders were the ones who were hurt very badly by Mexico's irregular history of payment, for that, in the final analysis, is what produced large capital losses. That, in turn, suggests that the elision between "conservative," "centralist," and "stability" was in reality primarily a fiscal notion, as far as markets were concerned. One suspects that foreign financial interests, especially those that comprised fixed-rent contracts, were largely indifferent to the merits, ideological or otherwise, of a particular regime. Even the putative British taste for free trade liberalism, at least in this context, seems to have had less to do with the interests of cotton manufacturers than with the financial claims of bondholders or convention debtors. The London market judged regimes on the probability of payment. In this context, the conservatives rather than the liberals were again the better bet (as had been centralists as opposed to federalists), but almost only in this context.

None of this is to say that decisions to pay or not to pay were made in a fiscal or political vacuum. It is difficult to avoid the impression that Mexico worked most to placate British interests when international politics in the 1830s and 1840s required. Or to put it differently, in times of international stress, when Mexico's leadership – especially Santa Anna – sought

228 Blázquez Domínguez, *Veracruz Liberal*, pp. 173–188.

British protection from the aggression or territorial ambitions of the United States, Mexico either paid or made gestures in the direction of the bond-holders. When such gestures became less useful, or altogether nugatory, policy and its nuance would change. As Marcela Terrazas Basante observes, the outbreak of the Crimean War in 1854 decisively altered the international context in which British policy was made and finally relegated the interests of the bondholders to the back burner.[229] It showed that, for after 1854, the bondholders were to endure the longest payment moratorium since the hostilities with Texas in 1836. Under such conditions, drift rather than progress was the more likely outcome, with pressures from the United States and domestic creditors largely dominant. Thus in the 1850s, the growing involvement of the United States in Mexican affairs, particularly during the Three Years' War, marked a genuine shift in international political commitments, a shift reflected in the bond market as well. Yet in the peculiar circumstances of the day, drift translated into a higher probability of European intervention or the realization of the long-held conservative monarchist project, neither of which possibility was repugnant to the bondholders. It was, after all, Murphy – a staunch monarchist – who styled himself the true Mexican friend of the London bondholders. And no one in Mexico underestimated Murphy's skill, influence, or determination.[230] Thus the puzzling reaction of the bond market to Civil War and the onset of national dissolution in Mexico once more in the late 1850s. Its established preference for "conservative" "centralizing" regimes was thus emphasized. But "conservative liberalism," the Porfirian synthesis, was not as yet on the horizon.

Domestic and international fiscal and monetary factors also figured in Mexico's decisions about payment: decision makers faced sharply binding constraints. While it is conventional to assume that early nineteenth-century Mexico was distinguished by some kind of expansive policy regime – military spending run amok – nothing, in reality, could have been further from the truth. The painfully slow macroeconomic growth, which virtually all agree occurred, could not have been the product of anything other than the systematic export of purchasing power under a fixed exchange rate, something that the Panic of 1837 and its aftershocks pushed into the early 1840s. At the same time, the overall budgets of the central governments tended to fall from the 1820s through the 1850s. Making any sort of real resource transfer abroad under these circumstances could

---

229 Or, alternatively, the Mexican default made the British government much less likely to do much for Mexico other than wring its hands over the actions of the United States in Mexico, another possibility Terrazas y Basante raises.

230 See especially Valentín Gómez Farías' monitoring of Murphy's publications in London. Valentín Gómez Farías to Benito Gómez Farías [?], Querétaro [1849], GF 3109, BLAC, UT.

have only been excruciatingly difficult, all the more so while retaining macroeconomic balance. How, indeed, could Mexico pay more and more while producing less and less? Or, in the long run, how could a country using tariffs and prohibitions to industrialize find the resources to fund the foreign debt, let alone borrow more? These were the fundamental dilemmas Mexico faced between the 1830s and the 1850s. By the 1850s, the tension had become unbearable. The "Mexico" that secured its independence with British loans in the 1820s no longer existed by the early 1850s, as the fiscal rebellion of the states decisively illustrates. The delicate political compromise worked out between conservatives and liberals, or centralists and federalists, for want of better terms, simply fell apart. Even in the face of large concessions from the British bondholders, the fiscal demands on Mexico seemed unsustainable. It was hard work keeping such arrangements together, like getting blood from the proverbial stone. Then time, inevitably, ran out.

4

A Monstrous Enterprise

An example now and then tends to keep the rest in order.

> —Viscount Palmerston (1856), as prime minister

In every-day life one is accustomed to see people who suspend payment owing to pecuniary embarrassments, yet nobody seeks to call them thieves.

> —Manuel de Zamacona (1861)

The object of England is clear enough. We go to claim reparation for the money of which we have been plundered.

> —*Times* (London) (1862)

Wild about Harry?

David Robertson, chairman of the Committee of Mexican Bondholders, was nothing, if not persistent. In 1857 and 1858, he literally besieged Viscount Palmerston and Derby and their foreign secretaries, Lords Clarendon and Malmesbury, with correspondence arguing the bondholders' case. Writing at least seven or eight times, Robertson asked that a share of expropriated church property be set aside on the bondholders' behalf. He pressed Malmesbury (successfully, if ineffectually) for the appointment of "interventors" in the Mexican ports to collect the bondholders' share of customs duties directly under the supervision of the British consuls. He (unsuccessfully) attempted to visit the conservative's minister in London, General Juan Almonte, in his sickbed. He complained incessantly about the bad faith of the Mexican government in meeting its commitments to the bondholders, although which government, during the Civil War, he sometimes failed to specify. He bemoaned the risible sums that the bondholders had actually received since 1854 – what was now becoming the lengthiest moratorium since the 1830s. He harassed then head of the Mexican Financial Agency in London, Francisco Facio, to near distraction. He argued that Mexico, the richest of the South American states (so he said), had uniquely failed to come to terms with Great Britain over its defaulted loans.

He complained that the British financial system was placed at risk by disturbances to Mexico's failure to remit silver that supported the exchanges. Robertson sometimes got his history wrong, and was especially deficient in financial history and the mechanics of the gold standard. But he certainly stirred things up. And he relentlessly flattered Palmerston.[1]

While it is obvious that Robertson was thoroughly overwrought, his letters do raise the important question of the relation between the demands of bondholders and British intervention, especially as one of the Tripartite Powers in 1862. At least one historian of diplomacy has argued that "the Mexican bondholders' agitation was . . . unusually successful in principle" in inducing British intervention.[2] To be sure, by 1858, the Committee of Bondholders was exerting considerable pressure on the Mexican Financial Agency in London, railing "against the Supreme Government, the Republic and the Financial Agency." And the committee passed resolutions by the fistful, petitioning the British government for assistance well into 1861, presenting the Foreign Office with a lengthy brief in November, and even asking the United States to assume a protectorate over Mexico and pay the London Debt![3] The Committee of Bondholders *never* relented, making one proposal after another for compensation, eventually resurrecting the idea of seizing Mexican territory that had appeared in the Conversion of 1837, even after it was clear that there was no support for this in the government.[4]

Yet a close study of events leading up to intervention in January 1862 makes the conclusion that this was an official response to the less-than-convincing demands of the bondholders. The British, along with the Spanish and French, were quite unable to define precisely what their interests in Mexico were, apart from a general concern with redress of grievances. There was much disagreement within the British commercial and mercantile

---

1 There is a précis of Robertson's 1857–1858 correspondence (May 28, 1858) in FO 97/275, PRO. An example of his effusions is David Robertson to the foreign secretary, Ladykirk, Berwyck upon Tweed, November 4, 1857, FO 97/275. For his Robertson's testy relations with the Mexican Financial Agency, see Francisco Facio to the finance minister, London, March 1, 1854, *Deuda Exterior*, vol. 13, AGNM.

2 E. D. Steele, "Palmerston's Foreign Policy and Foreign Secretaries 1855–1865," in Keith M. Wilson, ed., *British Foreign Secretaries and Foreign Policy: From Crimean War to First World War* (London, 1987), p. 51.

3 Francisco Facio to the finance minister, London, June 1, 1858, *Deuda Exterior*, vol. 13, AGNM. Also see the impressive profusion of communications from the Committee of Bondholders in FO 97/280, PRO. The brief, which is to be found there, runs to nearly thirty folio pages, and is dated November 22, 1861.

4 "Extract from Committee Report of 29 April 1861 pages 36 to 38," November 22, 1861, FO 97/280. The possibility that the United States might demand territorial concessions in return for aiding the Mexican liberals would seem to be the real motivation behind the reappearance of such an atavistic concern.

communities as to the wisdom of intervention, for some argued that direct involvement in Mexican affairs would end up costing far more than it could ever gain or that foreign holders of Mexican bonds would effectively be "free riders" on any actions taken by the British government.[5]

And, as we shall see, there is scant evidence that Juárez relished the prospect of suspension, either.[6]

Even more importantly, there is little indication that the Foreign Office regarded intervention in Mexico with anything other than deep suspicion. There is certainly *no* indication that the financial interests of anyone connected to the Foreign Office or sitting in Parliament led to intervention. There *was* considerable evidence that officials in the Foreign Office were much concerned about the kind of precedent intervention on behalf of the bondholders would set. More to the point, the British intervention in Mexico in 1862 was arguably more about the changes taking place in domestic British politics than about pressure from the bondholders, although the pressure that Robertson and his confrères exerted was considerable, if not especially coherent.

Certainly, by 1856, the effective suspension of dividend payments led no less a figure than Palmerston to consider the possibilities of an intervention. "These South American states are really beyond endurance in their Roguery and Impertinence. Although we have hitherto declined to intervene between our bondholders and the governments of these states, we have always told these States that the time might come when we were obliged to do so."[7] Yet what inevitably seemed to deter the British from active intervention in Mexico was the fear of setting a precedent, of making the Foreign Office a mere collection agency. Palmerston, in particular, thought that the circumstances in which an intervention could take place would be necessarily circumscribed.

If our diplomatic agent in Mexico or elsewhere should be invited by both parties to be witness to any agreement for the payment of interest on debt due to British subjects, I don't see why he need decline to do so and then if the agreement were afterwards broken we might interfere without setting an 'inconvenient' precedent. If Mexico or Peru decides to blockade there can be no reason for not giving them their desserts.

The key to understanding Britain's actions is, perhaps, less appropriately understood as a matter of the pressure exerted by the Mexican bondholders than as a political response to an outrage on British property at a time in

5 *Letters of Messrs. McCalmont, Brothers & Co and Reply Thereto by David Robertson* . . . (London, 1861).

6 See the detailed study of Carl Bock, *Prelude to Tragedy: The Negotiation and Breakdown of the Tripartite Convention of London, October 31, 1861* (Philadelphia, 1966).

7 Palmerston to the foreign secretary, London, June 27, 1856, *Clarendon Papers*, Bodleian Library, Oxford University, for this and what follows.

which the pressures on the Foreign Office were changing in response to process of broadening the electoral franchise. The "money" of which the *Times* (London) spoke in 1862 was *not* the now enormous arrears of interest owing to the bondholders, but a rather smaller sum, $660,000, that was extracted from the British legation in Mexico City on November 17, 1860 under orders of the conservative leader, Miguel Miramón.[8] These were dividend funds that had been segregated for remission to the bondholders by their agents in the ports and were, without doubt, British property. Everyone recognized the seriousness of the breach of British diplomatic rights that had occurred, but the action was justified by simple expediency: as the Civil War wound down, the conservative party needed money to pay its soldiers. It took what it could get where it could get it. Juárez and the liberals took cognizance of the claim of the British government once they had entered Mexico City in January 1861, and according to Manuel Payno, it "was not a subject of disagreement between Her British Majesty's Legation and the Constitutional Government."[9] As a consequence, when the British government recognized Juárez on February 22, 1861, it did so with the explicit understanding that the constitutional government would address the bondholders' claim, among others, but said nothing about the arrears of interest.[10]

There was, nevertheless, ample reason for optimism. While in possession of Veracruz, the liberals had signed two agreements, known as the Dunlop–Zamara Agreement and the Aldham–Ocampo Agreement, with the British government (actually, with the commander of British naval forces in the Gulf of Mexico). The major agreement, the Dunlop–Zamara (January 24, 1859), provided that 25 percent of all customs revenues were to be paid to the Mexican bondholders in London by "the party now in possession of Vera Cruz." The Aldham–Ocampo Agreement was to remedy "infraction of the Dunlop Convention."[11] The "infraction" of the Dunlop Convention was, according to Baring Brothers, "the additional assignment . . . have been applied to the sole benefit of the Diplomatic Convention and to the exclusion of the English Bondholders" – an arrangement regarded as inequitable, even though the exact interpretation of the Dunlop Convention was in dispute.[12] In any case, the liberals, by their actions, had committed

---

8 *Memoria de Hacienda, 1870,* pars. 1978–1982.

9 Payno, *México y sus cuestiones financieras,* p. 315.

10 George B. Mathew to the secretary of foreign relations, México, February 22, 1861, in Payno, *México y sus cuestiones financieras,* p. 319; Lord John Russell to the House of Commons, February 12, 1861, *Parliamentary Debates* (Commons), 3rd ser., vol. 161, col. 340.

11 "Agreements Entered into with the Constitutional Authorities at Veracruz by Captain Dunlop, R. N., and by Captain Aldham, R. N." (London, 1861).

12 "The Dunlop Convention," HC 4.5.36.3h, BBA. The rate at which customhouse assignments were made under the Otway (1858), Dunlop (1859), and Aldham conventions (1860) had steadily risen, from 16 to 29 percent, according to Mexican sources, or nearly doubling. "The Present Condition of Mexico," p. 332.

themselves to the payment of the London Debt and, even if only inadvertently, had raised the status to the claims of the bondholders to that of a diplomatic convention.[13] And as we previously noticed, the British government could intervene in the event of the violation of a diplomatic agreement. While the Foreign Office was in no hurry to interpret its obligation in this light, there was now presumption that the liberals' failure to live up to the agreement could have serious diplomatic consequences. In fact, when liberal finance minister Miguel Lerdo de Tejada pressed for the suspension of the foreign debt in May 1859, his proposal was resisted and immediately vetoed by Juárez on just these grounds.[14]

It was also for precisely this reason the French minister to Mexico, Dubois de Saligny, bluntly observed that Palmerston thought the liberals were more likely to pay the claims made against Mexico than were the conservatives, perhaps because the liberals never yielded control of the port of Veracruz and the resources it could generate even after repeated conservative sieges in 1859 and 1860. Here was yet another reason why Mexican bonds staged a mild rally as the liberals consolidated their hold over the central highlands in the waning months of the Three Years' War. The bondholders' representative explained, "With the victory of the [liberal] Government [in December 1860], [the bondholders] had reason to believe that some punctuality in the payment of interest would occur." But the explanation he gave for their optimism was different. The liberals would use the proceeds of the secularization of church properties to provide the resources with which the London Debt would be serviced, and this expectation had accounted for a rise of 20 percent in the value of Mexican bonds.[15] Indeed, Guillermo Prieto, in an especially Machiavellian analysis, thought the Dunlap Agreement *too* favorable to the bondholders. He believed that the conservative party was somehow behind it: the Juárez government, hard pressed for funds, would inevitably be driven into the hands of *agiotistas* like J. B. Jecker, Gregorio Mier y Terán, or Barron, Forbes.[16]

13 *Memorandum Relative to the Relations Existing between Great Britain and Mexico*, p. 3.

14 Blázquez Domínguez, *Veracruz Liberal*, p. 177.

15 Alexis de Gabriac to the minister of foreign affairs, México, June 10, 1859, in Díaz, ed., *Versión Francesa de México*, vol. 2: p. 111; Charles Whitehead to the finance minister, México, July 18, 1861, *Hacienda Pública*, unclassified papers, AGNM.

    Baring Brothers made precisely the point about the altered status of the bondholders' claims under convention status. See Baring Brothers to the foreign secretary, London, March 12, 1864, in the *Times* (London), April 12, 1864. So, too, did Lord John Russell. See Russell to the special commissioner to Mexico, London, March 30, 1861, in Gloria Grajales, ed., *México y la Gran Bretaña durante la Intervención, 1861–1862* (2nd ed., México, 1974), p. 47.

16 Martín Reyes Vayssade, *Jecker. El hombre que quiso vender México* (México, 2005), p. 182. Prieto also mentions "Iturbide" as a banker in his speculations. If this were Agustín Iturbide, Jr., his stint in the Mexican diplomatic service under the Lizardi as chargé d'affaires in London had certainly served him well. His widowed mother, lately empress, made do in modest housing on South Broad Street in Philadelphia.

Of course, British recognition did not last long and neither did optimism about the liberals' capacity and willingness to pay. Soon both the British and French officials on the scene openly expressed their conviction that the resources to service the foreign debt simply did not exist and that the ministers in Juárez's cabinet, not to mention Juárez himself, were not equal to the task.[17] By late June 1861, British naval officials were already drawing up plans for occupying maritime customs on the Gulf and Pacific coasts in preference to a costly blockade.[18] Relations with Mexico were suspended within seven days when the Congress passed a law (which Payno drafted and Juárez now approved) suspending payment of the foreign debt for two years on July 17, 1861.[19] It is difficult to see how the British had much choice in light of the Dunlop Convention, which is precisely the way the British minister was instructed to interpret matters, although, ironically, the Dunlop Convention undoubtedly hastened suspension by committing Juárez (or whoever was in power) to keep up simultaneous payments to *two* foreign masters: convention claimants *and* bondholders.[20] On the other hand, the Mexican response to British protests was equally adamant: in view of the fiscal circumstances of the government, there was no choice but to suspend payment. For the time being, the battle, with its accompanying fencing, was joined through the exchange of diplomatic correspondence.[21]

17 Blásquez Domínguez, *Veracruz Liberal*, pp. 208–210.

18 Wyke to the foreign secretary, México, June 24, 1861, FO97/280, PRO. Also Wyke to the foreign secretary, México, June 25, 1861, in Grajales, ed., *México y la Gran Bretaña*, pp. 66–68.

19 For the text of the suspension and its provisions, see Jorge Mario Magallón Ibarra, *Proceso y ejecucción vs. Fernando Maximiliano de Hapsburgo* (México, 2005), pp. 86–90. Also see Dubois de Saligny to the minister of foreign affairs, México, July 17, 1861, and August 9, 1861, in Díaz, ed., *Version Francesa de México*, vol. 2: pp. 261, 269. Dubois de Saligny asserted that he and Wyke learned of the decree from the newspapers, specifically *Siglo Diez y Nueve XIX*. Wyke affirmed this in a memorandum to the minister of foreign relations, México, July 19, 1861, in Grajales, ed., *México y la Gran Bretaña*, p 73. On the other hand, Charles Whitehead, the London bondholders' commissioner, claimed that a decree had been in effect since May 20, 1861, "occupying" the customs revenues of that port and effectively suspending payment. Another explanation, perhaps, of why formal suspensions of payments were usually anticipated by the London market. And yet Whitehead himself had taken possession of customs funds for remittance to London as late as July 13. Whitehead to the minister of finance, México, July 13, 1861, *Hacienda Pública*, unclassified papers, AGNM.

In view of Juárez' reluctance to take this step two years earlier, one can only conclude that it was a move born of desperation, or as Juárez put it on September 1861, "the imperatives of the law of necessity." See Grajales, ed., *México y la Gran Bretaña*, p. 99.

20 This possibility is suggested to me by a letter by Hugh Dunlop's successor once the Dunlop Convention went into effect. See Captain Charles Frederick to the secretary of the admiralty, on board HMS Casar, April 22, 1859, FO 97/275, PRO; C. Lennox Wyke to the minister for foreign affairs, México, June 13, 1861, FO 97/280, PRO; and finally "Question of Official Support to the Anglo-American Bondholders," Foreign Office, June 14, 1869, FO 97/282, PRO.

21 A good selection of documents relevant to the exchange from July through September 1861 was published by Grajales, ed., *México y la Gran Bretaña*, pp. 73–93. Foreign Minister Zamacona's response to Wyke was clearly based on the views of Manuel Payno, whom one can regard as the Mexican "voice" in the discussion.

The bondholders, of course, continued to press the Foreign Office for action into September. The Tripartite Convention was signed on October 31, 1861, but officials in the Foreign Office continued to debate the merits (and limits) of assistance to the bondholders. One undersecretary – A. H. Layard – questioned, "just how far the government is inclined to help the bondholders" and pressed for the British special commissioner and minister to Mexico, Sir Charles Wyke, to be given detailed instructions, "a complete answer" so as to avoid setting an unwanted precedent.[22] Even after the intervention occurred, Lord John Russell, defensively perhaps, wrote that Britain had no choice in joining France or Spain, lest it run the risk of coming into conflict with them: "As it is, we shall get our claims acknowledged by any government. But we have kept strictly as a government to no intervention and thereby secured our influence in Mexico." Such was the position to which Russell, at least publicly, continued to adhere in 1862.[23]

But most compelling, perhaps, was Layard's explanation for the Mexican intervention to his Parliamentary constituency. Layard, himself a distinguished scholar-turned-political reformer, worried about the implications of the Mexican question and criticisms of the government in the country and in Parliament. He saw the conservative (British) opposition attempting to make political capital of Britain's involvement in Mexico and specifically mentioned a speech by Lord Stanley at Lyme.[24] In November 1861, when Layard met his constituents at Southwark, he linked reform of the British political system, the rights of Englishmen to the preservation of their property, and the Mexican intervention in a most unusual way. "[W]e are not going to collect bad debts; English traders must take their own risks, but we are going to obtain redress for outrages committed on English subjects and English property . . . What would be thought of the English government if they were to allow English subjects to be outraged?" Or further, "the Government having been liberal in their foreign and colonial policy; it is not possible, when the proper time comes, that they will not pursue a liberal policy in domestic affairs."[25] The willingness of liberal ministers like Lord Russell to bring in further reform to the electoral system linked the domestic property rights of English citizens to their enjoyment of secure

22 A. H. Layard to the foreign secretary, London, November 20 and 27, 1861, Layard Papers, Add. Mss. 38987, British Library.

    Sir Charles Wyke (1815–1897) became minister to México in 1860. For more on Wyke, see *Foreign Office, Diplomatic and Consular Sketches* (London, 1883), pp. 146–149.

23 Lord John Russell to Layard, February [unknown], 1862, Layard Papers, Add. Mss. 38988, British Library. Also see *Times* (London), July 16, 1862, extract of correspondence with Sir Charles Wyke.

24 A. H. Layard to the foreign secretary, London, November 27, 1861, Layard Papers, Add. Mss. 3898, British Library.

25 *Times* (London), November 22, 1861.

property abroad. Here the full implications of Palmerston's historic "Civis Romanus Sum" speech regarding war against Greece in 1850 were realized: "A British subject, in whatever land he may be, shall feel confident that the watchful eye and the strong arm of England will protect him against injustice and wrong." Or as Layard put it in a speech to Parliament, "Her majesty's government have most distinctly stated from the commencement that their object in going to Mexico was not to interfere in internal affairs but solely for the purpose of claiming the due fulfillment of the engagements existing between the Mexican Government and this county and for the protection of English life and property."[26] With further broadening of the franchise just over the horizon in 1867, liberals like Palmerston and Russell saw Mexico in the context of electoral politics rather than financial hegemony. British ministers did not really discuss the implications of the Dunlop Convention for the Mexican bondholders, but they did worry about the appearance of British weakness in the face of Juárez's suspension of payments. Foreign investments gone bad through the vagaries of the market was a legitimate risk faced by capital, but the loss of assets through criminal conduct and the violation of diplomatic protection by the host country were another matter again.

There was also a fiscal and diplomatic context to Britain's ambivalent position toward intervention. As Chancellor of the Exchequer, Gladstone was associated with a policy of budgetary "retrenchment," the progressive reduction of home taxation and the elimination of unnecessary expenditure. His 1860 budget was famous for embodying just such principles, and certainly, the pressure to hold the line in the wake of the Crimean War informed any decision about Mexico. A large-scale military involvement in Mexico in the early 1860s was financially impossible, and the diplomatic consequences of French involvement were only all too apparent to the British as well, particularly with Palmerston's playing on naval tensions with France. The outbreak of the American Civil War in the spring of 1861 presented Britain with the opportunity to mediate a settlement between the Union and Confederate states, one presumably to Britain's advantage in reliving the distress of the cotton industry. Intervention in Mexico would cast doubt on Britain's neutrality, just as the French expedition had, at least in the mind of Gladstone, on France's.[27]

---

26 James Chambers, *Palmerston: The People's Darling* (London, 2004), p. 322; A. H. Layard to the House of Commons, March 10, 1862, *Parliamentary Debates*, 3rd ser., vol. 165 (1862), cols. 1268–1278. I have been unable to find the text of Stanley's speech in a search of the British press.

27 Martin Daunton, *Trusting Leviathan: The Politics of Taxation in Britain, 1799–1914* (Cambridge, 2001), pp. 169–171; Gladstone to the prime minister, Hawarden, September 25, 1862, in Philip Guedalla, ed., *Gladstone and Palmerstone, Being the Correspondence of Lord Palmerston with Mr. Gladstone, 1851–1865* (New York, 1928), p. 233.

Still, the fact that the Foreign Office did not exist to do the bond-holders' bidding does not mean that the market was insensitive to the actions of the Foreign Office. The mere rumors of an impending agreement between Spain, France, and Britain "created much excitement on the Stock Exchange" in late September 1861, as Mexican bonds relative to consols rose 20 percent in a month.[28] Yet not long before, the Committee of Bond-holders had succeeded in securing an interview with the foreign secretary, in which he promised "to take into consideration the question of the inter-ventors" as well as to "insist upon the agreements being faithfully kept which have been made by the Mexican Government with British subjects to Mexican bondholders." The market's sympathetic response was openly noted in the press: "Mexican [bonds have] improved . . . on the results of the deputation to Lord John Russell."[29] This came after a wave of increasingly negative commentary in which the prime minister himself was accused of temporizing and of creating a double standard for the behavior of the South American states. "It remains to be seen if the new system of keeping up a tremendous fleet which, while it is to be ever ready to operate for the protection of theological disputants in Syria, is never to protect English merchants or capitalists . . . who pay for it in the shape of an income tax."[30] The criticism cut very close to the bone and surely drove Palmerston (as prime minister) and his ministers to pay more attention to the bondhold-ers without committing to a specific course of action. Judging from the reaction of the bond market, the strategy worked, at least in the short run: Palmerston's promises, Gladstone's budgets, Russell's regard for the sensibilities of the French, and Layard's domestic political preoccupations induced Great Britain to intervene in Mexico, even if not for very long. And British withdrawal was motivated by a conviction that France had violated the Tripartite Convntion; the disposition of the bondholders was scarcely an issue. As Lord Montagu put it, "we considered [unilateral French military actions in Mexico] a slight to England and Spain, and withdrew."[31]

---

28 A. H. Layard to secretary of the Committee of Mexican Bondholders, London, September 27, 1861, Layard Papers, Add. Mss. 38987, British Library.

29 For a summary of the interview, see "Resolution Passed at an Adjourned Meeting of Mexican Bondholders Held at the London Tavern, July 16th, 1861," FO 97/280. *Times* (London), July 10 and July 12, 1861.

   It is a mystery how Robertson expected debt repayment to work during the war. Getting the assent of the conservatives in Mexico City to such a measure when the liberals controlled the port of Veracruz, for instance, would mean that Zuloaga or Miramón's government was agreeing to a measure it could not possibly enforce. Robertson, no fool, must have known that. The Foreign Office certainly did. See "Extract from Mr. Whitehead's Letter Dated Mexico, 19 February 1858," FO 97/275, PRO.

30 *Times* (London), July 11, 1861.

31 [James Howard Harris], *Memoirs of an Ex-Minister: An Autobiography by the Right Hon. The Earl of Malmesbury, G. C. B.* (New ed., London, 1885), p. 557. Malmesbury was foreign secretary in

Yet this was too much an oversimplification. Even after the British broke with the French over the legitimacy of the Jecker bonds or the desirability of bringing a foreign monarch to the "Mexican throne," Sir Charles Wyke continued negotiations with Manuel Doblado, Juárez's minister of foreign relations. Wyke's goal, for all intents and purposes, was a "separate peace," an arrangement that would recognize the bondholders' (and convention) interests with 59 percent of the customs of Veracruz and Tampico, along with some share of the Pacific revenues.[32] This "Puebla Convention" (1862) was ultimately rejected by the Foreign Office, not to say by Lord Russell himself, as too directly linking the bondholders, intervention in Mexico and the Foreign Office![33]

Of course, one might conclude, there was intervention, and there was *intervention*. Robertson, for all his bluster, was certain that none of this was setting a dreaded "precedent" in Mexican affairs. Britain's diplomats had *always* intervened on behalf of British interests, "but it was done in a different way . . . more in a private manner, by verbal, rather than written communication."[34] Somewhere, surely, Richard Pakenham and Percy Doyle were smiling. But something *had* changed in a quarter century. Unlike in 1837, diplomats put things in writing in 1862. So much the better for us.[35]

The Cupboard Was Bare

In December 1855, Payno remarked that he found 72,830 pesos on hand in the Mexican Treasury.[36] On the one hand, this was a considerable improvement over what was to be had a scant five years earlier, especially since Santa Anna was thought to have cleaned out the Treasury when his fall became inevitable. But Payno's finding was by no means the basis for an optimistic forecast. Prieto – who like his childhood friend and contemporary Payno

1858–1859 and was subject to lobbying by the bondholders. He scarcely mentions Mexico, which suggests that the Mexican intervention was really a minor episode from the British perspective, however important it might be from the Mexican side. Also see Montagu's speech to Parliament in *Times* (London), July 16, 1862.

32 Wyke to the foreign secretary, Puebla, April 29, 1862, in Grajales, ed., *México y la Gran Bretaña*, pp. 191–195.

33 Russell to the British minister to México, London, June 27, 1862, FO 50/363. Also see Grajales, ed., *México y la Gran Bretaña*, pp. 210–212.

34 David Robertson to the permanent undersecretary of state, n.p., June 20, 1857, FO 97/275, PRO.

35 For a contrasting view, see Reinhard Liehr, "La Deuda Exterior de México y los *Merchant Bankers* Británicos, 1821–1860," in Felix Becker, ed., *America Latina en las Letras y Ciencias Sociales Alemanas* (Caracas, 1984), pp. 339–370. Liehr perhaps underestimates the persistent intrusion of British diplomats in Mexican affairs prior to the intervention for just this reason: If it wasn't written down, it didn't happen. Some British diplomats, such as Percy Doyle, only described their activities decades after the fact.

36 Prieto, *Lecciones Elementales de Economía Política*, p. 696.

was one of nineteenth-century Mexico's protean literary, diplomatic, and ministerial figures – produced his own analysis of the condition of the public treasury on the eve of the intervention that was anything but optimistic.[37] While Prieto's brief study merits its own analysis, it was his consideration of the foreign debt that is relevant to our concerns. Prieto believed that a realistic budget for the national government would be no more than 9.5 million pesos after making a series of necessary reforms, including the reduction of the army and devolution of various powers to the states. Of that 9.5 million, 3 million would go to the public debt – an amount equal to what would be budgeted for the military. An amount of 3 million pesos, however, was scarcely £600,000, and this was for debt service of *all* kinds. Since the debt to the British bondholders was more than 51 million pesos in 1862, the interest on this sum *alone* at 5 percent was 2.5 million pesos per year, *equivalent to the entire amount received from the customhouses on account of the convention funds from 1852 through 1859*. Total *foreign* indebtedness was more than 80 million pesos, to say nothing of the internal debt.[38] Such data indicate that absent yet another write-down á la 1850, the London Debt could simply not be serviced. Exhausted by the Three Years' War, Mexico lacked the capacity to pay, something that Payno, for instance, had known and had clearly communicated to the British government. Even had the Mexican government diverted *all* the payments it made on convention debts, it could not have satisfied the bondholders' claims.[39]

Indeed, even Juárez's suspension of 1861 was couched in these terms. The constitutional government, the bondholders were told, recognized the legitimacy of the London Debt and even sympathized with the bondholders' protests. The issue was pragmatic, a question of timing. After three years of civil war, the resources to make payment were unavailable, including the funds raised by the secularization of church properties. If the British bondholders would only wait, they were told that the suspension would leave Juárez's administration in a stronger position to pay once it had reorganized its finances. It was a "temporary" (*pasajera*) measure, not a permanent denial of the bondholders' claim, the very notion of which Juárez said was repugnant to him. As legitimate head of state, he was compelled to recognize legitimate sovereign debts.[40] But all of this was not enough to mollify the British, who, perhaps, had heard a similar refrain in

37 On Prieto, see Malcolm D. McLean, *Vida y obra de Guillermo Prieto* (2nd. ed., México, 1998), p. 103. Guillermo Prieto, *Algunas ideas sobre la organización de la Hacienda Pública, basadas en el presupuesto de 1857* (México, 1861), pp. 21–22, for what follows.

38 Payno, *México y sus cuestiones financieras*, p. 306.

39 David Robertson to the Earl of Clarendon, Ladykirk, Berwyck upon Tweed, July 20, 1858, FO 97/275, PRO. "The Present Condition of Mexico," p. 335, table D, for convention funds.

40 Draft memorandum, [Finance Minister] to Charles Whitehead, México, [July 23, 1861], *Hacienda Pública*, unclassified papers, AGNM.

Table 4.1. *Silver Specie Shipments from Mexico to England, 1851–1868*

1851	5,210
1852	6,410
1853	5,810
1854	5,800
1855	5,430
1856	7,060
1858–1859	1,200–1,400
1860	4,518
1861	5,048
1862	6,242
1863	6,652
1864	7,002
1865	4,932
1866	5,032
1867	5,032
1868	3,204

Note: All values are in thousands of pounds sterling.
Sources: 1851–1856: Thomas Tooke and William Newmarch, *A History of Prices and of the State of Circulation from 1793 to 1837* ([1838–1857]; 6 vols., London, 1928), vol. 6: p. 769 ["Silver Chiefly and Includes West Indies, Peru and Partly California"]; 1858/1859: computed roughly from *Times* (London), March 14, 1858, and *Sunday Times*, July 3, 1859, with specific reference to the first shipment from Mexico in eighteen months occurring in July 1859; 1860–1868: computed value from *Report from the Select Committee on Depreciation of Silver* (London, 1876), Appendix No. 22, p. 163. Includes West Indies and South America excluding Brazil.

1850, only to be deceived once more. The bondholders continued to press for repayment, even to the extent of circulating a petition on the stock exchange supporting intervention in Mexico.[41] What was more, Britain would eventually support the French in their adventure and even more strikingly, so did the market, which rose from January to April 1864 in anticipation of the arrival of Maximilian.

If we examine Table 4.1, a reconstruction of the silver shipped from Mexico to Great Britain over the years 1853–1868, the persistence of the bondholders and the market's support for foreign intervention in Mexico

41 Charles Francis Adams to the secretary of state, London, September 19, 1861, in United States Congress, 37th Cong., 2nd sess., House, "The Present Condition of Mexico," p. 191.

may be slightly clearer. The usual caution extends to the accuracy of the figures in the table, perhaps to an even greater extent than customary: their trend is apt to be more reliable than their levels. Still, the magnitude of shipments to Britain in the interval 1851–1856 was surprisingly robust, reaching more than £7 million in 1856. But after this, it is all downhill and in 1858–1859, remission of specie fell to somewhere between £1.2 and £1.4 million. Of course, it can hardly be a coincidence that the contraction roughly follows the Three Years' War, and over eighteen months – from January 1858 through July 1859 – absolutely no shipments of silver from Mexico to Britain occurred. Once the liberals took over in 1860, a recovery began, but it was not until 1864 that the prewar total was nearly reattained. The surprising size of these shipments (and of their corresponding collapse in 1858–1859) could not have failed to impress the bondholders, for they were far in excess of what was needed to service the London Debt. But these were *private* remissions of silver, not public ones. Under the circumstances, it is logical to suppose that the bondholders and their representatives believed Mexico to be wealthy enough to pay its debts if its political system were so organized to do so.[42] In one way or another, this had been the position of the bondholders since 1850. Or as Sir Charles Wyke put matters, Mexico could treble its exports, specie included *and* treble its imports of British manufactures "with a Government formed by respectable men, if they were to be found."[43] Yet things had reached an obvious breaking point. There appeared no way that Mexico itself was capable of reorganizing in such a way as to permit a larger transfer of private resources to the government. Or as the *Times* (London) put it, "if there had been any visible approach to a better order of things, or any prospect of a sound political organization, this intervention would have never occurred."[44] But occur it did, and by May of 1862, Palmerston could report to Parliament that the French occupation of Mexico – by now mostly a French show – had improved the prospect for the conclusion of a convention for the satisfaction of British claims. And the British Convention payments had *always* been made, even during the Three Years' War. The interest was late, the capital portion suspended, and the amounts relatively small – but the convention debt had been, in this fashion, serviced.[45]

---

42 And, indeed, said as much. See David Robertson to Edmund Drummund, Ladykirk, Berwick upon Tweed, July 19, 1858, FO 97/275, PRO.

43 Wyke to the foreign secretary, México, July 26, 1861, in Grajales, ed., *México y la Gran Bretaña*, p. 84.

44 *Times* (London), January 31, 1862.

45 *Times* (London), May 17, 1862. See "The Present Condition of Mexico," table E, p. 335. One can understand better the anger of Mexican ministers such as Zamacona and Payno at the intervention if this simple fact is emphasized. In their minds, Mexico paid what it could when it could. On the other hand, Zamacona in particular was not above deliberately conflating payments made on the

The French Connection

For this reason, if not perhaps for this reason alone, the intervention of the French into Mexico affairs in 1862 was welcomed by the bond market. Nor was it, of course, a purely foreign imposition, for the intervention was openly "solicited" by a group of Mexican conservatives. Conservatives and monarchists had a long history of regarding the "royalist option" as the most plausible solution to the collapse of the Bourbon monarchy, and from a strictly political perspective there is no reason to regard Iturbide's imperial interregnum as anything other than one of a legitimate spectrum of possibilities open to the Mexican political elite at the time of independence.[46]

Although this is not the place for an extended analysis of France's motives for intervening in Mexico, few believed French financial claims to be anything other than a pretext. Indeed, "pretext" was very much used by Matías Romero in his discussions with officials in the Lincoln government.[47] Lincoln's minister to Paris, William Dayton, also wrote William H. Seward, the secretary of state, "that money or the recovery of debts was not the great object that took France and Spain to Mexico."[48] For that reason, perhaps, proposals advanced by the Lincoln government in the fall of 1861 to assume payment of Mexico's foreign debt for five year as of July 17, 1861, were met with no enthusiasm in Congress. The United States would take over Mexico's *funded* debt at 3 percent, with repayment guaranteed by a lien in some form on the states or public lands of Lower California, Chihuahua, Sonora, and Sinaloa. The agreement would be contingent on the willingness of England and France to refrain from actions against Mexico as long as debt service continued. Yet in the face of a general conviction that neither England nor France was acting *primarily* for financial reasons, such an agreement did not prosper and none was forthcoming.[49] The standard English-language history of Franco-Mexican affairs during the 1860s contends that Napoleon III's involvement had little to do with finance,

convention debts with dividends paid to the bondholders. A masterpiece of wounded innocence appears in Zamacona to the commandant of the British squadron in the Gulf of Mexico, Veracruz, January 5, 1859, FO 97/275, PRO.

46 María José Garrido Asperó, "Cada Quien Sus Héroes," *Estudios de Historia Contémporanea y Moderna de México*, 22 (2001), pp. 5–22.

47 Matías Romero, entry of August 31, 1861, in Thomas D. Schoonover, *Mexican Lobby: Matías Romero in Washington, 1861–1867* (Lexington, KY, 1986), p. 8.

48 Daniel B. Carroll, *Henri Mercier and the American Civil War* (Princeton, NJ, 1971), p. 281.

49 *Journal of the Executive Proceedings of the Senate of the United States of America*, 37th Cong., 2nd sess., 1887, vol. 12, pp. 122–126. Also Lord John Russell to the minister to France, London, September 27, 1861, in "The Present Condition of Mexico," p. 308; also see Matías Romero, entry of December 22, 1861, in Schonoover, ed., *Mexican Lobby*, p. 11.

but much more with a pseudo-Latin irredentism that aimed at checking the growing expansion of U.S. power in the hemisphere. Another study speaks of "an effort to carve out a French sphere of influence in Central America." A more recent French study essentially concurs. Bad debts of any sort were little more than a pretext for larger French "pan-Latinist" ambitions, although the baleful influence of the French minister to Mexico, de Saligny, comes in for severe scrutiny as well. Partisan hostility within France, particularly in the wake of Napoleon III's coup of 1857, may have prepared the way for foreign adventurism too. As A. J. P. Taylor put it, "Napoleon was convinced that he could avoid political concessions at home only by a striking success in foreign policy."[50]

But if the French intervention in Mexico had no real financial basis, it is not equally true that it had no financial implications, and not just for the British bondholders. The liberal assumption of power in 1860 coincided with a major financial crisis in Mexico City when the house of J. B. Jecker (previously known as Jecker, Torre) failed.[51] Characterized as "government bankers" and "the only large banking house in Mexico," Jecker had been the principal financier to the government of Ignacio Comonfort (1855–1858).[52] The house had also served the Zuloaga (1858) and Miramón (1859, 1860) (conservative) regimes. Its operations culminated in the eponymous (and notorious) Jecker bonds, an inflated obligation repudiated by the liberal Juárez government and rejected by the British government by early 1862.[53] Jecker's clients had, understandably, lost faith in the house and a "terrible" panic ensued, in which wealthy depositors such as the Béistegui, Iturbe, and Mier y Terán were compromised to well more than a million dollars.

---

50 Alfred Jackson Hanna and Kathryn Abbey Hanna, *Napoleon III and Mexico: American Triumph over Monarchy* (Chapel Hill, 1971), esp. pp. 3–9, 58–68, 182–208. Roger Price, *The French Second Empire: An Anatomy of Political Power* (Cambridge, UK, 2001), p. 315. Nancy M. Barker, "Monarchy in Mexico: Harebrained Scheme or Well-considered Prospect?" *The Journal of Modern History*, 41: 1(1976), pp. 51–68; Jean-Francois Lecaillon, *Napoléon III et le Mexique* (Paris, 1994), pp. 41, 44–47, 50–51. J. Albiot, *Les Campagnes Électorales, 1851–1869* (Paris, 1869), p. 201; A. J. P. Taylor, *The Struggle for Mastery in Europe, 1848–1918* (Oxford, 1954), p. 101.

51 *Bankers Magazine*, 20 (1860), pp. 494–495.

52 See Reyes Vayssade, *Jecker*, p. 159, who calculates that Jecker was responsible for nearly half the loans to Comonfort's government.

53 "The Jecker Bonds," HC 4.5.33, BBA. Also see "J. Martínez" (a pseudonym of Guillermo Prieto), "Bonos Títulados de Jecker" and "Más Sobre los Bonos de Jecker" in Guillermo Prieto, *Obras Completas* (32 vols., México, 1997), vol. 23: pp. 107–111, 116–122. [Friends of Mexico], *Historical and Financial Items* (n.p., [1866]), p. 11; Ana Rosa Suárez Argüello, "Los intereses de Jecker en Sonora," *Estudios de Historia Moderna y Contemporánea de México*, 9 (1983), pp. 21–34; Nancy N. Barker, "The Duke of Morny and the Affair of the Jecker Bonds," *French Historical Studies*, 6: 4 (1970), pp. 555–561; Reyes Vayssade, *Jecker*, pp. 174–192; Wyke to the foreign secretary, México, January 19, 1862, in Grajales, ed., *México y la Gran Bretaña*, pp. 133–137.

The notorious Jecker bonds consisted of 15,000,000 pesos obligation in return for 750,000 cash to the Miramón government by the Swiss financier of the same name.

Jecker was hoist by its own petard. Carrying $2 million of the bonds in its portfolio, they became virtually worthless as a result of the liberal victory and the house was forced into bankruptcy. Napoleon III's brother in law, the Duc de Morny, and the French minister to Mexico, de Saligny, had been implicated in trafficking in Jecker bonds too. All in all, financial fraud was a most fitting pastime for what Taylor called Napoleon's "gangster-followers."[54]

As a generalization, however, reports of French progress in subduing the liberal opposition in Mexico were greeted favorably by the bond market, especially the occupation of Querétaro and Mexico City. The *Times* (London) added that August 1863 saw "news of Mexico being declared an Empire and of the offer of the Crown to Maximilian 'without much improvement'." Some weeks later, the *Times* (London) added of the bonds, "they advanced to about 48 [from 36 and $3/4$]." Similarly, the *Times* (London) explained a fall of about 4 percent in October 1863 "on answer of Archduke Maximilian to Mexican delegation, specifying conditions for acceptance of the throne." These were, of course, discouragingly democratic, suggesting that Maximilian actually expected popular support in Mexico as a condition for taking up the throne.[55]

The behavior of the market recalls, to some extent, the support that the bondholders provided to Santa Anna in his turn to centralism and dictatorship. Logically, then, one asks, why did the market support conservatives and Mexican monarchists – indeed, parties whom one might assume to somehow seek to efface Mexican nationalism, especially in light of the historical equation of Juárez and the liberals with the resuscitation of the Mexican nation, and its defense against enemies, domestic or otherwise? There are a variety of answers to this question that run the gamut from a reevaluation of the official history of Mexico to a more nuanced appreciation of the way in which asset markets viewed their prospects under notional liberal or conservative regimes.

To begin, the involvement of France in Mexican affairs raised a significant question in the minds of the British bondholders. The failure of the Tripartite Convention and the withdrawal of the English and Spanish forces changed the nature of France's commitment in 1862. By choosing to remain in Mexico and connive at the creation of a monarchy, "the French chose to act as proprietors of the Mexican estate [and] there is not the least doubt that, even according to French law, an administrator or receiver . . . acting in that way would make himself liable for the charges on the estate." Thus, concluded one bondholder, "the French do now stand so as regards to

---

54 Taylor, *Struggle for Mastery*, p. 81n. See also Reyes Vayssade, *Jecker*, pp. 193–196, who attributes the failure to the house's overextension during the period of civil war.

55 *Times* (London), December 21 and December 23, 1863.

Mexico and its creditors." The legal status of France's administration aside, the bondholders believed "that the exactitude and liberality of the French government . . . can safely be relied upon: indeed it is *self-evident* [italics mine] that the more the Emperor of the French will be desirous to have and exercise influence in Mexico, the more he will profess and be ready to act most liberally in all pecuniary matters of Mexico affecting other nations, and especially England."[56] In other words, legal or diplomatic considerations would force the French to assume Mexican indebtedness. So the bondholders thought the French – or their client Maximilian – to be the more likely to pay than harried, bankrupt, flying Dutchman-like Juárez. In the long run, Juárez and the liberals might well cast their lot with the United States rather than with Europe. Thomas Corwin (diplomatic minister of the Union States) and the Lincoln Administration (studied neutrality aside) would guarantee only a limited portion of Mexico's external liabilities in exchange for additional Mexican territory: a reprise, essentially, of 1848.

There were some dissenters to the "French as saviors" view. Perhaps most eloquent and informed was George White, who glumly wrote Baring Brothers that

the prospects of the Bondholders, in any case, are as unsatisfactory as can well be . . . It is quite clear that the French government will enforce every claim which can be raked up . . . The £2,600,000 due to the Bondholders will be left to take its chances after all others have been satisfied . . . [T]he mere fact of the British government not interfering to place the Bondholders on an equal footing will amount to a tacit acquiescence in the wrong which will be inflicted on them.

Acting as agent and representative of the bondholders, White was in no mood to trust the French. "The only ray of hope . . . [is that] there may be heretofore such an increase in the revenues of the country that the assignments in favor of the Bondholders will be more than enough to cover the current interest and so leave some surplus applicable to the arrears."[57] But what White had apparently not counted on was the prospect of solvency and financial stability that French patronage would betoken. By December 1862, the Rothschilds' agent in Mexico was proposing that the house fund a consolidation loan on the foreign debt and claims against Mexico, "based on the supposition that [Mexico] will be entirely conquered and subdued either by the French alone or by the allied forces of the Three Powers."[58] For better or worse, French involvement in Mexico brought an unusual prospect

56 *Times* (London), July 2, 1863.
57 George White to Baring Brothers, México, August 11, 1862, HC 4.5.25, BBA.
58 John Walsham to the foreign secretary, México, December 7, 1862, FO 97/280, PRO; George White to Baring Brothers, México, December 8, 1862, HC 4.5.25, BBA.

of financial stability or serious international backing. It also brought the distinct whiff of competition to Baring Brothers, which may have been White's real concern. In the event, White did his job well, for the house acted as the agency through which dividends would be paid by the imperial Mexican government from 1864 through 1866 when they were available.[59]

To understand the effect that the French expedition and Maximilian's imperial moment had on the London Debt, it is best to be clear about what transpired. When Maximilian agreed to assume the throne, he did so via the Convention of Miramar[60] (April 10, 1864) between France and Mexico. Article 9 of the convention provided that the costs of the French expedition to Mexico that were to be reimbursed by the Mexican (imperial) government were fixed at 270 million francs up to July 1, 1864, securitized as a loan at 3 percent. Article 11 specified that Mexico would *immediately* pay France 66 million francs as security. In the event that the costs of the campaign exceeded 270 million francs, Mexico would repay an additional 25 million francs per year. The Mexican empire made its payment in bonds yielding 10 percent interest. The issue was largely held by Napoleon III's government, but some 12 million francs of the obligations ended up in the hands of private citizens.[61] At a stroke, Maximilian's government had agreed to saddle itself with another 50 *million* pesos in outstanding debts. To put this in perspective, Baring Brothers put the *overall* foreign debt in 1863 at near 80 million pesos. Alfred Hanna and Kathryn Hanna were absolutely correct in characterizing what Maximilian had assumed as a "staggering debt."[62]

Curiously, even though word of the Convention of Miramar reached London almost immediately, the enormous increase in Mexico's debt burden did not disturb the market. This was because one of Maximilian's first actions as emperor was an act of unparalleled largesse to the London

---

59 In general, see "Informe al E[xmo] Sr Almonte sobre los motivos legales que han impedídola ejecución del pago a cuenta de las $600,000 destinados al dividendo de Julio de 1866," *Segundo Imperio*, vol. 20, exp. 85, AGNM.

60 See Michele Cunningham, *Mexico and the Foreign Policy of Napoleon III* (Basingstroke, UK, 2001), Appendix 2, pp. 217–218.

61 *Discours de M. Berryer sur La Dette de Mexique et les Obligations Mexicains Prononces les 22 et 23 Juillet 1867 Au Corps Legislatif* (Paris, 1867), pp. 7, 28. The exact details of the issue appeared in the *Times* (London), April 18, 1864, "Anglo-French Six Per Cent Loan," as a commercial notice. Another report in *Times* (London) (May 24, 1864) suggested that French war expenses were expected to run 300 million francs – at least, or £60 million, nearly quadruple the existing foreign debt. Others estimated as much as 600 million francs! The numbers are so abysmal that they make the historian wonder if the French did not literally think the streets were paved with silver in Mexico, if not gold.

62 "Foreign Debt of Mexico," HC 4.5.36.3e, BBA; Hanna, *Napoleon III and Mexico*, pp. 126–127. Manuel Payno, *Cuentas, Gastos, Acreedores y otros Asuntos del Tiempo de la Intervención Francesa y del Imperio* (1868; México, 1981), p. 852, has an even higher figure.

bondholders, the so-called Conversion of 1864, in which the arrears of the Conversion of 1850 were converted at the rate of £100 bonds for £60 in coupons. Payno calculated that the value of the Conversion of 1864 was some 10 million pesos. Small wonder the London bondholders were happy in April 1864. As Payno put it, "Archduke Maximilian of Austria wanted to reign as Emperor of Mexico. To placate (*allanar*) the English Bondholders, he undertook the Conversion of 1864."[63]

But as the realization of what Maximilian and the French had done, the buoyancy of the market began to disappear. How could it not? The recognition of the London Debt and the credit opened to finance the expedition added 60 *million pesos* to Mexico's outstanding debt, which could now be arguably estimated at 140 *million* pesos. The temptation is strong to regard Maximilian as buying his way into the imperial throne, thereby adding profligacy to the long list of sins of omission and commission traditionally attributed to him. But by the same token, the fiscal pressures that were thereby created on the nascent Second Empire could only prove crushing. For how could Maximilian do anything less than be guided by policies that would make resources available to him? And one wonders, was the Convention of Miramar part of Napoleon III's larger vision of placating Britain by enriching the bondholders, even as the French went their own way in Mexico with British and Spanish acquiescence? Clearly, the arrangement with the Mexican bondholders had been under negotiation weeks *before* the convention had been signed.[64]

Even more remarkable was how rapidly sentiment turned against the Second Empire. If the market was pleased in April 1864 (see Figure 4.1), it underwent a sudden, sharp reversal in July, losing 35 percent in a month. The *Times* (London) remarked, "Mexican [bonds], notwithstanding the news of the reception of the Emperor Maximilian [are] now considerably under that to which the stock went a distant hope was first entertained that he might . . . be induced to accept the throne."[65] So from April through July 1864, the great hopes that the London bondholders had placed in a French reconstruction of Mexico under the Hapsburg prince had seemingly vanished.

The most straightforward explanation for this phenomenon may be summarized thusly: In the short run, George White of Barings was wrong. In the long run, White was right. The resources to service the London Debt were available in 1863 and 1864. In 1865 there was nothing. In 1866, there was an ample amount, but it would rapidly dry up. The evidence is crude,

63 Manuel Payno to the finance minister, México, October 14, 1868, *Deuda Exterior*, vol. 9, AGNM.
64 Cunningham, *Mexico and the Foreign Policy of Napoleon III*, pp. 155–173. See the notices, "To the Holders of Mexican Bonds," March 28 and 31, 1864, in *Times* (London).
65 July 13, 1864.

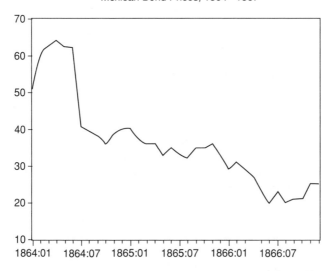

Mexican Bond Prices, 1864–1867

Figure 4.1. Mexican Bond Prices Relative to Consols, 1864–1866.

but compelling.[66] An OLS (ordinary least square) regression that uses the price of Mexican bonds relative to consols as the left-hand variable and on the right-hand side, dividend remissions and a dummy variable that takes on the value of "1" after Napoleon III announced his intention to withdraw all French forces in support of Maximilian from Mexico (May 31, 1866) explains 69 percent of the variation in relative price. The variables have the correct sign (dividends are directly related to the relative price of Mexican bonds, while Napoleon's withdrawal of French forces is negatively related) and the coefficient on the Napoleon III dummy is large and highly significant – even more so than on dividends. The F-statistic (14.22, $p = .99$) is large as well. In the highly charged circumstances of the Second Empire, where bondholders (correctly) perceived Napoleon III's support for Maximilian as absolutely crucial, troops (or their promised removal) mattered even more than dividends. One is inevitably reminded of Edouard Manet's famous "Execution of the Emperor Maximilian" in the National Gallery in London (1867), with the soldier to the right of the firing squad visibly resembling Napoleon III.

Two questions should be posed here. Why did dividends to the bondholders fluctuate in the way they did? And why did the bondholders

---

66 Dividend figures are from "Noticia de las cantidades entregadas por la Aduana Marítima de Veracruz por cuenta de la Deuda contraída en Londres," *Deuda Exterior*, vol. 9, AGNM.

Table 4.2. *Financing the French Expedition, 1864*

Estimates of Iglesias	
Loan through Convention of Miramar	40,000,000
Issued at 63	25,200,000
Less 50 percent of French war expenses as of 1864	21,000,000
Cash balance	4,200,000

Note: All values are in pesos.

conclude that the ostensible strength of the French, an ability to reorganize and revitalize the Mexican Treasury, was illusory?

One of the clearest attempts to address why the bondholders grew disillusioned with Maximilian so quickly was undertaken by José María Iglesias, Juárez's finance minister-in-exile (1864–1867).[67] Iglesias provided a variety of analyses, all of which led to a similar conclusion. From Table 4.2, which I have assembled from Iglesias' calculations, one can only conclude that the loan authorized by the Convention of Miramar would leave the Mexicans very little even if only half of the French war expenses were paid immediately. This, in essence, was the key. The price Napoleon III exacted from Maximilian for his support was to oblige the Mexican empire to pay the costs of the French expedition. Under even conservative assumptions, what remained would barely cover one month of the French army's costs. The interest on the loan, at 6 percent, itself required 2,400,000 pesos per year. In other words, Iglesias calculated that the loan of 1864 would barely last until 1865. Moreover, Iglesias emphasized that there were other fixed costs – dividends on the London Debt, the English Convention Debt, and the Spanish Convention Debt – which had yet to be considered. The interest on the loan authorized at Miramar would, in his judgment, essentially double these fixed costs![68] The total debt service of the empire, he concluded, implied a budget of 38–40 million pesos per year when careful students of the budget had warned that no more than 9 million pesos per year could be financed. Iglesias arrived at these conclusions by the end of April 1864. In his view, the French adventure was doomed from the beginning, a conclusion the London market rapidly came to share.

But, as usual, the definitive review of the loans made under the empire was produced by Payno, who termed the business "the most serious of the empire." It is a fitting compliment to his *Cuestiones financieras de México*, all the more striking for his broad concurrence with the judgment of Iglesias:

67 José María Iglesias, *Revistas históricas sobre la intervención francesa en México* ([1868–1869]; 3 vols., México, 1991), vol. 2: pp. 249–316.

68 Iglesias, *Revistas históricas*, vol. 2: pp. 278–279.

Table 4.3. *Disposition of Customs Revenue, Veracruz, 1862–1866*

Year	Bondholders/(Bondholders + Convention) (percent)	England/(England + France + Spain) (percent)	Creditors/All (percent)
1862		79	45
1863	77	31	43
1864	44	74	23
1865	0	67	14
1866	55	84	21

Sources and Notes: The "bondholders" share is computed from "Noticia de las cantidades entregadas por la Aduana Marítima de Veracruz por cuenta de la Deuda contraída en Londres," *Deuda Interior*, vol. 9, AGNM, and from Payno, *Cuentas, Gastos, Acreedores y otros Asuntos del Tiempo de la Intervención Francesa y del Imperio*, pp. 21–55. The English share of all creditor countries is inflated in 1865 and 1866 because of the way in which French appropriation of customs funds is recorded. From 1861 through 1866, Payno indicates that England accounted for 76 percent of all foreign *debt* payments made, or 46 percent if other forms of French "intervention" in the customs revenue are included. Depending on whether one uses the aggregated or disaggregated figures, 20–30 percent of all Veracruz customs revenue was turned over to foreign creditors.

"The French government buried Maximilian when he signed the treaty [*sic*] of Miramar."[69] Payno emphasizes some of the features that impress the modern student as well: the business is even more convoluted than most Mexican debt negotiations; the transactions almost completely lack transparency; the Mexican documentation – or the French documentation left in Mexico – is suspiciously sparse. Payno claims to have spent a year with the aid of several assistants trying to make sense out of what the French had done. He did not quite admit defeat, but he came close.[70] He does, however, supply us with the data to make a few plausible attempts at answering difficult questions.

As we show in Table 4.3, the reason why dividend payments to the London bondholders varied so much was because they were not the only payments made to English creditors. While in 1863, 77 percent of payments made from the Veracruz customs went to the London bondholders, in 1865, 100 percent of the payments went to British convention creditors. In 1864 and 1866, the division was rather more balanced. Since Great Britain formally recognized the Mexican empire in 1865, a likely possibility is that the diversion of resources to the convention debt in 1865 was related to

69 *Cuentas, Gastos, Acreedores y otros Asuntos del Tiempo de la Intervención Francesa y del Imperio*, pp. 757, 761.
70 *Cuentas, Gastos, Acreedores y otros Asuntos del Tiempo de la Intervención Francesa y del Imperio*, pp. 757, 933.

consolidating the broadest possible base of British support for Maximilian: prior to that, the London bondholders had enjoyed clear preference.[71]

Moreover, Payno's data only serves to emphasize the key role that imperial Mexico played in cementing diplomatic relations with Great Britain at a time of considerable diplomatic and military stress. Only in 1863 and late in 1866 did Britain cease to be the beneficiary of the Veracruz customs. For the rest of the interlude, Great Britain held pride of place.[72] One is tempted to recall that the bilateral agreement between Great Britain and France, the Cobden–Chevalier Treaty, was signed in 1860, customarily viewed as the inauguration of a free trade regime between the two nations, a commercial antidote to the possibility of war.[73] Even if the "traditional" view is an exaggeration, France's use of imperial Mexico to spread oil on the waters between the two nations seems only too obvious.

Indeed, it is difficult to avoid the conclusion that whatever the Foreign Office had said publicly, its representatives in Mexico were increasingly willing to leave the French to their own devices there as long as the bondholders were paid. As Sir Charles Wyke's successor, John Walsham, explained in 1863, "at all events, I will do what I can for the interests of the Bondholders." This involved suggesting to the French minister to Mexico, de Saligny, "the expediency of adopting some plan which would facilitate the system of Dividends and enable the Bondholders *to obtain their money at stated periods.*" The result of Walsham's intervention with de Saligny was quite positive. "So far from raising any objection to such an arrangement, Mr. de Saligny said that he should be glad to see it come into effect."[74] At the same time, Walsham remained in close touch with George White of Barings, to whom he communicated the relevant details. This is ironic, because as we have seen, White had warned Barings to expect little from the French in 1862.

But by June 1863, the French had occupied Mexico City, and were making strenuous efforts to convince the British to recognize the Confederate States as part of Napoleon III's version of a "Western Design." As

---

71 See Baring Brothers to the foreign secretary, London, June 22, 1866, FO 97/281, PRO, for independent confirmation of what the Mexican customs records indicate. Barings complained yet again of neglect of the bondholders in a letter to the Foreign Office, January 7, 1867, FO 97/281, PRO.

72 As Count Émile de Kératry put it, "'England has been the one to profit most by the sacrifices we made, thanks to the deductions made in her favour from the Mexican receipts during the whole time of the expedition.' *The Rise and Fall of Emperor Maximilian: A Narrative of the Mexican Empire, 1861–7* (London, 1868), p. 12.

73 Marc Flandreau, "Does Bilateralism Promote Trade? Nineteenth-Century Liberalization Revisited" (unpublished paper).

74 Walsham to the Foreign Secretary, México, July 12, 1863, FO 97/280, PRO. My emphasis. Walsham to the British interventor in Veracruz, México, July 22, 1863, and Walsham to George White, México, July 22, 1863, both in FO 97/280.

his propagandist Michel Chevalier argued, southern cotton was, if anything, even more vital to the future of French industrialization than it was to Great Britain's, if only because Britain had alternative sources of raw cotton in Brazil and India, while France had none.[75] It is not difficult to discern in French magnanimousness toward the British bondholders an attempt to solidify British support for French aims in Mexico, even as the British debate over whether or not to recognize the Confederacy reached its crescendo in July 1863. As always, larger international diplomatic, political, and economic concerns joined strictly domestic concerns in determining the fortunes of the London Debt. White would have undoubtedly agreed that a year was a long time in the politics of international debt negotiation.

Money Has No Smell?

It was one thing to collect revenues at Veracruz, even with the use of a British agent at the customs, but another still to put them into the hands of the British bondholders and convention debtors. How could Maximilian do what his predecessors had been unable to do, constrained as they were by a lack of resources? The details, to repeat, are murky, but in 1889, the French Bondholders' Association claimed that the loan authorized by the Convention of Miramar in 1864 immediately took £921,750 from the proceeds "in order to consolidate the capital and guarantee the interest of the Republican loan of 1850, issued for meeting the Veracruz indemnity."[76] In other words, part of the proceeds of the loan was used to anticipate customs revenue to service past debt with new debt. This sounds very familiar with Glynn Mills, a major holder of Mexican bonds (see Chapter 3) cast in the role of Baring Brothers in London and with the addition of Crédit Mobilier in Paris. Such tactics had been unsound forty years earlier, and they were no less so now, adding to the conviction that the rise in Mexican bonds in April 1864 was fundamentally unsustainable, as was the entire financial edifice of the empire.

In essence, what Maximilian did was to recognize that republican Mexico had defaulted on the Conversion of 1850. This default would make it impossible for imperial Mexico to raise a European loan. So Maximilian capitalized

75 [M. M. Chevalier] *France, Mexico and the Confederate States* (New York, 1863), pp. 8, 12, 15, 16, Americas Collection, MS 518, Woodson Research Center, Fondren Library, Rice University. Also see Sven Beckert, "Emancipation and Empire: Reconstructing the Worldwide Web of Cotton Production in the Age of the American Civil War," *American Historical Review*, 109: 5 (2004), pp. 1405–1438; Frenise A. Logan, "India: Britain's Substitute for American Cotton, 1861–1865," *The Journal of Southern History*, 24: 4 (1958), pp. 472–480.

76 *Times* (London), September 25, 1889. Also see Emilio Velasco to the *oficial mayor* of foreign relations, Paris, January 14, 1880, in Lucía de Robaina, ed., *Reconciliación de México y Francia (1870–1880)* (México, 1963), p. 160.

the arrears of 1850 as bonds bearing 3 percent interest, the so-called Conversion of 1864. For two years, Glynn Mills would pay the interest. This conversion created enormous problems after the fall of Maximilian. The liberal (Mexican) government would argue that the British had, in essence, bet on the wrong horse. Imperial Mexico had assumed the liability, but was unable, by virtue of Maximilian's fall, to meet it. As the Mexicans were to argue, in their view, under law, they owed the British nothing more.[77]

By late 1865, "money, the sinews of war, was already deficient."[78] Imperial Mexico – cash poor, but loaded down with new debts – could barely meet the expenses that its French masters imposed on it. This led to some remarkable maneuvers. In April 1865, another Mexican loan was raised in Paris, called and subsequently converted in September. But the Mexican expedition proved controversial in France, as did its financing, and by July of 1866, the Arroyo–Danó Convention directed that fully 50 percent of the Mexican customs after July 30, 1866, should be channeled to France to "repay" the loans of 1864 and 1865.[79]

Yet, fiscally at least, nothing proved more damaging than imperial Mexico's repudiation of the internal debt in 1866. Its status, which had bedeviled virtually every government since the close of the War of 1847, was again called into question. The details of the discussion were technical, but came down to whether internal debt converted into so-called "Zuloaga bonds" under the Plan of Tacubaya (which nullified the Constitution of 1857) remained current. Prior to February 1866, its legitimacy – or at least that of a large portion of it – had been recognized by the imperial government. The object of heavy speculation by commercial interests that supported Maximilian, these were deeply shocked by the refusal of government offices to continue negotiating the bonds. The language of their discontent could not have been plainer: "Really, we don't understand what is going on." And the aggrieved were not just anyone: one found Luis de Miranda e Iturbe, Jorge Murphy, and Antonio de Escandón – a member of the commission sent to Miramar to solicit Maximilian for the throne – among the signers of the complaint.[80] Evidently, the diversion of enormous

77 "Memorandum Relative to the Relations Existing between Great Britain and Mexico with Regard to the Claims of the British Bondholders," July 19, 1869, FO 97/282, pp. 15–16.

78 Keratry, *A Narrative of the Mexican Empire*, p. 90, for this and what follows.

79 *Discours de M. Berryear*, pp. 30–40; *Le Moniteur Universel*, September 28, 1865; F. Glennie to the British chargé d'Affaires, México, December 20, 1866, FO 97/281, PRO; Payno, *Cuentas, Gastos, Acreedores y otros Asuntos del Tiempo de la Intervención Francesa y del Imperio*, pp. 812–813. Also see Steven C. Topik, "When Mexico Had the Blues: A Transatlantic Tale of Bonds, Bankers, and Nationalists, 1862–1910," *American Historical Review*, 105: 3 (2000), pp. 714–738.

80 "Solicitud de varios comerciantes de esta capital en que piden una declaración expresa sobre el valor de los Bonos llamados de Zuloaga," México, February 28, 1866, *Indiferente general*, unclassified papers, AGNM.

    (*No comprendemos, en verdad, lo que sucede* is translated as "Really, we don't understand what is going on.")

sums in 1866 to pay the London bondholders came at the expense of some of the empire's major financiers! But with Napoleon III's government now enduring withering criticism of the Mexican affair and charges of corruption and favoritism to French banking interests in the air, the British bondholders' party would soon be over. One way or another, Benito Juárez would see to that.

Frustrated by the complexity and evident dishonesty of the financial shenanigans that went on during the Second Empire, Payno essentially threw up his hands in disgust. In 1868, he recommended that the republic should now consider the London Debt a tabula rasa. The Conversion of 1864 Payno held to be illegitimate, as were any obligations undertaken to the French after intervention. But the *payments* made to the bondholders had been genuine enough, and these Payno now deducted from the outstanding sum owed the British. After all was said and done, Payno calculated the London Debt as of January 2, 1869, at 73,156,489 pesos. To the French – and to the ostensible cause of all the trouble, a certain Monsieur Jecker – Payno concluded that Mexico owed nothing at all. Whatever legitimate debt there may have been, he thought, had been amply repaid in blood and treasure. "At the sad end of the reign of Maximilian, the financial situation was worse because of what France had done than it had been when Señor Juárez suspended payment in 1861." It was, Payno thought, the most shameful spectacle that the nineteenth century had yet witnessed.[81] The problems created had only just begun.

Back to Business

The fall of the Second Empire and the reestablishment of the constitutional government in Mexico brought the issue of the London Debt to the forefront. At the conclusion of the Arroyo–Danó Convention, payments to the London bondholders ceased after July 1866 and the price of Mexican bonds fell to levels unseen since the conclusion of the War of 1847. In January 1867, the Foreign Office reiterated its support for the claims of the bondholders.[82] Who could have imagined that it would be two decades before the bondholders were to see *anything* again? In fact, the initial contacts between the bondholders and the Juárez government were generally cordial. As they should have been. During the French intervention, the bondholders had received more than a *million* pesos in dividends,

81 Payno, *Cuentas, Gastos, Acreedores y otros Asuntos del Tiempo de la Intervención Francesa y del Imperio*, pp. 817–819, 852, 918, 926.

82 *Times* (London), March 9, 1867. Payno, *Cuentas, Gastos, Acreedores y otros Asuntos del Tiempo de la Intervención Francesa y del Imperio*, pp. 47–48, shows that the convention ended funding. Mariano Ortiz de Montellano, *Apuntes para la liquidación de la deuda contraída en Londres* (México, 1886), central foldout: "Cuadro General de la Deuda..." indicates no payment in July 1866, but is mistaken.

but the conservatives had been defeated – if not once and for all, at least as soundly as the liberals might have hoped. In London, there was open speculation that Mexico would cede further territory to the United States in an effort to raise revenues or, even worse, become its protectorate. Exaggerated stories about sovereign Mexican loans raised privately in the United States made the rounds.[83] And so the London bondholders were stuck. There was no one else with whom to do business. Thus, the bondholders' new agent, W. W. Holmes, emphasized their desire to find a resolution acceptable to Mexico. Mexico's finance minister – Romero – reciprocated, explaining that Mexico had every intention of discharging its legitimate debts, something stability and growth would presumably render less burdensome. Nevertheless, Romero pointedly reminded the bondholders that they had dealt with Maximilian and acquiesced to the Conversion of 1864. Maximilian – a usurper, Romero emphasized – had no right to negotiate any conversion at all. The bondholders for their part responded, albeit disingenuously, that they had no other choice under the circumstances even though their share in the Convention of Miramar was negotiated in advance.[84]

As far as Payno was concerned, there were both practical and political reasons for considering the connection between the London Debt and the Second Empire. First, the terms of the Conversion of 1864 were far less favorable to Mexico than the Conversion of 1850. Second, the French had used an unfavorable exchange rate in converting franc and pound liabilities into pesos. But third, and perhaps most importantly, to recognize the legitimacy of the Conversion of 1864 was to recognize implicitly the other debts the French had assumed in occupying Mexico and supporting Maximilian. The nature of these claims involved not only the obnoxious expenses of maintaining an extravagant imperial court. They also involved sums expended in making war on and killing Mexicans, "the sacrifices made in resisting foreign forces [and in] rejecting the exaggerated and unjust pretensions of the Intervention."[85] As Mariano Ortiz de Montellano put it, the bondholders had "hitched their fate to an interloping government."[86] Thus was the issue joined.

By late 1868, there is evidence that positions were beginning to harden on both sides. One look at a memo prepared for Juárez, and his cabinet

---

83 *Times* (London), November 20, 1867.

84 W. W. Holmes to the finance minister, London, April 14, 1868, and July 1, 1868, *Deuda Exterior*, vol. 9, AGNM; Romero's general response to the Committee of Bondholders was published in *Times* (London), June 30, 1868.

85 Manuel Payno to the finance minister, October 14, 1868, *Deuda Exterior*, vol. 9, AGNM. Payno, *Cuentas, Gastos, Acreedores y otros Asuntos del Tiempo de la Intervención Francesa y del Imperio*, pp. 599–623.

86 Ortiz de Montellano, *Liquidación de la Deuda*, p. 78.

reveals the uncertainty and increasing edginess of the Mexican government. Under pressure from the bondholders to be flexible, Finance Minister Romero prepared a draft response full of corrections, emendations, redactions, and finally, in the margins, the notation "Didn't go out" (*No corrió*), in which President Juárez apparently took a hard line. By cooperating with Maximilian, the bondholders had provided the emperor with "moral support, to an extent" (*por haberle dado, hasta cierto punto, fuerza moral*) that had prolonged the conflict. Moreover, the authority to come to an agreement with the bondholders lay with the Congress under the Constitution of 1857. In any event, the financial condition of the country, once more battered by civil war, could hardly support the regular resumption of debt service. Inserting the dagger and twisting it sharply, Romero pointed to the forbearance of his friends in the United States, who were only too willing to give Mexico at least two years to resolve the outstanding claims of its nationals. "The example should not go unnoticed (*desapercibido*) by Mexico's other creditors." So much for Romero's hitherto emollient words to the bondholders.[87]

For their part, the bondholders dropped the solicitous tone that characterized earlier communications.[88] In the same file as Romero's memo, a copy of their response is to be found. It is as abrasive as anything that group had produced in the late 1830s or 1850s. Romero was simply wrong, they explained, by Mexican law, by international law, and by English law. It didn't matter whether, as they memorably put it, "Mexico had the misfortune to have had 20 usurpers in a year." The arrangement made with Maximilian "was absolutely in no sense a *new conversion of the debt*" [italics in original],[89] but simply a continuation of existing obligations that Mexico had undertaken, most recently in 1850, and raised to the status of an international agreement by the Dunlop and Aldham conventions. Hence, in yet another nasty twist of phrase, "they were subsequently recognized under the joint intervention of the three powers, France, Spain, and England." Under international law, Maximilian was de facto head of state in 1864. They had no business questioning his authority to do business or the source of the funds that he employed, for that matter. And, finally, under English

---

87 This remarkable document is in *Deuda Exterior*, vol. 9, AGNM. It has been renumbered at least five times, but the stamped folio numbers run from 409 through 417. A version finally went out to the bondholders' commissioner on December 28, 1868, under Romero's signature. It maintains the tough tone of the draft. *Times* (London), February 9, 1869.

88 "Extracto de la opinión de un eminente Jurisconsulto respecto de la posición legal de los tenedores de Bonos Mexicanos (1851 y 1864)."

89 George White of Baring Brothers in his masterful summary of the London Debt, written in 1872, refers to the operation in detail as the Conversion of 1864. White had represented the bondholders in Mexico. So the bondholders were repudiating the one agent who had really gotten them something. White deserved better.

law, Queen Victoria was head of state. She (in theory) made the decision about whom to recognize as legitimate sovereign, not the bondholders. So, then, if Romero had agreed that the London Debt was a legitimate one, the matter should be decided by negotiations between the Queen's ministers and the Juárez government. Publicly, at least, the Bondholders Committee stressed that "too much importance should not be attached to the views . . . expressed by the Mexican government." Their private communications suggest that they took them seriously indeed. Moreover, in Parliament and at the Foreign Office, the bondholders continued to press for the reopening of diplomatic relations with Mexico and rumors of an imminent settlement with Mexico appeared in the London press. The bondholders repeatedly raised the question of diplomatic relations with Mexico in the House of Commons, pressed the foreign secretary Lord Clarendon (1865–1866, 1868–1870) for guidance, and issued optimistic estimates of Mexico's fiscal capacity based on customs collections at Veracruz. For its part, the Foreign Office echoed the position of the bondholders' chapter and verse, suggesting that the Mexicans may have been at odds over how to proceed, but the British were not.[90]

Indeed, and perhaps most remarkably, the bondholders went directly to the Mexican Congress to complain about Juárez and Romero's position. Their commissioner, Edward J. Perry,[91] in an appearance before that body dismissed Romero's response of December 28, 1868, as "sterile" and "theoretical" inasmuch as it admitted some responsibility to the bondholders, but suggested that Mexico had the right to repay if and when it suited the country. Perry told the Congress that Mexico was ruining whatever financial standing it had internationally. Rhetorically, he asked what would have happened if the bondholders had trailed Juárez to the northern frontier to ask his authorization for them to be paid out of Veracruz customs. Scornfully, Perry said that the request would have been dismissed as "addled"

90 *Times* (London), February 9; May 11 and 18; June 11 and 22; July 30; September 10, 1869.

At least in public. The "Memorandum Relative to the Relations Existing between Great Britain and Mexico" found in the PRO is full of marginal comments disputing the official positions of the government. There must have been a vigorous debate in the Foreign Office, but good soldiers all its officials kept their disagreements private.

91 There was an E. J. Perry and an Edward J. Perry participating in several of the earlier diplomatic conventions. His experience in Mexican finance went back to the Pakenham Convention in 1842. He also had an interest of more than $30,000 in the Doyle Convention (1851), which placed him in the company of some of Mexico's biggest financiers. The obituary of Edward Perry, aged 60, appeared in the *Times* (London) on March 5, 1883, and characterized him as official agent of the Mexican bondholders and resident in Mexico for nearly forty years. A seasoned professional thus represented the bondholders. See "The Present Condition of Mexico," pp. 333–334. Perry is also profiled in *Report of the Mexican Bondholders' Committee, May 6, 1869* ([London], 1869), p. 3. (*habría padecido de demencia* is translated as "addled.")

and, quite justly, impossible under the circumstances. While much of Perry's argument turned on points of international law, he insisted that the bondholders' actions had not been "voluntary" and that the capitalization of interest in 1864 had not been their doing. Moreover, there could be no denying that the debt was Mexico's. It could not be subrogated to Austria or France by virtue of Maximilian's actions.[92]

Perry's appearance before the Congress had the desired effect. The Budget Committee allocated funds for repayment of the London Debt, but without specifically "earmarking" as such. But the "Executive," meaning Juárez and the cabinet, simply refused to spend the money. "Only the custom of seeing the most anomalous things that take place in [Mexico] can explain how it is that the Executive, which is only an administrative power, should dictate legislative measures."[93] As one member of the committee bitterly complained, Juárez had usurped legislative prerogative in refusing to comply with the budget the Congress had provided. Perry reiterated that the Budget Committee had tried to bury funds for the renewal of the London Debt service in a domestic appropriation of 3.5 million pesos "so as not to tie the hands of the Government."[94] Nothing happened.

Perry was no fool. He knew that Romero, Juárez, the cabinet, and elements of the Congress were at odds over what to do about the London Debt. Romero responded to Perry that he had raised the subject in cabinet, "and the observations you have made with respect to it have not made [Juárez] change his mind." Perry persisted. Was this simply Juárez acting out of personal animus against people he thought had aided Maximilian? No, Romero answered, this was not merely Juárez's opinion, but the collective sense of the cabinet. Given Mexico's financial condition and the fact that it still faced a deficit and had to contend with violent resistance in some quarters and Indian depredations in the North, "this is not the most appropriate time to resume payment of the debt" – a reply that Perry and the Committee of Bondholders simply interpreted as a desire on Romero's part to temporize.[95] In any event, the Congress passed everything on to the Commission on Public Credit and the budget, from whence a proposal was set to emanate. And in 1870, it did.[96]

---

92 See Perry's petition during the session of April 17, 1869, in Pantaleón Tovar, *Historia parlamentaria del Cuarto Congreso Constitucional* (4 vols., México, 1872–1874), vol. IV: pp. 174–179.

93 *Report of the Mexican Bondholders' Committee, May 6, 1869,* p. 42.

94 E. J. Perry to the finance minister, México, January 7, 1869, *Deuda Exterior,* vol. 9, AGNM. (*por no poner trabas al Gobierno* is translated "so as not to tie the hands of the government.")

95 *Report of the Mexican Bondholders' Committee, May 6, 1869,* p. 13.

96 Tovar, *Historia parlamentaria,* vol. IV: pp. 64, 66. Much of what is printed here as "Expediente sobre Reclamación de Bonos Mexicanos en Londres" (pp. 50–66) is based word for word on the documents that appear in *Deuda Exterior,* vol. 9.

A Proposed Resolution in 1871

To practical, worldly politicians like Romero, a resolution of the difficulties with the bondholders was not simply a matter of restoring Mexico's good name, much less of an abstraction termed "public credit." "When we reestablish confidence in the solvency of the Treasury and pay our debts religiously, our financial paper will be taken seriously once more, and hundreds of millions of pesos will go into circulation. Invested in material improvements, mining, and other branches of our national wealth, the face of the Republic will be changed not only suddenly, but surprisingly."[97] In other words, Romero and others like him were aware of the changes taking place in the international economy and of the transforming effect that substantial capital investments could have on every facet of a country's life. He had spent time in the United States as a diplomat during the Civil War. He knew only too well how much the productive capacity of its economy had grown when financed by both domestic *and* international savings. This, rather than an abstract notion of national honor, was what was at stake.[98]

Accordingly, Mexico showed some flexibility in the position it took with the bondholders. There were, of course, certain principles from which Romero would not deviate. He roundly condemned the policy, followed by numerous predecessors, of servicing the domestic or foreign debt according to the political pressures of the moment. This was manifestly unfair to holders of the internal debt, which, because it was essentially unfunded, had become virtually worthless. On the other hand, "foreign" paper, such as the English convention bonds, funded in principle by customs continued to circulate at around 80 percent of its face value. There could be only class of debt, Romero argued, and this was the "public debt" – an obligation that carried one, not multiple, coupon rates, preferably at around 3 percent. And Romero firmly adhered to the idea that having collected dividends from Maximilian, the bondholders could not demand their repayment from the republic. Perhaps most difficult of all, he insisted, in modern parlance is that the bondholders have a "haircut," a reduction in the principal owed to them, by some 50 percent. When the first of these plans became public in May 1870, the market reacted badly and Mexican bonds, already depressed, fell to even lower levels in the coming months.[99]

---

97 *Exposición que el Ejecutivo Federal dirige al congreso de la Unión el 1° de Abril de 1871 sometiéndole un proyecto de arreglo de la deuda pública* ... (México, 1871), p. 7.

98 *Exposición que el Ejecutivo Federal dirige... de arreglo de la deuda pública*, p. 8.

99 *Exposición que el Ejecutivo Federal dirige... de arreglo de la deuda pública*, pp. 9–39, esp. pp. 15, 44, 53–54. In fact, "A" was even worse than it seemed, because it not only proposed to reduce the principal of the London bonds outstanding by 50 percent, but to put half of that on a deferred basis until 1881. That meant only 25 percent of the outstanding debt would remain current, and on an

In any event, the bondholders were given (or devised) a choice of eight "bases" under which the London Debt would be reorganized. Having rejected plans based on Romero's conditions – especially the sharp reduction in capital – as far too stringent, an "unofficial" negotiation continued between the bondholders and the Ministry of Foreign Relations, a sort of "back-channel" negotiation that surfaced only when the resulting proposals were finished. The resulting tangle of proposals and counterproposals is not made any easier to decipher by an apparent misprint that claims that Perry, the bondholders' commissioner, considered one plan acceptable, but that the bondholders did not, while in a footnote, Perry is said instead to have rejected the plan. What is very clear from Perry's correspondence with Romero in 1871 is that neither he nor the bondholders considered Mexico's position acceptable and that he would prefer to take his chances with the Mexican Congress.[100] Nor did the Juárez government find anything about which to be pleased. And there things stood, at an impasse, in 1871, as in 1868, and for much the same reasons, with the additional complication of the upcoming presidential elections muddying the waters further. In June 1871, Juárez was "reelected under the shadow of the rebellion of La Noria, lead by Porfirio Díaz." A little more than a year later, Júarez was dead of a heart attack. Perry made very little progress thereafter with Juárez's successor, Sebastián Lerdo de Tejada, and in 1875, he openly admitted defeat "with positive mortification."[101]

Normalcy?

While Mexico's debt to the London bondholders was, *sensu strictu*, a different matter than Great Britain's renewal of its diplomatic relations with Mexico, in practice, it was unlikely that London and Mexico City would come to terms without an agreement on the bonds. For one thing, Juárez had made Mexico's position clear. Foreign powers that had recognized Maximilian violated neutrality and voluntarily suspended relations with the republic. Thus, it would fall to those powers to renew relations under conditions of Mexico's choosing. Moreover, all treaties and agreements with these states would have to be renegotiated on terms satisfactory to Mexico. By 1879, Germany, Italy, Spain, Portugal, Belgium, and Bulgaria had renewed

---

interest-paying basis. It is no surprise that the bondholders rejected this plan as far too draconian. It was probably the worst news they had since the initial default.

100 For example, E. J. Perry to the finance minister, México, March 21, 1871, *Deuda Exterior*, vol. 9, AGNM.

101 *Exposición que el Ejecutivo Federal dirige . . . de arreglo de la deuda pública*, p. 23, par. 59, and 59n; *Third Annual General Report of the Council of the Corporation of Foreign Bondholders . . . for the Year 1875* (London, 1876), p. 26.

relations. The United States had never recognized Maximilian, or rather had recognized the liberal government since April 1859. England and France, it seemed, were out in the cold, but in 1880, France dropped its opposition to certain Mexican demands for guarantees against financial claims resulting from the intervention. Relations were thereupon restored. Crucially, it seems, France feared that its diplomatic isolation from Mexico would merely cement its commercial isolation, conceding to the United States precisely what the now-departed Napoleon III had feared: economic domination.[102]

Why things took so much longer to work out with England is an interesting question. One could of course simply respond by saying that things took longer because so much more was at stake. The London Debt had always been by far the largest of Mexico's external obligations. Resuming payment would place Mexican fiscal resources under substantial strain, especially as the political environment turned volatile once more in the early 1870s, so that traditional fiscal disincentives continued to outweigh concerns about access to international capital markets. Yet, *mutatis mutandis*, the bondholders had the most to lose by a continued stalemate, and their concerns could not simply be ignored. There were other factors at work as well. Britain's traditional financial, political, and diplomatic influence within Mexico would continue to erode only after the Civil War in the United States was settled, and by the late 1870s, the United States had actually surpassed Great Britain as Mexico's principal trading partner. Ironically, the Franco-Mexican trade also continued to grow, and had been increasing rapidly since the late 1850s.[103] So a stalemate over bonds and diplomatic recognition could not have come at a worse time for British commercial interests, who recognized the threat posed to British exploitation of Mexico's "vast resources."[104] And finally, the beginnings of the great depreciation of silver, and the Mexican peso, had begun around 1876. While this inevitably prejudiced Mexico's net barter terms of trade, it also logically reduced the cost of acquiring Mexican assets, rendering foreign direct investment in Mexico increasingly attractive.[105] For Mexico too, the

---

102 Emilio Velasco to the secretary of foreign relations, Rome, September 4, 1879 (reservada), in Robaina, ed., *Reconciliación de México y Francia (1870–1880)*, p. 120, and more generally, pp. 13–39. Many of the government ministers in France when relations were restored had been outspoken critics of the Mexican adventure as well.

103 Richard J. Salvucci, "The Origins and Progress of United States-Mexico Trade, 1825–1884: 'Hoc opus, hic labor est'," *Hispanic American Historical Review*, 71: 4 (1991), p. 720; Linda K. and Richard J. Salvucci, "Cuba and the Latin American Terms of Trade: Old Theories, New Evidence," *Journal of Interdisciplinary History*, 31: 2 (2000), p. 212n.

104 *Times* (London), June 1, 1883; August 15, 1884.

105 Edward Beatty, "The Impact of Foreign Trade on the Mexican Economy: Terms of Trade and the Rise of Industry, 1880–1923," *Journal of Latin American Studies*, 32: 2 (2000), p. 409.

continuing depreciation of silver meant that the sterling value of Mexican indebtedness would rise, making a timely resolution of the London Debt more attractive to both sides. It may be worth examining a few of these factors in an effort to understand when and how a settlement, the Dublán Convention, finally took place.

As far as British concern over growing foreign competition for Mexican trade and commerce, one has, as usual, to look no farther than what the Foreign Office heard. As early as 1868, Doyle, now an old Mexico hand, had written in dismay over the state of affairs. "Commerce cannot flourish as Merchants will not send goods where no Consuls are to be found."[106] In 1877, a delegation of British merchants pressed the foreign secretary, Lord Derby, about the need to restore relations with Mexico.

The number of British merchants had much decreased of late years and the trade of England was passing into the hands of the Germans, who had a Minister there. Spain had also a Minister there, while France was to a certain extent represented in the person of her Consul. [The Marquis of Huntly] and the deputation believed that the presence of a British Minister in Mexico would strengthen confidence very materially and induce British capital to be invested in Mexican enterprise, for which there was a large field.[107]

Certainly, the renewal of Anglo-Mexican relations would ultimately do little or nothing to change the rise of U.S. preeminence in the Mexican market – a transformation due to geography, factor endowments, Mexican import substitution and a corresponding change in its demand for imports from cottons to capital goods. Yet Sandra Kuntz has confirmed the observation of the delegation to Lord Derby. Between 1870 and 1909, Mexico's imports from the United States would grow at 6.2 percent per year, while those from Britain would increase at a mere 0.8 percent. A similar pattern would hold for the period 1870–1929 as well. Britain was losing the Mexican market, and the British knew it.[108]

But even as the British saw the growth of international competition as an incentive to reach a settlement with Mexico, the circumstances facing Mexico, at least until the accession of Porfirio Díaz (1876), were somewhat less unambiguous. Coming to terms with the London Debt and restoring full diplomatic relations with Britain had one very large cost in the minds of Mexican ministers, and they were not shy about voicing their doubts.

---

106 Percy Doyle to W. W. Barron (private and confidential) London, July 31, 1868, FO 97/282, PRO.
107 "Our Relations with Mexico," *Times* (London), June 26, 1877.
108 See Sandra Kuntz Ficker, "El Comercio México–Estados Unidos, 1870–1929: Reconstrucción Estadística y Tendencias Generales," *Mexican Studies/Estudios Mexicanos*, 17: 1 (2001), esp. pp. 80–84.

Romero put the matter with lapidary simplicity in 1870. Since independence, Mexico's public finances had been in disorder. Deficits were covered only with "help from abroad" (*ministraciones del extranjero*). Mexico's needs, as he put it, were "plentiful" (*cuantiosas*), but its taxpayers were "few" (*corta*). Endless rebellions and civil wars had only made things worse. Now Romero came straight to the point.

> At other times what made this situation even worse was that the major, most flourishing part of public revenues had been alienated or promised to foreigner creditors and their governments. That we are now free of such complications doubtless gives reason for hope that if we take advantage of current circumstances, we may once and for all (*radicalmente*) fix the evils that otherwise led us to a bottomless abyss.

It is nearly impossible not to take Romero at his word: suspension of debt service as a de facto "bridge" loan to the construction of a new fiscal regime. From expediency to policy, courtesy of widows and orphans? The bondholders' flirtation with Maximilian had given Juárez the political cover to walk away from a problem that had afflicted Mexican leaders almost from the beginning, *la deuda eterna*.[109]

Of course, the circumstances that Juárez and his government faced in 1870 and 1871 were nothing, if not difficult, with rebellions involving first Trinidad García de la Cadena in San Luis Potosi and then, in the face of Juárez's "reelection," Díaz himself in Oaxaca, a more "national" movement to which other powerful political figures were drawn.[110] Romero was quick to emphasize the large diversion of resources needed to put down the rebellions (the figure of a million dollars is mentioned in passing), but it is also clear that the loss of resources provided by such ports as Mazatlán that were occupied by the rebels hurt. Constrained as he was by financial stringency, international market pressures, and domestic political necessity, Romero was playing a double game. He could not appear to be unreasonable, but it was unreasonable to suppose that he could resume debt service. As Romero put it, he was not willing to continue "sacrificing the future to the present."[111]

Nor, apparently, was he willing to "sacrifice" the interests of an important domestic political constituency to those of the foreign bondholders. This was, we have repeatedly seen, a defining aspect of who was paid, when,

---

109 México. Ministerio de Hacienda y Crédito Público, *Exposición que el Ejecutivo dirige al Congreso de la Unión... del Estado que Guarda la Hacienda Federal* (México, 1870), p. 6. This was a report "voluntarily" prepared by Romero to smooth over Juarez's assumption of sweeping powers in 1870.

110 Laurens Ballard Perry, *Juárez and Díaz: Machine Politics in Mexico* (DeKalb, IL, 1978).

111 México. Ministerio de Hacienda y Crédito Público. *Exposición que el Ejecutivo Federal Dirige al Congreso de la Unión... del Estado que Guarda la Hacienda Federal en 1° de Abril de 1872* (México, 1872), pars. 1–11; *Memoria de Hacienda* (México, 1868), p. 41.

and why. With domestic politics in a state of flux, Romero consciously allocated the resources available to those who could be said to have formed the fiscal base of Juarismo during the intervention, creditors who were mostly, if not exclusively, domestic. As Francisco Calderón has argued, "the floating debt originated primarily during the Intervention, for which reason it was considered sacrosanct. The creditors were the same people who had supplied the [Liberal] army or who had themselves participated."[112] Thus, the *floating internal* debt was serviced in preference to the consolidated debt, to whose holders – whoever they were – the liberals felt less indebted.

In much the same way, what monies had been raised in the United States, mostly through small (effectively less than 3 million pesos) private placements, were made the preferred object of repayment as well and continued so as late as 1880. Thus the decision about whom to pay was also a decision about to whom the liberal government owed its existence in 1870. Here, naturally the British did not figure.[113] The calculation would inevitably change as post–intervention governments reduced their domestic borrowing. By the 1880s, the domestic debt was far less of a factor, and its political constituency correspondingly reduced.

Marcello Carmagnani has called this process a "fiscal aspect of economic convergence." By this he simply means that the desire of post–Maximilian regimes to gain international financial legitimacy (especially with the Europeans) drove falling fiscal deficits, *at least in the long run*. Iglesias, for example, points out that the restored republic reduced the active military from eighty thousand to eighteen thousand men and made a serious effort to prevent local military commanders from appropriating Treasury funds. A host of other administrative economies were undertaken as well.[114] Budget figures for this period appear a bit shaky, but Carmagnani is clearly on to something when he concludes that "[before 1867] all budgets had shown deficits [but] . . . in the following period of 1867–1911, when only 25 budgets (56.8) percent were negative [*sic*]."[115] As a consequence, in 1868, the domestic debt was 112 percent of the foreign debt. By 1880,

112 Francisco R. Calderón, "La Hacienda Pública," in Daniel Cosío Villegas, ed., *Historia Moderna de México* (8 vols., México, 1955–1965), vol. 2: p. 391.

113 *Memoria de Hacienda . . . 1880* (México, 1881), p. xii; "Segundo contrato del general Carvajal," New York, September 11, 1865, in *Correspondencia de la Legación Mexicana en Washington Durante La Intervención Extranjera, 1860–1868* (10 vols., México, 1871), vol. 5: pp. 621–622; *Contratos hechos en los Estados Unidos por los Comisionados de México durante los años 1865 y 1866* (México, 1868), esp. pp. 486–487.

114 José María Iglesias, *Autobiografía* (1893; 3rd ed., México, 2004), pp. 28–32.

115 Carlos Marichal and Marcello Carmagnani, "Mexico: From Colonial Fiscal Regime to Liberal Financial Order, 1750–1912," in Michael D. Bordo and Roberto Cortés-Conde, eds., *Transferring Wealth and Power from the Old to the New World* (New York, 2001), pp. 306, 312. An interesting contemporary comment on the reliability of fiscal data appears in Ángel M. Domínguez, "Memoria Estadística sobre las Rentas Públicas de la Nación," *Boletín de la Sociedad de Geografía y Estadística de la República Mexicana* (1890), pp. 572–582.

when the British began serious efforts to reestablish relations with Mexico, the domestic debt was 67 percent of the foreign debt – a decline of some 40 percent. It is clear that serious measures were taken to reduce government spending.[116]

As a proportion of GDP, the decline is even more striking: from about 26 percent of GDP to about 10 percent.[117] One speculates that this must have been the smallest share of total output claimed by the internal debt at almost any time since 1800. For sure, this was a moment – an opportunity – and it would pass, as Carmagnani freely admits. As we will see, budget problems nearly derailed the settlement anyway. Thus in terms of the opposition to a settlement from domestic interests, for Díaz, this was a question of *carpe diem*, and seize the moment Díaz did.

A balanced budget was then a prerequisite for resuming substantial payments to the British bondholders.[118] During the 1870s and 1880s, Mexico's ability to produce a balanced budget emerged by fits and starts, in much the same way negotiations with the British would proceed. In early 1875, for instance, one British informant declared, "there is great opposition in the Chambers [of Deputies] towards making any arrangement towards paying part interest of the debt, on the pretence that the country cannot afford it." By the spring of 1876, the market price of Mexican bonds fell to its lowest level of the nineteenth century, a scant 5.

This may very well have been a reflection of how politically divisive in Mexico the London Debt had become. In Díaz's *Plan de Tuxtepec* (March 21, 1876), Díaz explicitly condemned any recognition of the debt as "immoral" and accused Sebastián Lerdo de Tejada's government of planning to do just that. "In Mexico, there is no compensation for damages caused by the Intervention."[119] Indeed, Díaz did not and perhaps could not establish a commission to study the issue of resolving the foreign debt until 1880, the last year of his first administration, for the debt seems to have become the Mexican equivalent of "waving the bloody shirt." For practical purposes, Mexico's London Debt would remain worthless until the domestic fiscal situation could be stabilized, which is to say, until the early 1880s. Even then the stability was subject to sudden, large disturbances.

Nor, for all that, did things move quickly from the British side, at least publicly. Unofficial contact between Mexico and Britain regarding the reestablishment of diplomatic relations appears to have taken place in

116 Assuming that Carmagnani figures are correct. In an address to Congress of June 2, 1883, Diputado Genaro Raygosa put the internal debt at 20 million pesos and the foreign debt at 89 million, an even lower ratio than Carmagnani indicates. See *El Monitor Republicano*, June 7, 1883.

117 For GDP figures, I use http://biblioteca.itam.mx/recursos/ehm.html#pib (accessed July 24, 2007).

118 *Memoria de Hacienda . . . 1880* (México, 1881), pp. 45–52, for this and what follows on Diaz.

119 See the text in Román Iglesias González, *Planes Políticos, Proclamas, Manifiestos y Otros Documentos de la Independencia al México Moderno, 1812–1940* (México, 1998), p. 487.

Paris late in 1880 through the Mexican minister there. By early 1881, the British government had taken steps to determine "to find out from the Mexican government itself whether there is any real desire to renew relations with Great Britain."[120] The decisive change in Mexico, nevertheless, would originate on the demand side in the desire of the federal government to reenter the international capital markets. The Mexican minister in Paris, Velasco, reported that his government "was bent upon making railroads and upon developing the resources of the country. Now to carry his plans into effect he must attract foreign capital to Mexico; while in order to attract foreign capital, it would be necessary to reestablish the credit of the country and this could not be done *without coming to an equitable settlement with the present creditors*"[121] [italics mine]. Rail development in Mexico in the 1880s, when trackage increased ninefold, provided the proximate cause for the resolution of an issue that had dragged on for six decades. In 1880, Mexico had less than 10 percent of the total stock of track in Latin America. By 1890, the share had risen to 25 percent.[122]

Another factor weighing on Mexican policy, according to the same source, was Mexico's felt desire to counterbalance the growing influence of the United States in Mexican economic affairs. This influence, to which we previously alluded, had become considerably more substantial by the 1880s than it had been even a decade earlier, with the U.S. share of merchandise trade reaching nearly 50 percent by the end of the decade.[123] As Velasco put it, "the one consideration, the one anxiety which overruled all others in the minds of Mexicans was . . . the independence of their country from encroachments from their all-powerful neighbor."[124] This was at almost precisely the moment that a treaty of commercial reciprocity with Mexico was being considered in the United States, a treaty that regarded "Mexico and the United States as integral parts of one commercial system."[125] So the

120 Lord Lyons (British minister to France) to the foreign secretary, Paris, December 14, 1880, and Lord Tenterden (permanent undersecretary, 1873–1882) to the British minister in Paris, [London] February 18, 1881, in *Correspondence Respecting the Renewal of Diplomatic Relations with Mexico, 1880–1883* ([London], 1884), pp. 3, 9.

121 Lord Lyons to the foreign secretary, Paris, December 28, 1880, in *Correspondence Respecting the Renewal of Diplomatic Relations with Mexico*, p. 8. This point is also emphasized by Priscilla Connolly, *El contratista de don Porfirio. Obras públicas, deuda y desarrollo desigual* (México, 1997), p. 87. She refers to the settlement as "absolutely indispensable" for attracting fresh funds on p. 119.

122 For a convenient survey, see William R. Summerhill, "The Development of Infrastructure," in Victor Bulmer-Thomas, John Coatsworth, and Roberto Cortés Conde, eds., *The Cambridge Economic History of Latin America* (2 vols., 2006), vol. 2: pp. 302, 305.

123 Kuntz Ficker, "El Comercio México–Estados Unidos, 1870–1929," p. 82.

124 Viscount Lyons to the foreign secretary, Paris, January 10, 1882, in *Correspondence Respecting the Renewal of Diplomatic Relations with Mexico*, p. 48.

125 Speech of Hon. Abram S. Hewitt of New York, February 27, 1885, 48th Cong., 2nd sess., *Congressional Record*, 16, Appendix 172.

notion of using restored relations with Great Britain as a way of diversifying trade with the United States was very much on the minds of ministers in Mexico.

By spring 1883, it is clear that commercial interests in Great Britain were all but unanimous in urging the Foreign Office to reestablish diplomatic relations with Mexico. In a remarkable petition to the foreign secretary, the Association of Chambers of Commerce of the United Kingdom attributed much of the commercial success of the United States in the Mexican market to Great Britain's absence of diplomatic relations with Mexico, "a very serious disadvantage." The situation regarding Mexican trade the Association characterized as "disastrous and anomalous," and even more remarkably, "the Association cannot regard the bondholders' claims as being a bar to diplomatic relations, or a just and conclusive ground under any circumstances for disregarding the commercial interests of Great Britain in which Her Majesty's subjects are so largely involved." This was seemingly the first time that anyone accused the government of putting the interests of British finance ahead of trade and industry, but it would certainly not be the last.[126]

Private negotiations would, then, consume the better part of the following year. In principle, the British decision to initiate discussions weakened their bargaining position, but accurately reflected growing British commercial interests. At precisely the time that Sir Spenser St. John was appointed Special Envoy (May 29, 1883) to Mexico to carry on negotiations, the British vice-consul at Havana, Lionel Carden, was in Mexico carrying out an unprecedented survey of Mexican resources, commercial policy, trade, and the like. So, if as the foreign secretary – Earl Granville (1870–1874, 1880–1885) – admitted, "Her Majesty's Government desire to take a first step towards the renewal of diplomatic relations,"[127] it was a calculated policy of *reculer pour mieux sauter*. The British were especially anxious that recognition not be made contingent on a solution to the London Debt, a position they feared the Mexicans would adopt. Ignacio Mariscal, the secretary of foreign affairs (1880–1883, 1885–1910), assured them that it was not.[128] From that point on, the negotiations for the settlement of the London Debt as opposed to those relating to the reestablishment of diplomatic relations were essentially separate affairs.

126 Or as Winston Churchill famously put it after the return to the gold standard in 1925, "I would rather see Finance less proud and Industry more content." See D. E. Moggridge, *British Monetary Policy 1924–1931* (Cambridge, UK, 1972), p. 76.

127 Earl Granville to the secretary of foreign relations, [London], April 19, 1883, in *Correspondence Respecting the Renewal of Diplomatic Relations with Mexico*, p. 70.

128 Memorandum by Lord Fitzmaurice, [London], August 1, 1883, in *Correspondence Respecting the Renewal of Diplomatic Relations with Mexico*, p. 122.

The first public indications of change took place when the Mexican National Congress was inaugurated by President Manuel González and at the Queen's Speech at the opening of Parliament. In the Queen's Speech, read by the Lord Chancellor on February 5, 1884, a brief paragraph was inserted that read, "Arrangements are in progress for the resumption of diplomatic relations with Mexico, and Special Envoys have been dispatched by each Government to promote that end."[129] González had alluded to the same thing in identical terms in his message: "The Envoys were appointed on the 29th May in accordance with [an] Agreement."[130] But more importantly, González revealed that the Mexican government had made another proposal to the London bondholders and, no less significantly, was seeking to contract a loan of up to $20,000,000.

Inevitably, the prospect of an agreement, however remote, had a dramatic effect on the market for Mexican bonds. By late 1879, Mexican bonds were quoted at 10. There seems to be little doubt that however "secret" the communication between Great Britain and Mexico ostensibly was, word had somehow gotten out. Market quotations jumped 50 percent between December 1880 and January 1881, from 18 to 27, almost precisely the time at which back-channel negotiations had begun – and this was true of the price relative to British consols as well. By the moment that British businessmen were openly pushing the Foreign Office to resume relations with Mexico, the bonds had pushed into the low 30s. But they would get no higher, at least for a while. Again, the coincidence between what was occurring behind the scenes and what the London Stock Exchange "knew" is little short of astounding. Once British and Mexican diplomats had agreed that the reestablishment of diplomatic relations *did not require* an agreement on the London Debt to be reached simultaneously, bond prices started to recede. Not even the "public" announcement of negotiations in the Queen's Speech (nor González's somewhat earlier disclosure) could arrest the fall. If these discussions were, in fact, supposed to be secret, they were – at best – a secret badly kept.[131]

The fact that negotiations with the Committee of Mexican Bondholders were to proceed on a separate track from those involving diplomatic relations did not mean that Mexico assigned any less importance to them. To the contrary, President González sent his personal secretary, Carlos Rivas, to Paris in April 1883 to respond to an informal settlement advanced by

---

129 *Times* (London), February 6, 1884.

130 See *Correspondence Respecting the Renewal of Diplomatic Relations with Mexico*, p. 151.

131 British correspondence manifests a concern with secrecy that is hard to understand. Since a separate negotiation was taking place over the settlement of the London Debt, it would stand to reason that the issues of the debt and recognition had been separated. Any bondholder would have known that – or, at least, any senior member of the Committee of Bondholders.

the leadership of the Committee of Bondholders the preceding fall, something Rivas had accomplished within a month.[132] A sharp increase in bond prices followed – some 20 percent between April and May – so the broader market responded favorably to the Mexican offer. The chairman and vice-chairman of the committee had recommended a debt settlement of £18 million, with £2 million deducted for "all the expenses connected with the recognition." The dividend was to commence at 1 percent in the first year, and thereafter to be incrementally raised to 3 percent after six years "should the resources of Mexico prove sufficient." The only items to be recognized as legitimately convertible were the bonds originating in the conversions of 1850 and 1864 (suggesting the influence of Glynn Mills on the committee, since Payno had already emphatically denied the legitimacy of the Conversion of 1864). Rivas was (so he claimed) authorized to revise and enlarge the bondholders' informal proposal.[133] What resulted from this process was "substantially different," a settlement of £20 million with £4.7 million to be deducted to pay off outstanding convention bonds (£2 million) and the remainder expected to cover costs of approximately 1 percent. Significantly, the new issue was scheduled to mature in 1903, but Mexico retained the right to purchase bonds at a maximum of 50 percent of their market price. All dividends were due in London and payable in sterling to avoid exchange risk.[134]

On the face of it, Mexico had obtained a remarkably favorable agreement from the Committee of Bondholders, or its leadership, at least. So favorable, indeed, that a disinterested observer might wonder exactly what the committee was thinking. Essentially, it had accepted a deal based on the Conversion of 1850 and the arrears of interest on the 3 percents it issued from 1867 through 1883. This the Mexicans calculated at $76.5 million. Now, in 1869, Payno had, on the basis of painstaking calculations, put the London Debt at $73 million, after discounting what had transpired during the intervention. *What the bondholders had agreed to in 1883 was less in nominal terms than Payno had fixed in 1869!* And this ostensibly *included* the arrears of interest accrued since 1867, which, in effect, were written off entirely. The bondholders were also conceding that Mexico would never pay more than 50 for bonds it purchased on the open market even though they had already doubled to 33 during negotiations – from 1881 to 1883.

132 *Times* (London), September 20, 1883; Ortiz de Montellano, *Apuntes Para la Liquidación de la Deuda Contraída en Londres* p. 411–415. The initial negotiations were handled by Jesús Cervantes, probably an associate of Rivas from Jalisco. *Times* (London), May 19, 1883.

133 The historian of Manuel González's presidency, Don Coerver, suggests that González tried to distance himself from Rivas' work by claiming that Rivas lacked negotiating authority. See Don M. Coerver, *The Porfirian Interregnum: The Presidency of Manuel González of Mexico, 1880–1884* (Ft. Worth, Texas, 1979), pp. 258–259n.

134 Ortiz de Montellano, *Deuda de México Contraída en Londres*, pp. 411–418.

So one could conclude that if the prospects for Mexico were as glowing as the leadership of the Committee of Bondholders suggested, further appreciation was likely – gains that the Committee of Bondholders had agreed to foreswear. For Mexico, it was a triumph of what had become known as the "Juárez doctrine," the idea that the intervention had effectively invalidated any agreements that the belligerents had previously signed. No one, of course, said as much. But, in essence, this was what had occurred.

There is one very large mystery surrounding the fate of the Sheridan–Rivas proposal. The mystery is twofold and can be expressed quite simply: Why would the British bondholders ever accept such an agreement, indeed praising its "handsome terms"?[135] And why would the government of González, having negotiated what could only be described as remarkably generous terms, ultimately abandon the agreement, as it did? To be sure, there were individual bondholders who were highly critical of what the committee had negotiated, and one particularly astute investor, a certain Captain Pavy,

maintained that every word [of the Sheridan–Rivas proposal] was against the bondholders accepting the proposal. They were asked to accept 3 percent, to cut off nearly the whole of their back interest and nearly the whole of their capital. He objected to the Mexican government having the power to buy or draw the bonds at 50 percent of their nominal value.

Another Mr. Bulman observed that Mexico was being treated "as if she were a bankrupt state," which Mexico was not. But the leadership of the Committee of Bondholders seemed determined to ignore any opposition to the proposal and moved that a resolution supporting it should be carried unanimously.

Trying to uncover the reasons for such a strange turn of events is, unfortunately, almost all speculation. The recent and definitive study of the bondholders themselves provides some data on the composition of the Committee of Bondholders at the time, but accurately admits that we know very little about who the bondholders were in the 1880s, let alone anything about a "typical" one.[136] The leadership of the Committee of Bondholders had always been subject to the charge that it represented the great and the good, those with large sums at risk, or those whose positions were largely speculative. The Select Committee of the House of Commons on Loans

---

135 *Times* (London), May 19, 1883, for discussion of the proposal.
136 Costeloe, *Bonds and Bondholders*, pp. 231, 234–235, 294. Trollope's *The Way We Live Now* was published in 1875. Augustus Melmotte's great phantom project was, emblematically, the South Central Pacific and Mexican Railway, which would "civilize" Mexico by linking it to California. The Mexican debt question also outlived Anthony Trollope, who died in 1882.

to Foreign States indeed heard one witness declare that "90 out of 100 transactions in Mexican stock are gambling transactions."[137] It would be easy to tell a kind of Trollopian story in which a group of monied men, speculators, some with Parliamentary connections, or even in Parliament, used their connections, wealth, and influence to buy the Mexican bonds when they were nearly worthless, only to sell them at substantial profits once the possibility of British recognition of Mexico and new funding had been realized. For such people, virtually any settlement *could* have been profitable, for these were not the long-suffering bona fide investors whose tales of woe had graced the columns of London's newspapers from the 1830s onward. Sunk cost or no, any individual who had somehow managed to hold on to Mexican bonds for more than twenty years (for the clock began ticking again only in 1867) might very well have felt defrauded and deceived.

But, of course, twenty years is a long time. Thirty is longer. And sixty is longer still. Perry, who had represented the bondholders in their negotiations with Mexico after the intervention, would not live to see the final resolution of the debt, but he had been born in the 1820s, more or less coincident with the original issue of the Barclay and Goldschmidt loans. It was thus very unlikely that there were many original holders of the bonds left alive in 1884, although, to be sure, the bonds sometimes stayed in certain families after the death of the original purchaser. But again, it is difficult to know how outraged a third-generation bondholder might have felt over his or her grandparents' loss in the 1830s: opportunity cost is not subject to infinite regress. There was clearly some division over whether or not the Sheridan–Rivas proposal was in *everyone's* best interest. It is pretty clear that it was in the best interests of the leadership of the Committee of Bondholders, who passed it over dissenting voices.

It is, then, *possible* to think of a plausible explanation for the conduct of the British in 1883. What is a bit harder to justify is the conduct of Mexico, which on the face of it seems almost *impossible* to understand. Don Coerver, the historian of the González presidency, suggests that the timing of the agreement embarrassed González, for it demonstrated that the prior negotiations had taken place without the requisite congressional approval, which occurred only after word of the agreement reached Mexico.[138] This may well have been part of the problem, for one of the explanations offered at the time for congressional opposition to agreement was that it simply provided González's antagonists with an issue around which to rally. Another was

---

137 *Times* (London), April 30, 1875.
138 Coerver, *Porfirian Interregnum*, pp. 245–247, 258–259; *El Siglo Diez y Nueve*, November 14, 21, 1887. For a guide to what follows, the November 1887 *Siglo Diez y Nueve* is a useful, if partisan, guide. Apart from what is cited, see especially November 4, 8, 15, 21, and 29.

that *porfiristas* in the Congress believed the debt should now be left to Díaz to settle, particularly once it was obvious that Díaz would be president again in 1884. But perhaps a more compelling reason for Mexico's stalling not just in 1883, but through 1885, was the state of the macroeconomy. The international effects of the Panic of 1883 hit Mexico hard, and the finances of the federal government, delicately balanced at best, deteriorated quickly. The fiscal deficit ballooned to 14 million pesos in 1883–1884, which, if one trusts the numbers, was in absolute terms the worst it had been in sixty years, and the government again resorted to seigniorage as it had in the 1830s to make ends meet. A report written for the Committee of Bondholders on the state of the economy labeled the financial situation in 1884 a "disaster" and blamed rising federal expenditures and disturbances associated with opening the economy for what had occurred.[139] Whatever the political costs of an agreement with Great Britain, they would be high; or however corrupt the González administration might be, the obstacle to reaching an agreement with the Committee of Bondholders, even a very favorable one, was the state of public finance. Mexico might well agree to a settlement in 1883 or 1884, but the prospects of Mexico resuming payment under the international financial circumstances of the day were virtually nil. But this is getting ahead of the story.

The official explanation from Mexico was that the agreement negotiated by Rivas did not conform in detail to the guidelines that congressional legislation had specified. Specifically, the amount scheduled for conversion exceeded the outstanding value of the 1851 3 percents, and was therefore excessive. The clause allowing Mexico to redeem the converted bonds at 50 percent of par was apt to depress the market value of the issue even further. The internal and external debt must be dealt with in an evenhanded fashion. And there was to be absolutely no provision made for converting the 1864 issue made under Maximilian's government, since only obligations recognized as legitimate by the republic were to be included. The government's rejection of the Sheridan–Rivas proposal contained some extraordinary language, especially referring to errors committed by past Mexican administrations and to the reluctance of Mexico to do anything that would cast doubt on its probity and seriousness in international financial markets. This, presumably, related to the £4.7 million in additional funds that were earmarked to pay off the "expenses" of conversion, something that

139 http://biblioteca.itam.mx/recursos/ehm.html#finanzas (accessed September 13, 2007), table 17.3.1; and E. Kozhevar, *Informe Sobre la República Mexicana* (México, 1887), p. 57. For more on the impact of 1884, see "Informe del Consejo de Administración," 14 de Abril de 1885, in Luis Cerda, ed., *Historia Financiera del Banco Nacional de México. Porfiriato 1884–1910* (2 vols., México, 1997), vol. 2: p. 519; and "The Mexican Economy in 1884," in *Review of the Economic Situation of Mexico*, 60: 703 (1984), pp. 175–216.

contemporary foreign observers openly called the "stealing clause" of the agreement. The reputation of the González's government for profligacy, corruption, and outright dissolution had apparently forced this quaint *nostra culpa* into the official record. And, indeed, doubts as to what exactly the purpose of the £4.7 million was later said to have been the principal reason that the Sheridan–Rivas proposal failed.[140]

The London market reacted predictably to circumstances. Mexican bonds fell 37 percent between June and December 1883. "[I]t is generally understood that the negotiations upon the basis proposed by [Rivas] are at an end and that the business will be undertaken upon different lines and under the direction of other houses and intermediaries than have up to the present time been concerned in the matter." So with those words, the Sheridan–Rivas proposal was declared dead, the very public protest of the Committee of Bondholders notwithstanding. The outcome of the negotiations, diplomatic niceties aside, would later be termed a "fiasco."[141]

The Battles of the Mountain and the Plain

With the failure of the Sheridan–Rivas proposal, the focus of public interest turned to Eduardo Noetzlin and to an eponymous agreement that would remedy the defects of its predecessor. The reaction to this proposal, the Sheridan–Noetzlin Agreement, was of historic proportions in Mexico. The debate ended in gunshots outside the Chamber of Deputies and disorder within. Troops were called out to quell student disturbances, and photos from the era reveal the distinctly confident, comfortably bourgeois mien of some of the youthful scholars imprisoned. Since President-Elect Díaz had a history of opposition to a settlement, and was rumored to be no less opposed to the one at hand, the historian inevitably speculates how "spontaneous" the demonstrations had been.[142] But even more arresting than the circumstances of the debate or than of the Noetzlin–Sheridan proposal itself, which we will examine in due course, was the *substance* of the debate. A Joint Committee of Finance and Public Credit had been appointed to present a study to the Chamber of Deputies on the history of the London Debt beginning, as it were, in the beginning. And so on

---

140 Ortiz de Montellano, *Apuntes Para la Liquidación de la Deuda Contraída en Londres*, pp. 447–459; *Times* (London), September 13, 1884; [T. S. Van Dyke], "Mexican Politics," *Harper's New Monthly Magazine* (October 1885), pp. 761–769, with p. 765 for the phrase "stealing clause." Strictly speaking, the phrase was applied to the Sheridan–Noetzlin proposal, described later. If so, it applies, a fortiori, to the Sheridan–Rivas proposal as well.

141 *Times* (London), December 7, 12, and 14, 1883; and February 18, 1884.

142 "Mexico's Debts," *The Nation*, August 13, 1885, pp. 129–130; "Mexican Politics," pp. 766–768; Alejandro Rivas and José Manuel Villalpando, *Los Presidentes de México* (México, 2001), p. 125, for a striking sepia photograph of a group of students apprehended.

November 7, 1884, there commenced the first reading of a report that would ultimately form the basis of Joaquín Casasus' *Historia de la Deuda Contraída en Londres* (México, 1885), a work rightly regarded as the seminal study of the question. But the committee's report differed somewhat in tone from Casasus' by-no-means-dispassionate account of events.[143] What made the committee's report so explosive was its open analysis, whose style might be best described as "let the chips fall where they may." After briefly describing the Barclay, Herring, Richardson and Goldschmidt loans, default, the conversions of 1830, 1837, and 1850, the committee concluded that

it has always been said that the debt had an unseemly origin, that it was undertaken in iniquitous circumstances, and that the lenders delivered a few thousand old rifles, two broken-down boats, and the remains of English army uniforms. Added to this, there was an issue of fraudulent bonds, and they made the Republic pay both what it owed and it didn't.

There was a brief account of independence, the accompanying flight of capital, and the need for "sovereignty." "The first friend of Mexico was England. Mexico went not to its government, but to its subjects with the idea of obtaining the sums needed for the economic establishment of the State. This was the origin of the debt, and presented in its historical context, no one can find anything corrupt about it." As far as stories about old guns, broken-down ships, and useless uniforms are concerned, "this was always a grotesque slander to divert and distract the masses. The English Stock [Exchange] has always been honorable . . . [and not] some 'gyp joint' (*baratillo*) set up to swindle foreign governments." If there had been any swindling, "the [Mexican] Government had been despoiled by its own agents; the bondholders had nothing to do with the distribution of the proceeds of the loans – which is as it should be." The report went on to mention the events of the 1840s, the scandals surrounding the Conversion of 1846, and the remarkable twists and turns of several governments desperate for funds. Before turning to the Conversion of 1850, the report emphasized that none of these shenanigans were the bondholders' doings. The principal reason why the debt had exploded was "failure to make timely interest payments, which has occasioned various capitalizations." There was only one way to avoid such fiscal disasters: pay what you owed when due. Do not capitalize arrears.

When the committee considered what opposition there could be to resolving the impasse, it pointed to the evident change that had taken

143 *Diario de los Debates de la Cámara de Diputados. Año de 1884* (México, 1884), vol. 1, pp. 178–182, for this and what follows. [Hereafter, *Diario 1884*, with relevant pages.] (*puede descubrir una impureza* is translated as "find anything corrupt about it.")

place in the Mexican economy between 1863 and 1883, and especially to the financial deepening that had occurred. There were, the committee averred, more than 400 million pesos in outstanding capital in Mexican banking, mining, agricultural colonization, and railroads. The resolution of the public debt in all its aspects was an integral part of the development of financial markets that Mexico now required if progress were to be institutionalized. If some were demanding that the internal debt be placed on an equal footing as the international, that was a reasonable demand. And even if the Treasury was passing through a rough patch in 1884, the committee predicted that it would be past it in five months. None of these were compelling reasons for delaying a settlement with English creditors any longer.[144]

The settlement to which the committee was referring was twofold: one diplomatic and the other financial. The Sheridan–Noetzlin proposal[145] formed the basis of the financial settlement, and had been substituted for the now-defunct Sheridan–Rivas proposal. The Sheridan–Noetzlin proposal was based on the Conversion of 1850 and consisted mostly of the capital of the conversion (£10,241,650), arrears of interest from January 1, 1867 through January 1, 1885 (£5,684,115), and that part of the Conversion of 1864 that represented unpaid interest on the Conversion of 1850 from July 1, 1851, through July 1, 1873 (£2,918,880). New bonds worth £17,200,000 were to be issued, with coupon rates gradually increasing from 2 to 3 percent. Of this £17 million, £14.5 million were to be used to fund the conversion; the remainder was earmarked for fees and costs. Again, Mexico retained the option of purchasing the bonds at 50 percent. So while part of the Conversion of 1864, notoriously carried out during the intervention, was admitted to conversion through a technicality, and while the discretionary funds for expenses had been reduced even further, the capital funded through the Sheridan–Noetzlin (£14.5 million) proposal was even *less* than the Sheridan–Rivas (£15.2 million). For Mexico, things had only gotten better. For Great Britain, it seemed things could only get worse: as one pained writer to the *Times* (London) put it, "no good will come to Mexico or the Bondholders by the present scheme." Mexico celebrated by restoring diplomatic relations with Britain on September 17, 1884, by offering to pay *at most* about 70 percent of what it owed, and most likely, a

---

144 *Diario 1884*, pp. 185–189.

145 *Diario 1884*, pp. 191–195. Also see Ortiz de Montellano, *Apuntes Para la Liquidación de la Deuda Contraída en Londres*, pp. 461–472, which shows the various iterations the proposal went through from June to November 1884 before reaching Mexico for debate. The Sheridan–Noetzlin agreement was (accurately) criticized at a meeting of the bondholders in London as "infinitely worse" than the Sheridan–Rivas proposal. It passed anyway. See *Times* (London), September 25, 1884. Also see "Debt of the Republic of Mexico in London," London, September 18, 1884, *Deuda Exterior*, vol. 9, AGNM.

good deal less. At the prices current on the London Exchange in September 1884, the offer was worth about 35 percent of what the Mexicans owed.[146]

Another element in the Sheridan–Noetzlin proposal was the role of the Banco Nacional de Mexico (BNDM) and of its founder Noetzlin.[147] The BNDM was one of the crucial links in the chain of financial institutions that ultimately engineered Mexico's reentry into the international credit markets. While the BNDM had no obligation to lend to the government of Mexico, it nevertheless did so and maintained a current account on its behalf, as well as a close working relationship with the Finance Ministry. Effectively, the BNDM financed a significant share of the federal government's budget. Under González, the BNDM seems to have retained a significant degree of independence, although González himself owed the BNDM a considerable sum of money.

The BNDM was given a role in the Sheridan–Noetzlin proposal. At a basic level, it was to act as a collection agent for the government, receiving 10 percent of the customs for the purpose of making dividend payments. But the function of the BNDM went well beyond that and came to absorb some of the functions that the Mexican Financial Agency in London had exercised for earlier issues. The BNDM ultimately purchased bonds for its own portfolio, so it was exposed to a substantial political risk, as Luis Cerda is at pains to explain. Whether this would make subsequent defaults more or less likely is arguable, but for whatever the reason, a mechanism subjecting Mexicans to the effects of a sovereign default was now clearly in place: an impairment in the bank's assets would require a corresponding reduction in its liabilities, such as the notes it issued.[148]

It would be hard to think of a previous occasion, other than in the early 1820s, when the merits of Mexico's participation in the international financial markets were discussed in greater detail, with more acuity or with more impassioned rhetoric, than they were to be in November 1884. The gallery was noisy, sometimes interfering with the speakers. Some of the speakers were among the notable figures of the mid- to late nineteenth century: Salvador Díaz Mirón, poet; Guillermo Prieto, now 70 years of age,

---

146 The preliminary agreement was signed on August 6, 1884. It reached Mexico by late October. See Edourd Noetzlin to the finance minister, Paris, October 1, 1884, *Deuda Exterior*, vol. 9, AGNM.
  The Oaxacan Ignacio Mariscal presented his credentials to Queen Victoria in early December. She had, presumably, recovered from her irritation at the Mexicans for shooting Maximilian some seventeen years earlier. Hidalgo, *Representantes de México en Gran Bretaña*, pp. 61–62; *Times* (London), September 16 and 24, 1884. I have used data from the September 24 "Money Market and City Intelligence" column to calculate the 70 percent figure, which seemingly depends on the bonds being purchased at a maximum of 50. In September 1884, they were trading at half of that!
147 Cerda, *Banco Nacional*, pp. 257–271, Extracts of the Weekly Minutes of the Council of Administration of BNDM, April 22–December 2, 1884.
148 Cerda, *Banco Nacional*, pp. 244–245.

his perspective on the history of the century unmatched, but his health
a bit uncertain; Justo Sierra; and not least, Francisco Bulnes, polymath,
polemicist, politician, his appreciation of Mexico's economic potential as
great as anyone's in attendance. They were an appropriately qualified group
to discuss their country's full reentry into the nineteenth-century economy,
with its awesome flows of migrants, money, materials, and merchandise.
So lengthy was the exchange – its record takes up more than a hundred
double-column pages of very small print – that it is impossible to give any
detailed account of it here. But it is not impossible to reprise the principal
points or suggest the flavor of what was said, such as "Señor Bulnes is not
the Pope. I mean, he is not infallible."[149]

Díaz Mirón and Prieto, among others, were critical of the agreement.
Bulnes argued in favor. Over and over again, opponents of the Sheridan–
Noetzlin proposal asserted that they were in principle not opposed to
repayment. What Mexico owed, Mexico should pay. As one of them put
it, "the Deputies opposed do not deny the legitimacy of the English debt
in its origin . . . Again, the Deputies opposed want to pay."[150] But exactly
how much to pay, on what schedule, with what sources – all the devilish
details – these escaped consensus. Indeed, the opponents even dragged out
the "obsolete ships and threadbare uniforms" charge once more. Yet all
of these disagreements were to be expected, and in reality, some of them
were essentially technical. Occasionally, a poet may argue on less-than-
convincing fiscal grounds. Indeed, the acting president of the chamber, who
opposed the agreement, came to a historically bizarre amount that Mexico
owed England – about £5.2 million – by employing an unusual method of
calculating *simple* interest over sixty years. The magic of compound interest
held no charms for him. The sums included for payments of expenses and
commissions came in for criticism as well, pared down as they might have
been. Yet one cannot quite shake the feeling that what was really at stake
was the old question of who gets paid first, domestic or foreign bondholders.

This was phrased in various ways and couched in terms of a nationalism
not unusual for the time, but in essence, here was an updated version of
conflict that had been going on since the 1840s, if not earlier. *Why should we
pay London first?* It was not even so much a matter of paying *Englishmen* first,
although there was the standard "the Intervention began with the Treaty
of *London*" harangue and the English were eagerly offered up as sacrificial
victims. Some of the disputants were sophisticated enough to know that
the nationality of the holders of bearer bonds could be, and was, almost
anything by 1884. They also knew that for every widow and orphan whose
living had been threatened by the default, there were speculators who no

149 *Diario 1884*, p. 342.
150 *Diario 1884*, p. 322.

doubt had profited handsomely from the purchase of depreciated stock. As one deputy put it, "as far as the original bondholders, those who bought at 55 and 86, well, what about the current bondholders who bought at 10, 15 or 25, who'll generously agree to limit themselves to making 1,600 percent [from the Sheridan-Noetzlin proposal]."[151] The debate seemed, to put it in slightly more modern terms, whether the Mexican government should have access to international capital markets, or whether its financing should be restricted to domestic ones – perhaps nationality, while politically potent, also involved economic efficiency. It might be drawing too stark a distinction to say the debate was about inefficient domestic lenders who could charge monopoly rents versus efficient foreign lenders who offered considerably more competitive terms. Yet this very crucial difference did come up in the debate, albeit in language suited to the time and place.

Specifically, as another supporter of the proposal – Francisco Cosmes – observed,[152]

we have to understand something. Our financial situation is such that we won't get out of it without getting a loan. It can be a domestic loan, or a foreign loan, but we have got to borrow to get by. Now, if we want to continue with this endless business that our governments have of going to borrow from domestic lenders . . . the conditions are more ruinous for the Country than the arrangement of the debt we are looking at. . . . Now we all know who the lenders are in [Mexico] and what they do . . . *agiotistas* and usurers with no love of country or sense of public interest . . . [T]hey live, grow, and fatten while the Nation grows thin and starves . . . If you look at the majority of fortunes that exist in Mexico, all or most of them have come at the expense of the public treasury. . . . Well, señores deputies, do you want me to tell you why this agreement is so unpopular?

It's because the *agiotistas* have gone around spreading rumors among the public about the nation's dignity, or damage to it, so that the debt will not be settled. So that they can keep on devouring the country.

They're afraid that the prize will slip from their hands, because they understand when Mexico has its credit abroad, then Mexico can go to foreign capital and get the money it needs on terms far less onerous than the *agiotistas*' . . . Anyone who has browsed through the financial press knows that fabulous reputation this country has for wealth will draw foreign capitalists who want to exploit this wealth as long as they are offered guarantees and security.

This interesting intervention closed with something of a warning. If you want to keep the domestic monopolists happy, vote against this agreement.

---

151 *Diario 1884*, p. 253.

152 *Diario 1884*, pp. 257–263. (*eterna rutina* is translated as "endless business" and *capitales nacionales* as "domestic lenders.")

Of course, Cosmes' analysis makes sense. It is a bit difficult to think in terms of British versus Mexican creditors in an international capital market, especially when there was nothing to prevent Mexicans from buying 1850 3 percents on the London Stock Exchange. So the older formulation, one going back to Robert Wyllie in the 1840s, had set Mexican *agiotistas* against the British bondholders in the competition for the state's limited resources. Now, with the emergence of global international financial markets and the existence of bearer bonds, it probably made more sense to think in terms of domestic and foreign lenders. While there is no guarantee that everyone understood that the world was changing in precisely this way, the rhetoric was a perfect device for shielding domestic lenders from foreign competition. Why allow the English to dictate to Mexico how much to pay? What allows someone of indefinite nationality[153] like Noetzlin to play a central role in the proceedings? Questions like this were wholly congruent with the matrix of Mexico's historic experiences in the nineteenth century, where foreign armies, foreign agents, foreign diplomats, foreign emperors, and foreign debts provided a natural point for the definition of Mexico's inchoate but nevertheless critical questions of nationality, nationhood, and national institutions. A patriot would find the language of economic nationalism logical, natural, and seductive. So would a lender accustomed to a closed financial market. The last refuge of a scoundrel? Perhaps.[154]

There is another possibility. Recent historiography has cast what we are accustomed to call "insider lending" in Mexico in a rather more benign light. Noel Maurer, in particular, has argued that such lending was an efficient response to imperfections in the capital market, especially where entrepreneurial groups maintained their traditional predominance.[155] The problem, he readily admits, is that these networks acted to restrain entry. During this and later debates, critics of the government would point out that privileged insiders, such as the financer and military contractor Juan Llamedo, seemed more than able to survive even when domestic payments were suspended in favor of the London Debt. Llamedo was an important domestic financier – a "vampire," as it was said – who lent on the anticipated customs revenues of Veracruz.[156] When the question was raised about

---

153 Described by Deputy Eduardo Viñas as *"el Sr. Noetzlin, cuya nacionalidad no conozco y cuyos antecedentes ignoro." Diario 1884*, p. 323: "Mr. Noetzlin, of Unknown Ancestry and Nationality."

154 One thinks, for example, of the ostensibly odd pairing of Carlos Slim and Andrés Manuel López Obrador in contemporary (ca. 2006) Mexican politics. Why would a billionaire businessman in Mexico support a "populist" candidate for president? One would not immediately associate a López Obrador *sexenio* with greater emphasis on an open economy.

155 Noel Maurer, "Banks and Entrepreneurs in Porfirian Mexico: Inside Exploitation or Sound Business Strategy?" *Journal of Latin American Studies*, 31 (1999), pp. 331–361.

156 *El Monitor Republicano*, July 3, 1885.

whom to pay, Llamedo – a Spanish immigrant – counted as a "domestic" lender – an *agiotista* even – whose insider connections trumped repayment of the London Debt. So the emerging network of insider lending that Maurer identifies in the 1880s may well have been using its congressional influence under cover of defense of local ("domestic") interests as a tool for preserving or enlarging its rents. Again, the discourse was cast in nationalistic terms, which is true enough. Yet this was a common enough tactic of rent-seeking elites and hardly limited to Mexico, or even finance alone.[157]

At all odds, as the debate wore on, civility and patience wore thin. The presence of Díaz, on the verge of reassuming the presidency from González, never far removed from the discussion, was invoked to provide the Sheridan–Noetzlin proposal with sufficient political cover. Díaz was quoted as saying that the agreement was not everything he would want, but that he could live with it. To which one deputy – Eduardo Viñas – archly responded, "The Bondholders have asked for ratification by Congress. They have not asked for the ratification of Sr. General Díaz. General Díaz has no business in this affair."[158] But no matter. On Saturday, November 15, 1884, the Chamber of Deputies took a vote on the first reading of the commission's report, in effect, adopting the Sheridan–Noetzlin proposal without modification. It carried 93 to 58. As Viñas later put it, the battle "on the plain" had been lost. But the battle "in the mountains" was just beginning. By this, Viñas meant the parliamentary maneuvering to have each article of the Sheridan–Noetzlin proposal considered and voted on separately. Not quite the French Revolution, perhaps, but important nonetheless.

This began on November 17 and almost immediately turned disorderly when Francisco Bulnes denied that the chamber had any right to consider and vote on the articles of the debt agreement individually.[159] The atmosphere rapidly deteriorated as police began to cart off protesters in the gallery. Prieto shouted that the disorder was being caused by the police, but he was himself drowned out by the growing din in the chamber. One truly dramatic moment came when Prieto stood and said,

Sir: at the time of the American war, the treaty of peace was submitted to the Congress as a single article. Those of us in opposition strongly insisted that this treaty be discussed by parts, but the Commission [handing the treaty in Congress] refused to give way. The result was that a third of the National Territory was lost (*Prolonged applause*).[160]

157 Pedro Fraile Balbín, *Industrialización y grupos de presión: la economía política y grupos de presión en España, 1900–1950* (Madrid, 1991) yields an interesting comparative perspective.
158 *Diario 1884*, p. 339.
159 *Diario 1884*, p. 346.
160 *Diario 1884*, p. 352.

In the heated atmosphere, the acting president of the chamber cleared the galleries and took the meeting into secret session, something he was within his procedural rights to do. But the disorder simply spilled out onto the streets of Mexico City, where the army opened fire on demonstrating students and, it was said, spilled blood.[161] As a result, when the deputies met again on November 18, everything was in an uproar. Some deputies commented on an atmosphere of intimidation, the possibility of police agents in the galleries, and an armed battalion stationed outside the chamber. It then emerged that the acting president claimed that he had asked for the troops to be stationed outside on his own authority. More heated discussion. And another vote: this one to consider and vote on each article separately. It failed, by a vote of seventy-two in favor to eighty-one against.

At that point, it seemed as if opponents of the Sheridan–Noetzlin proposal had simply lost. And perhaps they had. But here the record of the session becomes tumultuous. Pistol shots were heard outside the chamber, and cries of "They are murdering the People" went up from the floor as deputies scurried around in disarray. Díaz Mirón and the acting president went outside in an effort to prevent further bloodshed and then returned to beg for order inside the chamber. But the acting president then made an unfortunate error. Asked how many dead there were, he explained that "a bunch of riffraff" had attacked the police, who were forced to defend themselves, which elicited a shouted response from the floor and the galleries, "It's the People, not a bunch of riffraff!" At that point, the session simply dissolved into chaos, and as a witness laconically put it, "It was impossible to continue."[162]

It was 6:00 P.M., November 19, 1884. The battle of the mountain was over. Later, in Paris, Noetzlin contacted his superiors, urging them to let him know precisely what he was to tell the Committee of Bondholders about the state of negotiations. Finance Minister Manuel Dublán laconically noted in reply, "Congress closed the newspapers today without resolving the Noetzlin agreement."[163]

A Punters' Conversion

With the end of the presidency of González in December 1884, the Sheridan–Noetzlin proposal fell squarely into the hands of Díaz once more. If Díaz had alternately denounced the London Debt in the marketplace

161 *Diario 1884*, pp. 353, 355 (Guillermo Prieto).
162 *Diario 1884*, pp. 366–368 (*Es el Pueblo, no el populacho*).
163 Noetzlin to the minister of finance, London, December 14, 1884, and Dublán to the Mexican minister in London, México, December 15, 1884, *Deuda Exterior*, vol. 9, AGNM.

of *pronunciamientos*, then temporized with it in his first trip to the palace, he now had no choice but to confront it directly. His position during the congressional debate had been ambiguous and Díaz's relation to the popular tumult that ensued was uncertain. But circumstances now conspired to place him, willingly or not, at the center of the controversy. The draft report of his finance minister – Dublán (1884–1891) – to the Congress made it clear that Mexico's debt, foreign and national, was perceived as the key to the country's international economic position. Nothing symbolizes this more clearly than the provenance of the draft, to be found among the papers of Section 6 of the finance ministry, "Public Credit" in a file labeled "English Debt."[164] In 1885, the London Debt *was* public finance.

Once the Congress failed to ratify the Sheridan–Noetzlin proposal, Noetzlin was almost immediately relieved of his responsibility. Indeed Dublán informed Noetzlin that Díaz "was convinced that, surely, one of his first duties was for Mexico to arrange recognition of its legitimate debts by paying its creditors the interest stipulated" and that Noetzlin's role was "terminated by the inaction of the Congress."[165] One source of opposition in the Congress to Noetzlin's arrangement had nominally, as we have seen, been its failure to put Mexican creditors on an equal footing with foreign nationals or to provide for a comprehensive settlement of the national debt and its refunding in a more evenhanded way. Now, by coincidence or not, this was the route that the Díaz government was to take, adopting the position of those "on the mountain" rather than on the plain.

For forty years, such arrangements almost nearly always commenced with a total suspension of payments by the central government as it took stock of its resources and decided which of its creditors to penalize and which to pay – the calculation historically phrased in terms of *agiotistas* versus bondholders. The fiscal crisis that had engulfed Mexico under González continued to wreak havoc with Dublán's calculations of Mexico's capacity to pay. His draft report to the Congress could, naturally, offer little certainty as to precisely what revenues in 1885 would be; the working projection was $27 million pesos. Budgeted expenses for the year were $38 million, which Dublán termed an "overwhelming imbalance." Sixty percent of "probable" revenues would go to servicing the floating debt alone. The payment of ordinary expenses was in doubt, and there seemed little possibility that the country's institutions could weather the fiscal crisis without disruption. Under the circumstances, extraordinary measures to reduce, defer, and reschedule expenses would have to be taken, the first of which was the

164 "Originales y anexos del informe que dio el Señor Dublán al Congreso de la Unión acerca de las leyes de 22 de Junio último" [1885], *Deuda Exterior*, vol. 9, AGNM.
165 Dublán to Noetzlin, México, January 21, 1885, *Deuda Exterior*, vol. 9, AGNM.

suspension of short-term debt payments on June 22, 1885.[166] While Carlos Marichal's pioneering account of the Dublán Convention suggests that the suspension helped create a "furor" in foreign money markets, quite the opposite seems to have been true on the London Stock Exchange. There Mexican bonds relative to consols held more or less steady at 27–28 in June and July and then began a slow but steady rise of 25 percent over the following year. In reality, the market had learned from long experience that the suspension of Mexican debt payments and other measures of domestic austerity usually betokened better – not worse – treatment for the holders of Mexican sovereign debt.

Certainly by fall, 1885, the bondholders in London were once again pressing Mexico for action.[167] Their reaction to what had transpired in Mexico was nothing, if not complex. On the one hand, they confessed grave disappointment that the Mexican Congress had failed to ratify the Sheridan–Noetzlin Agreement. On the other, they quite frankly admitted that if the Sheridan–Noetzlin Agreement had passed the Congress, such was Mexico's fiscal situation that "it must be confessed that there would have been no means of paying it." Yet having said that, there were aspects of the Díaz government's approach to the problem that left the bondholders uneasy. On the one hand, the bondholders (literally) cheered when Díaz's plan "to issue Six Per Cent Treasury Bonds to provide for the whole floating debt of the country which had hampered so long the whole revenue and the whole prosperity of the country." But they were far less encouraged by the way the decree of June 22 would handle the London Debt. In its essentials, the plan called for the conversion of the 1850 3 percents at par. In so doing, it recognized the principle of this conversion and *previous ones* to which Mexican bonds had been admitted while explicitly rejecting ostensibly spurious claims such as the Jecker bonds or issues occurring under the Second Empire. While there were potential problems with the approach (e.g., with the Lizardi's unauthorized issue of 1842 or the status of the deferred bonds of 1837), the major sticking point was the handling of arrears. As the bondholders put it, "the very serious fact in regard to these arrears was that the Mexican government proposed nothing, but said it was a matter for something to be left to be agreed upon." This was so: Section 3, Article 19A of the decree of June 22 flatly stated that "other unpaid interest as of this date will be deferred and its mode of payment the object

166 Carlos Marichal, "Debt Strategies in the Porfiriato: The Conversion Loan of 1888 and the Role of Banamex as Government Banker" [1999]. This remarkably concise discussion should be supplemented by Leonor Ludlow's authoritative "Manuel Dublán: La Administración Puente en la Hacienda Pública Porfiriana," in Ludlow, ed., *Los Secretarios de Hacienda*, vol. 2: pp. 141–174. (*desnivel . . . abrumador* is translated as "overwhelming imbalance.")

167 *Times* (London), September 10, 1885, for this and what follows.

of special arrangement with the creditors."[168] So, again, the arrears, which the bondholders calculated to represent nearly half of the total debt or some £45–£50 million alone (out of some £100 million), had disappeared. What had represented a sticking point in so many negotiations over the course of the nineteenth century was, again, simply discarded. If the point of long-term investment is to garner the returns from compound interest, the entire point of holding Mexican bonds had been lost – *unless the calculation was that so few long-term holders remained that the arrears were a sunk cost to recent purchasers of the bonds*. In other words, Mexico seems to have assumed that its bonds had long ago become instruments of mere speculation and traded more on the basis of prospective capital gains and losses rather than the almost entirely illusory prospect of accumulating wealth based on the income they provided. If this were indeed the case, Mexico was engaging in a hard-nosed but not unrealistic negotiating strategy. And whatever the grandiloquent accusations of a Díaz Mirón or even a Prieto, this ultimate attempt to reach agreement could never be fairly classified as a financial species of *entreguismo*. What the British had stated in the House of Commons about laying short-term bets on Mexico was fairly taken up by the Mexican side as well. It was, as the British might have said, a punters' conversion.

While there was much lip service paid at the meeting to the question of the arrears, the bondholders came only to the conclusion that the matter should be "pressed." There was also agreement that "some arrangement" be made to consider the interests of those who held the bonds issued under Maximilian in 1864. But the one serious dissent, which moved that the negotiation be taken out of the hands of the Committee of Mexican Bondholders and placed under the somewhat less suspect jurisdiction of the Council of the Corporation of Foreign Bondholders, was ruled "not in order." H. P. Sheridan and his handpicked successor, E. P. Bouverie, certainly knew how to run a meeting. Or as one of the dissident

---

168 All references to Dublán and Lozano's *Legislacción Mexicana* from this point on are to the printed "Official Edition" of 1887. The searchable edition available online through the UNAM extends only as far as 1866. http://biblioweb.dgsca.unam.mx/dublanylozano/ (accessed September 13, 2007).

Technically, the deferred bonds were excluded from the Conversion of 1846 and thus the Conversion of 1850. In 1856, Mexico made an agreement with Lizardi and Company to call in all the deferred bonds, but Lizardi evaded the agreement. Detailed accounts of the complexities thus created appear in "Case of the Holders of Deferred Bonds of 1837 Shut Out from the Conversion of 1846," London, November 22, 1861, and "Mexican Deferred Bonds," México, May 22, 1862, FO 97/280, PRO.

Ibarra Bellon, *El Comercio y el poder*, p. 46, cites Jan Bazant to the effect that the Conversion of 1850 disposed of the question of the arrears through the United States indemnity payment. But the arrears in question in 1850 were only those accruing since *1846*, not *all* the arrears. See my discussion of the Conversion of 1850 in Chapter 3. Thus this *cannot* be the explanation for why the arrears disappeared in the final settlement.

1837 bondholders subsequently put it, "particular interests had been left in the cold, while the larger bondholders had taken care of themselves."[169]

And take care of themselves they did. Within six weeks, record time by the standards of the history of the London Debt, the Finance Ministry could report that its agent in London, General Francisco Z. Mena (Noetzlin's successor), had reached agreement with *both* the Council of Foreign Bondholders and the Committee of Mexican Bondholders on all necessary grounds, remarkably considering that the supervision of the Council of the Corporation of Foreign Bondholders had been "out of order" to a protesting Mexican bondholder not long before.[170] With the lines of communication thus tightly controlled, "a satisfactory arrangement that merits the uniform approval of the Council of Ministers" was struck. Its specifics were as follows: The highly controversial Jecker bonds and the Conversion of 1864 under Maximilian were actually recognized, but only to the extent of 50 percent of their principal. It is not really clear what effect this provision had, since, as we have seen, most of the Jecker bonds were held in the portfolio of Jecker, Torre when the firm went bankrupt in 1860. Since the Conversion of 1864 had capitalized unpaid interest accruing on the 1851 3 percents from 1854 through 1863 at 60, taking these bonds at 50 percent amounted to cutting the interest paid under the republic to 30 *percent* of its total. From 1863 through 1866, the interest was capitalized at only 9 percent in new bonds. Moreover, the Díaz government reserved the right to delay the exchange of the 1851 3 percents until 1891 and to purchase outstanding bonds in the secondary market at 40 percent of their nominal value until 1891, and at 50 percent thereafter. This was the extent to which the arrears were recognized. In every other respect, it was the Sheridan–Noetzlin Agreement, but with fees and costs capped at £200,000. All told, Finance Minister Dublán calculated that a settlement along these lines would reduce the outstanding London Debt by the staggering sum of 41 million pesos, or £8.2 million. Depending on how one figures the outstanding debt in 1886, that would be a reduction of 40–50 percent.[171]

If, in fact, this settlement was, at least, no less advantageous to Mexico than its predecessor, it would be easy to conclude that the thing explained itself – the Congress had complained about the previous agreement and gotten a better one. But this perhaps underestimates the role that Díaz himself played in the transformation of the political system. As Friedrich Katz has emphasized, during his second term in office, Díaz effectively

169 *Times* (London), July 1, 1886.
170 *Diario de los Debates de la Cámara de Diputados. Año de 1886* (México, 1888), vol. 1, p. 85. [Hereafter, *Diario 1886*, with relevant pages.]
171 *Diario 1886*, pp. 86–87.

prevented the election of any opponent to the Congress, and by 1888, that institution "had for all practical purposes become a rubber stamp."[172] This, of course, does not prove that Díaz organized the opposition to ratification in 1884, or even had anything to do with it. But it does suggest that a remarkable change in the political and fiscal landscape was well under way by 1886 – one that, no matter what one thinks of the results, played a role in freeing up a significant quantity of domestic resources for economic development and made foreign lending once again likely. Indeed, one might well conclude that one of the principal obstacles to economic growth in nineteenth-century Mexico, hitherto all but ignored, was a very nasty case of what is today called "debt overhang." Debt-overhang theories (fundamentally associated with Jeffrey Sachs) show that if there is some likelihood that in the future, debt will be larger than the country's repayment ability, expected debt-service costs will discourage further domestic and foreign investment and thus harm growth. Potential investors will fear that the more a country produces, the more it will be "taxed" by creditors to service the external debt, and thus they will be less willing to incur costs today for the sake of increased output in the future. Why invest if the returns will all be eaten up by creditors? By implication, large stocks of debt will reduce growth by depressing investment: in a nutshell, Mexico in the nineteenth century.[173]

The Role of Bleichroeder

While Mexico had steadfastly maintained during the Sheridan–Noetzlin negotiations that it sought no fresh capital, the realities of its public finance dictated otherwise. As the finance ministry put it in 1887,[174] "our bonds are quoted at prices never before reached, but that does not mean the financial crisis is behind us." This statement was quite accurate. Mexican bond prices reached their highest levels in a quarter century in London. Yet there were outstanding debts of 22 million pesos alone in railroad subsidies. To the extent that these were obligations payable in sterling in London, they were effectively indexed to the depreciation of the peso, which was far from over by the late 1880s. Any comprehensive restructuring of the national debt in Mexico – including but not limited to the London Debt – would inevitably raise the question of stabilizing debt service at sustainable levels.

172 Friederich Katz, "Mexico: Restored Republic and Porfiriato, 1867–1910," in Leslie Bethell, ed., *The Cambridge History of Latin America* (11 vols., New York, 1984–1996), vol. 5: p. 35.
173 Catherine Pattillo, Hélène Poirson and Lucca Ricci, "External Debt and Growth," *Finance and Development*, 39: 2 (2002). http://www.imf.org/external/pubs/ft/fandd/2002/06/pattillo.htm (accessed August 14, 2007).
174 *Memoria de Hacienda . . . 1887*, XXXX, LVIII, for this and what follows.

Typically, the issue in Latin America was one of debt maturing before the underlying productive assets did. Mexico was unexceptional in this regard. Something akin to a "bridge loan" would be needed to give the Dublán Convention a chance to work.

Such a loan was forthcoming in 1888, but from an unlikely source, the German house of Bleichroeder. Marichal suggests that substantial German financial interests in Mexico made Bleichroeder a likely candidate, but other sources suggest that Noetzlin, who represented the BNDM in the negotiations in Berlin, brought in Bleichroeder and drew up the loan agreement.[175] What is clear is that Bleichroeder, German chancellor Bismarck's personal banker, financed the Dublán Convention, or at least, could be regarded as financing the conversion of the London Debt, which is not quite the same. The total value of bonds and certificates that qualified for conversion as part of the London Debt in 1885 was £14.6 million. Of that, about £11 million was the capital and interest of the Conversion of 1850. Bleichroeder's loan to Mexico was £10.5 million or approximately the same amount. Indeed, the capital amount recognized in 1885 from the Conversion of 1850 was *identical* (£10,241,650). So again it was as if Bleichroeder had simply purchased the issue whole, without having to pay out the interest as well. Bleichroeder had cut a very good deal indeed.[176]

So good, in fact, that even Díaz's presumably tame Congress showed distinct signs of discomfort in recommending it. The Finance Committee in the Senate acknowledged that it had taken very little time to study the plan.[177] Echoing the words that had authorized a foreign loan more than sixty years before, the committee concluded that "the evil lies not in the need to borrow, but in the impossibility of calling on the means of doing so . . . with the help of credit." The Federation could not balance the budget while financing the floating debt and resuming service on the foreign debt. It was simply a necessity to look for help from a source beyond ordinary means, "either at home or in foreign markets." "The only and necessary solution is that proposed by the President . . . whose sole aim is to facilitate the progress of public administration." In Porfirio we trust, in other words.

The tone of the discussion in the Chamber of Deputies was slightly less abashed, but nevertheless radically different from what had prevailed only three years earlier.[178] Calling the loan "an efficient means" of providing

---

175 Carlos Marichal, "Foreign Loans, Banks, and Capital Markets in Mexico, 1880–1910," in Reinhard Lehr, ed., *The Public Debt in Latin America in Historical Perspective* (Madrid, 1995), pp. 362–363; *Times* (London), February 28, 1888.

176 *Memoria de Hacienda . . . 1886*, "Estado General de los Créditos reconocidos por la Deuda Contraída en Londres . . . ," XLVII.

177 Cámara de Senadores, *Dictamen de la Comisión de Hacienda autorizando al Ejecutivo para contraer un empréstito de diez millones y quinientas mil libras esterlinas* (México, 1887).

178 See *Diario de los Debates de la Cámara de Diputados. Año de 1887* (México, 1890), vol. 3: pp. 693–696.

"fertile results" for Mexico, the speakers limited themselves to the conclusion that Mexico would pay less after the Dublán Convention than before, albeit at an exaggerated reduction of 70 percent! The economies would come primarily from the simplification of interest rates, maturities, and the overhead required by servicing a number of debt instruments simultaneously. It was all very decorous. The proposed loan passed the Chamber of Deputies by voice vote 150 to 0.

To repeat, beneath it all was the fact that Bleichroeder had managed to negotiate a profitable agreement. Too profitable to avoid, apparently, as the British concluded that the Germans were seeking to diversify their portfolio geographically. Having loaded up on assets from the Old World, they were now – so the reasoning went – prepared to explore the New. Of the £10.5 million, Bleichroeder committed to take £3.7 million at 70. Of the balance (£6.8 million), Bleichroeder had the option through July 1, 1889, at 86.5. Here things became truly interesting, because Bleichroeder could pay for the balance with 1850, and 1886 converted bonds at 40. Of course, the announcement drove the market price of Mexican in London bonds to exactly 40 in February 1888, but over the previous six months, they had traded at an (monthly) average of 33. If Bleichroeder had done nothing else but bought up the 1850s, the house could have sold them for a 17.5 percent gain in merely six months. Or Bleichroeder could have rolled the 17.5 percent over into the new issue, effectively reducing their price to 69. In theory, Bleichroeder could have purchased a nominal £6.8 million for £4.69 million. Since the bonds were publicly available to Bleichroeder at 86.5, it seems reasonable that the house could have resold them at or near that price. In so doing, Bleichroeder would have made £1.8 million. Since Bleichroeder could, at least in theory, have purchased the entire 1850 issue for £3.4 million, one could argue that the potential profits on the deal to Bleichroeder could have been more than 50 percent! Now, certainly, this is the best of all possible worlds, but it explains why Marichal speculates on "the obscure financial juggling [taking place here] . . . in which the profit margins tend to be quite high."[179]

Such profits themselves tend to address another problem with the Bleichroeder loan: what would have induced *any* merchant bank in the late 1880s to lend a country that still suffered from serious fiscal imbalances and that had been in default for sixty years *anything*? Economic historians emphasize the growing credibility of the state under Díaz, but for however much truth the argument holds there is also a whiff of the teleological about it. There were severe riots in Mexico City over the London Debt only four years earlier. And while there is certainly a dramatic change in the tenor

---

179 Marichal, *Foreign Loans, Banks and Capital Markets*, p. 362. The specifics of the contract are described in the *Times* (London), February 28, 1888.

of congressional proceedings regarding foreign borrowing between 1884 and 1887, there is still more than a hint of uncertainty about them. Does the conclusion of the Finance Committee of the Senate, "in this case the pecuniary result of the convention would probably be genuinely plausible" sound particularly confident?[180] When Finance Minister José Yves Limantour completed arrangements for the conversion of the public debt in 1893 (one of his first initiatives) he publicly admitted that a number of loose ends dating back to 1883 had yet to be settled.[181] Among these was the persistent problem of the floating debt, which Limantour contended was the greatest obstacle to a balanced budget. So the actions of Bleichroeder in 1887 seem less an affirmation of faith in a now-credible regime than pure opportunism. Certainly British criticisms of the operation were pointed as "not good finance."[182]

Nevertheless, apart from the profitability of the operation, something else may have induced Bleichroeder to take the plunge. According to Katz, Bleichroeder was effectively given a monopoly over Mexico's external borrowing by being given the right of first refusal (secretly) to loans. Actually, if this was a secret, it was not particularly well guarded, because there was a similar clause in the public contract of the 1887 loan.[183] Again, such a concession is a signal of weakness, not strength, or of debility, not credibility. As the *Times* (London) waspishly but astutely put it, "such a scheme certainly seems like a relapse of the old hand-to-mouth-system." The British bondholders were said to disapprove. But the Federation received an immediate infusion of 17 million pesos, which is what Finance Minister Dublán urgently required. And this his predecessors, great and not so great, would have understood only too well.

Conclusions

In 1850, Prieto set out to convert Mexico's national debt and resume payments on the London Debt. He failed. In 1887, Dublán set out to convert Mexico's national debt and resume payment on the London Debt. He succeeded. It is instructive to consider why Dublán succeeded, but Prieto did not.

---

180 Cámara de Senadores, *Dictamen de la Comisión de Hacienda autorizando al Ejecutivo para contraer un empréstito de diez millones y quinientas mil libras esterlinas*, p. 37.

181 "Exposición de Motivos de la Iniciativa de Ley para Completar el Arreglo de la Deuda Nacional," México, May 23, 1893, in Secretaria de Hacienda y Crédito Público, *Colección de Leyes y Disposiciones Relacionadas con la Deuda Exterior de México* ([1925] México, 1989), pp. 167–169.

182 *Times* (London), February 28, 1888.

183 *Memoria de Hacienda... 1887*, LXV, LXVII, LXVIII; Friedrich Katz, *Deutschland, Diaz und die mexicanische Revolution. Die deutsche Poltitik in México, 1870–1920* (Berlin, 1964), pp. 98–108.

Perhaps most importantly as Prieto (and his successor Payno) soon realized, the resources with which Prieto had to work were far smaller than
those offered Dublán. Prieto took the war indemnity from the United
States, $15 million, and transferred it to foreign creditors, of whom the
London bondholders were but one group. The money, as a contemporary
put it, "went up in smoke." Bleichroeder financed Dublán at more than $60
million, and the first tranche alone amounted to more than $17 million
or more in nominal terms than the entire war indemnity. But that was
sufficient to convert the bulk of the London Debt in 1887, whereas Prieto
and Payno scarcely made a dent. The great debt reduction that Dublán
achieved, his predecessors could only dream of, and Dublán engineered a
virtual cancellation of the arrears of interest. His predecessors were no less
able, but much less fortunate. In 1888, the Committee of Bondholders
rode roughshod over its constituency. There were probably few if any "bona
fide" bondholders left and the committee made do with the speculative
profits from capital gains. In 1850 there were undoubtedly more than
a few original bondholders left. Rational or not, they entertained hopes
that some more substantial part of their investment could be salvaged. In
the late 1880s, such hopes were sunk, and had become sunk costs. "1850
versus 1888" was thus ultimately a matter of supply and demand: the
cost of a settlement had fallen, so a settlement was more likely to take
place.

Of course the international and political context had also changed dramatically. Díaz was, credible or no, a figure of considerably greater weight
than Joaquín Herrera – no one would have ever dreamed of calling Herrera
the "greatest man in the Americas," as James Creelman said of Díaz in
1908. Nor was the sheer volume of capital on the move in 1850 as it was
in 1888. British investment in Latin America in 1865 was £80 million. In
1885, it was £250 million.[184] With the specific entry of German finance
into Mexico, there was, again, an increase in the supply of capital seeking
a higher return. If Finance Minister Dublán had been seeking a settlement
after the Baring Crisis (1890), he may have encountered greater difficulties,
but as it was, the timing was good. For a settlement to take place, both
sides must be willing and able to settle.

Carmagnani has vigorously argued that this was a "fiscal aspect of
economic convergence." By this he simply means that desire of post–
Maximilian regimes to gain international financial legitimacy drove falling
fiscal deficits, at least in the long run. Budget figures in Mexico are perhaps
not good enough to support Carmagnani's generalizations, but he is clearly
on to something when he concludes that "[before 1867] all budgets had

184 Miller, *Britain and Latin America*, p. 122.

shown deficits [but] . . . in the following period of 1867–1911, when only 25 budgets (56.8) percent were negative [*sic*]."[185] As a consequence, in 1868, the domestic debt was 112 percent of the foreign debt. By 1880, when the British began serious efforts to reestablish relations with Mexico, the domestic debt was 67 percent of the foreign debt – a decline of some 40 percent. As a proportion of GDP, the decline is even more striking: from about 26 percent of GDP to about 10 percent.[186] One speculates (there is little more to do) that this must have been the smallest share of total output claimed by the internal debt at almost any time since 1800. Indeed, this is *precisely* what Rivas argued in justifying his negotiations: "The internal debt is . . . relatively insignificant."[187] For sure, this was a moment – an opportunity – and it would pass, as Carmagnani freely admits. Yet the moment coincided almost exactly with the effort to settle the London Debt. Thus in terms of the opposition to a settlement from domestic interests, for Díaz, this was a question of *carpe diem*, and seize the moment Díaz did – whether by dint of adroitness or good fortune is an open question. The fact is that Dublán could address Mexico's entire debt in the conversion, not just the London Debt – a possibility his predecessors never really enjoyed.

The Dublán Convention also brought an end to a problem that had plagued Mexico for most of the nineteenth century, one called "debt overhang." Mexico was a textbook case, one in which economic decline and mounting international debt interact to discourage new investment. While debt relief obviously brings short-term costs, in the long run, the debtor and all creditors are better off for the reduction in debt, for new lending stimulates fresh investment. Fresh investment, in turn, raises economic growth and lowers the cost of borrowing as well. As Taylor points out, this was exactly the sequence that Mexico followed during the 1880s, when its external bond spread fell and gross British capital flows quintupled.[188] Thus the London Stock Exchange saw the relative price of Mexican assets rise as it had done so only twice before in the nineteenth century – in and around 1835, when the transition to centralism was well advanced, and in 1864, when Maximilian was paying the bondholders dividends. In the later 1880s, rising bond prices reflected the optimism that fiscal breathing room provided: "an upswing associated with Mexico's renewed access to international capital markets."[189] By 1896, when Limantour balanced

---

185 Marichal and Carmagnani, "Mexico: Colonial Regime to Liberal Order," pp. 306, 312.

186 For GDP figures, I use http://biblioteca.itam.mx/recursos/ehm.html#pib (accessed July 24, 2007).

187 *Monitor Republicano*, November 21, 1883.

188 Alan Taylor, "Foreign Capital Flows," in Victor Bulmer-Thomas et al., eds., *Cambridge Economic History of Latin America*, vol. 2: pp. 74–79.

189 Marco Aiolfi, Luis Catão, and Allan Timmermann, "Common Factors in Latin America's Business Cycles," IMF Working Paper WP/06/49, p. 17.

the budget, the sentiment would have seemed justified. By one estimate, fresh funds amounting to £14 million (105 million pesos) would flow into Mexico during the Porfiriato.[190] Mexico's first debt crisis, which had lasted more than sixty years, was finally over.

190 Connolly, *El contratista de don Porfirio*, p. 127.

Conclusions

Lessons for the Past: The London Debt
in a Modern Mirror

Stylized History?

The crises of the 1980s sparked a revolution in historical studies or, at least, in historical studies of sovereign debt. To even a casual reader, the explicit recourse to past episodes of heavy lending, default, and subsequent adjustment for insights into contemporary events was striking. If anything, economic and financial historians learned – or remembered – that such crises had occurred before and that whatever their consequences, fiscal annihilation was not inevitable. After the pain of default and adjustment, lenders, in some case, with suitable changes in character and nationality, stood ready to lend again. The world did not come to an end. Nor would it.

Yet for the historian, however brilliant and provocative some of these studies were, there was usually something missing. Economists in the policymaking community were seeking to draw lessons *from* the past, useful knowledge sometimes drawn from what they termed "stylized facts." Yet a stylized fact often seemed to be a convenient assumption, a too-neat generalization, or an altogether unrealistic aggregation of data drawn from different cases, sources, and research programs. Useful the results may have been in a purely pragmatic way: they provided ministers and the bureaucracies they headed with some guidelines, however imperfect, about how to proceed in real markets and the real world. That is, these studies helped reduce complete uncertainty into more manageable notions of risk, and as such, were a natural propaedeutic toward meaningful actions and workable policies by lenders. To paraphrase Crane Brinton's famous formulation about revolutions, no ideas, no Baker Plan, no Brady Bonds. This was, I think, one of the more impressive contributions of financial and economic historians to something other than purely academic discourse. One can argue with the results and many critics, like Jeffrey Sachs or Joseph Stiglitz, certainly did.[1] Not to put too fine a point on it, but the business

---

1 Joseph E. Stiglitz, *Globalization and Its Discontents* (New York, 2002); Jeffrey D. Sachs, "Resolving the Debt Crisis of Low-Income Countries," *Brookings Papers on Economic Activity*, 1 (2002): pp. 257–286.

of international finance was far too important to be left to international bankers.

Historians, however, distrust stylized facts, models, and above all, economic theory. Whether such skepticism is justified or not is beside the point. It is a reality that economic historians must confront. And confront it here we must. One important result of this study is to underscore exactly how fruitful economists' discussion of the debt crises have been, not simply for understanding the present, but for understanding the *past*. The standard, if often unspoken judgment about Mexico before 1870, is that there is no heuristic structure, no way of understanding the rapid political alterations that makes any sense, particularly when labels like "Liberal" and "Conservative" are employed. In other words, there is no coherent analytical framework, hence the seeming randomness or chaos of "political instability." But this is simply not true. There are lessons in the present for the past, and these lessons, with such exotic names as "debt overhang," "debt intolerance," and, most amusingly, "original sin," can help us understand what transpired in Mexico *if we are willing to concede the integrity of historical experience*. Economists want to dismiss the charge of lack of realism in models by pointing to the canonical text of Milton Friedman: realism doesn't matter, but the ability to predict or retrodict (in historical terms) does.[2] Moreover the process whereby phenomena occur is not simply a "black box" for historians. It is the essence of historical explanation itself: what we don't know about the world matters as much as what we do. A model may be elegant, clever, or even pretty. But if it is a model of nothing that ever transpired, it is not history. In the film *History Boys*, one character raises the question, "Do you want to be clever or thoughtful?" Historians, immersed in evidence – creating evidence in a pragmatic sense is *their job* – have generally wanted to be thoughtful. They generally do not regard the world as a "black box," which may be "usefully regarded" "as if" it were something else unless they are lazy, sloppy, or cynical. Famously, they want to "get it right."

If we consider the impressive results of the best work on the debt crisis in the 1980s, we will be compelled to admit that it makes nineteenth-century Mexico a lot less "other" and considerably more comprehensible. True, we want to be very specific about the way in which a clear historical accounting will differ from a "stylized" one and why this matters. But that is just our intention here.

Let us review once more the idea of "debt intolerance," the idea that a developing country seems prone to default at levels of indebtedness that a more developed country could easily handle. Mexico has been cited, to

---

2 Milton Friedman, "The Methodology of Positive Economics," in *Essays in Positive Economics* ([1953] Chicago, 1970), pp. 3–43.

good effect, as one of the key cases of "debt intolerance." We have shown that the characterization is strikingly correct, even to the point of showing that Mexico would default at a ratio of debt to GDP that was only around 15 percent. But the model of debt intolerance does not really specify the genetic basis of the intolerance: *why are some countries more prone to serial default than others?*

In the Mexican case, the roots of debt intolerance are historical. They are clearly based on the fiscal modifications that accompanied the shift to a federal republic after independence. They were the result of decisions by federalist politicians about the extent to which the national government would be supplied with the coercive power to supply itself with resources. The decisions to abolish the indigenous tribute, the tobacco monopoly, and to hand the alcabala revenues over to the states all deprived the Federation of vital revenues. As a result, whereas the late Bourbons could, according to Humboldt, predictably count on 20 million pesos a year as a reasonable basis for public finance, the first republic and most of its successors could, at most, count on *nominally* half as much. Mexico could not consistently count on budgeting expenditures at 20 million pesos again until the 1870s and, realistically, until the 1880s – *and it was in the 1880s that the London Debt was resolved.*[3]

Here was the root of the conflict. The Mexicans argued that they lacked the *capacity to pay*. The British, especially the Committee of Bondholders, contended that Mexico lacked the *willingness to pay*. Mexico contended that it could not pay although it wanted to. The British argued that Mexico could pay but lacked the political will to do so. As a result, two nations largely talked past each other for sixty years, basing their arguments on very different assumptions. And both, in their own way, were correct. With a Bourbon financial structure, Mexico could have paid. But under federalism, no such structure was available. Hence the centralists (an oversimplified term, for sure) looked backward, or at least, to the fiscal arrangements of the Bourbons, as a way of recovering national financial equilibrium. The financial markets clearly understood this distinction. By and large, this is why the price of the London Debt (both in nominal terms or relative to British consols) rose and fell with the prospects of centralist reorganization and control, even if centralism itself contained elements (such as trade prohibitions or sops to domestic financiers) that were less than congenial to the prospects of repayment on Mexican bonds.

Let us, for the sake of clarity, engage in a brief thought experiment or counterfactual exercise. The interest payments on the initial loans required about 1.5 million pesos per year. At 20-million-pesos income per year, these payments would have consumed about 7.5 percent of total expenditure. Of

---

3 http://biblioteca.itam.mx/recursos/ehm.html#finanzas (17.1.xls) (accessed August 19, 2007).

course, with federal income at 10 million pesos, at most, debt service consumed 15 percent. At 15 percent, the republic defaulted. Would it have defaulted at 7.5 percent? As Carlos Marichal and Matilde Souto have shown, the viceroyalty of New Spain averages *situado* payments of about 1.2 million pesos yearly after 1780. So, in a sense, Mexico was, albeit with difficulty (and no choice), producing a similar flow of revenue before 1810. Unless one is prepared to argue that there was a sustained fall in domestic output of more than 50 percent annually from the late colonial period through the first republic, and there is absolutely no such evidence this occurred, it seems obvious that Mexico *could* have serviced such the London Debt. This, then, is why Lucas Alamán, Anastasio Bustamante (by the 1830s, although not before), and the centralists were pointing to a sort of neo–Bourbon fiscal regime in the 1830s. Ideological the choice may well have been, the preferred regime of what Michael Costeloe has called the *hombres de bien*, but it was also the best chance for Mexico to put its fiscal house in order. As it happened, the catastrophe of Texas meant this was the *last* chance for any such restructuring to occur. After that, events simply intervened and the opportunity was lost. So, yes, Mexico was "debt intolerant," but the causes of the syndrome *are rooted in Mexican history* and not some mysterious predisposition to default. Debt intolerance, in other words, was a historical phenomenon before it was an economic one. Or so a historian might object.

Let us now pass to a reconsideration of what was truly a significant problem in the economic history of nineteenth-century Mexico, "debt overhang." One of the lessons that a reconsideration of the London Debt teaches us is that precisely how important an "obstacle" to Mexican development debt overhang was, along with the usual suspects of high transportation and transaction costs. To repeat, "debt overhang" basically occurs when the foreign debt rises more quickly than domestic output: investment will be suppressed because successively larger increments to its returns will be devoted to debt service. There is no point in investing if the best that can happen is that a foreign tax on the result lowers its marginal benefit. But within the limits imposed by diminishing returns, increased investment is the basis for economic growth. Therefore, we have only to illustrate that "debt overhang" did occur as a result of the London Debt.

The procedure we use is, admittedly, pretty crude. But it makes the point, which is all that is required. Federico Sturzenegger and Jeromino Zettle-meyer use a static sustainability debt equation in the presence of a known interest rate and growth path.[4] By employing their equation and interpolating, it appears that if the ratio of the public debt to GDP is 15 percent,

4 Federico Sturzenegger and Jeronimo Zettlemeyer, *Debt Default and Lessons from a Decade of Crisis* (Cambridge, MA, 2006), pp. 308–313.

the growth rate of GDP is 1 percent, and the interest rate is 7 percent, a permanent primary surplus of something less than 1 percent would be required to make debt sustainable. Given an average interest rate of 6 percent on the loans, we might conclude that a permanent 1 percent primary surplus is a reasonable target. Once again, nineteenth-century budget figures are very shaky and most amount to mere guesses. Yet there is really no evidence that other than in anything other than an isolated year or two before 1850, the government achieved anything resembling a permanent primary surplus even *1 percent of GDP!* The London Debt was growing too quickly to be sustained, let alone include the other components of the public debt omitted here. The only way nineteenth-century Mexico could grow was by some combination of lower interest rates, reductions of current expenditure, and, therefore, reduction of the public debt. To repeat the conclusion of the final chapter, this did not and perhaps could not occur until the 1880s. Therefore, we conclude that the fundamental *financial* obstacle to growth in nineteenth-century Mexico was the London Debt. It was not the only obstacle to growth. Indeed, there are those who would argue that financial obstacles to growth were probably not even the most important *real* obstacles to economic growth in the sense that low agricultural productivity was demonstrably (logically) more important. But if we are going to use economics to draw lessons *for* the past, then we must conclude that the London Debt produced "debt overhang."

As to the final notion, the somewhat exotically named "original sin," this is a concept framed by Barry Eichengreen and Ricardo Hausmann primarily to refer to debtors unable to borrow abroad in their own currencies, or to contract long-term loans domestically. There is also a sense in which *original sin* refers to countries that have otherwise strong financial institutions and sound macroeconomic policies, but are nevertheless penalized for the behavior of other debtors.[5] On the whole, original sin has little real meaning for the London Debt, unless one were to count Mexico as one of the "original sinners." Until well into the 1870s, the depreciation of the peso against sterling was never a problem. To the contrary, in the introduction, we noted that there was a tendency for the peso to appreciate, at least in nominal terms, during the initial half of our study. Moreover, Mexico's sins were largely those of commission, and the price it paid for them a matter of the evolution of bond finance in the nineteenth century.[6] For example, the worst error the Mexicans made was to permit the capitalization of arrears, for this led to a rapid multiplication of principal between 1827 and 1847,

---

5 Barry Eichengreen, Ricardo Hausmann and Ugo Panizza, "Currency Mismatches, Debt Intolerances and Original Sin: Why They Are Not the Same and Why It Matters," NBER Working Paper 10036. http://www.nber.org/papers/w10036 (accessed August 20, 2007).

6 Sturzenegger and Zettlemeyer, *Debt Default*, p. 15.

when most of the damage was done. But even a cursory examination of the precedent-setting rescheduling, in 1830, suggests that the Mexican government (and Alamán) largely got the agreement it wanted from the British bondholders. There was no coercion by the British to speak of, and if anything, the Mexican side played the British rather well. Moreover, such arrangements were common at this stage in the evolution of international lending. With Sor Juana we may ask, who was the greater sinner: one who paid for sin (the Mexicans) or one who sinned for pay (the British)? Then again if "original sin" means the "the source of a fundamentally flawed nature," perhaps, what Lorenzo de Zavala had in mind when he said, "I've looked carefully at many of the conflicts that have agitated and may agitate [Mexico], but none deserve the more careful attention of governments than abuses like this."[7] Original sin, indeed.

One of the most widely cited "second-generation" works on debt crises is the work of Paolo Mauro, Nathan Sussman, and Yishay Yaffeh (MSY).[8] To put their conclusion most baldly, wars and violence are bad for bond markets, or as the distinguished financial historian Larry Neal put it after persistent questioning about whether or not this generalization was really quite so robust, "My faith in bond markets is restored."[9] One of the more revealing findings of this study is that MSY are in general correct but that there are exceptions. In Mexico, there were revolts, violence, and instability that did *not* depress Mexican bond prices. In fact, the result suggests that the market was even more discriminating than is usually supposed. Since the London Debt was mostly in default, the result depends more on the price of the bonds (or their price relative to British consols) than anything else, but "instability" associated with a higher probability of centralist government meant that bondholders became more likely to be repaid rather than less. This was, as we emphasized, a consequence of the financial reorganization with which centralism was associated – a response to the diffuse responsibilities and fiscal voluntarism of Mexican federalism. By and large, when centralists took the upper hand in Mexico, Mexican bonds tended to rise, even if the events accompanying the prospect of centralist government were accompanied by "political instability." There were exceptions to this pattern, of course, but perhaps the most striking example was the rise in bond prices during the early phase of the Tripartite Intervention. Here the French struck a deal with the British and the cynosure of the Conservative Party's hopes in Mexico, the prospect of a European prince on the Mexican throne, was realized. A cynic may object that here the rise in Mexican bonds was, for all intents, a sort of bribe to purchase the acquiescence of the

7 Zavala, *Ensayo histórico de las Revoluciones de México*, p. 269.
8 *Emerging Markets and Financial Globalization*.
9 Private conversation with the author, spring 2006.

British Foreign Office in the realization of Napoleon III's "Latin" vision. No matter. Bribes have a distinguished history in international diplomacy, although they are usually termed something else. The fact is that "conservatives" and "centralists" in Mexico were usually responsible for raising bond prices on the London Stock Exchange. In the words of Francisco Madero, Porfirio Díaz was one more "centralist," so the pattern was preserved into the settlement of the default as well. From Alamán to Díaz, these were the sorts of figures who compelled the respect of the international financial markets in the nineteenth century – for better or worse. So, to repeat, MSY may be correct with their stylized history. The real thing was a bit more complicated.

England's Treasure by Foreign Trade?

In thinking about England, Mexico, and the London Debt, then, a certain sense of how things worked becomes clearer. For whatever the reason – diplomatic and political being the usual justifications – Mexican borrowing in Britain was intended to consolidate independence and bind the two nations to each other. The extent to which they actually embraced has long been questioned.[10] On the one hand, in the 1970s, a generation of scholars – deeply influenced by Stanley and Barbara Stein's *The Colonial Heritage of Latin America* – tended to see early manifestations of British influence everywhere, but nowhere so much as in international trade. Here, depending on the interpretation, the British made decisive, new breakthroughs into the markets of the newly independent Spanish-American republics, or were able to transform long-standing "informal" or "direct" networks of trade that existed in the Spanish empire into the backbone of an imperium of free trade in which American silver continued to finance the purchase of British cottons, albeit now in light of day rather than under moonlit skies. While the *dependentistas* regarded the disruptive effects of this new wave of globalization as largely axiomatic – especially on the fragile structure of America's widely diffused, if low-productivity, textile industry – there were others who were not so sure.

The most strident, if not precisely eloquent, figure of this group was the British commercial historian D. C. M. Platt. Platt was a Holocaust-by-free trade denier par excellence. For most of the nineteenth century, he suggested, the volume and value of British exports to Spanish America was trivial. In particular, the penetration of these goods was shallow in

10 Richard J. Salvucci, "1829 and All That: Great Britain, Mexico and Silver Reconsidered," in *The Burden of Spanish Silver: The Impact on American Labor and Europe's Economy: A Workshop of the Atlantic History Seminar* (Harvard University, October 29, 2005), for more detailed summary of this controversy. http://www.fas.harvard.edu/~atlantic/spansilver.html (accessed August 22, 2007).

American markets because their capacity to import was relatively limited: in the traditional British account, the balance of payments was *always* a constraint on economic growth, or, perhaps, it was the other way around. If the American economies were not growing much before 1870, they surely could not have been large markets either. While this is not the place to rehearse once more the arguments for and against these positions, the controversy may have died down, but it was never really settled.

One thing Platt seemed to have established quite conclusively was that the degree of British interference in the American economies, or, perhaps, the extent to which Her Majesty's government shaped the policies of the new republics or even limited their scope for choice, was quite restricted. If there was little free trade, there was no imperialism of free trade either. The British government largely stood back as the subjects of the realm poured their puny merchandise and private capitals into the American sinkhole. And especially as far as lending went, the British followed the classic Palmerstonian position that it was no affair of the crown to rescue private investors from themselves. If the crown's subjects lost money in American speculations, that was between the investor and the host government. The logic was interesting: if it was minding you wanted, then you invested your capital at home. With very few exceptions, notably the diplomatic conventions, the Foreign Office had no intention of intervening in American affairs to save the fool and his or her money from finance ministers in Colombia, Peru, Chile, or Mexico, who specialized in converting sterling into near-worthless paper.

Yet a close reading of the history of Anglo-Mexican relations and the diplomacy of the London Debt suggests, again, considerably greater complexity and subtlety than Platt allowed, as if the relevant spectrum of policy choices ran from "A" to "B," but no further. While it is true that Great Britain did not physically intervene until the Tripartite Convention, British ministers to Mexico had a long history of suggesting, lobbying, cajoling, arguing, and, yes, threatening. It was the British minister who suggested the mechanism of the customs funds in the early 1830s as a means of servicing the London Debt. It was the British who considered recognizing the independence of Texas if the tariff of 1838 was allowed to operate against British cottons. It was the British who effectively pressured the Mexicans into using the indemnity from the War of 1847 to service the British Convention debts. It was the British who effectively raised the status of the bondholders' claims to a diplomatic agreement under the Dunlop and Aldham Conventions that made an open diplomatic clash well-nigh inevitable. To paraphrase Edward Said, Great Britain provided the "structure of reference and meaning" in defining the diplomatic possibilities open to Mexico in dealing with its domestic financiers and, indeed, with the growing power of an aggressive United States. Platt argued that the British did nothing *to* Mexico. Certainly, they did nothing *for* Mexico either. Their looming presence as possible allies against the United States in the 1830s and 1840s produced nothing for all the treasure, Manuel Payno complained, that Mexico shipped to Great Britain before intervention. Would Mexico have fought the United States over Texas and the northern territories in 1846 if the Conversion of 1837 had not held out the prospect of escape from fiscal catastrophe by offering the British bondholders land warrants there as an alternative? These territories had already been lost as far as Mexico was concerned. The *only* tangible reason for fighting to retain them was as a means of resolving the London Debt, for they were nothing, if not a drain on the resources of central Mexico. Finally, Mexico may have been little more than an electoral issue for Liberal ministers in Great Britain in the early 1860s rather than a true *casus belli*, but the British record of collaboration with the French after 1863 was nothing of which to be proud, either.

Nevertheless, the question remains, what exactly was England's stake in Mexico in the era of the London Debt? Perhaps where Platt went awry was in arguing that if Britain had limited commercial and financial interests in Mexico, it then had effectively little interest *at all*. But this seems misleading, if only because there was another possibility: that there was a *monetary* link between Britain, Mexico, and the East, which left Mexico a role in construction of the British empire in the nineteenth century. And, among others, it was the bondholders and their agents who suggested the link. They were, after all, the ones who monitored the flow of liquid resources from Veracruz and the ports. They saw, with some frustration, precisely how much specie Mexico was producing. The problem, to summarize brutally, was that they had no claim on it. These were, apparently, private flows that comprised the bulk of Mexican silver exports (and therefore exports) for most of the nineteenth century. Where were they going, and to whom did they belong?

Mexico played a part in the creation and functioning of the British empire in the nineteenth century because a major part of the British empire, India, and a closely associated trading partner, China, were on the silver standard. We do not have a comprehensive account of this nexus, although, some day, we no doubt shall. But we can sketch out a few of its broad features here, raise some questions, and then explain the relation of these to the London Debt. In Table C.1, we assemble a few statistics concerning the visible trade balance of Great Britain with India and China in the early 1850s extracted from the work of the political economist J. R. McCulloch. These are compared with data on silver shipments from Mexico to England that I have reconstructed in Table 4.1. No one should place too much emphasis on the strict accuracy of the numbers, but instead look to the rough magnitudes.

Table C.1. *UK Visible Trade Deficit on India and China and
Mexico Silver to England*

	Deficit on India and China	Silver to England
1854	9,947,598	5,800,000
1855	10,130,598	5,430,000
1856	13,855,871	7,020,000
1857	16,026,065	0

Note: Values are in current pounds sterling.
Source: J. R. McCulloch, "Precious Metals," in D. P. O'Brien, ed., *The
Collected Works of J. R. McCulloch* (8 vols., London, 1995), 7: 471, for
UK Visible Trade Deficit; Table 4.1, this volume, for Mexico Silver to
England.

McCulloch painted a picture of India and China together running a
substantial visible surplus on Great Britain in the early 1850s, a conclusion
that seems consistent with more modern analyses. Obviously, Britain must
have settled a part of its deficit with the East by the usual means of invisibles,
but again recent analysis has placed this item on the smaller end of the
spectrum. The obvious point is that in 1854–1856, Britain made half of its
eastern balances, in effect, with silver from Mexico. In 1857 and 1858, once
the Three Years' War had overtaken Mexico, there were no silver shipments
for nineteen months, leading one to wonder what the British did in this
instance, precisely as the mutiny was occurring in India. At this point,
we draw no conclusions about the Indian mutiny and Mexican silver other
than to notice the coincidence, intriguing however it may be. But there
is another, somewhat less neat, coincidence as well. It was *after* the major
interruption in silver shipments to Britain that the Dunlop Convention
(1859) was signed, the agreement that paved the way for the Foreign Office
to regard the affairs of the British bondholders as an "official" diplomatic
matter rather than as a private affair between borrower and lender. It is
quite tempting to regard the London bondholders as a sort of canary in the
mine here. Their complaints – more than three decades of them – failed to
produce anything like gunboat diplomacy in Mexico, until what was really
at stake, Mexico's ability to grease the wheels of the eastern project with
silver, was compromised. Then, along with the newly important threat
to the property rights of a putatively reformed British electorate, Her
Majesty's Government ... swung is too strong a word ... but moved a bit
more rapidly into action may not be putting it unfairly. It is almost as if
the bondholders in Mexico were a kind of British sideshow to the main
event, the silver nexus, whose workings were subterranean and therefore
hardly visible. When these were threatened, matters with the bondholders
suddenly heated up.

Even so, Mexican silver did not cover Britain's balances with India and China. But then so what of it? A possible answer is that with a fixed exchange rate, the India and China surplus would have comprised what contemporaries called the "drain" on these economies. In reality, in the absence of anything approaching balanced trade between Britain, Mexico, India, and China, there would have been monetary disturbances in India and China. At the very least, there could only have been consistent pressure on prices there to fall – deflation – in the absence of a gross rise in the nominal (silver) value of British demand. And, of course, this is precisely what the tenor of modern discussions of the period leading up to 1857 suggests. D. A. Washbrook calls the period 1818–1860 in India on in which "a long-term depression saw the prices of all commodities . . . falling in some case to barely half their pre-1820s levels. . . . [driven by] an effective contraction of the money supply." The distinguished Indian historian K. N. Chaudhuri does not scruple in defining "deflation" as a basic characteristic of the pre-1857 era. It would, on the whole, seem to fit.[11] In essence, then, Mexican silver facilitated British colonialism, or at the very least, may have rendered it less disruptive and burdensome to India.

Of course, the result was ironic, not to say unintentional. Neither the British bondholders nor their government had anything other than self-interest in mind when bonds, politics, and diplomacy famously inspired George Canning to call the New World into existence to redress the balance of the Old. They were seeking to draw no lessons from Mexico – just profits. And perhaps the one "lesson" the episode of the London Debt offers is one that has been repeated time and time again: unfettered and unsupervised, financial markets produce excess speculation.[12] It would be pleasant to report that we have learned this much from history, but as any financial prospectus inevitably cautions, past performance is no guide to future results.

11 D. A. Washbrook, "India, 1818–1860: The Two Faces of Colonialism," in Wm Roger Louis, ed., *The Oxford History of the British Empire* (5 vols., Oxford, 1999), 5: pp. 408–409; K. N. Chaud-huri, "India's Foreign Trade and the Cessation of the East India Company's Trading Activities, 1828–1840," *Economic History Review*, new series (1966), vol. 19 (2): pp. 345–363 and especially p. 361.

12 Gillian Tett, "Doomed to Repeat it? A Crash History Lesson in Crashes for Wall Street?" *Financial Times*, August 27, 2007.

Bibliography

Primary Sources

Archives and Libraries

Mexico

Archivo General de la Nación
  Deuda Exterior, vols. 5, 9, 12, 13, 15
  Gobernación, leg. 61, exp. 38; leg. 91, caja 151, exp. 1;
  Gobernación, vol. 377, exp. 1
  Hacienda Pública, 1ª Sección, 1850
  Hacienda Pública, 2ª, Sección de Carpetas Azules, 1824, 1825, 1827, 1828–
    1839, 1835–1836
  Hacienda Pública, 4ª, Sección de Carpetas Azules, 1804, 1804–1824, 1820–
    1824, 1824
  Hacienda Pública, 6ª, Sección, 1857–1858
  Hospital de Jesús, leg. 440, exps. 1, 2
  Indiferente General, unclassified
  Segundo Imperio, vols. 16, 20
  Suprema Corte de Justicia de la Nación, Asuntos Económicos, 1852, 1855
Archivo Histórico del Senado
  Cámara de Senadores (1825), vol. 1
Secretaría de Relaciones Exteriores, Archivo Histórico Diplomático
  Legajos Encuadernados 1062, 1063, 1064

United Kingdom

Baring Brothers (subsequently acquired by ING Bank NV)
  House Correspondence (HC) 4.5.2; 4.5.4; 4.5.21; 4.5.22; 4.5.24; 4.5.25; 4.5.33;
    4.5.36; 4.5.59
British Library Manuscript Collections
  Additional Manuscripts 13126, 38987, 38988, 43170
The Guildhall Library Manuscripts Section
Oxford University, Bodleian Library
  Clarendon Papers
Public Record Office (now called The National Archives)
  FO 50/35, 36, 37, 62, 63, 64, 74, 80A, 80B, 93, 99, 110, 113, 134, 144, 149,
    150, 153, 161, 363

FO 83/2303, 2305
FO 97/203, 273, 274, 275, 280, 281, 282
FO 203/14, 16
The Rothschild Archive
RAL/XI/112/124

United States

Haverford College Quaker and Special Collections
  Stokes-Evans-Cope Papers
Harvard Business School Baker Library
Harvard Law School Library Special Collections
Historical Society of Pennsylvania
  Dreer Collection
  Meredith Family Papers
  Samuel Chew Papers, 1826–1850
  Td*1851, vol. 3
Institute Archives and Special Collections, Rensellaer Polytechnic Institute
  Skilton Family Papers, 1798–1917
Rice University, Woodson Research Center, Fondren Library
  Americas Collection, MS 518
Sutro Library Mexicana Collection
University of California, Berkeley Bancroft Library
University of Texas, Austin, Benson Latin American Collection (BLAC)
  Juan E Hernández y Dávalos Collection (HD)
  Manning and Mackintosh Papers, 1714–1894
  Valentín Gómez Farías Papers (GF)
University of Texas, San Antonio, Rare Books and Fine Press Collection, John Peace
    Library
Yale University Library, Mexican Collection

Newspapers

Bankers Circular and Monetary Times
Bankers Magazine
Bee (New Orleans)
El Financiero (Mexico)
El Monitor Republicano
El Siglo Diez y Nueve
El Sol and supplements
El Universal
Financial and Commercial Record
Financial and Commercial Review
Financial Times (London)
Gaceta del Gobierno Supremo de la Federación Mexicana
Gaceta del Gobierno Supremo de México
Le Moniteur Universel
Niles Weekly Register
Sunday Times (London)
Times (London)

All Other Printed Primary Sources

Alamán, Lucas, *Historia de México desde los primeros momentos que prepararon su Independencia en el año de.* 1808 *hasta la época presente.* A facsimile edition of the first edition published between 1849 and 1852. 5 volumes. México: Fondo de Cultura Económica, 1985–.

————, *Liquidación general de la deuda esterior de la República Mexicana hasta fin de diciembre de* 1841: *Precedida de la relación histórica de los préstamos de que procede y de las diversas modificaciones que han tenido hasta la formación del fondo consolidado, con un résumen de todos los puntos que han quedado pendientes y requieren resolución del supremo Gobierno.* México: Imprenta de I. Cumplido, 1845.

[Anonymous], *A los Españoles en Londres. Un Mexicano Contestando al Número 20 de su Periódico.* México: [n.p.], 1826.

————, *Reestablecimiento del Estanco dela Siembra y Cultivo del Tabaco en los Puntos Cosecheros: Contrato entre el Banco Nacional y la compañía empresaria de México haciendo estensivo por toda la República por cinco años el arrendamiento de la renta y disposiciones del Supremo Gobierno de estas materias.* México: Imprenta del Iris, 1839.

————, *Ecsamen analítico del préstamo de* 130,000 *libras esterlinas: vindicación de los supremos poderes de la República que intervinieron en la declaración de su nulidad que hizo el conservador.* México: Imprenta de Ignacio Cumplido, 1840.

————, *Representación dirigida al Ecsmo. Sr. Presidente de la República por los apoderados de los acreedores que tienen hipotecas sobre las aduanas marítimas.* México: Imprenta de Ignacio Cumplido, 1842.

————, *Observaciones imparciales acerca de la administración financiera en la época del gobierno provisional.* México: J. M. Lara, 1845.

————, *Préstamo forzoso de dos millones de pesos que se hace por intermedio del venerable clero para ayudar al sostenimiento de la guerra contra los Estados Unidos del Norte.* Toluca: [Unknown], 1846.

————, *Cuestión del Día. Reflexiones Sobre La Hacienda Pública y el Crédito, Escritas con motivo del proyecto presentado al Supremo Gobierno para la formación de un Banco Nacional y arrendamiento o administración de las rentas.* México: Imprenta de Ignacio Cumplido, 1853.

————, *Contratos hechos en los Estados Unidos por los comisionados del gobierno de México durante los años de.* 1865 *y* 1866. *Contratos celebrados por los generales D. José M. de J. Carvajal y D. Gaspar Sánchez Ochoa, e intervencion del Sr. Romero en los mismos.* México: Imprenta del Gobierno, en Palacio, 1868.

————, *Annual Report of the American Historical Association,* 1908, 2 volumes. Washington, DC: Government Printing Office, 1911.

Berryer [Pierre Antoine], *Discours de M. Berryer sur La Dette de Mexique et les Obligations Mexicains Prononces les* 22 *et* 23 *Juillet* 1867 *Au Corps Legislatif.* Tours: Imprimerie-Librairie E. Mazereau, 1867.

Bocanegra, José María, *Memoria para la historia de México independiente,* 1822–1846. A facsimile edition of the first edition published in 1892. 3 volumes. México: Fondo de Cultura Económica, 1987.

Bosch García, Carlos, *Material para la historia diplomática de México (México y los Estados Unidos,* 1820–1848). México: Universidad Nacional Autónoma de México, 1957.

Bustamante, Carlos María, *Diario Histórico de México,* 1822–1848. A CD-ROM edition edited by Josefina Vázquez et al. México: El Colegio de México, 2001.

Casasus, Joaquín D., *Historia de la Deuda Contraída en Londres Con Un Apéndice Sobre el Estado Actual de la Hacienda Pública.* México: Imprenta del Gobierno Federal en Palacio, 1885.

Committee of Mexican Bondholders, Report of the Committee of Mexican Bondholders, presented to the general meeting of bondholders, at the London tavern, on May 15, 1854. London: Letts, Son, and Steer, 1854.

———, Report of the Committee of Mexican Bondholders, presented to the general meeting of bondholders, at the London tavern. London: Letts, Son, and Steer, 1855.

———, Report of the Committee of Mexican Bondholders Committee, presented on May 6, 1869. London: Letts, Son and Co., 1869.

Committee of Spanish American Bondholders, *Statement of Proceedings in Relation to the Mexican Debt Published By the Committee of Spanish American Bondholders*. London: Baily Bros., 1850.

Curtis, Goerge Ticknor, *Life of Daniel Webster*, 2 volumes. New York: D. Appleton and Company, 1870.

Cutler, Wayne, editor, *Correspondence of James K. Polk*, 10 volumes. Nashville, TN: Vanderbilt University Press, 1969–.

Díaz, Lilia, *Versión Francesa de México*, 3 volumes. México: El Colegio de México, 1963.

Espinosa, J., *Bases del plan de Hacienda Pública, que en clase de especiales de diversos ramos de ella deben fijar la marcha en desarroyo a consecuencia del establecimiento de la última de la tres bases generales que fijó la commission de arreglo del ramo, en sessión del 22 de noviembre de 1841*. México: Imprenta de A. Díaz, 1841.

Esteva, José Ignacio, *Contestación a las observaciones del señor contador de crédito público sobre la cuenta y memoria del ramo: referente a las ocho primeros meses del año de 1825*. México: Imprenta Del Aguila, 1828.

Forbes, Alexander, *California: A History of Upper & Lower California; from their first discovery to the present time, comprising an account of the climate, soil, natural productions, agriculture, commerce, &.; a full view of the missionary establishments and condition of the free & domesticated Indians; with an appendix relating to steam-navigation in the Pacific; illustrated with a new map, plans of the harbors and numerous engravings*. Original published in 1839. San Francisco: T. C. Russell, 1919.

García, Genaro, editor, *Documentos inéditos o muy raros para la historia de México*. Documentary series originally published between 1905 and 1911. México: Editorial Porrúa, 2006.

Grajales, Gloria, editor, *México y la Gran Bretaña durante la intervención, 1861–1862*, 2nd edition. México: Secretaría de Relaciones Exteriores, 1974.

Great Britain. Foreign Office, *Circular Addressed by Viscount Palmerston to His Majesty's Representatives in Foreign States Respecting the Debts Due by Foreign States to British Subjects*. London: T. R. Harrison, 1849.

———, *The Foreign Office List and Diplomatic and Consular Year Book*. London: Harrison and Sons, 1852.

———, *Correspondence Respecting the Renewal of Diplomatic Relations with Mexico*. London: n.p., 1884.

———, *Further Correspondence Respecting the Renewal of Diplomatic Relations with Mexico*. London: n.p., 1885.

Great Britain. Parliament, House of Commons, *Correspondence between Great Britain and Foreign Powers and Communications from the British Government Relative to Loans Made by British Subjects, 1823–1847*. London: T. R. Harrison, 1847.

———, *Correspondence between Great Britain and Foreign Powers and Communications from the British Government Relative to Loans Made by British Subjects, 1847–1853*. London: T. R. Harrison, 1853.

———, *Correspondence Respecting British Claims on Mexico*. London: Harrison and Sons, 1861.

———, *Report from the Select Committee on the Depreciation of Silver*. London: His Majesty's Stationery Office, 1876.

Great Britain. Post Office, *The Post Office Directory for 1836 Being a List of the Merchants, Traders & of London and Parts Adjacent*, 37th edition. London: E. Lowe, 1836.

Green, Duff, *Facts and Suggestions: Biographical, Historical, Financial and Political Addressed to the People of the United States*. New York: C. S. Wescott and Company's Union Printing Office, 1866.

Guedalla, Philip, editor, *Gladstone and Palmerston: Being the Correspondence of Lord Palmerston with Mr. Gladstone, 1851–1865*. New York: Harper, 1928.

[Haro y Tamariz, Antonio], *Estracto del espediente sobre la conversión de la deuda esterior*. México: Imprenta de I. Cumplido, 1846.

[Harris, James Howard], *Memoirs of an Ex-Minister: An Autobiography by the Right Hon. The Earl of Malmesbury*, G. C. B. New edition. London: Longman's, Green and Company, 1885.

Huskisson, William, *The Speeches of the Right Honorable William Huskisson with a Biographical Supplied to the Editor from Authentic Sources*, 3 volumes. London: J. Murray, 1831.

Iglesias, José María, *Revistas históricas sobre la intervención francesa en México*. An edition of the 1868–1869 publication. 3 volumes. México: Consejo Nacional para la Cultura y las Artes, 1991.

———, *Autobiografía*, 3rd edition. Based on the 1893 edition. México: Senado de la República, 2004.

Iglesias González, Román, editor, *Planes Políticos, Proclamas, Manifiestos y Otros Documentos dela Independencia al México Moderno, 1812–1940*. México: Universidad Nacional Autónoma de México, 1998.

Jacob, William, *An Historical Inquiry into the Production and Consumption of the Precious Metals*. Philadelphia: Carey and Lea, 1832.

Jenkins, John H., editor, *Papers of the Texas Revolution, 1835–1836*, 10 volumes. Austin, TX: Presidial Press, 1973.

Kératry, Emile, *The Rise and Fall of Emperor Maximilian: A Narrative of the Mexican Empire, 1861–7*. London: Sampson, Low, Son and Marston, 1868.

Kinder, Thomas, *Mexican Justice and British Diplomacy: The Case of Thomas Kinder as Regards the Parras Estate Purchased by Him in Joint Account with Messrs. Baring Bros and Co.*, 2nd edition. London: R. Taylor, 1841.

Mansfield, Edward Deering, *Life and Services of General Winfield Scott: including the siege of Vera Cruz, the battle of Cerro Gordo, and the battles in the valley of Mexico, to the conclusion of peace, and his return to the United States*. New York: A. S. Barnes and Co., 1852.

M'Calmont Brothers and Company, *Letters of Messrs. M'Calmont, Brothers, & Co., and reply thereto, by David Robertson, Esq., M. P., honorary chairman*. London: Letts, Son and Co., 1861.

México, *Leyes, decretos y convenios relativos a la deuda estrangera, que se reunen para la fácil inteligencia del dictámen de la Comision de crédito público de la Cámara de diputados*. [México, 1848].

———, *Mexican National Debt, Contracted in London: Decrees and Regulations Since the Adjustment of October 14th, December 23rd, 1850*. London: Letts, Son and Co., 1860.

———, *Actas constitucionales mexicanas (1821–1824)*. A facsimile edition edited by José Barragán Barragán for the Instituto de Investigaciones Jurídicas. México: Universidad Nacional Autónoma de México, 1980.

México. Congreso. Cámara de Diputados. Comisión de Hacienda, *Dictamen de la Primera Comisión de Hacienda de la Caámara de Diputados sobre la propuesta de los socios de la estinguida {sic} Casa de Barclay, Herring, Richardson y compañia*. México: Imprenta del Aguila, 1828.

———, *Cámara de Diputados. Comisión de Crédito Público, Dictámen de la Comisión de Crédito Público de la Cámara de Diputados sobre el arreglo de la deuda inglesa*. México: Imprenta De I. Cumplido, 1850.

———, 12ª Legislatura. Cámara de Diputados. *Diario de los debates de la Cámara de Diputados. Año de 1884*, 4 volumes. México: n.p., 1884.

———, 13ª Legislatura Cámara de Diputados. *Diario de los debates de la Cámara de Diputados. Año de 1886*, 4 volumes. México: n.p., 1888.

————, 13ª Legislatura Cámara de Diputados. *Diario de los debates de la Cámara de Diputados. Año de 1887*, 4 volumes. México: n.p., 1890.

México Congreso. Cámara de Senadores, *Analysis of the Memorial Presented by the Secretary of the Treasury to the First Constitutional Congress of the United Mexican State, Being the Substance of a Report of the Financial Committee of a the Chamber of Senators*. London: G. Cowie and Co., 1825.

————, *Dictamen de la Comisión de Hacienda autorizando al Ejecutivo para contraer un empréstito de diez millones y quinientas mil libras esterlinas*. México: Imprenta del Gobierno Federal, 1887.

México. Junta de Gobernadores, *Documentos relativos a la reunión en esta capital de los gobernadores de los estados, convocados para proveer a las exigencias del erario federal*. México: Imprenta de J. M. Lara, 1851.

México. Legación (U.S.),. *Correspondencia de la Legación Mexicana en Washington durante la intervención extranjera. 1860–1868: colección de documentos para formar la historia de la Intervención*, 10 volumes. México: Imprenta del Gobierno, en Palacio, 1870–1892.

México Secretaría de Hacienda Pública, *Memoria que el Secretario de Estado y del Despacho de Hacienda presentó al soberano Congreso Constituyente sobre los ramos del Ministerio de su cargo leída en la sesión del día 12 de noviembre de 1823*. México: Imprenta del Supremo Gobierno, 1823.

————, *Memoria sobre el estado de la hacienda pública*. México: Imprenta del Supremo Gobierno, 1825.

————, *Memoria del ramo de hacienda federal de los Estados Unidos Mexicanos*. México: Imprenta del Supremo Gobierno, 1828.

————, *Razón de los préstamos que ha negociado el supremo gobierno de la federacion, en virtud de la autorizacion concedida por los decretos del Congreso general de 21 de noviembre y 24 de diciembre del año de 1827, 3 de octubre y 20 de noviembre de 1828, que se publica con autorización del escmo. Sr. ministro de hacienda, ciudadano Lorenzo de Zavala*. México: Imprenta del Correo, 1829.

————, *Memoria de la Secretaría del Despacho de Hacienda*. México: Imprenta del Supremo Gobierno, 1831.

————, *Memoria de la Secretaría del Despacho de Hacienda*. México: Imprenta del Supremo Gobierno, 1832.

————, *Decreto sobre préstamo forzoso de dos millones y medio de pesos para pagar la deuda reconocida al Gobierno de los Estados Unidos de América*. México: Imprenta de J. M. F. de Lara, 1843.

————, *Memoria de la Hacienda Nacional de la República*. México: Imprenta del Supremo Gobierno, 1845.

————, *Memoria de la Hacienda Nacional de la República*. México: Imprenta del Supremo Gobierno, 1848.

————, *Esposición del secretario del despacho de hacienda : leída en Consejo de Ministros con asistencia de los gobernadores de los estados, en 17 de agosto de 1851*. México: Imprenta de J. M. Lara, 1851.

————, *Informe que presenta el Secretario de Hacienda sobre el estado que guarda la Deuda Extranjera Pidiéndose cobra el deficiente estraordinario de 1.300.000 pesos para el pago de los dividendos que se adeudan*. México: Tipografía de Vicente García Torres, 1852.

————, *Informes leídos en la Cámara de Diputados por el Secretario de Hacienda : sobre el estado que guarda el erario público, y sobre las últimas operaciones practicadas en la deuda esterior e interior de la República Mexicana*. México: Imprenta de I Cumplido, 1852.

————, *Memoria en que Manuel Payno da cuenta al público de su manejo en el desempeño del Ministerio de Hacienda, y de las comisiones que le confió el supremo gobierno en Inglaterra acompañándose los documentos relativos al pago del primer dividendo de la deuda esterior y las comunicaciones dirigidas á Lord Palmerston sobre la ley de 30 denoviembre de 1850*. México: Imprenta de Cumplido, 1852.

México. Secretaría de Hacienda y Crédito Público, *Memoria que el Secretario de Estado y del Despacho de Hacienda y Crédito Público presenta al Congreso dela Union, el 31 de enero de 1868.* México: Imprenta del Gobierno, en Palacio, 1868.

————, *Exposición que el Ejecutivo dirige al Congreso de la Unión, dando cuenta del uso que hizo de las facultades que le concedió el articulo 11 de la ley de 17 de enero de 1870, y del estado que guarda la hacienda federal.* México: Imprenta del Gobierno, 1870.

————, *Memoria de Hacienda y Crédito Público, correspondiente al cuadragésimoquinto año económico. Presentada por el Secretario de Hacienda al Congreso de la Union. El 16 de setiembre de 1870.* México: Imprenta del Gobierno, 1870.

————, *Exposición que el Ejecutivo federal dirige al Congreso dela Unión el 10. de abril de 1871 sometiéndole un proyecto de arreglo de la deuda pública, y dándole cuenta del estado de la hacienda federal en el primer semestre del año económico cuadragésimosexto.* México: Imprenta del Gobierno, 1871.

————, *Memoria de la secretaría de hacienda correspondiente al año fiscal de 1880 a 1881.* México: Imprenta del Gobierno, 1881.

————, *Memoria de hacienda correspondiente al ejercicio fiscal de 1886 a 1887 presentado por el ministro del ramo.* México: Imprenta del Gobierno, 1888.

————, *Colección de leyes y disposiciónes relaciónadas con la deuda exterior de Mexico.* A facsimile of the 1925 edition. México: Universidad Nacional Autonoma de México, 1989.

Michelena, José Mariano, *Esplicación de la conducta de Michelena en algunos puntos.* México: Imprenta Galván a cargo de M. Arévalo, 1827.

[Mier y Terán, Manuel de], *Memoria que el Secretario de Estado y del despacho de marina presenta al soberano Congreso Constituyente Mexicano. Leída en sesión pública de 13 de Noviembre de 1823.* México: Imprenta del Supremo Gobierno, en palacio, [1824].

Mora, José María Luis, *Escritos del obispo Abad y Queipo: disertación sobre bienes eclesiásticos presentada al gobierno de Zacatecas. Diversos proyectos para el arreglo del crédito público.* A facsimile of the 1837 edition. México: Miguel Angel Porrúa, 1986.

————, *Obras Completas*, 8 volumes. México: Secretaría de Educación Pública and Instituto de Investigaciones Dr. José María Luis Mora, 1986–1988.

————, *Revista política de las diversas administraciones que ha tenido la república hasta 1837.* A facsimile of the 1837 edition. México: Miguel Angel Porrua, 1986.

Murphy, Tomás, *Memoria sobre la deuda esterior de la Republica Mexicana desde su creación hasta fines de 1847.* Paris: Imprenta de A. Blondeau, 1848.

O'Brien, D. P., editor, *The Collected Works of J. R. McCulloch*, 8 volumes. London: Routledge/Thoemmes Press, 1995.

Ortiz de Montellano, Mariano, *Apuntes para la liquidación de la deuda contraída en Londres.* México: Imprenta del Gobierno Federal en Palacio, 1886.

Paula Arrangóiz y Berzábal, Francisco de and Guillermo Parish Robertson *Piezas justificativas del arreglo de la Deuda de México.* México: Tipografía de R. Rafael, 1849.

Payno, Manuel, *Reseña sobre los principales ramos de la Hacienda Pública.* México: Imprenta de I. Cumplido, 1851.

————, *México y el Sr. embajador Don Joaquín Francisco Pacheco.* México: Imprenta De J. Abadiano, 1862.

————, *La deuda interior de México.* México: Imprenta Económica, 1865.

————, *Cuentas, gastos, acreedores y otros asuntos del tiempo de la intervención francesa y del imperio de 1861 a 1867.* A facsimile of the edition of 1868. México: Secretaría de Hacienda y Crédito Público and Miguel Angel Porrúa, 1981.

————, *México y sus Cuestiones Financieras con La Inglaterra, La España y La Francia.* A facsimile of the 1862 edition. México: Miguel Angel Porrua and Secretaría de Hacienda y Crédito Público, 1982.

Presas, Josef de, *Memoria sobre el estado y situación política en que se hallaba el reino de Nueva España en agosto de 1823.* Madrid: Imprenta Real, 1824.

Prieto, Guillermo, *Memoria de mis tiempos*. An edition of the original printing of 1906. México: Editorial Porrúa, 1985.

———, *Lecciones elementales de economía política*. A facsimile of the second enlarged edition of 1876. México: Consejo Nacional para la Cultura y las Artes, 1989.

———, *Obras Completas*, 32 volumes. México: Consejo Nacional para la Cultura y las Artes, 1992–1997.

Robaina, Lucía de, editor, *Reconciliación de México y Francia (1870–1880)*. México: Secretaría de Relaciones Exteriores, 1963.

Robertson, W. Parish, *The Foreign Debt of Mexico; Being the Report of a Special Mission to That State, Undertaken on Behalf of the Bondholders*. London: Smith Elder and Co., 1850.

Romero, Matías, *Diario Personal de Matías Romero (1855–1865)*. Edited by Emma Cosío Villegas. México: El Colegio de México, 1960.

———, *La promoción de las relaciones comerciales entre México y los Estados Unidos de Ameérica*. Reedition of a publication of 1879. México: Banco Nacional de Comercio Exterior, 1961.

Schoonover, Thomas D., editor, *Mexican Lobby. Matías Romero in Washington, 1861–1867*. Lexington, KY: University Press of Kentucky, 1986.

Sheppard, Edgar, editor, *George, Duke of Cambridge, a Memoir of His Private Life*, 2 volumes. London: Longmans, Green and Co., 1906.

Smith, Ashbel, "Reminiscences of the Texas Republic," 1875. http://www.tamu.edu/ccbn/dewitt/smithasbel1.htm.

United States. Bureau of Statistics, *American Commerce. Commerce of South America, Central America, Mexico, and West Indies, with Share of the United States and Other Leading Nations Therein, 1821–1898*. Washington, DC: Government Printing Office, 1898.

United States. Congress, *Congressional Record*. United States: Congress, 1885.

United States. House, *37th Congress, 2nd session, The Present Condition of Mexico. Message from the President of the United States, in answer to resolution of the House of 3rd of March last, transmitting report from the Department of State regarding the present condition of Mexico*. Washington, DC: Government Printing Office, 1862.

United States. Senate, *32nd Congress, 1st session. Message from the President of the United States, Communicating a Report from the Secretary of State, urging an early appropriation to pay the instalment (sic) due to Mexico under the Treaty of Gaudalupe (sic) Hidalgo*. Washington, DC: A. Boyd Hamilton, 1852.

United States, *Statutes at Large, 1789–1875*, 18 volumes. Washington, DC: Government Printing Office, 1875.

Van Dyke, T. S., "Mexican Politics," *Harper's New Monthly Magazine*, vol. 71, 1885, pp. 761–769.

Vázquez, Josefina, editor, *La Gran Breteña frente al México amenazado, 1835–1848*. México: Secretaría de Relaciones Exteriores, 2002.

Vega, Mercedes de and María Cecilia Zulueta, *Testimonios de una Guerra: 1846–1848*, 2 volumes. México: Secretaría de Relaciones Exteriores, 2001.

Ward, Henry George, *México en 1827*. A translation of the original edition of 1828. México: Fondo de Cultura Económica, 1981.

Webster, Fletcher, editor, *The Private Correspondence of Daniel Webster*. Boston: Little Brown and Company, 1857.

Wyllie, Robert Crichton, *México, noticia sobre su hacienda pública bajo el gobierno español y después de la independencia: probabilidades sobre su aumento o mejora, cálculos sobre la deuda interior y esterior, presupuestos aprocsimados de sus ingresos y egresos, a lo que se han añadido tablas ilustrativas sobre sistema mercantil, manufacturero y prohibitivo, y observaciones sobre la colonización. Todo formado para el conocimiento e instrucción de los mercaderes, emigrantes, y tenedores de bonos mexicanos*. A facsimile of the 1845 edition published within *Documentos para el estudio de la industrialización en México, 1837–1845*. México: Secretaría de Hacienda y Crédito Público y Nacional Financiera, 1977.

Zavala, Lorenzo de, *Esposición del Secretario del Despacho de Hacienda, D. Lorenzo de Zavala: a las Cámaras de la Unión, a su ingreso al despacho del ramo*. México: Imprententa Del Aguila, 1829.

_____, *Ensayo histórico de las revoluciones de México desde 1800 hasta 1830*. A facsimile of the 1845 edition. México: Fondo de Cultura Económica, 1985.

Secondary Sources

[Anonymous], *Foreign Office, Diplomatic and Consular Sketches*. London: W. H. Allen and Co., 1883.

_____, "The Mexican Economy in 1884," *Review of the Economic Situation of Mexico*, 1984.

_____, "Mexico's Debts," *The Nation*, 1885.

_____, "Thomas & Francis Bellamy, Heart Attack in Refectory of Ryan ca 1823, Imperial Highness Prince Eterbyde (Iturbide), Emperor of Mexico's Son, Arundel, Clifford, Stourton, Peter (Petre)." *Ampleforth Journal*, 1896.

Alatriste, Oscar, "El capitalismo Británico en los inicios del México independiente," *Estudios de historia moderna y contemporánea de México*, 1977.

Albiot, J., *Les Campagnes Électorales, 1851–1869*. Paris: A. Le Chevalier, 1869.

Andrews, Catherine, "Discusiones en torno de la reforma de la Constitución Federal de 1824 durante el primer gobierno de Anastasio Bustamante (1830–1832)," *Historia Mexicana*, 2006.

Anna, Timothy E., *Forging Mexico, 1821–1835*. Lincoln, NE: University of Nebraska Press, 1998.

Aoilfi, Marco, Luis Catão and Allan Timmermann, "Common Factors in Latin America's Business Cycles," IMF Working Paper WP/06/49 (unpublished paper, 2006).

Aquino Sánchez, Faustino A., *Intervención Francesa, 1838–1839. La diplomacia Mexicana y el imperialismo de libre comercio*. México: Instituto Nacional de Antropologiae Historia, 1997.

Arnold, Linda, editor, *Directorio de Burócratas en la Ciudad de México 1761–1832*. México: Archivo General de la Nación, 1980.

Balbín, Pedro Fraile. *Industrialización y grupos de presión: la economía política y grupos de presión en España, 1900–1950*. Madrid: Alianza Editorial, 1991.

Barker, Nancy M., "The Duke of Morny and the Affair of the Jecker Bonds," *French Historical Studies*, 1970.

_____, "Monarchy in Mexico: Harebrained Scheme or Well-Considered Prospect," *The Journal of Modern History*, 1976.

Bazant, Jan, *Historia de la deuda exterior de México (1823–1946)*, 2nd edition. México: El Colegio de México, 1981.

Beatty, Edward, "The Impact of Foreign Trade on the Mexican Economy: Terms of Trade and the Rise of Industry, 1880–1923," *Journal of Latin American Studies*, 2000.

Bécker, Felix, editor, *America Latina en las Letras y Ciencias Sociales Alemanas*. Caracas: Monte Avila Editoras, 1984.

Beckert, Sven, "Emancipation and Empire: Reconstructing the Worldwide Web of Cotton Production in the Age of the American Civil War," *American Historical Review*, 2004.

Bethell, Leslie, editor, *The Cambridge History of Latin America*, 11 volumes. New York: Cambridge University Press, 1984–1996.

Blake, Robert, *Benjamin Disraeli*. Originally published in 1966. London: Prion, 1998.

Blázquez Domínguez, Carmen, *Veracruz Liberal, 1858–1860*. México: El Colegio de México, 1986.

Bock, Carl, *Prelude to Tragedy: The Negotiation and Breakdown of the Tripartite Convention of London, October 31, 1861*. Philadelphia: University of Pennsylvania Press, 1966.

Bordo, Michael D. and Roberto Cortés-Conde, editors, *Transferring Wealth and Power from the Old to the New World. Monetary and Fiscal Institutions in the 17th through the 19th Centuries*. New York: Cambridge University Press, 2001.

Bulmer-Thomas, Victor, John Coatsworth and Roberto Cortés-Conde, editors, *The Cambridge Economic History of Latin America*, 2 volumes. New York: Cambridge University Press, 2006.

Cárdenas Sánchez, Enrique, *Cuando se originó el atraso económico de México. La economía mexicana en el largo siglo xix, 1780–1920*. Madrid: Biblioteca Nueva-Fundación Ortega y Gassett, 2003.

Carroll, Daniel B., *Henri Mercier and the American Civil War*. Princeton, NJ: Princeton University Press, 1971.

Carus-Wilson, E[leanora] M[ary], editor, *Essays in Economic History*, 3 volumes. London: E. Arnold, 1966.

Cerda, Luis, *Historia Financiera del Banco Nacional de México*, 2 volumes. México: Fomento Cultural Banamex, 1997.

Chambers, James, *Palmerston: The People's Darling*. London: John Murray, 2005.

Chaudhuri, K. N., "India's Foreign Trade and the Cessation of the East India Company's Trading Activities, 1828–1840," *Economic History Review*, 1966.

Clarke, John, *British Diplomacy and Foreign Policy, 1782–1865: The National Interest*. London: Hyman, 1989.

Cline, William R., *International Debt Reexamined*. Washington, DC: Institute for International Economics, 1995.

Coerver, Don M., *The Porfirian Interregnum: The Presidency of Manuel González of Mexico, 1880–1884*. Fort Worth, TX: Texas Christian University Press, 1979.

Cohen, Henry, *Business and Politics in America from the Age of Jackson to the Civil War: The Career Biography of W. W. Corcoran*. Westport, CT: Greenwood, 1971.

Collins, Michael, "The Langton Papers: Banking and Bank of England Policy in the 1830s," *Economica*, 1972.

Connolly, Priscilla, *El contratista de Don Porfirio. Obras Públicas, deuda y desarrollo desigual*. México: Fonde de Cultura Económica, 1997.

Cosío Villegas, Daniel, editor, *Historia Moderna de México*, 8 volumes. México: Editorial Hermes, 1955–1965.

————, *La cuestión arancelaria en México*. A facsimile of the 1932 edition. México: Universidad Nacional Autónoma de México, Facultad de Economía, 1989.

Costeloe, Michael P., *La primera republica federal de México (1824–1835)*. México: Fondo de Cultura Económica, 1975.

————, "The Extraordinary Case of Mr. Falconnet and the 2,500,000 Silver Dollars: London and Mexico, 1850–1853," *Estudios Mexicanos/Mexican Studies*, 1999.

————, *Bonds and Bondholders: British Investors and Mexico's Foreign Debt, 1824–1888*. Westport, CT: Praeger, 2003.

Covarrubias, José Enrique, *La moneda de cobre en México, 1760–1842: Un problema administrativo*. México: El Colegio de México, 2000.

Cunningham, Michelle, *Mexico and the Foreign Policy of Napoleon III*. Basingstroke, UK: Palgrave, 2001.

Daunton, Martin, *Trusting Leviathan: The Politics of Taxation in Britain, 1799–1914*. Cambridge, UK: Cambridge University Press, 2001.

Diebold, Francis X., *Elements of Forecasting*, 4th edition. Mason, OH: South-Western, 2007.

Domínguez, Angel M., "Memoria Estadística sobre las Rentas Públicas de la Nación," *Boletín de la Sociedad de Geografía y Estadística de la República Mexicana*, 1890.

Eichengreen, Barry, Ricardo Hausmann and Ugo Panizza, "Currency Mismatches, Debt Intolerances and Original Sin: Why They Are Not the Same and Why It Matters," NBER Working Paper 10036. http://www.nber.org/papers/w10036.

Engelson, Lester G., "Proposals for the Colonization of California by England in Connection with the Mexican Debt to British Bondholders, 1837–1846," *California Historical Society*, 1939.

Engerman, Stanley and Robert E. Gallman, *The Cambridge Economic History of the United States*, 3 volumes. Cambridge, UK: Cambridge University Press, 2000.

Ferguson, Niall, *The House of Rothschild. Money's Prophets, 1798–1848*. New York: Viking, 1998.

Fevearyear, A[lbert] E[dgar], *The Pound Sterling: A history of English Money*. Oxford: Clarendon Press, 1931.

Fishlow, Albert, "Lessons from the Past: Capital Markets during the Nineteenth Century and the Interwar Period," *International Organization*, 1985.

Flandreau, Marc, "Does Bilateralism Promote Trade? Nineteenth-Century Liberalization Revisited" (unpublished paper, 2006).

———, and Juan Flores, "Resources and Reputations: Historical Precedents for Recent Banking Crises," *Annual Review* (Rothschild Archive), 2007. http://www.rothschildarchive.org/ib/articles/AR2007BankingCrises.pdf.

Florescano, Enrique, *Precios del maíz y crisis agrícolas en México (1708–1810)*. México: El Colegio de México, 1969.

Fowler, Will, "Joseph Welsh: A British Santanista (Mexico, 1832)," *Journal of Latin American Studies*, 2004.

Friedman, Benjamin M., *The Moral Consequences of Economic Growth*. New York: Random House, 2005.

Friedman, Milton, *Essays in Positive Economics*. Chicago, IL: University of Chicago Press, 1970.

Garber, Paul Neff, *The Gadsden Treaty*. Gloucester, MA: Peter Smith, 1959.

García, Irma Lombardo, *El siglo de Cumplido. La emergencia del periodismo mexicano de opinión (1832–1857)*. México: Universidad Nacional Autónoma de México, 2002.

Garrido Asperó, María José, "Cada Quien Sus Héroes," *Estudios de Historia Contémporanea y Moderna de México*, 2001.

Gartner, Manfred, *A Primer in European Macroeconomics*. London: Prentice Hall, 1997.

Gleijeses, Piero, "A Brush with Mexico," *Diplomatic History*, 2005.

Goschen, George J., *The Theory of the Foreign Exchanges*, 16th edition. London: E. Wilson, 1894.

Hanna, Alfred Jackson and Kathryn Abbey Hanna, *Napoleon III and Mexico: American Triumph over Monarchy*. Chapel Hill, NC: University of North Carolina Press, 1971.

Haber, Stephen and Armando Razo, "Political Instability and Economic Performance: Evidence from Revolutionary Mexico," *World Politics*, 1998.

Heath, Hilary, "Mexicanos e ingleses: xenofobia y racismo," *Secuencia*, 1992.

Hidalgo, Delia, *Representantes de México en Gran Bretaña, 1822–1980*. México: Secretaría de Relaciones Exteriores, 1981.

Hidy, Ralph W., "Cushioning a Crisis in the London Money Market," *Bulletin of the Business Historical Society*, 1946.

———, *The House of Baring in American Trade and Finance*. Cambridge, MA: Harvard University Press, 1949.

Hobsbawn, E[ric] J. and George Rudé, *Captain Swing*. Harmondsworth: Penguin, 1973.

Ibarra Bellon, Araceli, *El comercio y el poder en México, 1821–1864. La lucha por las fuentes financieras entre el Estado central y las regiones*. México: Fonde de Cultura Económica, 1998.

[Instituto Nacional de Estadística, Geografía e Informática], *Catálogo de documentos históricos de la estadística en México (Siglos XVI–XIX)*. Aguascalientes: INEGI, 2005.

———, *Estadísticas históricas de México*, 2 volumes. Aguascalientes: INEGI, 1985.

Johnston, Henry McKenzie, *Missions to Mexico: A Tale of British Diplomacy in the 1820s*. London: British Academic Press, 1992.

Jones, Raymond A., *The British Diplomatic Service, 1815–1914*. Waterloo, Ontario: Wilfrid Laurier University Press, 1983.

Katz, Friedrich, *Deutschland, Diaz und die mexicanische Revolution. Die deutsche Poltitik in México, 1870–1920*. Berlin: Deutscher Verlag der Wissenschaften, 1964.

Kozhevar, E. *Informe sobre la República Mexicana, presentado al consejo de tenedores de bonos, extranjeros*. Translated by Joaquín Casasus. México: Secretaría de Fomento, 1887.

Kuntz Ficker, Sandra, "El Comercio México–Estados Unidos, 1870–1929: Reconstrucción Estadística y Tendencias Generales," *Mexican Studies/Estudios Mexicanos*, 2001.

Lecaillon, Jean-Francois, *Napoleón III et le Mexique: les illusions d'un grand dessein*. Paris: L'Harmattan, 1994.

Liehr, Reinhard, *The Public Debt in Latin America in Historical Perspective*. Madrid: Iberoamericana, 1995.

———, editor, *Empresas y modernización en Meéxico desde las reformas borbónicas hasta el Porfiriato*. Madrid: Iberoamericana, 2006.

López de Roux, María Eugenia, editor, *El reconocimiento de la independencia de México*. México: Secretaría de Relaciones Exteriores, 1995.

Louis, Wm. Roger, editor, *The Oxford History of the British Empire*, 5 volumes. Oxford, UK: Oxford University Press, 1999.

Ludlow, Leonor and Carlos Marichal, editors, *Los secretarios de Hacienda y sus proyectos*, 2 volumes. México: Universidad Nacional Autónoma de México, 2002.

Madero, Francisco, *La sucesion presidencial en 1910*. A reprint of the 1908 edition. México: CEID, 1985.

Magallón Ibarra, Jorge Mario, *Proceso y ejecución vs Fernando Maximiliano de Hapsburgo*. México: Universidad Nacional Autónoma de México, 2005.

Marichal, Carlos, *La bancarrota del virreinato. Nueva España y las finanzas del Imperio español, 1780–1810*. México: Fondo de Cultura Económica, 1992.

———, "Debt Strategies in the Porfiriato: The Conversion Loan of 1888 and the Role of Banamex as Government Banker" (unpublished paper, 1999).

——— and Daniela Moreno, editors, *De Colonia a Nación. Impuestos y politicos en México, 1750–1860*. México: El Colegio de México, 2001.

Mateos, Juan Antonio, *Historia Parlamentaria de los Congresos Mexicanos*, 13 volumes, México: Editorial Miguel Angel Porrúa, 1997.

Maurer, Noel, "Banks and Entrepreneurs in Porfirian Mexico: Inside Exploitation or Sound Business Strategy?" *Journal of Latin American Studies*, 1999.

Mauro Paolo, Nathan Sussman and Yishay Yafeh, *Emerging Markets and Financial Globalization: Sovereign Bond Spreads in 1870–1913 and Today*. New York: Oxford University Press, 2006.

McClean, Malcom, *Vida y obra de Guillermo Prieto*, 2nd edition. México, D.F.: El Colegio de México and Consejo Nacional para la Cultura y las Artes, 1998.

Miller, Rory. *Britain and Latin America in the Nineteenth and Twentieth Centuries*. London: Longman, 1993.

Moggridge, D. E., *British Monetary Policy, 1924–1931: The Norman Conquest of $4.86*. Cambridge, UK: Cambridge University Press, 1972.

Nicholson, Harold, *Diplomacy*, 3rd edition. London: Oxford University Press, 1963.

Noriega Elío, Cecilia, *El Constituyente de 1842*. México: Universidad Nacional Autónoma de México, 1986.

Olliff, Donathon, C., *Reforma Mexico and the United States: A Search for Alternatives to Annexation, 1854–1861*. Albama: University of Alabama Press, 1981.

Patillo, Catherine, Hélène Poirson and Lucca Ricci, "External Debt and Growth," *Finance and Development*, 2002. http://www.imf.org/external/pubs/ft/fandd/2002/06/pattillo.htm.

Perry, Laurens Ballard, *Juárez and Díaz: Machine Politics in Mexico*. DeKalb, IL: Northern Illinois University Press, 1978.

Peterson, Merrill D., *The Great Triumvirate: Webster, Clay, and Calhoun*. New York: Oxford University Press, 1987.

Platt, D. C. M., *Finance, Trade, and Politics in British Foreign Policy 1815–1914*. Oxford: Clarendon Press, 1968.

Potash, Robert, *Mexican Government and Industrial Development in the Early Republic: The Banco de Avío*. Expanded and updated from the Mexican edition of 1959. Amherst, MA: University of Massachusetts Press, 1983.

Price, Roger, *The French Second Empire: An Anatomy of Political Power*. Cambridge, UK: Cambridge University Press, 2001.

Reinhart, Carmen, Kenneth Rogoff and Michael Savastano, "Debt Intolerance," *Brookings Papers on Economic Activity*, 2003.

Reyes Vayssade, Martín, *Jecker. El hombre que quiso vender México*. México: Editorial Joaquín Mortiz, 2005.

Ridley, Jasper, *Maximilian and Juárez*. New York: Ticknor and Fields, 1992.

Rippy, J. Fred, "Latin America and the British Investment Boom of the 1820s," *The Journal of Modern History*, 1947.

Rivas, Alejandro and José Manuel Villalpando, *Los Presidentes de México*. México: Planeta Editores, 2001.

Roekell, Lelia M., "Bonds over Bondage: British Opposition to the Annexation of Texas," *Journal of the Early Republic*, 1999.

Rojas, Rafael, "Iturbide: La Primera Traición," *Nexos*, 2001.

Roland, Alex, *Undersea Warfare in the Age of Sail*. Bloomington, IN: Indiana University Press, 1978.

Romero Sotelo, María Eugenia and Luis Jáuregui, *Las contingencias de una larga recuperación. La economía mexicana, 1821–1867*. México: Universidad Nacional Autónoma de México, 2003.

Rostow, W[alt] W[hitman]., *British Economy of the Nineteenth Century: Essays*. Oxford: Oxford University Press, 1948.

Rowe, Kenneth, *The Postal History and Markings of Forward Agents*. Louisville, KY: Leonard H. Hartman, 1996.

Sachs, Jeffrey D., "Resolving the Debt Crisis of Low-Income Countries," *Brookings Papers on Economic Activity*, 2002.

Salvucci, Richard J., "The Origins and Progress of United States-Mexican Trade, 1825–1884: 'Hoc opus, hic labor est'," *Hispanic American Historical Review*, 1992.

———, "Algunas Consideraciones Económicas (1836). Análisis Mexicano de la Depresión a Principios del Siglo XIX," *Historia Mexicana*, 2005.

———, "1829 and All That: Great Britain, Mexico and Silver Reconsidered," *The Burden of Spanish Silver: The Impact on American Labor and Europe's Economy: A Workshop of the Atlantic History Seminar* (unpublished paper, 2005). http://www.fas.harvard.edu/~atlantic/spansilver.html.

Schmitz, Joseph William, *Texan statecraft, 1836–1845*. San Antonio: Naylor, 1941.

[Secretaría de Hacienda y Crédito Público], *Deuda externa pública mexicana*. México: Fondo de Cultura Económica, 1988.

———, *Fobaproa: la verdadera historia*. México: Secretaría de Hacienda y Crédito Público, 1998.

[Secretaría de Relaciones Exteriores], *Los primeros consulados de México, 1823–1872*. México: Secretaría de Relaciones Exteriores, 1974.

──────, *Representantes diplomáticos de México en Washington, 1822–1973*. México: Secretaría de Relaciones Exteriores, 1974.

──────, *Los Cancilleres de México*, 2 volumes. México: Secretaría de Relaciones Exteriores, 1992.

Serrano Ortega, José and Luis Jaúregui, editors, *Hacienda y Política. Las finanzas públicas y los grupos de poder en la primera república federal mexicana*. México: Instituto Mora: El Colegio de Michoacán: El Colegio de México: Instituto de Investigaciones Históricas-UNAM, 1998.

Smith, Walter Buckingham, *Economic Aspects of the Second Bank of the United States*. Cambridge, MA: Harvard University Press, 1953.

Solares Robles, María Laura. *Una revolución pacífica. Biografía de Manuel Gómez Pedraza, 1789–1851*. México: Instituto de Investigaciones Dr. José María Luis Mora: Acervo Diplomático de la Secretaría de Relaciones Exteriores; [Querétaro]: Consejo Estatal para la Cultura y las Artes del Gobierno del Estado de Querétaro, 1996.

Sordo Cedeño, Reynaldo, *El Congreso en la primera república centralista*. México: El Colegio de México, 1993.

Stephen, Leslie and Sidney Lee, *Dictionary of National Biography*, 21 volumes. London: Oxford University Press, 1921–1922. Supplemented by *Oxford Dictionary of National Biography* (2004).

Stiglitz, Joseph E., *Globalization and Its Discontent*. New York: W. W. Norton and Co., 2002.

Sturzenegger, Federico and Jeronimo Zettlemeyer, *Debt Default and Lessons from a Decade of Crisis*. Cambridge, MA: MIT, 2006.

Suárez Argüello, Ana Rosa, "Los intereses de Jecker en Sonora," *Estudios de Historia Moderna y Contemporanea de México*, 1983.

──────, *La batalla por Tehuantepec: el peso de los intereses privados en la relación México-Estados Unidos, 1848–1854*. México: Secretaría de Relaciones Exteriores, 2003.

Taylor, A. J. P., *The Struggle for Mastery in Europe, 1848–1918*. Oxford: Oxford University Press, 1954.

Teichova, Alice, Ginette Kurgan van Hentenryk and Dieter Ziegler, editors, *Banking, Trade, and Industry: Europe, America, and Asia from the Thirteenth to the Twentieth Centuries*. New York: Cambridge University Press, 1997.

Tena Ramírez, Felipe, *Leyes fundamentals de México*, 12th edition. México: Editorial Porrúa, 1983.

Tenenbaum, Barbara, *The Politics of Penury: Debts and Taxes in Mexico, 1821–1856*. Albuquerque, NM: University of New México Press, 1986.

Terrazas y Basante, Marcela, *Inversiones, Especulaciones y Diplomacia. Las Relaciones Entre México y Estados Unidos Durante La Dictadura Santanista*. México: Universidad Nacional Autónoma de México, 2000.

────── and Ana Rosa Suárez Argüello, editors, *Política y negocios. Ensayos sobre la relación entre México y los Estados Unidos en el siglo XIX*. México: Universidad Nacional Autónoma de Mexico/Instituto Mora, 1997.

Tinkler, Robert, *James Hamilton of South Carolina*. Baton Rouge, LA: LSU Press, 2004.

Tooke, Thomas and William Newmarch, *A History of Prices and of the State of Circulation from 1793 to 1837*. Reprint edition. London: P. S. King and Son, 1928.

Topik, Steven C., "When Mexico Had the Blues: A Transatlantic Tale of Bonds, Bankers, and Nationalists, 1862–1910," *American Historical Review*, 2000.

Trujillo Bolio, Mario and José María Contreras Vaídez, eds., *Formacion empresarial y compañías agrícolas en el México del siglo xix*. México, 2003.

Vargas Rangel, Virginia, "El Primer Presidente de la Sociedad Mexicana de Geografía e Estadística," *Elementos*, 2006. http://www.elementos.buap.mx/portadas/portadas.html

Vázquez, Josefina, *México, Gran Bretaña y otros paises, 1821–1848*. México: Senado de la República, 1990.

———, editor, *La Gran Bretaña frente al México amenazado, 1835–1848*. México: Secretaría de Relaciones Exteriores, 2002.

Walker, David W., "Business as Usual: The Empresa del Tabaco in Mexico, 1837–1844," *Hispanic American Historical Review*, 1984.

———, *Kinship, Business, and Politics: The Martínez del Río family in Mexico, 1824–1867*. Austin, TX: University of Texas Press, 1986.

Wallace, Laura, "Ahead of His Time," *Finance and Development*, 2006.

Wilson, Keith M., editor, *British Foreign Secretaries and Foreign Policy: From Crimean War to First World War*. London: Croon Helm, 1987.

Worley, J. L., "The Diplomatic Relations of England and the Republic of Texas," *Quarterly of the Texas State Historical Association*, 1906.

Zaragoza, José, *Historia de la deuda externa de México, 1823–1861*. México: Universidad Nacional Autónoma de México, 1996.

Index